Reprints of Economic Classics

THE THEORY OF MORAL SENTIMENTS

Also published in

REPRINTS OF ECONOMIC CLASSICS

BY ADAM SMITH

LECTURES ON JUSTICE, POLICE, REVENUE AND ARMS [1896]
THE WEALTH OF NATIONS, 2 volumes [1776] *Facsimile*
THE EARLY WRITINGS OF ADAM SMITH [1966]

THE
THEORY
OF
MORAL SENTIMENTS.

BY

ADAM SMITH *1723 - 1790.*

REPRINTS OF ECONOMIC CLASSICS

AUGUSTUS M. KELLEY · PUBLISHERS
NEW YORK · 1966

FIRST PUBLISHED 1759

LIBRARY OF CONGRESS CATALOGUE CARD NUMBER

66 - 15558

PRINTED IN THE UNITED STATES OF AMERICA
by SENTRY PRESS, NEW YORK, N. Y. 10019

THE

THEORY

OF

MORAL SENTIMENTS;

OR,

AN ESSAY TOWARDS AN ANALYSIS OF THE PRINCIPLES BY WHICH MEN NATURALLY
JUDGE CONCERNING THE CONDUCT AND CHARACTER, FIRST OF THEIR
NEIGHBOURS, AND AFTERWARDS OF THEMSELVES.

TO WHICH IS ADDED,

A DISSERTATION ON THE ORIGIN OF LANGUAGES.

BY

ADAM SMITH, LL.D., F.R.S.

NEW EDITION.

WITH A BIOGRAPHICAL AND CRITICAL MEMOIR OF THE AUTHOR,

BY DUGALD STEWART.

LONDON:
HENRY G. BOHN, YORK STREET, COVENT GARDEN.
1853.

CONTENTS.

PART I.

Page

OF THE PROPRIETY OF ACTION, . . . 1

SECTION I.

OF THE SENSE OF PROPRIETY, ... 3
CHAP. I. Of Sympathy, ... *ib.*
... II. Of the Pleasure of mutual Sympathy, . 10
... III. Of the Manner in which we judge of the Propriety or
Impropriety of the Affections of other Men, by
their concord or dissonance with our own, . 14
... IV. The same Subject continued, . . 19
... V. Of the amiable and respectable Virtues, . 26

SECTION II.

OF THE DEGREES OF THE DIFFERENT PASSIONS WHICH ARE CONSIS-
TENT WITH PROPRIETY, ... 31
Introduction, ... *ib.*
CHAP. I. Of the Passions which take their origin from the Body, 33
... II. Of those Passions which take their origin from a parti-
cular turn or habit of the Imagination, . 39
... III. Of the Unsocial Passions, ... 44

                                                              Page
CHAP. IV. Of the Social Passions,   .   .   .   52
    ...   V. Of the Selfish Passions,   .   .   .   55

                    SECTION III.

OF THE EFFECTS OF PROSPERITY AND ADVERSITY UPON THE JUDG-
    MENT OF MANKIND WITH REGARD TO THE PROPRIETY OF ACTION;
    AND WHY IT IS MORE EASY TO OBTAIN THEIR APPROBATION IN THE
    ONE STATE THAN IN THE OTHER, ... 60

CHAP. I. That though our sympathy with Sorrow is generally
              a more lively sensation than our sympathy with
              Joy, it commonly falls much more short of the
              violence of what is naturally felt by the person
              principally concerned,   .   .   .   ib.
    ...   II. Of the origin of Ambition, and of the distinction of
              Ranks, ...   70
         III. Of the corruption of our Moral Sentiments, which
              is occasioned by this disposition to admire the
              rich and the great, and to despise or neglect per-
              sons of poor and mean condition,   .   84

                    PART II.

OF MERIT AND DEMERIT ; OR, OF THE OBJECTS OF REWARD
    AND PUNISHMENT, ...   91

                    SECTION I.

OF THE SENSE OF MERIT AND DEMERIT,   .   .   .   93
Introduction, ...   ib.
CHAP. I. That whatever appears to be the proper object
              of gratitude appears to deserve reward ; and
              that, in the same manner, whatever appears to be
              the proper object of resentment appears to de-
              serve punishment,   .   .   .   94
         II. Of the proper Objects of Gratitude and Resentment, 97
        III. That where there is no approbation of the conduct
              of the person who confers the benefit, there is
              little sympathy with the gratitude of him who
              receives it; and that, on the contrary, where there

Page

is no disapprobation of the motives of the person who does the mischief, there is no sort of sympathy with the resentment of him who suffers it, ... 100

CHAP. IV. Recapitulation of the foregoing Chapters, 103

V. The Analysis of the Sense of Merit and Demerit, 105

SECTION II.

OF JUSTICE AND BENEFICENCE, ... 112

CHAP. I. Comparison of those two Virtues, . . . *ib.*

.. II. Of the sense of Justice, of Remorse, and of the consciousness of Merit, . . . 119

... III. Of the utility of this constitution of Nature, 124

SECTION III.

OF THE INFLUENCE OF FORTUNE UPON THE SENTIMENTS OF MANKIND, WITH REGARD TO THE MERIT OR DEMERIT OF ACTIONS, . 133

Introduction, ... *ib.*

CHAP. I. Of the Causes of this Influence of Fortune, . 136

... II. Of the Extent of this Influence of Fortune, . 141

... III. Of the final Cause of this Irregularity of Sentiments, ... 152

PART III.

OF THE FOUNDATION OF OUR JUDGMENTS CONCERNING OUR OWN SENTIMENTS AND CONDUCT, AND OF THE SENSE OF DUTY, ... 159

CHAP. I. Of the Principle of Self-approbation and Self-disapprobation, ... 161

... II. Of the love of Praise, and of that of Praise-worthiness; and of the dread of Blame, and of that of Blame-worthiness, . . 166

... III. Of the Influence and Authority of Conscience, . 191

... IV. Of the Nature of Self-deceit, and of the Origin and Use of general Rules, . . . 221

... V. Of the Influence and Authority of the general

Page

Rules of Morality, and that they are justly regarded as the Laws of the Deity, . . 229
CHAP. VI. In what cases the Sense of Duty ought to be the
sole principle of our Conduct ; and in what cases
it ought to concur with other Motives, 243

PART IV.

OF THE EFFECT OF UTILITY UPON THE SENTIMENT OF
APPROBATION, ... 255
CHAP. I. Of the Beauty which the Appearance of Utility bestows upon all the Productions of Art, and of
the extensive Influence of this Species of
Beauty, ... 257
.. II. Of the Beauty which the Appearance of Utility bestows upon the Characters and Actions of Men ;
and how far the Perception of this Beauty may
be regarded as one of the original Principles of
Approbation, ... 269

PART V.

OF THE INFLUENCE OF CUSTOM AND FASHION UPON THE
SENTIMENTS OF MORAL APPROBATION AND DISAPPRO-
BATION, ... 279
CHAP. I. Of the Influence of Custom and Fashion upon our
notions of Beauty and Deformity, . 281
... II. Of the Influence of Custom and Fashion upon Moral
Sentiments, ... 290

PART VI.

OF THE CHARACTER OF VIRTUE 307
Introduction, ... 309

SECTION I.

OF THE CHARACTER OF THE INDIVIDUAL SO FAR AS IT AFFECTS HIS
OWN HAPPINESS ; OR OF PRUDENCE, . . 310

CONTENTS.

SECTION II.

Page

OF THE CHARACTER OF THE INDIVIDUAL SO FAR AS IT CAN AFFECT
THE HAPPINESS OF OTHER PEOPLE, ... 319

Introduction, ... *ib.*

CHAP. I. Of the Order in which Individuals are recommended
by Nature to our care and attention, . . 321

... II. Of the Order in which Societies are by Nature recommended to our Beneficence, . . . 334

... III. Of Universal Benevolence, . . . 345

SECTION III.

OF SELF-COMMAND, ... 349

CONCLUSION OF THE SIXTH PART, ... 385

PART VII.

OF SYSTEMS OF MORAL PHILOSOPHY, . . . 389

SECTION I.

OF THE QUESTIONS WHICH OUGHT TO BE EXAMINED IN A THEORY
OF MORAL SENTIMENTS, ... 391

SECTION II.

OF THE DIFFERENT ACCOUNTS WHICH HAVE BEEN GIVEN OF THE
NATURE OF VIRTUE, ... 393

Introduction, ... *ib.*

CHAP. I. Of those Systems which make Virtue consist in
Propriety. 395

... II. Of those Systems which make Virtue consist in
Prudence, ... 431

... III. Of those Systems which make Virtue consist in
Benevolence, ... 440

... IV. Of Licentious Systems 449

CONTENTS.

SECTION III.

Page

OF THE DIFFERENT SYSTEMS WHICH HAVE BEEN FORMED CONCERN-
ING THE PRINCIPLE OF APPROBATION, . . . 461

Introduction, ... *ib.*

CHAP. I. Of those Systems which deduce the Principle of Approbation from Self-love, . . . 463

... II. Of those Systems which make Reason the Principle
of Approbation, ... 467

... III. Of those Systems which make Sentiment the Principle of Approbation, ... 472

SECTION IV.

OF THE MANNER IN WHICH DIFFERENT AUTHORS HAVE TREATED OF
THE PRACTICAL RULES OF MORALITY, . . . 482

CONSIDERATIONS CONCERNING THE FIRST FORMATION OF
LANGUAGES, &c. 505

ACCOUNT OF THE LIFE AND WRITINGS

OF

ADAM SMITH, LL.D.,

BY

DUGALD STEWART.

———◆———

FROM HIS BIRTH TILL THE PUBLICATION OF THE HEORY
OF MORAL SENTIMENTS.

ADAM SMITH, author of the Inquiry into the Nature and
Causes of the Wealth of Nations, was the son of Adam Smith,
comptroller of the customs at Kirkaldy,* and of Margaret Douglas,
daughter of Mr. Douglas of Strathenry. He was the only child of
the marriage, and was born at Kirkaldy, on the 5th of June, 1723,
a few months after the death of his father.

His constitution during infancy was infirm and sickly, and required all the tender solicitude of his surviving parent. She was
blamed for treating him with an unlimited indulgence ; but it
produced no unfavourable effects on his temper or his disposition : and he enjoyed the rare satisfaction of being able to repay
her affection, by every attention that filial gratitude could dictate,
during the long period of sixty years.

---

* Mr. Smith, the father, was a native of Aberdeenshire, and, in the
earlier part of his life, practised at Edinburgh as a writer to the signet.
He was afterwards private secretary to the Earl of Loudoun (during the
time he held the offices of principal secretary of state for Scotland, and
of keeper of the great seal), and continued in this situation till 1713 or
1714, when he was appointed comptroller of the customs at Kirkaldy.
He was also clerk to the courts-martial and councils of war for Scotland ; an office which he held from 1707 till his death. As it is now
seventy years since he died, the accounts I have received of him are
very imperfect ; but, from the particulars already mentioned, it may be
presumed, that he was a man of more than common abilities.

An accident which happened to him when he was about three years old, is of too interesting a nature to be omitted in the account of so valuable a life. He had been carried by his mother to Strathenry, on a visit to his uncle Mr. Douglas, and was one day amusing himself alone at the door of the house, when he was stolen by a party of that set of vagrants who are known in Scotland by the name of tinkers. Luckily he was soon missed by his uncle, who, hearing that some vagrants had passed, pursued them, with what assistance he could find, till he overtook them in Leslie wood ; and was the happy instrument of preserving to the world a genius, which was destined, not only to extend the boundaries of science, but to enlighten and reform the commercial policy of Europe.

The school of Kirkaldy, where Mr. Smith received the first rudiments of his education, was then conducted by Mr. David Miller, a teacher, in his day, of considerable reputation, and whose name deserves to be recorded, on account of the eminent men whom that very obscure seminary produced while under his direction. Of these were Mr. Oswald, of Dunikeir ;* his brother, Dr. John Oswald, afterwards Bishop of Raphoe ; and our late excellent colleague, the Rev. Dr. John Drysdale : all of them nearly contemporary with Mr. Smith, and united with him through life by the closest ties of friendship. One of his schoolfellows is still alive ;† and to his kindness I am principally indebted for the scanty materials which form the first part of this narrative.

Among these companions of his earliest years, Mr. Smith soon attracted notice, by his passion for books, and by the extraordinary powers of his memory. The weakness of his bodily constitution prevented him from partaking in their more active amusements ; but he was much beloved by them on account of his temper, which, though warm, was, to an uncommon degree,

* The late James Oswald, Esq.—for many years one of the most active, able, and public-spirited of our Scottish representatives in Parliament. He was more particularly distinguished by his knowledge in matters of finance, and by his attention to whatever concerned the commercial or the agricultural interests of the country. From the manner in which he is mentioned in a paper of Mr. Smith's, which I have perused, he appears to have combined, with that detailed information which he is well known to have possessed, as a statesman and man of business, a taste for the more general and philosophical discussions of political economy. He lived in habits of great intimacy with Lord Kames and Mr. Hume ; and was one of Mr. Smith's earliest and most confidential friends.

† George Drysdale, Esq., of Kirkaldy, brother of the late Dr. Drysdale.

friendly and generous. Even then he was remarkable for those habits which remained with him through life, of speaking to himself when alone, and of *absence* in company.

From the grammar-school of Kirkaldy, he was sent, in 1737, to the university of Glasgow, where he remained till 1740, when he went to Baliol College, Oxford, as an exhibitioner on Snell's foundation.

Dr. Maclaine, of the Hague, who was a fellow-student of Mr. Smith's at Glasgow, told me some years ago, that his favourite pursuits while at that university were mathematics and natural philosophy; and I remember to have heard my father remind him of a geometrical problem of considerable difficulty, about which he was occupied at the time when their acquaintance commenced, and which had been proposed to him as an exercise by the celebrated Dr. Simpson.

These, however, were certainly not the sciences in which he was formed to excel; nor did they long divert him from pursuits more congenial to his mind. What Lord Bacon says of Plato may be justly applied to him : " Illum, licet ad rempublicam non accessisset, tamen naturâ et inclinatione omnino ad res civiles propensum, vires eo præcipue intendisse ; neque de Philosophia Naturali admodum sollicitum esse ; nisi quatenus ad Philosophi nomen et celebritatem tuendam, et ad majestatem quandam moralibus et civilibus doctrinis addendam et aspergendam sufficeret." * The study of human nature in all its branches, more particularly of the political history of mankind, opened a boundless field to his curiosity and ambition ; and while it afforded scope to all the various powers of his versatile and comprehensive genius, gratified his ruling passion of contributing to the happiness and the improvement of society. To this study, diversified at his leisure hours by the less severe occupations of polite literature, he seems to have devoted himself almost entirely from the time of his removal to Oxford ; but he still retained, even in advanced years, a recollection of his early acquisitions, which not only added to the splendour of his conversation, but enabled him to exemplify some of his favourite theories concerning the natural progress of the mind in the investigation of truth, by the history of those sciences in which the connection and succession of discoveries may be traced with the greatest advantage. If I am not mistaken, too, the influence of his early taste for the Greek Geometry may be remarked in the elementary clearness and fulness, bordering sometimes upon prolixity, with which he frequently states his political reasonings. The lectures of the profound and eloquent Dr. Hutcheson, which he had attended

* Redargutio Philosophiarum.

previous to his departure from Glasgow, and of which he always spoke in terms of the warmest admiration, had, it may be reasonably presumed, a considerable effect in directing his talents to their proper objects.*

I have not been able to collect any information with respect to that part of his youth which was spent in England. I have heard him say, that he employed himself frequently in the practice of translation (particularly from the French), with a view to the improvement of his own style : and he used often to express a favourable opinion of the utility of such exercises to all who cultivate the art of composition. It is much to be regretted, that none of his juvenile attempts in this way have been preserved ; as the few specimens which his writings contain of his skill as a translator, are sufficient to show the eminence he had attained in a walk of literature, which, in our country, has been so little frequented by men of genius.

It was probably also at this period of his life, that he cultivated with the greatest care the study of languages. The knowledge he possessed of these, both ancient and modern, was uncommonly extensive and accurate ; and, in him, was subservient, not to a vain parade of tasteless erudition, but to a familiar acquaintance with every thing that could illustrate the institutions, the manners, and the ideas of different ages and nations. How intimately he had once been conversant with the more ornamental branches of learning, in particular, with the works of the Roman, Greek, French, and Italian poets ; appeared sufficiently from the hold which they kept of his memory, after all the diffe-

---

* Those who have derived their knowledge of Dr. Hutcheson solely from his publications, may, perhaps, be inclined to dispute the propriety of the epithet *eloquent,* when applied to any of his compositions; more particularly, his *System of Moral Philosophy,* which was published after his death. His talents, however, as a public speaker, must have been of a far higher order than what he has displayed as a writer ; all his pupils whom I have happened to meet with (some of them, certainly, very competent judges) having agreed exactly with each other in their accounts of the extraordinary impression which they made on the minds of his hearers.

Dr. Hutcheson's Inquiry into our Ideas of Beauty and Virtue ; his Discourse on the Passions; and his Illustrations of the Moral Sense, are much more strongly marked with the characteristical features of his genius, than his posthumous work. His great and deserved fame, however, rests *now* chiefly on the traditionary history of his academical lectures, which appear to have contributed very powerfully to diffuse, in Scotland, that taste for analytical discussion, and that spirit of liberal inquiry, to which the world is indebted for some of the most valuable productions of the eighteenth century.

rent occupations and inquiries in which his maturer faculties had been employed.* In the English language, the variety of poetical passages which he was not only accustomed to refer to occasionally, but which he was able to repeat with correctness, appeared surprising even to those whose attention had never been directed to more important acquisitions.

After a residence at Oxford of seven years, he returned to Kirkaldy, and lived two years with his mother ; engaged in study, but without any fixed plan for his future life. He had been originally destined for the Church of England, and with that view had been sent to Oxford ; but not finding the ecclesiastical profession suitable to his taste, he chose to consult, in this instance, his own inclination, in preference to the wishes of his friends ; and abandoning at once all the schemes which their prudence had formed for him, he resolved to return to his own country, and to limit his ambition to the uncertain prospect of obtaining, in time, some one of those moderate preferments, to which literary attainments lead in Scotland.

In the year 1748, he fixed his residence at Edinburgh, and during that and the following years, read lectures on rhetoric and belles lettres, under the patronage of Lord Kames. About this time, too, he contracted a very intimate friendship, which continued without interruption till his death, with Mr. Alexander Wedderburn, now Lord Loughborough, and with Mr. William Johnstone, now Mr. Pulteney.

At what particular period his acquaintance with Mr. David Hume commenced, does not appear from any information that I have received ; but from some papers, now in the possession of Mr. Hume's nephew, and which he has been so obliging as to allow me to peruse, their acquaintance seems to have grown into friendship before the year 1752. It was a friendship on both sides founded on the admiration of genius, and the love of simplicity ; and which forms an interesting circumstance in the history of each of these eminent men, from the ambition which both have shown to record it to posterity.

In 1751, he was elected Professor of Logic in the University of Glasgow ; and the year following, he was removed to the Profes-

---

* The uncommon degree in which Mr. Smith retained possession, even to the close of his life, of different branches of knowledge which he had long ceased to cultivate, has been often remarked to me by my learned colleague and friend, Mr. Dalzel, Professor of Greek in this University.——Mr. Dalzel mentioned particularly the readiness and correctness of Mr. Smith's memory on philological subjects, and the acuteness and skill he displayed in various conversations with him on some of the *minutiæ* of Greek grammar.

sorship of Moral Philosophy in the same University, upon the death of Mr. Thomas Craigie, the immediate successor of Dr. Hutcheson. In this situation he remained thirteen years ; a period he used frequently to look back to, as the most useful and happy of his life. It was indeed a situation in which he was eminently fitted to excel, and in which the daily labours of his profession were constantly recalling his attention to his favourite pursuits, and familiarising his mind to those important speculations he was afterwards to communicate to the world. In this view, though it afforded, in the meantime, but a very narrow scene for his ambition, it was probably instrumental, in no inconsiderable degree, to the future eminence of his literary character.

Of Mr. Smith's lectures while Professor at Glasgow, no part has been preserved, excepting what he himself published in the Theory of Moral Sentiments, and in the Wealth of Nations. For the following short account of them, I am indebted to a gentleman who was formerly one of Mr. Smith's pupils, and who continued till his death to be one of his most intimate and valued friends.*

" In the Professorship of Logic, to which Mr. Smith was appointed on his first introduction into this University, he soon saw the necessity of departing widely from the plan that had been followed by his predecessors, and of directing the attention of his pupils to studies of a more interesting and useful nature than the logic and metaphysics of the schools. Accordingly, after exhibiting a general view of the powers of the mind, and explaining so much of the ancient logic as was requisite to gratify curiosity with respect to an artificial method of reasoning, which had once occupied the universal attention of the learned, he dedicated all the rest of his time to the delivery of a system of rhetoric and belles lettres. The best method of explaining and illustrating the various powers of the human mind, the most useful part of metaphysics, arises from an examination of the several ways of communicating our thoughts by speech, and from an attention to the principles of those literary compositions which contribute to persuasion or entertainment. By these arts, everything that we perceive or feel, every operation of our minds, is expressed and delineated in such a manner, that it may be clearly distinguished and remembered. There is, at the same time, no branch of literature more suited to youth at their first entrance upon philosophy than this, which lays hold of their taste and their feelings.

" It is much to be regretted, that the manuscript containing

* Mr. Millar, the late celebrated Professor of Law in the University Glasgow.

Mr. Smith's lectures on this subject was destroyed before his death. The first part, in point of composition, was highly finished ; and the whole discovered strong marks of taste and original genius. From the permission given to students of taking notes, many observations and opinions contained in these lectures have either been detailed in separate dissertations, or engrossed in general collections, which have since been given to the public. But these, as might be expected, have lost the air of originality and the distinctive character which they received from their first author, and are often obscured by that multiplicity of common-place matter in which they are sunk and involved.

"About a year after his appointment to the Professorship of Logic, Mr. Smith was elected to the chair of Moral Philosophy. His course of lectures on this subject was divided into four parts. The first contained Natural Theology ; in which he considered the proofs of the being and attributes of God, and those principles of the human mind upon which religion is founded. The second comprehended Ethics, strictly so called, and consisted chiefly of the doctrines which he afterwards published in his Theory of Moral Sentiments. In the third part, he treated at more length of that branch of morality which relates to *justice*, and which, being susceptible of precise and accurate rules, is for that reason capable of a full and particular explanation.

" Upon this subject he followed the plan that seems to be suggested by Montesquieu ; endeavouring to trace the gradual progress of jurisprudence, both public and private, from the rudest to the most refined ages, and to point out the effects of those arts which contribute to subsistence, and to the accumulation of property, in producing correspondent improvements or alterations in law and government. This important branch of his labours he also intended to give to the public ; but this intention, which is mentioned in the conclusion of the Theory of Moral Sentiments, he did not live to fulfil.

" In the last part of his lectures, he examined those political regulations which are founded, not upon the principle of *justice*, but that of *expediency*, and which are calculated to increase the riches, the power, and the prosperity of a State. Under this view, he considered the political institutions relating to commerce, to finances, to ecclesiastical and military establishments. What he delivered on these subjects contained the substance of the work he afterwards published under the title of An Inquiry into the Nature and Causes of the Wealth of Nations.

" There was no situation in which the abilities of Mr. Smith appeared to greater advantage than as a Professor. In delivering his lectures, he trusted almost entirely to extemporary elocution. His manner, though not graceful, was plain and unaffected ; and, as he seemed to be always interested in the subject, he never failed to interest his hearers. Each discourse consisted commonly of several distinct propositions, which he successively endeavoured to prove and illustrate. These propositions, when announced in general terms, had, from their extent, not unfrequently something of the air of a paradox. In his attempts to explain them, he often appeared, at first, not to be sufficiently possessed of the subject, and spoke with some hesitation. As he advanced, however, the matter seemed to crowd upon him, his manner became warm and animated, and his expression easy and fluent. In points susceptible of controversy, you could easily discern, that he secretly conceived an opposition to his opinions, and that he was led upon this account to support them with greater energy and vehemence. By the fulness and variety of his illustrations, the subject gradually swelled in his hands, and acquired a dimension which, without a tedious repetition of the same views, was calculated to seize the attention of his audience, and to afford them pleasure, as well as instruction, in following the same object, through all the diversity of shades and aspects in which it was presented, and afterwards in tracing it backwards to that original proposition or general truth from which this beautiful train of speculation had proceeded.

"His reputation as a Professor was accordingly raised very high, and a multitude of students from a great distance resorted to the University, merely upon his account. Those branches of science which he taught became fashionable at this place, and his opinions were the chief topics of discussion in clubs and literary societies. Even the small peculiarities in his pronounciation or manner of speaking, became frequently the objects of imitation."

While Mr. Smith was thus distinguishing himself by his zeal and ability as a public teacher, he was gradually laying the foundation of a more extensive reputation, by preparing for the press his system of morals. The first edition of this work appeared in 1759, under the title of "The Theory of Moral Sentiments."

Hitherto Mr. Smith had remained unknown to the world as an author ; nor have I heard that he had made a trial of his powers in any anonymous publications, excepting in a periodical work called *The Edinburgh Review*, which was begun in the year 1755, by some gentlemen of distinguished abilities, but which they were prevented by other engagements from carrying further than the two first numbers. To this work Mr. Smith contributed a review of Dr. Johnson's Dictionary of the English Language, and also a letter, addressed to the editors, containing some general observations on the state of literature in the different countries of Europe. In the former of these papers he points out some defects in Dr. Johnson's plan, which he censures as not sufficiently grammatical. "The different significations of a word (he observes) are indeed collected ; but they are seldom digested into general classes, or ranged under the meaning which the word principally expresses: And sufficient care is not taken to distinguish the words apparently synonymous." To illustrate this criticism, he copies from Dr. Johnson the articles BUT and HUMOUR, and opposes to them the same articles digested agreeably to his own idea. The various significations of the word BUT are very nicely and happily discriminated. The other article does not seem to have been executed with equal care.

The observations on the state of learning in Europe are written with ingenuity and elegance ; but are chiefly interesting, as they show the attention which the Author had given to the philosophy and literature of the Continent, at a period when they were not much studied in this island.

In the same volume with the Theory of Moral Sentiments, Mr. Smith published a Dissertation " On the Origin of Languages, and on the different Genius of those which are original and compounded." The remarks I have to offer on these two discourses, I shall, for the sake of distinctness, make the subject of a separate section.

———◆———

Of the Theory of Moral Sentiments, and the Dissertation on the Origin of Languages.

THE science of Ethics has been divided by modern writers into two parts ; the one comprehending the theory of Morals, and the other its practical doctrines. The questions about which the former is employed, are chiefly the two following : *First*, By what *principle* of our constitution are we led to form the notion of moral distinctions ;—whether by that faculty which, in the other branches of human knowledge, perceives the distinction between truth and falsehood ; or by a peculiar power of perception (called by some the Moral Sense) which is *pleased* with one set of qualities, and *displeased* with another ? *Secondly*, What is the proper *object* of moral approbation ? or, in other words, What is the common quality or qualities belonging to all the different modes of virtue ? Is it benevolence ; or a rational self-love ; or a disposition (resulting from the ascendancy of Reason over Passion) to act suitably to the different relations in which we are placed ? These two questions seem to exhaust the whole theory of Morals.

The scope of the one is to ascertain the origin of our moral ideas; that of the other, to refer the phenomena of moral perception to their most simple and general laws.

The practical doctrines of morality comprehend all those rules of conduct which profess to point out the proper ends of human pursuit, and the most effectual means of attaining them; to which we may add all those literary compositions, whatever be their particular form, which have for their aim to fortify and animate our good dispositions, by delineations of the beauty, of the dignity, or of the utility of Virtue.

I shall not inquire at present into the justness of this division. I shall only observe, that the words Theory and Practice are not, in this instance, employed in their usual acceptations. The theory of Morals does not bear, for example, the same relation to the practice of Morals, that the theory of Geometry bears to practical Geometery. In this last science, all the practical rules are founded on theoretical principles previously established. But in the former science, the practical rules are obvious to the capacities of all mankind; the theoretical principles form one of the most difficult subjects of discussion that have ever exercised the ingenuity of metaphysicians.

In illustrating the doctrines of practical morality (if we make allowance for some unfortunate prejudices produced or encouraged by violent and oppressive systems of policy), the ancients seem to have availed themselves of every light furnished by nature to human reason; and indeed those writers who, in later times, have treated the subject with the greatest success, are they who have followed most closely the footsteps of the Greek and the Roman philosophers. The theoretical question, too, concerning the essence of virtue, or the proper *object* of moral approbation, was a favourite topic of discussion in the ancient schools. The question concerning the *principle* of moral approbation, though not entirely of modern origin, has been chiefly agitated since the writings of Cudworth, in opposition to those of Hobbes; and it is this question accordingly (recommended at once by its novelty and difficulty to the curiosity of speculative men) that has produced most of the theories which characterise and distinguish from each other the later systems of moral philosophy.

It was the opinion of Dr. Cudworth, and also of Dr. Clarke, that moral distinctions are perceived by that power of the mind, which distinguishes truth from falsehood. This system it was one great object of Dr. Hutcheson's philosophy to refute, and in opposition to it, to show that the words Right and Wrong express certain agreeable and disagreeable qualities in actions, which it is not the province of reason but of feeling to perceive; and to that power of perception which renders us susceptible of pleasure or of pain from the view of virtue or of vice, he gave the name of the Moral Sense. His reasonings upon this subject are in the main acquiesced in, both by Mr. Hume and Mr. Smith ; but they differ from him in one important particular,—Dr. Hutcheson plainly supposing, that the moral sense is a simple principle of our constitution, of which no account can be given ; whereas the other two philosophers have both attempted to analyze it into other principles more general. Their systems, however, with respect to it are very different from each other. According to Mr. Hume, all the qualities which are denominated virtuous, are useful either to ourselves or to others, and the pleasure which we derive from the view of them is the pleasure of utility. Mr. Smith, without rejecting entirely Mr. Hume's doctrine, proposes another of his own, far more comprehensive ; a doctrine with which he thinks all the most celebrated theories of morality invented by his predecessors coincide in part, and from some partial view of which he apprehends that they have all proceeded.

Of this very ingenious and original theory, I shall endeavour to give a short abstract. To those who are familiarly acquainted with it as it is stated by its author, I am aware that the attempt may appear superfluous ; but I flatter myself that it will not be wholly useless to such as have not been much conversant in these abstract disquisitions, by presenting to them the leading principles of the system in one connected view, without those interruptions of the attention which necessarily arise from the author's various and happy illustrations, and from the many eloquent digressions which animate and adorn his composition.

The fundamental principle of Mr. Smith's theory is, that the primary objects of our moral perceptions are the actions of other men ; and that our moral judgments with respect to our own conduct are only applications to ourselves of decisions which we have already passed on the conduct of our neighbour. His work accordingly includes two distinct inquiries, which, although sometimes blended together in the execution of his general design, it is necessary for the reader to discriminate carefully from each other, in order to comprehend all the different bearings of the argument. The aim of the former inquiry is, to explain in what manner we learn to judge of the conduct of our neighbour ; that of the latter, to show how, by applying these judgments to ourselves, we acquire *a sense of duty*, and a feeling of its paramount authority over all our other principles of action.

Our moral judgments, both with respect to our own conduct and that of others, include two distinct perceptions : *first*, A perception of conduct as right or wrong ; and, *secondly*, A perception of the merit or demerit of the agent. To that quality of conduct

which moralists, in general, express by the word Rectitude, **Mr.**
Smith gives the name of Propriety; and he begins his theory
with inquiring in what it consists, and how we are led to form
the idea of it. The leading principles of his doctrine on this subject are comprehended in the following propositions :—

1. It is from our own experience alone, that we can form any
idea of what passes in the mind of another person on any particular occasion; and the only way in which we can form this
idea, is by supposing ourselves in the same circumstances with
him, and conceiving how we should be affected if we were so
situated. It is impossible for us, however, to conceive ourselves
placed in any situation, whether agreeable or otherwise, without
feeling an effect of the same kind with what would be produced
by the situation itself; and consequently the attention we give
at any time to the circumstances of our neighbour, must affect us
somewhat in the same manner, although by no means in the
same degree, as if these circumstances were our own.

That this imaginary change of situation, is the real source
of the interest we take in their fortunes, Mr. Smith attempts
to prove by various instances. "When we see a stroke aimed,
and just ready to fall upon the leg or arm of another person,
we naturally shrink and draw back our own leg or our own
arm; and when it does fall, we feel it in some measure, and are
hurt by it as well as the sufferer. The mob, when they are gazing
at a dancer on the slack-rope, naturally writhe and twist and
balance their own bodies, as they see him do, and as they feel
that they themselves must do if in his situation." The same
thing takes place, according to Mr. Smith, in every case in which
our attention is turned to the condition of our neighbour. Whatever is the passion which arises from any object in the person
principally concerned, an analogous emotion springs up, at the
thought of his situation, in the breast of every attentive spectator.
In every passion of which the mind of man is susceptible, the
emotions of the bystander always correspond to what, by bringing
the case home to himself, he imagines should be the sentiments of
the sufferer.

To this principle of our nature which leads us to enter into the
situations of other men, and to partake with them in the passions
which these situations have a tendency to excite, Mr. Smith gives
the name of *sympathy* or *fellow-feeling*, which two words he
employs as synonymous. He acknowledges that, upon some occasions, sympathy arises merely from the view of a certain emotion in
another person; but that in general it arises, not so much from the
view of the emotion, as from that of the situation which excites it.

2. A sympathy or fellow-feeling between different persons is
always agreeable to both. When I am in a situation which ex-

cites any passion, it is pleasant to me to know, that the spectators
of my situation enter with me into all its various circumstances,
and are affected with them in the same manner as I am myself.
On the other hand, it is pleasant to the spectator to observe this
correspondence of his emotions with mine.

3. When the spectator of another man's situation, upon
bringing home to himself all its various circumstances, feels
himself affected in the same manner with the person principally
concerned, he approves of the affection or passion of this person
as just and proper, and suitable to its object. The exceptions
which occur to this observation are, according to Mr. Smith, only
apparent. "A stranger, for example, passes by us in the street
with all the marks of the deepest affliction : and we are immediately told, that he has just received the news of the death of
his father. It is impossible that, in this case, we should not approve of his grief ; yet it may often happen, without any defect
of humanity on our part, that, so far from entering into the violence of his sorrow, we should scarce conceive the first movements
of concern upon his account. We have learned, however, from
experience, that such a misfortune naturally excites such a degree
of sorrow ; and we know, that if we took time to examine his
situation fully, and in all its parts, we should, without doubt, most
sincerely sympathise with him. It is upon the consciousness of
this conditional sympathy that our approbation of his sorrow is
founded, even in those cases in which that sympathy does not
actually take place ; and the general rules derived from our preceding experience of what our sentiments would commonly correspond with, correct upon this, as upon many other occasions,
the impropriety of our present emotions."

By the *propriety* therefore of any affection or passion exhibited
by another person, is to be understood its suitableness to the
object which excites it. Of this suitableness I can judge only
from the coincidence of the affection with that which I feel,
when I conceive myself in the same circumstances ; and the perception of this coincidence is the foundation of the sentiment of
moral approbation.

4. Although, when we attend to the situation of another person, and conceive ourselves to be placed in his circumstances, an
emotion of the same kind with that which he feels naturally
arises in our own mind, yet this sympathetic emotion bears but a
very small proportion, in point of degree, to what is felt by the
person principally concerned. In order, therefore, to obtain the
pleasure of mutual sympathy, nature teaches the spectator to
strive, as much as he can, to raise his emotion to a level with
that which the object would really produce : and, on the other
hand, she teaches the person whose passion this object has ex-

cited, to bring it down, as much as he can, to a level with that of the spectator.

5. Upon these two different efforts are founded two different sets of virtues. Upon the effort of the spectator to enter into the situation of the person principally concerned, and to raise his sympathetic emotions to a level with the emotions of the actor, are founded the gentle, the amiable virtues; the virtues of candid condescension and indulgent humanity. Upon the effort of the person principally concerned to lower his own emotions, so as to correspond as nearly as possible with those of the spectator, are founded the great, the awful, and respectable virtues ; the virtues of self-denial, of self-government, of that command of the passions, which subjects all the movements of our nature to what our own dignity and honour, and the propriety of our own conduct, require.

As a farther illustration of the foregoing doctrine, Mr. Smith considers particularly the degrees of the different passions which are consistent with propriety, and endeavours to show, that, in every case, it is decent or indecent to express a passion strongly, according as mankind are disposed, or not disposed, to sympathize with it. It is unbecoming, for example, to express strongly any of those passions which arise from a certain condition of the body ; because other men, who are not in the same condition, cannot be expected to sympathize with them. It is unbecoming to cry out with bodily pain ; because the sympathy felt by the spectator bears no proportion to the acuteness of what is felt by the sufferer. The case is somewhat similar with those passions which take their origin from a particular turn or habit of the imagination.

In the case of the unsocial passions of hatred and resentment, the sympathy of the spectator is divided between the person who feels the passion, and the person who is the object of it. " We are concerned for both, and our fear for what the one may suffer damps our resentment for what the other has suffered." Hence the imperfect degree in which we sympathise with such passions ; and the propriety, when we are under their influence, of moderating their expression to a much greater degree than is required in the case of any other emotions.

The reverse of this takes place with respect to all the social and benevolent affections. The sympathy of the spectator with the person who feels them, coincides with his concern for the person who is the object of them. It is this redoubled sympathy which renders these affections so peculiarly becoming and agreeable.

The selfish emotions of grief and joy, when they are conceived on account of our own private good or bad fortune, hold a sort of middle place between our social and our unsocial passions. They are never so graceful as the one set, nor so odious as the other. Even when excessive, they are never so disagreeable as excessive resentment ; because no opposite sympathy can ever interest us against them : and when most suitable to their objects, they are never so agreeable as impartial humanity and just benevolence ; because no double sympathy can ever interest us for them.

After these general speculations concerning the propriety of actions, Mr. Smith examines how far the judgments of mankind concerning it are liable to be influenced, in particular cases, by the prosperous or the adverse circumstances of the agent. The scope of his reasoning on this subject is directed to show (in opposition to the common opinion), that when there is no envy in the case, our propensity to sympathise with joy is much stronger than our propensity to sympathise with sorrow ; and, of consequence, that it is more easy to obtain the approbation of mankind in prosperity than in adversity. From the same principle he traces the origin of ambition, or of the desire of rank and pre-eminence ; the great object of which passion is, to attain that situation which sets a man most in the view of general sympathy and attention, and gives him an easy empire over the affections of others.

Having finished the analysis of our sense of propriety and of impropriety, Mr. Smith proceeds to consider our sense of merit and demerit ; which he thinks has also a reference, in the first instance, not to our own characters, but to the characters of our neighbours. In explaining the origin of this part of our moral constitution, he avails himself of the same principle of sympathy, into which he resolves the sentiment of moral approbation.

The words *propriety* and *impropriety*, when applied to an affection of the mind, are used in this theory (as has been already observed) to express the suitableness or unsuitableness of the affection to its exciting *cause*. The words *merit* and *demerit* have always a reference (according to Mr. Smith) to the *effect* which the affection tends to produce. When the tendency of an affection is beneficial, the agent appears to us a proper object of reward ; when it is hurtful, he appears the proper object of punishment.

The principles in our nature which most directly prompt us to reward and to punish, are gratitude and resentment. To say of a person, therefore, that he is deserving of reward or of punishment, is to say, in other words, that he is a proper object of gratitude or of resentment ; or, which amounts to the same thing, that he is to some person or persons the object of a gratitude or of a resentment, which every reasonable man is ready to adopt and sympathize with.

It is, however, **very necessary** to observe, that we do not thoroughly sympathize with the gratitude of one man towards another, merely because this other has been the cause of his good fortune, unless he has been the cause of it from motives which we entirely oppose. Our sense, therefore, of the good desert of an action, is a compounded sentiment, made up of an indirect sympathy with the person to whom the action is beneficial, and of a direct sympathy with the affections and motives of the agent. The same remark applies, *mutatis mutandis*, to our sense of demerit, or of ill-desert.

From these principles, it is inferred, that the only actions which appear to us deserving of reward, are actions of a beneficial tendency, proceeding from proper motives ; the only actions which seem to deserve punishment, are actions of a hurtful tendency, proceeding from improper motives. A mere want of beneficence exposes to no punishment ; because the mere want of beneficence tends to do no real positive evil. A man, on the other hand, who is barely innocent, and contents himself with observing strictly the laws of justice with respect to others, can merit only, that his neighbours, in their turn, should observe religiously the same laws with respect to him.

These observations lead Mr. Smith to anticipate a little the subject of the second great division of his work, by a short inquiry into the origin of our sense of justice, *as applicable to our own conduct;* and also of our sentiments of remorse, and of good desert.

The origin of our sense of justice, as well as of all our other moral sentiments, he accounts for by means of the principle of sympathy. When I attend only to the feelings of my own breast, my own happiness appears to me of far greater consequence than that of all the world besides. But I am conscious, that, in this excessive preference, other men cannot possibly sympathize with me, and that to them I appear only one of the crowd, in whom they are no more interested than in any other individual. If I wish, therefore, to secure their sympathy and approbation (which, according to Mr. Smith, are the objects of the strongest desire of my nature), it is necessary for me to regard my happiness, not in that light in which it appears to myself, but in that light in which it appears to mankind in general. If an unprovoked injury is offered to me, I know that society will sympathize with my resentment ; but if I injure the interests of another, who never injured me, merely because they stand in the way of my own, I perceive evidently, that society will sympathize with *his* resentment, and that I shall become the object of general indignation.

When, upon any occasion, I am led by the violence of passion to overlook these considerations, and in the case of a competition of interests, to act according to my own feelings, and not according to those of impartial spectators, I never fail to incur

the punishment of remorse. When my passion is gratified, and I begin to reflect coolly on my conduct, I can no longer enter into the motives from which it proceeded ; it appears as improper to me as to the rest of the world ; I lament the effects it has produced ; I pity the unhappy sufferer whom I have injured ; and I feel myself a just object of indignation to mankind. "Such," says Mr. Smith, "is the nature of that sentiment which is properly called remorse. It is made up of shame from the sense of the impropriety of past conduct ; of grief for the effects of it ; of pity for those who suffer by it ; and of the dread and terror of punishment from the consciousness of the justly provoked resentment of all rational creatures."

The opposite behaviour of him who, from proper motives, has performed a generous action, inspires, in a similar manner, the opposite sentiment of conscious merit, or of deserved reward.

The foregoing observations contain a general summary of Mr. Smith's principles with respect to the origin of our moral sentiments, in so far at least as they relate to the conduct of others. He acknowledges, at the same time, that the sentiments of which we are conscious, on particular occasions, do not always coincide with these principles ; and that they are frequently modified by other considerations, very different from the propriety or impropriety of the affections of the agent, and also from the beneficial or hurtful tendency of these affections. The good or bad consequences which accidentally follow from an action, and which, as they do not depend on the agent, ought undoubtedly, in point of justice, to have no influence on our opinion, either of the propriety or the merit of his conduct, scarcely ever fail to influence considerably our judgment with respect to both ; by leading us to form a good or a bad opinion of the prudence with which the action was performed, and by animating our sense of the merit or demerit of his design. These facts, however, do not furnish any objections which are peculiarly applicable to Mr. Smith's theory ; for whatever hypothesis we may adopt with respect to the origin of our moral perceptions, all men must acknowledge, that, in so far as the prosperous or the unprosperous event of an action depends on fortune or on accident, it ought neither to increase nor to diminish our moral approbation or disapprobation of the agent. And accordingly it has, in all ages of the world, been the complaint of moralists, that the actual sentiments of mankind should so often be in opposition to this equitable and indisputable maxim. In examining, therefore, this irregularity of our moral sentiments, Mr. Smith is to be considered, not as obviating an objection peculiar to his own system, but as removing a difficulty which is equally connected with **every** theory on the subject which has ever been proposed. So far as I know, he is the first philosopher who has been fully aware of the importance of the difficulty, and he has indeed treated it with great ability and success. The explanation which he gives of it is not warped in the least by any peculiarity in his own scheme ; and, I must own, it appears to me to be the most solid and valuable improvement he has made in this branch of science. It is impossible to give any abstract of it in a sketch of this kind ; and therefore I must content myself with remarking, that it consists of three parts. The first explains the causes of this irregularity of sentiment ; the second, the extent of its influence ; and the third, the important purposes to which it is subservient. His remarks on the last of these heads are more particularly ingenious and pleasing ; as their object is to show, in opposition to what we should be disposed at first to apprehend, that when nature implanted the seeds of this irregularity in the human breast, her leading intention was, to promote the happiness and perfection of the species.

The remaining part of Mr. Smith's theory is employed in showing, in what manner *our sense of duty* comes to be formed, in consequence of an application to ourselves of the judgments we have previously passed on the conduct of others.

In entering upon this inquiry, which is undoubtedly the most important in the work, and for which the foregoing speculations are, according to Mr. Smith's theory, a necessary preparation, he begins with stating *the fact* concerning our consciousness of merited praise or blame ; and it must be owned, that the first aspect of the fact, as he himself states it, appears not very favourable to his principles. That the great object of a wise and virtuous man is not to act in such a manner as to obtain the actual approbation of those around him, but to act so as to render himself the *just* and *proper* object of their approbation, and that his satisfaction with his own conduct depends much more on the consciousness of *deserving* this approbation than from that of really enjoying it, he candidly acknowledges ; but still he insists, that although this may seem, at first view, to intimate the existence of some moral faculty, which is not borrowed from without, our moral sentiments have always some secret reference, either to what are, or to what upon a certain condition would be, or to what we imagine ought to be, the sentiments of others ; and that if it were possible that a human creature could grow up to manhood without any communication with his own species, he could no more think of his own character, or of the propriety or demerit of his own sentiments and conduct, than of the beauty or deformity of his own face. There is indeed a tribunal within the breast, which is the supreme arbiter of all our actions, and which often mortifies us amidst the applause, and supports us under the censure of the world ; yet still, he contends, that if we inquire into the origin of its institution, we shall find, that its jurisdiction is, in a great measure, derived from the authority of that very tribunal whose decisions it so often and so justly reverses.

When we first come into the world, we, for some time, fondly pursue the impossible project of gaining the good-will and approbation of everybody. We soon however find, that this universal approbation is unattainable ; that the most equitable conduct must frequently thwart the interests or the inclinations of particular persons, who will seldom have candour enough to enter into the propriety of our motives, or to see that this conduct, how disagreeable soever to them, is perfectly suitable to our situation. In order to defend ourselves from such partial judgments, we soon learn to set up in our own minds, a judge between ourselves and those we live with. We conceive ourselves as acting in the presence of a person, who has no particular relation, either to ourselves, or to those whose interests are affected by our conduct ; and we study to act in such a manner as to obtain the approbation of this supposed impartial spectator. It is only by consulting him that we can see whatever relates to ourselves in its proper shape and dimensions.

There are two different occasions, on which we examine our own conduct, and endeavour to view it in the light in which the impartial spectator would view it. First, when we are about to act ; and, secondly, after we have acted. In both cases, our views are very apt to be partial.

When we are about to act, the eagerness of passion seldom allows us to consider what we are doing with the candour of an indifferent person. When the action is over, and the passions which prompted it have subsided, although we can undoubtedly enter into the sentiments of the indifferent spectator much more coolly than before, yet it is so disagreeable to us to think ill of ourselves, that we often purposely turn away our view from those circumstances which might render our judgment unfavourable. Hence that self-deceit which is the source of half the disorders of human life.

In order to guard ourselves against its delusions, nature leads us to form insensibly, by our continual observations upon the conduct of others, certain general rules concerning what is fit and proper either to be done or avoided. Some of their actions shock all our natural sentiments ; and when we observe other people affected in the same manner with ourselves, we are confirmed in the belief, that our disapprobation was just. We naturally, therefore, lay it down as a general rule, that all such actions are to be avoided, as tending to render us odious, contemptible, or punishable ; and we endeavour, by habitual reflection, to fix this

general rule in our minds, in order to correct the misrepresentations of self-love, if we should ever be called on to act in similar
circumstances. The man of furious resentment, if he were to
listen to the dictates of that passion, would, perhaps, regard the
death of his enemy as but a small compensation for a trifling
wrong. But his observations on the conduct of others have
taught him how horrible such sanguinary revenges are; and he has
impressed it on his mind as an invariable rule, to abstain from
them upon all occasions. This rule preserves its authority with
him, checks the impetuosity of his passion, and corrects the
partial views which self-love suggests; although, if this had been
the first time in which he considered such an action, he would
undoubtedly have determined it to be just and proper, and what
every impartial spectator would approve of. A regard to such
general rules of morality constitutes, according to Mr. Smith,
what is properly called *the sense of duty.*

I before hinted, that Mr. Smith does not reject entirely from
his system that principle of *utility*, of which the perception in
any action or character constitutes, according to Mr. Hume, the
sentiment of moral approbation. That no qualities of the mind
are approved of as virtues, but such as are useful or agreeable,
either to the person himself or to others, he admits to be a proposition that holds universally; and he also admits, that the
sentiment of approbation with which we regard virtue, is enlivened by the perception of this utility, or, as he explains the
fact, it is enlivened by our sympathy with the happiness of those
to whom the utility extends: But still he insists, that it is not
the view of this utility which is either the first or principal
source of moral approbation.

To sum up the whole of his doctrine in a few words. "When
we approve of any character or action, the sentiments which we
feel are derived from four different sources. First, we sympathize with the motives of the agent; secondly, we enter into the
gratitude of those who receive the benefit of his actions; thirdly,
we observe that his conduct has been agreeable to the general
rules by which those two sympathies generally act; and, lastly,
when we consider such actions as making a part of a system of
behaviour which tends to promote the happiness either of the individual or of society, they appear to derive a beauty from this
utility, not unlike that which we ascribe to any well-contrived
machine." These different sentiments, he thinks, exhaust completely, in every instance that can be supposed, the compounded
sentiment of moral approbation. "After deducting," says he,
"in any one particular case, all that must be acknowledged to
proceed from some one or other of these four principles, I should
be glad to know what remains; and I shall freely allow this

overplus to be ascribed to a moral sense, or to any other peculiar faculty, provided anybody will ascertain precisely what this overplus is."

Mr. Smith's opinion concerning the nature of virtue, is involved in his theory concerning the principle of moral approbation. The idea of virtue, he thinks, always implies the idea of propriety, or of the suitableness of the affection to the object which excites it ; which suitableness, according to him, can be determined in no other way than by the sympathy of impartial spectators with the motives of the agent. But still he apprehends that this description of virtue is incomplete ; for although in every virtuous action propriety is an essential ingredient—it is not always the sole ingredient. Beneficent actions have in them another quality, by which they appear, not only to deserve approbation, but recompense, and excite a superior degree of esteem, arising from a double sympathy with the motives of the agent, and the gratitude of those who are the objects of his affection. In this respect beneficence appears to him to be distinguished from the inferior virtues of prudence, vigilance, circumspection, temperance, constancy, firmness, which are always regarded with approbation, but which confer no merit. This distinction, he apprehends, has not been sufficiently attended to by moralists ; the principles of some affording no explanation of the approbation we bestow on the inferior virtues ; and those of others accounting as imperfectly for the peculiar excellency which the supreme virtue of beneficence is acknowledged to possess.

Such are the outlines of Mr. Smith's Theory of Moral Sentiments ; a work which must be allowed by all to be a singular effort of invention, ingenuity, and subtilty.*

It contains a large mixture of important truth and, although the author has sometimes been misled by too great a desire of generalizing his principles, he has had the merit of directing the attention of philosophers to a view of human nature which had

* According to Dr. Gillies, the learned English translator of "Aristotle's Ethics and Politics," the general idea which runs through Mr. Smith's Theory, was obviously borrowed from the following passage of Polybius : " From the union of the two sexes, to which all are naturally inclined, children are born. When any of these, therefore, being arrived at perfect age, instead of yielding suitable returns of gratitude and assistance to those by whom they have been bred, on the contrary, attempt to injure them by words or actions, it is manifest that those who behold the wrong, after having also seen the sufferings and the anxious cares that were sustained by the parents in the nourishment and education of their children, must be greatly offended and displeased at such proceeding. For man, who among all the various kinds of animals is alone endowed with the faculty of reason, cannot, like the rest, pass over such

formerly in a great measure escaped their notice. Of the great proportion of just and sound reasoning which the theory involves, its striking plausibility is a sufficient proof; for, as the author himself has remarked, no system in morals can well gain our assent, if it does not border, in some respects, upon the truth. "A system of natural philosophy (he observes) may appear very plausible, and be for a long time very generally received in the world, and yet have no foundation in nature; but the author who should assign as the cause of any natural sentiment, some principle which neither had any connection with it, nor resembled any other principle which had some connection, would appear absurd and ridiculous to the most injudicious and inexperienced reader." The merit, however, of Mr. Smith's performance does not rest here. No work, undoubtedly, can be mentioned, ancient or modern, which exhibits so complete a view of those facts with respect to our moral perceptions, which it is one great object of this branch of science to refer to their general laws; and, upon

actions: but will make reflection on what he sees; and comparing likewise the future with the present, will not fail to express his indignation at this injurious treatment; to which as he foresees, he may also, at some time, be exposed. Thus again, when any one who has been succoured by another in the time of danger, instead of showing the like kindness to this benefactor, endeavours at any time to destroy or hurt him; it is certain that all men must be shocked by such ingratitude, through sympathy with the resentment of their neighbour; and from an apprehension also, that the case may be their own. And from hence arises, in the mind of every man, a certain *notion* of the nature and force of duty, in which consists both the beginning and the end of justice. In like manner, the man who, in defence of others, is seen to throw himself the foremost into every danger, and even to sustain the fury of the fiercest animals, never fails to obtain the loudest acclamations of applause and veneration from all the multitude; while he who shows a different conduct is pursued with censure and reproach. And thus it is, that the people begin to discern the nature of things honourable and base, and in what consists the difference between them; and to perceive that the former, on account of the advantage that attends them, are to be admired and imitated, and the latter to be detested and avoided."

"The doctrine," says Dr. Gillies, "contained in this passage, is expanded by Dr. Smith into a theory of moral sentiments. But he departs from *his author,* in placing the perception of right and wrong, in sentiment or feeling, ultimately and simply.————Polybius on the contrary, maintains with Aristotle, that these notions arise from reason, or intellect, operating on affection or appetite; or, in other words, that the moral faculty is a compound, and may be resolved into two simpler principles of the mind."—(Gilles's Aristotle, vol. i. pp. 302, 303, second edition).

The only expression I object to in the two preceding sentences, is the this account it well deserves the careful study of all whose taste leads them to prosecute similar inquiries. These facts are indeed frequently expressed in a language which involves the author's peculiar theories : But they are always presented in the most happy and beautiful lights ; and it is easy for an attentive reader, by stripping them of hypothetical terms, to state them to himself with that logical precision, which, in such very difficult disquisitions, can alone conduct us with certainty to the truth.

It is proper to observe farther, that with the theoretical doctrines of the book, there are everywhere interwoven, with singular taste and address, the purest and most elevated maxims concerning the practical conduct of life ; and that it abounds throughout with interesting and instructive delineations of characters and manners. A considerable part of it, too, is employed in collateral inquiries, which, upon every hypothesis that can be formed concerning the foundation of morals, are of equal importance. Of this kind is the speculation formerly mentioned, with respect to the influence of fortune on our moral sentiments, and another speculation, no less valuable, with respect to the influence of custom and fashion on the same part of our constitution.

phrase *his author*, which has the appearance of insinuating a charge of plagiarism against Mr. Smith ; a charge which, I am confident he did not deserve. It exhibits, indeed, an instance of a curious coincidence between two philosophers in their views of the same subject ; and as such, I have no doubt that Mr. Smith himself would have remarked it, had it occurred to his memory, when he was writing his book. Of such accidental coincidences between different minds, examples present themselves every day to those, who, after having drawn from their internal resources all the lights they could supply on a particular question, have the curiosity to compare their own conclusions with those of their predecessors. And it is extremely worthy of observation, that, in proportion as any conclusion approaches to the truth, the number of previous approximations to it may be reasonably expected to be multiplied.

In the case before us, however, the question about originality is of little or no moment ; for the peculiar merit of Mr. Smith's work does not lie in his general principle, but in the skilful use he has made of it to give a systematical arrangement to the most important discussions and doctrines of Ethics. In this point of view, the Theory of Moral Sentiments may be justly regarded as one of the most original efforts of the human mind in that branch of science to which it relates ; and even if we were to suppose that it was first suggested to the author by a remark of which the world was in possession for two thousand years before, this very circumstance would only reflect a stronger lustre on the novelty of his design, and on the invention and taste displayed in its execution.

The style in which Mr. Smith has conveyed the fundamental principles on which his theory rests, does not seem to me to be so perfectly suited to the subject as that which he employs on most other occasions. In communicating ideas which are extremely abstract and subtile, and about which it is hardly possible to reason correctly, without the scrupulous use of appropriated terms, he sometimes presents to us a choice of words, by no means strictly synonymous, so as to divert the attention from a precise and steady conception of his proposition : and a similar effect is, in other instances, produced by that diversity of forms which, in the course of his copious and seducing composition, the same truth insensibly assumes. When the subject of his work leads him to address the imagination and the heart, the variety and felicity of his illustrations ; the richness and fluency of his eloquence ; and the skill with which he wins the attention and commands the passions of his readers, leave him, among our English moralists, without a rival.

The Dissertation on the Origin of Languages, which now forms a part of the same volume with the Theory of Moral Sentiments, was, I believe, first annexed to the second edition of that work. It is an essay of great ingenuity, and on which the author himself set a high value ; but, in a general review of his publications, it deserves our attention less, on account of the opinions it contains, than as a specimen of a particular sort of inquiry, which, so far as I know, is entirely of modern origin, and which seems, in a peculiar degree, to have interested Mr. Smith's curiosity. Something very similar to it may be traced in all his different works, whether moral, political, or literary ; and on all these subjects he has exemplified it with the happiest success.

When, in such a period of society as that in which we live, we compare our intellectual acquirements, our opinions, manners, and institutions, with those which prevail among rude tribes, it cannot fail to occur to us as an interesting question, by what gradual steps the transition has been made from the first simple efforts of uncultivated nature, to a state of things so wonderfully artificial and complicated. Whence has arisen that systematical beauty which we admire in the structure of a cultivated language ; that analogy which runs through the mixture of languages spoken by the most remote and unconnected nations ; and those peculiarities by which they are all distinguished from each other ? Whence the origin of the different sciences and of the different arts ; and by what chain has the mind been led from their first rudiments to their last and most refined improvements ? Whence the astonishing fabric of the political union : the fundamental principles which are common to all governments ; and the different forms which civilized society has assumed in different ages of

the world ? On most of these subjects very little information is
to be expected from history ; for long before that stage of society
when men begin to think of recording their transactions, many of
the most important steps of their progress have been made. A
few insulated facts may, perhaps, be collected from the casual observations of travellers, who have viewed the arrangements of
rude nations ; but nothing, it is evident, can be obtained in this
way, which approaches to a regular and connected detail of
human improvement.

In this want of direct evidence, we are under a necessity of
supplying the place of fact by conjecture ; and when we are
unable to ascertain how men have actually conducted themselves
upon particular occasions, of considering in what manner they
are likely to have proceeded, from the principles of their nature,
and the circumstances of their external situation. In such inquiries, the detached facts which travels and voyages afford us,
may frequently serve as land-marks to our speculations ; and
sometimes our conclusions, *a priori*, may tend to confirm the cre-
dibility of facts, which, on a superficial view, appeared to be
doubtful or incredible.

Nor are such theoretical views of human affairs subservient
merely to the gratification of curiosity. In examining the history of mankind, as well as in examining the phenomena of the
material world, when we cannot trace the process by which an
event *has been* produced, it is often of importance to be able to
show how it *may have been* produced by natural causes. Thus, in
the instance which has suggested these remarks, although it is
impossible to determine with certainty what the steps were by
which any particular language was formed, yet if we can show,
from the known principles of human nature, how all its various
parts might gradually have arisen, the mind is not only to a certain degree satisfied, but a check is given to that indolent philosophy, which refers to a miracle, whatever appearances, both in
the natural and moral worlds, it is unable to explain.

To this species of philosophical investigation, which has no appropriated name in our language, I shall take the liberty of giving
the title of *Theoretical* or *Conjectural History;* an expression
which coincides pretty nearly in its meaning with that of *Natural
History*, as employed by Mr. Hume,* and with what some French
writers have called *Histoire Raisonnée.*

The mathematical sciences, both pure and mixed, afford, in
many of their branches, very favourable subjects for theoretical
history ; and a very competent judge, the late M. d'Alembert,
has recommended that arrangement of their elementary principles,

* See his Natural History of Religion.

which is founded on the natural succession of inventions and discoveries, as the best adapted for interesting the curiosity and
exercising the genius of students.   The same author points out
as a model a passage in Montucla's History of Mathematics,
where an attempt is made to exhibit the gradual progress of philosophical speculation, from the first conclusions suggested by a
general survey of the heavens, to the doctrines of Copernicus.   It
is somewhat remarkable, that a theoretical history of this very
science (in which we have, perhaps, a better opportunity than in
any other instance whatever, of comparing the natural advances
of the mind with the actual succession of hypothetical systems)
was one of Mr. Smith's earliest compositions, and is one of the
very small number of his manuscripts which he did not destroy
before his death.

I have already hinted, that inquiries perfectly analogous to these
may be applied to the modes of government, and to the municipal
institutions which have obtained among different nations.   It is
but lately, however, that these important subjects have been considered in this point of view ; the greater part of politicians before the time of Montesquieu having contented themselves with
an historical statement of facts, and with a vague reference of
laws to the wisdom of particular legislators, or to accidental circumstances, which it is now impossible to ascertain.   Montesquieu, on the contrary, considered laws as originating chiefly
from the circumstances of society ; and attempted to account,
from the changes in the condition of mankind, which take place
in the different stages of their progress, for the corresponding
alterations which their institutions undergo.   It is thus that, in
his occasional elucidations of the Roman jurisprudence, instead
of bewildering himself among the erudition of scholiasts and of
antiquaries, we frequently find him borrowing his lights from the
most remote and unconnected quarters of the globe, and combining the casual observations of illiterate travellers and navi-
gators, into a philosophical commentary on the history of law
and of manners.

The advances made in this line of inquiry since Montesquieu's
time have been great.   Lord Kames, in his Historical Law Tracts,
has given some excellent specimens of it, particularly in his
Essays on the History of Property and of Criminal Law, and
many ingenious speculations of the same kind occur in the works
of Mr. Millar.

In Mr. Smith's writings, whatever be the nature of his subject,
he seldom misses an opportunity of indulging his curiosity, in
tracing from the principles of human nature, or from the circumstances of society, the origin of the opinions and the institutions
which he describes.   I formerly mentioned a fragment concerning

the History of Astronomy which he has left for publication ; and I have heard him say more than once, that he had projected, in the earlier part of his life, a history of the other sciences on the same plan. In his Wealth of Nations, various disquisitions are introduced which have a like object in view, particularly the theoretical delineation he has given of the natural progress of opulence in a country ; and his investigation of the causes which have inverted this order in the different countries of modern Europe. His lectures on jurisprudence seem, from the account of them formerly given, to have abounded in such inquiries.

I am informed by the same gentleman who favoured me with the account of Mr. Smith's lectures at Glasgow, that he had heard him sometimes hint an intention of writing a treatise upon the Greek and Roman republics. "And after all that has been published on that subject, I am convinced (says he) that the observations of Mr. Smith would have suggested many new and important views concerning the internal and domestic circumstances of those nations, which would have displayed their several systems of policy, in a light much less artificial than that in which they have hitherto appeared."

The same turn of thinking was frequently, in his social hours, applied to more familiar subjects ; and the fanciful theories which, without the least affectation of ingenuity, he was continually starting upon all the common topics of discourse, gave to his conversation a novelty and variety that were quite inexhaustible. Hence, too, the minuteness and accuracy of his knowledge on many trifling articles, which, in the course of his speculations, he had been led to consider from some new and interesting point of view ; and of which his lively and circumstantial descriptions amused his friends the more, that he seemed to be habitually inattentive, in so remarkable a degree, to what was passing around him.

I have been led into these remarks by the Dissertation on the Formation of languages, which exhibits a very beautiful specimen of theoretical history, applied to a subject equally curious and difficult. The analogy between the train of thinking from which it has taken its rise, and that which has suggested a variety of his other disquisitions, will, I hope, be a sufficient apology for the length of this digression ; more particularly, as it will enable me to simplify the account which I am to give afterwards, of his inquiries concerning political economy.

I shall only observe farther on this head, that when different theoretical histories are proposed by different writers, of the progress of the human mind in any one line of exertion, these theories are not always to be understood as standing in opposition

to each other. If the progress delineated in all of them be plausible, it is possible at least, that they may all have been realized ;
for human affairs never exhibit, in any two instances, a perfect
uniformity. But whether they have been realized or no, is often
a question of little consequence. In most cases it is of more importance to ascertain the progress that is most simple, than the
progress that is most agreeable to fact ; for, paradoxical as the
proposition may appear, it is certainly true that the real progress
is not always the most natural. It may have been determined
by particular accidents, which are not likely again to occur, and
which cannot be considered as forming any part of that general
provision which nature has made for the improvement of the
race.

In order to make some amends for the length (I am afraid I
may add for the tediousness) of this section, I shall subjoin to it
an original letter of Mr. Hume's addressed to Mr. Smith, soon
after the publication of his Theory. It is strongly marked with
that easy and affectionate pleasantry which distinguished Mr.
Hume's epistolary correspondence, and is entitled to a place in
this Memoir, on account of its connection with an important
event of Mr. Smith's life, which soon after removed him into a
new scene, and influenced, to a considerable degree, the subsequent course of his studies. The letter is dated from London,
12th April, 1759.

" I give you thanks for the agreeable present of your Theory.
Wedderburn and I made presents of our copies to such of our
acquaintances as we thought good judges, and proper to spread
the reputation of the book. I sent one to the Duke of Argyll, to
Lord Lyttleton, Horace Walpole, Soame Jennyns, and Burke, an
Irish gentleman, who wrote lately a very pretty treatise on the
Sublime. Millar desired my permission to send one in your
name to Dr. Warburton. I have delayed writing to you till I
could tell you something of the success of the book, and could
prognosticate with some probability, whether it should be finally
damned to oblivion, or should be registered in the temple of im-
mortality. Though it has been published only a few weeks, I
think there appear already such strong symptoms, that I can
almost venture to foretell its fate. It is in short this ———. But I
have been interrupted in my letter by a foolish impertinent visit
of one who has lately come from Scotland. He tells me that the
University of Glasgow intend to declare Rouet's office vacant,
upon his going abroad with Lord Hope. I question not but you
will have our friend Ferguson in your eye, in case another project for procuring him a place in the University of Edinburgh
should fail. Ferguson has very much polished and improved his

treatise on Refinement,* and with some amendments it will make an admirable book, and discovers an elegant and a singular genius. The Epigoniad, I hope, will do ; but it is somewhat up-hill work. As I doubt not but you consult the reviews sometimes at present, you will see in the Critical Review a letter upon that poem ; and I desire you to employ your conjectures in finding out the author. Let me see a sample of your skill in knowing hands by your guessing at the person. I am afraid of Lord Kames's Law Tracts. A man might as well think of making a fine sauce by a mixture of wormwood and aloes, as an agreeable composition by joining metaphysics and Scotch law. However, the book, I be-lieve, has merit ; though few people will take the pains of diving into it. But to return to your book. and its success in this town, I must tell you ——. A plague of interruptions ! I ordered myself to be denied ; and yet here is one that has broke in upon me again. He is a man of letters, and we have had a good deal of literary conversation. You told me that you was curious of literary anec-dotes, and therefore I shall inform you of a few that have come to my knowledge. I believe I have mentioned to you already Helvetius's book *de l'Esprit*. It is worth your reading, not for its philosophy, which I do not highly value, but for its agreeable composition. I had a letter from him a few days ago, wherein he tells me that my name was much oftener in the manuscript, but that the Censor of books at Paris obliged him to strike it out. Voltaire has lately published a small work called *Candide, ou l'Optimisme.* I shall give you a detail of it——. But what is all this to my book ? say you.—My dear Mr. Smith have patience : Compose yourself to tranquillity : Show yourself a philosopher in practice as well as profession : Think on the emptiness, and rash-ness, and futility of the common judgments of men : How little they are regulated by reason in any subject, much more in philo-sophical subjects, which so far exceed the comprehension of the vulgar.

————————Non si quid turbida Roma,
Elevet, accedas : examenve improbum in illa
Castiges trutina : nec te quæsiveris extra.

A wise man's kingdom is his own breast ; or, if he ever looks farther, it will only be to the judgment of a select few, who are free from prejudices, and capable of examining his work. Nothing, indeed, can be a stronger presumption of falsehood than the ap-probation of the multitude ; and Phocion, you know, always sus-pected himself of some blunder when he was attended with the applauses of the populace.

* Published afterwards under the title of " An Essay on the History of Civil Society."

" Supposing, therefore, that you have duly prepared yourself
for the worst by all these reflections, I proceed to tell you the
melancholy news, that your book has been very unfortunate ; for
the public seem disposed to applaud it extremely.   It was looked
for by the foolish people with some impatience ; and the mob of
literati are beginning already to be very loud in its praises.   Three
Bishops called yesterday at Millar's shop in order to buy copies, and
to ask questions about the author.   The Bishop of Peterborough said
he had passed the evening in a company where he heard it ex-
tolled above all books in the world.   The Duke of Argyll is more
decisive than he uses to be in its favour.   I suppose he either
considers it as an exotic, or thinks the author will be serviceable
to him in the Glasgow elections.   Lord Lyttleton says, that Robertson and Smith and Bower are the glories of English literature.   Oswald protests he does not know whether he has reaped
more instruction or entertainment from it.   But you may easily
judge what reliance can be put on his judgment who has been
engaged all his life in public business, and who never sees any
faults in his friends.   Millar exults and brags that two-thirds of
the edition are already sold, and that he is now sure of success.
You see what a son of the earth that is, to value books only by
the profit they bring him.   In that view, I believe, it may prove
a very good book.
   " Charles Townsend, who passes for the cleverest fellow in England, is so taken with the performance, that he said to Oswald
he would put the Duke of Buccleuch under the author's care, and
would make it worth his while to accept of that charge. As soon as
I heard this I called on him twice, with a view of talking with him
about the matter, and of convincing him of the propriety of send-
ing that young Nobleman to Glasgow : For I could not hope that
he could offer you any terms which would tempt you to renounce
your Professorship.   But I missed him.   Mr. Townsend passes
for being a little uncertain in his resolutions : so perhaps you
need not build much on this sally.
   " In recompense for so many mortifying things, which nothing
but truth could have extorted from me, and which I could easily have
multiplied to a greater number, I doubt not but you are so good a
Christian as to return good for evil ; and to flatter my vanity by
telling me that all the godly in Scotland abuse me for my account
of John Knox and the Reformation.   I suppose you are glad to
see my paper end, and that I am obliged to conclude with
                                    Your humble servant,
                                          DAVID HUME."

FROM THE PUBLICATION OF THE THEORY OF MORAL SENTIMENTS, TILL THAT OF THE WEALTH OF NATIONS.

AFTER the publication of the Theory of Moral Sentiments, Mr. Smith remained four years at Glasgow, discharging his official duties with unabated vigour, and with increasing reputation. During that time the plan of his lectures underwent a considerable change. His ethical doctrines, of which he had now published so valuable a part, occupied a much smaller portion of the course than formerly ; and accordingly, his attention was naturally directed to a more complete illustration of the principles of jurisprudence and of political economy.

To this last subject his thoughts appear to have been occasionally turned from a very early period of life. It is probable that the uninterrupted friendship he had always maintained with his old companion Mr. Oswald, had some tendency to encourage him in prosecuting this branch of his studies ; and the publication of Mr. Hume's political discourses, in the year 1752, could not fail to confirm him in those liberal views of commercial policy which had already opened to him in the course of his own inquiries. His long residence in one of the most enlightened mercantile towns in this island, and the habits of intimacy in which he lived with the most respectable of its inhabitants, afforded him an opportunity of deriving what commercial information he stood in need of, from the best sources ; and it is a circumstance no less honourable to their liberality than to his talents, that notwithstanding the reluctance so common among men of business to listen to the conclusions of mere speculation, and the direct opposition of his leading principles to all the old maxims of trade, he was able, before he quitted his situation in the university, to rank some very eminent merchants in the number of his proselytes.*

Among the students who attended his lectures, and whose minds were not previously warped by prejudice, the progress of his opinions, it may be reasonably supposed, was much more rapid. It was this class of his friends accordingly that first adopted his system with eagerness, and diffused a knowledge of its fundamental principles over this part of the kingdom.

Towards the end of 1763 Mr. Smith received an invitation from Mr. Charles Townsend to accompany the Duke of Buccleuch on his travels ; and the liberal terms in which the proposal was made to him, added to the strong desire he had felt of visiting

---

* I mention this fact on the respectable authority of James Ritchie, Esq., of Glasgow.

the Continent of Europe, induced him to resign his office at Glasgow. With the connection which he was led to form in consequence of this change in his situation, he had reason to be satisfied in an uncommon degree, and he always spoke of it with pleasure and gratitude. To the public it was not, perhaps, a change equally fortunate ; as it interrupted that studious leisure for which nature seems to have destined him, and in which alone he could have hoped to accomplish those literary projects which had flattered the ambition of his youthful genius.

The alteration, however, which, from this period, took place in his habits, was not without its advantages. He had hitherto lived chiefly within the walls of an university; and although to a mind like his, the observation of human nature on the smallest scale is sufficient to convey a tolerably just conception of what passes on the great theatre of the world, yet it is not to be doubted, that the variety of scenes through which he afterwards passed, must have enriched his mind with many new ideas, and corrected many of those misapprehensions of life and manners which the best descriptions of them can scarcely fail to convey. But whatever were the lights that his travels afforded to him as a student of human nature, they were probably useful in a still greater degree, in enabling him to perfect that system of political economy, of which he had already delivered the principles in his lectures at Glasgow, and which it was now the leading object of his studies to prepare for the public. The coincidence between some of these principles and the distinguishing tenets of the French economists, who were at that very time in the height of their reputation, and the intimacy in which he lived with some of the leaders of that sect, could not fail to assist him in methodizing and digesting his speculations ; while the valuable collection of facts, accumulated by the zealous industry of their numerous adherents, furnished him with ample materials for illustrating and confirming his theoretical conclusions.

After leaving Glasgow, Mr. Smith joined the Duke of Buccleuch at London early in the year 1764, and set out with him for the Continent in the month of March following. At Dover they were met by Sir James Macdonald, who accompanied them to Paris, and with whom Mr. Smith laid the foundation of a friendship, which he always mentioned with pleasure, and of which he often lamented the short duration. The panegyrics with which the memory of this accomplished and amiable person has been honoured by so many distinguished characters in the different countries of Europe, are a proof how well fitted his talents were to command general admiration. The esteem in which his abilities and learning were held by Mr. Smith, is a testimony to his extraordinary merit of still superior value. Mr. Hume, too, seems, in this instance, to have partaken of his friend's enthusiasm. " Were you and I together (says he in a letter to Mr. Smith), we should shed tears at present for the death of poor Sir James Macdonald. We could not possibly have suffered a greater loss than in that valuable young man."

In this first visit to Paris the Duke of Buccleuch and Mr. Smith employed only ten or twelve days,* after which they proceeded to Toulouse, where they fixed their residence for eighteen months ; and where, in addition to the pleasure of an agreeable society, Mr. Smith had an opportunity of correcting and extending his information concerning the internal policy of France, by the intimacy in which he lived with some of the principal persons of the Parliament.

From Toulouse they went, by a pretty extensive tour, through the south of France to Geneva. Here they passed two months. The late Earl of Stanhope, for whose learning and worth Mr. Smith entertained a sincere respect, was then an inhabitant of that republic.

About Christmas 1765 they returned to Paris, and remained there till October following. The society in which Mr. Smith

---

* The day after his arrival at Paris, Mr. Smith sent a formal resignation of his Professorship to the Rector of the University of Glasgow. " I never was more anxious," says he in the conclusion of this letter, "for the good of the College, than at this moment ; and I sincerely wish, that whoever is my successor may not only do credit to the office by his abilities, but be a comfort to the very excellent men with whom he is likely to spend his life, by the probity of his heart, and the goodness of his temper."

The following extract from the records of the University, which follows immediately after Mr. Smith's letter of resignation, is at once a testimony to his assiduity as a Professor, and a proof of the just sense which that learned body entertained of the talents and worth of the colleague they had lost :

" The meeting accept of Dr. Smith's resignation, in terms of the above letter, and the office of Professor of Moral Philosophy in this University is therefore hereby declared vacant. The University, at the same time, cannot help expressing their sincere regret at the removal of Dr. Smith, whose distinguished probity and amiable qualities procured him the esteem and affection of his colleagues ; and whose uncommon genius, great abilities, and extensive learning, did so much honour to this society ; his elegant and ingenious Theory of Moral Sentiments having recommended him to the esteem of men of taste and literature throughout Europe. His happy talent in illustrating abstracted subjects, and faithful assiduity in communicating useful knowledge, distinguished him as a Professor, and at once afforded the greatest pleasure and the most important instruction to the youth under his care."

spent these ten months, may be conceived from the advantages he enjoyed, in consequence of the recommendations of Mr. Hume. Turgot, Quesnai, Necker, d'Alembert, Helvetius, Marmontel, Madame Riccoboni, were among the number of his acquaintances ; and some of them he continued ever afterwards to reckon among his friends. From Madame d'Anville, the respectable mother of the late excellent and much lamented Duke of Rochefoucauld, he received many attentions, which he always recollected with particular gratitude.

It is much to be regretted that he preserved no journal of this very interesting period of his history : and such was his aversion to write letters, that I scarcely suppose any memorial of it exists in his correspondence with his friends. The extent and accuracy of his memory, in which he was equalled by few, made it of little consequence to himself to record in writing what he heard or saw ; and from his anxiety before his death to destroy all the papers in his possession, he seems to have wished that no materials should remain for his biographers, but what were furnished by the lasting monuments of his genius, and the exemplary worth of his private life.

The satisfaction he enjoyed in the conversation of Turgot may be easily imagined. Their opinions on the most essential points of political economy were the same ; and they were both animated by the same zeal for the best interests of mankind. The favourite studies, too, of both, had directed their inquiries to subjects on which the understandings of the ablest and the best informed are liable to be warped, to a great degree, by prejudice and passion ; and on which, of consequence, a coincidence of judgment is peculiarly gratifying. We are told by one of the biographers of Turgot, that after his retreat from the ministry, he occupied his leisure in a philosophical correspondence with some of his old friends ; and, in particular, that various letters on important subjects passed between him and Mr. Smith. I take notice of this anecdote chiefly as a proof of the intimacy which was understood to have subsisted between them ; for in other respects, the anecdote seems to me to be somewhat doubtful. It is scarcely to be supposed that Mr. Smith would destroy the letters of such a correspondent as Turgot ; and still less probable, that such an intercourse was carried on between them without the knowledge of any of Mr. Smith's friends. From some inquiries that have been made at Paris by a gentleman of this Society since Mr. Smith's death, I have reason to believe, that no evidence of the correspondence exists among the papers of M. Turgot, and that the whole story has taken its rise from a report suggested by the knowledge of their former intimacy. This circumstance I think it of importance to mention, because a good deal of curiosity has been excited by the passage in question, with respect to the fate of the supposed letters.

Mr. Smith was also well known to M. Quesnai, the profound and original author of the Economical Table ; a man (according to Mr. Smith's account of him) " of the greatest modesty and simplicity;" and whose system of political economy he has pronounced " with all its imperfections," to be " the nearest approximation to the truth that has yet been published on the principles of that very important science." If he had not been prevented by Quesnai's death, Mr. Smith had once an intention (as he told me himself) to have inscribed to him his " Wealth of Nations."

It was not, however, merely the distinguished men who about this period fixed so splendid an era in the literary history of France, that excited Mr. Smith's curiosity while he remained in Paris. His acquaintance with the polite literature, both of ancient and modern times, was extensive ; and amidst his various other occupations, he had never neglected to cultivate a taste for the fine arts ;—less, it is probable, with a view to the peculiar enjoyments they convey (though he was by no means without sensibility to their beauties), than on account of their connection with the general principles of the human mind ; to an examination of which they afford the most pleasing of all avenues. To those who speculate on this very delicate subject, a comparison of the modes of taste that prevail among different nations, affords a valuable collection of facts ; and Mr. Smith, who was always disposed to ascribe to custom and fashion their full share in regulating the opinions of mankind with respect to beauty, may naturally be supposed to have availed himself of every opportunity which a foreign country afforded him of illustrating his former theories.

Some of his peculiar notions, too, with respect to the imitative arts, seem to have been much confirmed by his observations while abroad. In accounting for the pleasure we receive from these arts, it had early occurred to him as a fundamental principle, that a very great part of it arises from the difficulty of the imitation ; a principle which was probably suggested to him by that of the *difficulté surmontée*, by which some French critics had attempted to explain the effect of versification and of rhyme.* This principle Mr. Smith pushed to the greatest possible length, and referred to it, with singular ingenuity, a great variety of phenomena in all the different fine arts. It led him, however, to some conclusions, which appear, at first view at least, not a little paradoxical ; and I cannot help thinking that it warped his judgment in many of the opinions which he was accustomed to give on the subject of poetry.

* See the Preface to Voltaire's *Oedipe,* edit. of 1729.

The principles of dramatic composition had more particularly attracted his attention ; and the history oi the theatre, both in ancient and modern times, had furnished him with some of the most remarkable facts on which his theory of the imitative arts was founded. From this theory it seemed to follow as a consequence, that the same circumstances which, in tragedy, give to blank verse an advantage over prose, should give to rhyme an advantage over blank verse ; and Mr. Smith had always inclined to that opinion. Nay, he had gone so far as to extend the same doctrine to comedy ; and to regret that those excellent pictures of life and manners which the English stage affords, had not been executed after the model of the French school. The admiration with which he regarded the great dramatic authors of France tended to confirm him in these opinions ; and this admiration (resulting originally from the general character of his taste, which delighted more to remark that pliancy of genius which accommodates itself to established rules, than to wonder at the bolder flights of an undisciplined imagination) was increased to a great degree, when he saw the beauties that had struck him in the study, heightened by the utmost perfection of theatrical exhibition. In the last years of his life he sometimes amused himself, at a leisure hour, in supporting his theoretical conclusions on these subjects, by the facts which his subsequent studies and observations had suggested : and he intended, if he had lived, to have prepared the result of these labours for the press. Of this work he has left for publication a short fragment ; but he had not proceeded far enough to apply his doctrine to versification and to the theatre. As his notions, however, with respect to these were a favourite topic of his conversation, and were intimately connected with his general principles of criticism, it would have been improper to pass them over in this sketch of his life ; and I have even thought it proper to detail them at greater length than the comparative importance of the subject would have justified, if he had carried his plans into execution. Whether his love of system, added to his partiality for the French drama, may not have led him, in this instance, to generalize a little too much his conclusions, and to overlook some peculiarities in the language and versification of that country, I shall not take upon me to determine.

In October, 1766, the Duke of Buccleuch returned to London. His Grace, to whom I am indebted for several particulars in the foregoing narrative, will, I hope, forgive the liberty I take in transcribing one paragraph in his own words : " In October, 1766, we returned to London, after having spent near three years together, without the slightest disagreement or coolness ;—on my part, with every advantage that could be expected from the

society of such a man. We continued to live in friendship till
the hour of his death ; and I shall always remain with the impression of having lost a friend whom I loved and respected, not
only for his great talents, but for every private virtue."

The retirement in which Mr. Smith passed his next ten years,
formed a striking contrast to the unsettled mode of life he had
been for some time accustomed to, but which was so congenial to
his natural disposition, and to his first habits, that it was with the
utmost difficulty he was ever persuaded to leave it. During the
whole of this period (with the exception of a few visits to Edinburgh and London), he remained with his mother at Kirkaldy; occupied habitually in intense study, but unbending his mind at times
in the company of some of his old school-fellows, whose "sober
wishes" had attached them to the place of their birth. In the
society of such men Mr. Smith delighted ; and to them he was
endeared, not only by his simple and unassuming manners, but
by the perfect knowledge they all possessed of those domestic
virtues which had distinguished him from his infancy.

Mr. Hume, who (as he tells us himself) considered "a town as
the true scene for a man of letters," made many attempts to
seduce him from his retirement. In a letter, dated in 1772, he
urges him to pass some time with him in Edinburgh. "I shall
not take any excuse from your state of health, which I suppose
only a subterfuge invented by indolence and love of solitude.
Indeed, my dear Smith, if you continue to hearken to complaints
of this nature, you will cut yourself out entirely from human
society, to the great loss of both parties." In another letter,
dated in 1769, from his house in James's Court (which commanded a prospect of the Frith of Forth, and of the opposite
coast of Fife), "I am glad (says he) to have come within sight of
you ; but as I would also be within speaking terms of you, I wish
we could concert measures for that purpose. I am mortally sick at
sea, and regard with horror and a kind of hydrophobia the great
gulf that lies between us. I am also tired of travelling, as much
as you ought naturally to be of staying at home. I therefore
propose to you to come hither, and pass some days with me in
this solitude. I want to know what you have been doing, and
propose to exact a rigorous account of the method in which you
have employed yourself during your retreat. I am positive you
are in the wrong in many of your speculations, especially where you
have the misfortune to differ from me. All these are reasons for
our meeting, and I wish you would make me some reasonable
proposal for that purpose. There is no habitation in the island
of Inchkeith, otherwise I should challenge you to meet me on
that spot, and neither of us ever to leave the place till we were
fully agreed on all points of controversy. I expect General Con-
way here to-morrow, whom I shall attend to Roseneath, and I

shall remain there a few days. On my return I hope to find a
letter from you, containing a bold acceptance of this defiance."

At length (in the beginning of the year 1776) Mr. Smith accounted
to the world for his long retreat, by the publication of his "Inquiry
into the Nature and Causes of the Wealth of Nations." A letter
of congratulation on this event, from Mr. Hume, is now before me.
It is dated 1st April, 1776 (about six months before Mr. Hume's
death), and discovers an amiable solicitude about his friend's literary fame. "*Euge! Belle!* Dear Mr. Smith : I am much pleased
with your performance, and the perusal of it has taken me from
a state of great anxiety. It was a work of so much expectation,
by yourself, by your friends, and by the public, that I trembled
for its appearance ; but am now much relieved. Not but that
the reading of it necessarily requires so much attention, and the
public is disposed to give so little, that I shall still doubt for some
time of its being at first very popular. But it has depth and
solidity and acuteness, and is so much illustrated by curious facts,
that it must at last take the public attention. It is probably
much improved by your last abode in London. If you were here
at my fire-side I should dispute some of your principles. . . .
But these, and a hundred other points, are fit only to be discussed
in conversation. I hope it will be soon ; for I am in a very bad
state of health, and cannot afford a long delay."

Of a book which is now so universally known as " The Wealth
of Nations," it might be considered perhaps as superfluous to
give a particular analysis ; and, at any rate, the limits of this
essay make it impossible for me to attempt it at present. A few
remarks, however, on the object and tendency of the work, may,
I hope, be introduced without impropriety. The history of a philosopher's life can contain little more than the history of his speculations ; and in the case of such an author as Mr. Smith, whose
studies were systematically directed from his youth to subjects of
the highest importance to human happiness, a review of his writings,
while it serves to illustrate the peculiarities of his genius, affords
the most faithful picture of his character as a man.

Of the Inquiry into the Nature and Causes of the Wealth of Nations.[*]

.An historical view of the different forms under which human
affairs have appeared in different ages and nations, naturally
suggests the question, Whether the experience of former times
may not now furnish some general principles to enlighten and

[*] At the period when this memoir was read before the Royal Society
of Edinburgh, it was not unusual, even among men of some talents and

direct the policy of future legislators? The discussion, however, to which this question leads, is of singular difficulty: as it requires an accurate analysis of by far the most complicated class of phenomena that can possibly engage our attention, those which result from the intricate and often imperceptible mechanism of political society;—a subject of observation which seems, at first view, so little commensurate to our faculties, that it has been generally regarded with the same passive emotions of wonder and submission, with which, in the material world, we survey the effects produced by the mysterious and uncontrollable operation of physical causes. It is fortunate that upon this, as upon many other occasions, the difficulties which had long baffled the efforts of solitary genius begin to appear less formidable to the united exertions of the race ; and that in proportion as the experience and the reasonings of different individuals are brought to bear upon the same objects, and are combined in such a manner as to illustrate and to limit each other, the science of politics assumes more and more that systematical form which encourages and aids the labours of future inquirers.

In prosecuting the science of politics on this plan, little assistance is to be derived from the speculations of ancient philosophers, the greater part of whom, in their political inquiries, confined their attention to a comparison of the different forms of government, and to an examination of the provisions made for perpetuating their own existence, and for, extending the glory of the state. It was reserved for modern times to investigate those universal principles of justice and of expediency, which ought, under every form of government, to regulate the social order ; and of which the object is, to make as equitable a distribution as possible, among all the different members of a community, of the advantages arising from the political union.

The invention of printing was perhaps necessary to prepare the way for these researches. In those departments of literature and of science, where genius finds within itself the materials of its labours ; in poetry, in pure geometry, and in some branches of moral philosophy ; the ancients have not only laid the foundations on which we are to build, but have left great and finished

information, to confound, studiously, the speculative doctrines of political economy with those discussions concerning the first principles of Government, which happened, unfortunately, at that time to agitate the public mind. The doctrine of Free Trade was itself represented as of a revolutionary tendency ; and some who had formerly prided themselves on their intimacy with Mr. Smith, and on their zeal for the propagation of his liberal system, began to call in question the expediency of subjecting to the disputations of philosophers, the arcana of State Policy, and the unfathomable wisdom of the feudal ages.

models for our imitation. But in physics, where our progress depends on an immense collection of facts, and on a combination of the accidental lights daily struck out in the innumerable walks of observation and experiment; and in politics, where the materials of our theories are equally scattered, and are collected and arranged with still greater difficulty, the means of communication afforded by the press have, in the course of two centuries, accelerated the progress of the human mind, far beyond what the most sanguine hopes of our predecessors could have imagined.

The progress already made in this science, inconsiderable as it is in comparison of what may be yet expected, has been sufficient to show, that the happiness of mankind depends, not on the share which the people possesses, directly or indirectly, in the enactment of laws, but on the equity and expediency of the laws that are enacted. The share which the people possesses in the government is interesting, chiefly to the small number of men whose object is the attainment of political importance; but the equity and expediency of the laws are interesting to every member of the community; and more especially to those whose personal insignificance leaves them no encouragement but what they derive from the general spirit of the government under which they live.

It is evident, therefore, that the most important branch of political science is that which has for its object to ascertain the philosophical principles of jurisprudence; or (as Mr. Smith expresses it) to ascertain "the general principles which ought to run through and be the foundation of the laws of all nations."* In countries where the prejudices of the people are widely at variance with these principles, the political liberty which the constitution bestows, only furnishes them with the means of accomplishing their own ruin: And if it were possible to suppose these principles completely realized in any system of laws, the people would have little reason to complain that they were not immediately instrumental in their enactment. The only infallible criterion of the excellence of any constitution is to be found in the detail of its municipal code; and the value which wise men set on political freedom, arises chiefly from the facility it is supposed to afford for the introduction of those legislative improvements which the general interests of the community recommend. I cannot help adding, that the capacity of a people to exercise political rights with utility to themselves and to their country, presupposes a diffusion of knowledge and of good morals, which can only result from the previous operation of laws favourable to industry, to order, and to freedom.

* See the conclusion of his Theory of Moral Sentiments.

Of the truth of these remarks enlightened politicians seem now to be in general convinced ; for the most celebrated works which have been produced in the different countries of Europe, during the last thirty years, by Smith, Quesnai, Turgot, Campomanes, Beccaria, and others, have aimed at the improvement of society,—not by delineating plans of new constitutions, but by enlightening the policy of actual legislators. Such speculations, while they are more essentially and more extensively useful than any others, have no tendency to unhinge established institutions, or to inflame the passions of the multitude. The improvements they recommend are to be effected by means too gradual and slow in their operation, to warm the imaginations of any but the speculative few ; and in proportion as they are adopted, they consolidate the political fabric, and enlarge the basis upon which it rests.

To direct the policy of nations with respect to one most important class of its laws, those which form its system of political economy, is the great aim of Mr. Smith's *Inquiry :* And he has unquestionably had the merit of presenting to the world, the most comprehensive and perfect work that has yet appeared, on the general principles of any branch of legislation. The example which he has set will be followed, it is to be hoped, in due time, by other writers, for whom the internal policy of states furnishes many other subjects of discussion no less curious and interesting ; and many accelerate the progress of that science which Lord Bacon has so well described in the following passage : " Finis et scopus quem leges intueri, atque ad quem jussiones et sanctiones suas dirigere debent, non alius est, quam ut cives feliciter degant ; id fiet, si pietate et religione recte instituti ; moribus honesti ; armis adversus hostes externos tuti ; legum auxilio adversus seditiones et privatas injurias muniti ; imperio et magistratibus obsequentes ; copiis et opibus locupletes et florentes fuerint.——Certe cognitio ista ad viros civiles proprie spectat ; qui optime nôrunt, quid ferat societas humana, quid salus populi, quid æquitas naturalis, quid gentium mores, quid rerumpublicarum formæ diversæ : ideoque possint de legibus, ex principiis et præceptis tam æquitatis naturalis, quam politices decernere. Quamobrem id nunc agatur, ut fontes justitiæ et utilitatis publicæ petantur, et in singulis juris partibus character quidam et idea justi exhibeatur, ad quam particularium regnorum et rerumpublicarum leges probare, atque inde emendationem moliri, quisque, cui hoc cordi erit et curæ, possit."

The enumeration contained in the foregoing passage, of the different objects of law, coincides very nearly with that given by Mr. Smith in the conclusion of his Theory of Moral Sentiments ; and the precise aim of the political speculations which he then announced, and of which he afterwards published so valuable a part in his Wealth of Nations, was to ascertain the general principles of justice and of expediency, which ought to guide the institutions of legislators on these important articles;—in the words of Lord Bacon, to ascertain those *leges legum*, "ex quibus informatio peti possit, quid in singulis legibus bene aut perperam positum aut constitutum sit."

The branch of legislation which Mr. Smith has made choice of as the subject of his work, naturally leads me to remark a very striking contrast between the spirit of ancient and of modern policy in respect to the Wealth of Nations.* The great object of the former was to counteract the love of money and a taste for luxury, by positive institutions ; and to maintain in the great body of the people, habits of frugality, and a severity of manners. The decline of states is uniformly ascribed by the philosophers and historians, both of Greece and Rome, to the influence of riches on national character ; and the laws of Lycurgus, which, during a course of ages, banished the precious metals from Sparta, are proposed by many of them as the most perfect model of legislation devised by human wisdom. How opposite to this is the doctrine of modern politicians ! Far from considering poverty as an advantage to a state, their great aim is to open new sources of national opulence, and to animate the activity of all classes of the people, by a taste for the comforts and accommodations of life.

One principal cause of this difference between the spirit of ancient and of modern policy, may be found in the difference between the sources of national wealth in ancient and in modern times. In ages when commerce and manufactures were yet in their infancy, and among states constituted like most of the ancient republics, a sudden influx of riches from abroad was justly dreaded as an evil, alarming to the morals, to the industry, and to the freedom of a people. So different, however, is the case at present, that the most wealthy nations are those where the people are the most laborious, and where they enjoy the greatest degree of liberty. Nay, it was the general diffusion of wealth among the lower orders of men, which first gave birth to the spirit of independence in modern Europe, and which has produced under some of its governments, and especially under our own, a more equal diffusion of freedom and of happiness than took place under the most celebrated constitutions of antiquity.

Without this diffusion of wealth among the lower orders, the important effects resulting from the invention of printing would have been extremely limited ; for a certain degree of ease and in-

* Filangieri, La Scienza della Legislazione, L. i. cap. 13.

dependence is necessary to inspire men with the desire of know-ledge, and to afford them the leisure which is requisite for acquiring it ; and it is only by the rewards which such a state of society holds up to industry and ambition, that the selfish pas-sions of the multitude can be interested in the intellectual im-provement of their children. The extensive propagation of light and refinement arising from the influence of the press, aided by the spirit of commerce, seems to be the remedy provided by nature, against the fatal effects which would otherwise be pro-duced, by the subdivision of labour accompanying the progress of the mechanical arts: Nor is anything wanting to make the remedy effectual, but wise institutions to facilitate general instruction, and to adapt the education of individuals to the stations they are to occupy. The mind of the artist, which, from the limited sphere of his activity, would sink below the level of the peasant or the savage, might receive in infancy the means of intellectual enjoyment, and the seeds of moral improvement ; and even the insipid uniformity of his professional engagements, by presenting no object to awaken his ingenuity or to distract his attention, might leave him at liberty to employ his faculties, on subjects more interesting to himself, and more extensively useful to others.

These effects, notwithstanding a variety of opposing causes which still exist, have already resulted, in a very sensible degree, from the liberal policy of modern times. Mr. Hume, in his Essay on Commerce, after taking notice of the numerous armies raised and maintained by the small republics in the ancient world, ascribes the military power of these states to their want of com-merce and luxury. " Few artizans were maintained by the labour of the farmers, and therefore more soldiers might live upon it." He adds, however, that " the policy of ancient times was VIOLENT, and contrary to the NATURAL course of things ;"—by which, I presume, he means, that it aimed too much at modifying, by the force of positive institutions, the order of society, accord-ing to some preconceived idea of expediency ; without trusting sufficiently to those principles of the human constitution, which, wherever they are allowed free scope, not only conduct mankind to happiness, but lay the foundation of a progressive improve-ment in their condition and in their character. The advantages which modern policy possesses over the ancient, arise principally from its conformity, in some of the most important articles of political economy, to an order of things recommended by nature ; and it would not be difficult to show, that, where it remains im-perfect, its errors may be traced to the restraints it imposes on the natural course of human affairs. Indeed, in these restraints may be discovered the latent seeds of many of the prejudices and follies which infect modern manners, and which have so long bid defiance to the reasonings of the philosopher and the ridicule of the satirist.

The foregoing very imperfect hints appear to me to form, not only a proper, but in some measure a necessary introduction to the few remarks I have to offer on Mr. Smith's Inquiry; as they tend to illustrate a connection between his system of commercial politics, and those speculations of his earlier years, in which he aimed more professedly at the advancement of human improvement and happiness. It is this view of political economy that can alone render it interesting to the moralist, and can dignify calculations of profit and loss in the eye of the philosopher. Mr. Smith has alluded to it in various passages of his work, but he has nowhere explained himself fully on the subject; and the great stress he has laid on the effects of the division of labour in increasing its productive powers, seems, at first sight, to point to a different and very melancholy conclusion;—that the same causes which promote the progress of the arts, tend to degrade the mind of the artist; and, of consequence, that the growth of national wealth implies a sacrifice of the character of the people.

The fundamental doctrines cf Mr. Smith's system are now so generally known, that it would be tedious to offer any recapitulation of them in this place; even if I could hope to do justice to the subject, within the limits which I have prescribed to myself. I shall content myself, therefore, with remarking, in general terms, that the great and leading object of his speculations is, to illustrate the provisions made by nature in the principles of the human mind, and in the circumstances of man's external situation, for a gradual and progressive augmentation in the means of national wealth; and to demonstrate that the most effectual plan for advancing a people to greatness, is to maintain that order of things which nature has pointed out; by allowing every man, as long as he observes the rules of justice, to pursue his own interest in his own way, and to bring both his industry and his capital into the freest competition with those of his fellow-citizens. Every system of policy which endeavours, either by extraordinary encouragements to draw towards a particular species of industry a greater share of the capital of the society than what would naturally go to it, or, by extraordinary restraints, to force from a particular species of industry some share of the capital which would otherwise be employed in it, is, in reality, subversive of the great purpose which it means to promote.

What the circumstances are, which, in modern Europe, have contributed to disturb this order of nature, and, in particular, to encourage the industry of towns, at the expense of that of the country, Mr. Smith has investigated with great ingenuity ; and in such a manner, as to throw much new light on the history of that state of society which prevails in this quarter of the globe. His observations on this subject tend to show, that these circumstances were, in their first origin, the natural and the un-avoidable result of the peculiar situation of mankind during a certain period ;· and that they took their rise, not from any general scheme of policy, but from the private interests and pre-judices of particular orders of men.

The state of society, however, which at first arose from a sin-gular combination of accidents, has been prolonged much beyond its natural period, by a false system of political economy, propa-gated by merchants and manufacturers ; a class of individuals, whose interest is not always the same with that of the public, and whose professional knowledge gave them many advantages, more particularly in the infancy of this branch of science, in defending those opinions which they wished to encourage. By means of this system a new set of obstacles to the progress of national pros-perity has been created. Those which arose from the disorders of the feudal ages, tended directly to disturb the internal arrange-ments of society, by obstructing the free circulation of labour and of stock, from employment to employment, and from place to place. The false system of political economy, which has been hitherto prevalent, as its professed object has been to regulate the commercial intercourse between different nations, has produced its effect in a way less direct and less manifest, but equally preju-dicial to the states that have adopted it.

On this system, as it took its rise from the prejudices or rather from the interested views of mercantile speculators, Mr. Smith bestows the title of the Commercial or Mercantile System ; and he has considered at great length its two principal expedients for enriching a nation ; restraints upon importation, and encourage-ments to exportation. Part of these expedients, he observes, have been dictated by the spirit of monopoly, and part by a spirit of jealousy against those countries with which the balance of trade is supposed to be disadvantageous. All of them appear clearly, from his reasonings, to have a tendency unfavourable to the wealth of the nation which imposes them. His remarks with respect to the jealousy of commerce are expressed in a tone of indignation, which he seldom assumes in his political writings.

" In this manner," says he, " the sneaking arts of underling tradesmen are erected into political maxims for the conduct of a great empire. By such maxims as these, nations have been taught that their interest consisted in beggaring all their neighbours. Each nation has been made to look with an invidious eye upon the prosperity of all the nations with which it trades, and to consider their gain as its own loss. Commerce, which ought naturally to be, among nations as among individuals, a bond of union and friendship, has become the most fertile source of discord and animosity. The capricious ambition of kings and ministers has not, during the present and the preceding century, been more fatal to the repose of Europe, than the impertinent jealousy of merchants and manufacturers. The violence and injustice of the rulers of mankind is an ancient evil, for which, perhaps, the nature of human affairs can scarce admit of a remedy. But the mean rapacity, the monopolizing spirit of merchants and manufacturers, who neither are nor ought to be the rulers of mankind, though it cannot perhaps be corrected, may very easily be prevented from disturbing the tranquillity of anybody but themselves."

Such are the liberal principles which, according to Mr. Smith, ought to direct the commercial policy of nations ; and of which it ought to be the great object of legislators to facilitate the establishment. In what manner the execution of the theory should be conducted in particular instances, is a question of a very different nature, and to which the answer must vary in different countries, according to the different circumstances of the case. In a speculative work, such as Mr. Smith's, the consideration of this question did not fall properly under his general plan ; but that he was abundantly aware of the danger to be apprehended from a rash application of political theories, appears not only from the general strain of his writings, but from some incidental observation which he has expressly made upon the subject. "So unfortunate," says he, in one passage, "are the effects of all the regulations of the mercantile system, that they not only introduce very dangerous disorders into the state of the body politic, but disorders which it is often difficult to remedy, without occasioning, for a time at least, still greater disorders. In what manner, therefore, the natural system of perfect liberty and justice ought gradually to be restored we must leave to the wisdom of future statesmen and legislators to determine." In the last edition of his Theory of Moral Sentiments, he has introduced some remarks, which have an obvious reference to the same important doctrine. The following passage seems to refer more particularly to those derangements of the social order which derived their origin from the feudal institutions :

The man whose public spirit is prompted altogether by humanity and benevolence, will respect the established powers and privileges even of individuals, and still more of the great orders and societies into which the state is divided. Though he should consider some of them as in some measure abusive, he will content himself with moderating what he often cannot annihilate without great violence. When he cannot conquer the rooted prejudices of the people by reason and persuasion, he will not attempt to subdue them by force ; but will religiously observe what, by Cicero, is justly called the divine maxim of Plato, never to use violence to his country any more than to his parents. He will accommodate, as well as he can, his public arrangements to the confirmed habits and prejudices of the people ; and will remedy, as well as he can, the inconveniences which may flow from the want of those regulations which the people are averse to submit to. When he cannot establish the right, he will not disdain to ameliorate the wrong ; but, like Solon, when he cannot establish the best system of laws, he will endeavour to establish the best that the people can bear.

These cautions with respect to the practical application of general principles were peculiarly necessary from the author of "The Wealth of Nations ;" as the unlimited freedom of trade, which it is the chief aim of his work to recommend, is extremely apt, by flattering the indolence of the statesman, to suggest to those who are invested with absolute power, the idea of carrying it into immediate execution. "Nothing is more adverse to the tranquillity of a statesman," says the author of an Eloge on the Administration of Colbert, " than a spirit of moderation ; because it condemns him to perpetual observation, shows him every moment the insufficiency of his wisdom, and leaves him the melancholy sense of his own imperfection ; while, under the shelter of a few general principles, a systematical politician enjoys a perpetual calm. By the help of one alone, that of a perfect liberty of trade, he would govern the world, and would leave human affairs to arrange themselves at pleasure, under the operation of the prejudices and the self-interests of individuals. If these run counter to each other, he gives himself no anxiety about the consequence ; he insists that the result cannot be judged of till after a century or two shall have elapsed. If his contemporaries, in consequence of the disorder into which he has thrown public affairs, are scrupulous about submitting quietly to the experiment, he accuses them of impatience. They alone, and not he, are to blame for what they have suffered ; and the principle continues to be inculcated with the same zeal and the same confidence as before." These are the words of the ingenious and eloquent author of the Eloge on Colbert, which obtained the prize from the French Academy in the year 1763 ; a performance which, although confined and erroneous in its speculative views, abounds with just and important reflections of a practical nature. How far his remarks apply to that particular class of politicians whom he evidently aimed at in the foregoing passage, I shall not presume to decide.

It is hardly necessary for me to add to these observations, that they do not detract in the least from the value of those political theories which attempt to delineate the principles of a perfect legislation. Such theories (as I have elsewhere observed*) ought to be considered merely as descriptions of the ultimate objects at which the statesman ought to aim. The tranquillity of his administration, and the immediate success of his measures, depend on his good sense and his practical skill ; and his theoretical principles only enable him to direct his measures steadily and wisely, to promote the improvement and happiness of mankind, and prevent him from being ever led astray from these important ends, by more limited views of temporary expedience. " In all cases," says Mr. Hume, " it must be advantageous to know what is most perfect in the kind, that we may be able to bring any real constitution or form of government as near it as possible, by such gentle alterations and innovations as may not give too great disturbance to society."

The limits of this Memoir make it impossible for me to examine particularly the merit of Mr. Smith's work in point of originality. That his doctrine concerning the freedom of trade and of industry coincides remarkably with that which we find in the writings of the French Economists, appears from the slight view of their system which he himself has given. But it surely cannot be pretended by the warmest admirers of that system, that any one of its numerous expositors has approached to Mr. Smith in the precision and perspicuity with which he has stated it, or in the scientific and luminous manner in which he has deduced it from elementary principles. The awkwardness of their technical language, and the paradoxical form in which they have chosen to present some of their opinions, are acknowledged even by those who are most willing to do justice to their merits : whereas it may be doubted, with respect to Mr. Smith's Inquiry, if there exists any book beyond the circle of the mathematical and physical sciences, which is at once so agreeable in its arrangement to the rules of a sound logic, and so accessible to the examination of ordinary readers. Abstracting entirely from the author's peculiar and original speculations, I do not know that, upon any subject whatever, a work has been produced in our times, containing so methodical, so comprehensive, and so judicious a digest of all the most profound and enlightened philosophy of the age.

In justice also to Mr. Smith, it must be observed, that although some of the economical writers had the start of him in publishing their doctrines to the world, these doctrines appear, with respect to him, to have been altogether original, and the result of his own

* Elements of the Philosophy of the Human Mind, p. 261.

re...ections. Of this, I think, every person must be convinced, who reads the Inquiry with due attention, and is at pains to examine the gradual and beautiful progress of the author's ideas : But in case any doubt should remain on this head, it may be proper to mention, that Mr. Smith's political lectures, comprehending the fundamental principles of his Inquiry, were delivered at Glasgow as early as the year 1752 or 1753 ; at a period, surely, when there existed no French performance on the subject, that could be of much use to him in guiding his researches.* In the year 1756, indeed, M. Turgot (who is said to have imbibed his first notions concerning the unlimited freedom of commerce from an old merchant, M. Gournay) published in the *Encyclopédie*, an article which sufficiently shows how completely his mind was emancipated from the old predjudices in favour of commercial regulations : but that even then, these opinions were confined to a few speculative men in France, appears from a passage in the *Mémoires sur la Vie et les Ouvrages de M. Turgot ;* in which, after a short quotation from the article just mentioned, the author adds : " These ideas were *then* considered as paradoxical ; they are since become common, and they will one day be adopted universally."

The Political Discourses of Mr. Hume were evidently of greater use to Mr. Smith, than any other book that had appeared prior to his lectures. Even Mr. Hume's theories, however, though always plausible and ingenious, and in most instances profound and just, involve some fundamental mistakes ; and, when compared with Mr. Smith's, afford a striking proof, that, in considering a subject so extensive and so complicated, the most penetrating sagacity, if directed only to particular questions, is apt to be led astray by first appearances ; and that nothing can guard us effectually against error, but a comprehensive survey of the whole field of discussion, assisted by an accurate and patient analysis of the ideas about which our reasonings are employed. It may be worth while to add, that Mr. Hume's Essay " on the Jealousy of Trade," with some other of his Political Discourses, received a very flattering proof of M. Turgot's approbation, by his undertaking the task of translating them into the French language.†

* In proof of this, it is sufficient for me to appeal to a short history of the progress of political economy in France, published in one of the volumes of *Ephemerides du Citoyen,* See the first part of the volume for the year 1769. The paper is entitled, *Notice abrégée des différens Ecrits Modernes, qui ont concouru en France à former la science de l'économie politique.*

† When this memoir was first written, I was not fully aware to what an extent the French economists had been anticipated, in some of their most important conclusions, by writers (chiefly British) of a much earlier

It does not belong to my present undertaking (even if I were qualified for such a task) to attempt a separation of the solid and important doctrines of Mr. Smith's book from those which appear exceptionable or doubtful. I acknowledge that there are some of his conclusions to which I would not be understood to subscribe implicitly ; more particularly in that chapter, where he treats of the principles of taxation ;—a subject which he has certainly examined in a manner more loose and unsatisfactory than most of the others which have fallen under his review.*

It would be improper for me to conclude this section without

date. I had often, indeed, been struck with the coincidence between their reasonings concerning the advantages of their territorial tax, and Mr. Locke's speculations on the same subject, in one of his political discourses published sixty years before ; as well as with the coincidence of their argument against corporations and exclusive companies, with what had been urged at a still earlier period, by the celebrated John de Witt, Sir Josiah Child, John Cary, of Bristol, and various other speculative men, who appeared in the latter part of the seventeenth century. To these writers, my attention had been directed by some quotations of the Abbé Morellet, in his very able Memoir on the East India Company of France, printed in 1769. Many passages, however, much more full and explicit than those which had fallen in his way, have been pointed out to me by the Earl of Lauderdale, in his curious and valuable collection of rare English Tracts relating to political economy. In some of these, the argument is stated in a manner so clear and so conclusive, as to render it surprising, that truths of which the public has been so long in in possession, should have been so completely overborne by prejudice and misrepresentation, as to have had, to a large proportion of readers, the appearance of novelty and paradox, when revived in the philosophical theories of the present age.

That the writers of this Island should have had the start of those in the greater part of Europe, in adopting enlightened' ideas concerning commerce, will not appear surprising, when we consider that " according to the Common Law of England, the freedom of trade is the birthright of the subject." For the opinions of Lord Coke and of Lord Chief-Justice Fortescue, on this point, see a pamphlet by Lord Lauderdale, entitled, " Hints to the Manufacturers of Great Britain," &c., (printed in 1805) ; where also may be found a list of statutes containing recognitions and declarations of the above principle,

* Among the questionable doctrines to which Mr. Smith has lent the sanction of his name, there is perhaps none that involves so many important consequences as the opinion he has maintained concerning the expediency of legal restrictions on the rate of interest. The inconclusiveness of his reasoning on this point, has been demonstrated, with a singular degree of logical acuteness, by Mr. Bentham, in a short treatise entitled *Defence of Usury ;* a performance to which (notwithstanding the

taking notice of the manly and dignified freedom with which the author uniformly delivers his opinions, and of the superiority which he discovers throughout, to all the little passions connected with the factions of the times in which he wrote. Whoever takes the trouble to compare the general tone of his composition with the period of its first publication, cannot fail to feel and acknowledge the force of this remark. It is not often that a disinterested zeal for truth has so soon met with its just reward. Philosophers (to use an expression of Lord Bacon's) are "the servants of posterity;" and most of those who have devoted their talents to the best interests of mankind, have been obliged, like Bacon, to "bequeath their fame" to a race yet unborn, and to console themselves with the idea of sowing what another generation was to reap :

Insere Daphni pyros, carpent tua poma nepotes.

Mr. Smith was more fortunate ; or rather, in this respect, his fortune was singular. He survived the publication of his work only fifteen years ; and yet, during that short period, he had not only the satisfaction of seeing the opposition it at first excited, gradually subside, but witnessing the practical influence of his writings on the commercial policy of his country.

CONCLUSION OF THE NARRATIVE.

ABOUT two years after the publication of "The Wealth of Nations," Mr. Smith was appointed one of the Commissioners of his Majesty's Customs in Scotland ; a preferment which, in his esti-

long interval that has elapsed since the date of its publication), I do not know that any answer has yet been attempted ; and which a late writer (Sir Francis Baring, in his Pamphlet on the Bank of England), eminently acquainted with the operations of commerce, has pronounced (and, in my opinion, with great truth) to be "perfectly unanswerable." It is a remarkable circumstance, that Mr. Smith should, in this solitary instance, have adopted, on such slight grounds, a conclusion so strikingly contrasted with the general spirit of his political discussions, and so manifestly at variance with the fundamental principles which, on other occasions, he has so boldly followed out, through all their practical applications. This is the more surprising, as the French Economists had, a few years before, obviated the most plausible objections which are apt to present themselves against this extension of the doctrine of commercial freedom. See, in particular, some observations in Mr. Turgot's Reflections on the Formation and Distribution of Riches; and a separate Essay, by the same author, entitled, " Mémoire sur le prêt à intérêt, et sur le Commerce des ' Fers.' "

mation, derived an additional value from its being bestowed on him at the request of the Duke of Buccleuch. The greater part of these two years he passed in London, enjoying a society too extensive and varied to afford him any opportunity of indulging his taste for study. His time, however, was not lost to himself; for much of it was spent with some of the first names in English literature. Of these no unfavourable specimen is preserved by Dr. Barnard, in his well-known "Verses addressed to Sir Joshua Reynolds and his friends."

> If I have thoughts, and can't express 'em,
> Gibbon shall teach me how to dress 'em
>   In words select and terse :
> Jones teach me modesty and Greek,
> Smith how to think, Burke how to speak,
>   And Beauclerc to converse.*

In consequence of Mr. Smith's appointment to the Board of Customs, he removed, in 1778, to Edinburgh, where he spent the last twelve years of his life ; enjoying an affluence which was more than equal to all his wants ; and, what was to him of still greater value, the prospect of passing the remainder of his days among the companions of his youth.

His mother, who, though now in extreme old age, still possessed a considerable degree of health, and retained all her faculties unimpaired, accompanied him to town ; and his cousin Miss Jane Douglas (who had formerly been a member of his family at Glasgow, and for whom he had always felt the affection of a brother) while she divided with him those tender attentions which her aunt's infirmities required, relieved him of a charge for which he was peculiarly ill qualified, by her friendly superintendence of his domestic economy.

The accession to his income which his new office brought him, enabled him to gratify, to a much greater extent than his former circumstances admitted of, the natural generosity of his disposition ; and the state of his funds at the time of his death, compared with his very moderate establishment, confirmed, beyond a doubt, what his intimate acquaintances had often suspected, that a large proportion of his annual savings was allotted to offices of secret charity. A small, but excellent library, which he had gradually formed with great judgment in the selection, and a simple, though hospitable table, where, without the formality of an invitation, he was always happy to receive his friends, were the only expenses that could be considered as his own.†

* See Annual Register for the year 1776.

† Some very affecting instances of Mr. Smith's beneficence, in cases where he found it impossible to conceal entirely his good offices, have

The change in his habits which his removal to Edinburgh produced, was not equally favourable to his literary pursuits. The duties of his office, though they required but little exertion of thought, were yet sufficient to waste his spirits and to dissipate his attention ; and now that his career is closed, it is impossible to reflect on the time they consumed, without lamenting, that it had not been employed in labours more profitable to the world, and more equal to his mind.

During the first years of his residence in this city, his studies seemed to be entirely suspended ; and his passion for letters served only to amuse his leisure, and to animate his conversation. The infirmities of age, of which he very early began to feel the approaches, reminded him at last, when it was too late, of what he yet owed to the public, and to his own fame. The principal materials of the works which he had announced, had been long collected ; and little probably was wanting, but a few years of health and retirement, to bestow on them that systematical arrangement in which he delighted ; and the ornaments of that flowing, and apparently artless style, which he had studiously cultivated, but which, after all his experience in composition, he adjusted, with extreme difficulty, to his own taste.*

The death of his mother in 1784, which was followed by that of Miss Douglas, in 1788, contributed, it is probable, to frustrate these projects. They had been the objects of his affection for more than sixty years ; and in their society he had enjoyed, from his infancy, all that he ever knew of the endearments of a family.†

been mentioned to me by a near relation of his, and one of his most confidential friends, Miss Ross, daughter of the late Patrick Ross, Esq., of Innernethy. They were all on a scale much beyond what might have been expected from his fortune ; and were accompanied with circumstances equally honourable to the delicacy of his feelings and the liberality of his heart.

* Mr. Smith observed to me, not long before his death, that after all his practice in writing, he composed as slowly and with as great difficulty as at first. He added, at the same time, that Mr. Hume had acquired so great a facility in this respect, that the last volumes of his History were printed from his original copy, with a few marginal corrections.

It may gratify the curiosity of some readers to know, that when Mr. Smith was employed in composition, he generally walked up and down his apartment, dictating to a secretary. All Mr. Hume's works (I have been assured) were written with his own hand. A critical reader may, I think, perceive in the different styles of these two classical writers, the effects of their different modes of study.

† In the early part of Mr. Smith's life it is well known to his friends, that he was for several years attached to a young lady of great beauty

He was now alone, and helpless ; and, though he bore his loss with equanimity, and regained apparently his former cheerfulness, yet his health and strength gradually declined till the period of his death, which happened in July, 1790, about two years after that of his cousin, and six after that of his mother. His last illness, which arose from a chronic obstruction in his bowels, was lingering and painful ; but had every consolation to soothe it which he could derive from the tenderest sympathy of his friends, and from the complete resignation of his own mind.

A few days before his death, finding his end approach rapidly, he gave orders to destroy all his manuscripts, excepting some detached essays, which he intrusted to the care of his executors ; and they were accordingly committed to the flames. What were the particular contents of these papers is not known even to his most intimate friends ; but there can be no doubt that they consisted, in part, of the letters on rhetoric, which he read at Edinburgh in the year 1748, and of the lectures on natural religion and on jurisprudence, which formed part of his course at Glasgow. That this irreparable injury to letters proceeded, in some degree, from an excessive solicitude in the author about his posthumous reputation, may, perhaps, be true ; but with respect to some of his manuscripts, may we not suppose, that he was influenced by higher motives ? It is but seldom that a philosopher, who has been occupied from his youth with moral or with political inquiries, succeeds completely to his wish in stating to others, the grounds upon which his own opinions are founded ; and hence it is, that the known principles of an individual, who has approved to the public his candour, his liberality, and his judgment, are entitled to a weight and an authority, independent of the evidence which he is able, upon any particular occasion, to produce in their support. A secret consciousness of this circumstance, and an apprehension that, by not doing justice to an important argument, the progress of truth may be rather retarded than advanced, have probably induced many authors to withhold from the world the unfinished results of their most valuable labours ; and to content

and accomplishment. How far his addresses were favourably received, or what the circumstances were which prevented their union, I have not been able to learn ; but I believe it is pretty certain that, after this disappointment, he laid aside all thoughts of marriage. The lady to whom I allude died also unmarried. She survived Mr. Smith for a considerable number of years, and was alive long after the publication of the first edition of this Memoir. I had the pleasure of seeing her when she was turned of eighty, and she still retained evident traces of her former beauty. The powers of her understanding and the gaiety of her temper seemed to have suffered nothing from the hand of time.

themselves with giving the general sanction of their suffrages to truths which they regarded as peculiarly interesting to the human race.*

The additions to the Theory of Moral Sentiments, most of which were composed under severe disease, had fortunately been sent to the press in the beginning of the preceding winter ; and the author lived to see the publication of the work. The moral and serious strain that prevails through these additions, when connected with the circumstance of his declining health, adds a peculiar charm to his pathetic eloquence, and communicates a new interest, if possible, to those sublime truths, which in the academical retirement of his youth, awakened the first ardours of his genius, and on which the last efforts of his mind reposed.

In a letter addressed, in the year 1787, to the Principal of the University of Glasgow, in consequence of being elected Rector of that learned body, a pleasing memorial remains of the satisfaction with which he always recollected that period of his literary career, which had been more peculiarly consecrated to these important studies. "No preferment," says he, "could have given me so

* Since writing the above, I have been favoured by Dr. Hutton with the following particulars.

"Some time before his last illness, when Mr. Smith had occasion to go to London, he enjoined his friends, to whom he had intrusted the disposal of his manuscripts, that, in the event of his death, they should destroy all the volumes of his lectures, doing with the rest of his manuscripts what they pleased. When now he had become weak, and saw the approaching period of his life, he spoke to his friends again upon the same subject. They entreated him to make his mind easy, as he might depend upon their fulfilling his desire. He was then satisfied. But some days afterwards, finding his anxiety not entirely removed, he begged one of them to destroy the volumes immediately. This accordingly was done ; and his mind was so much relieved, that he was able to receive his friends in the evening with his usual complacency.

"They had been in use to sup with him every Sunday ; and that evening there was a pretty numerous meeting of them. Mr. Smith, not finding himself able to sit up with them as usual, retired to bed before supper ; and, as he went away, took leave of his friends by saying, ' I believe we must adjourn this meeting to some other place.' He died a very few days afterwards."

Mr. Riddell, an intimate friend of Mr. Smith's, who was present at one of the conversations on the subject of the manuscripts, mentioned to me, in addition to Dr. Hutton's note, that Mr. Smith regretted "he had done so little." " But I meant," said he, " to have done more ; and there are materials in my papers, of which I could have made a great deal. But that is now out of the question."

That the idea of destroying such unfinished works as might be in his possession at the time of his death, was not the effect of any sudden or much real satisfaction. No man can owe greater obligations to a society than I do to the University of Glasgow. They educated me ; they sent me to Oxford. Soon after my return to Scotland, they elected me one of their own members ; and afterwards preferred me to another office, to which the abilities and virtues of the never-to-be-forgotten Dr. Hutcheson had given a superior degree of illustration. The period of thirteen years which I spent as a member of that society, I remember as by far the most useful, and therefore as by far the happiest and most honourable period of my life ; and now after three-and-twenty years absence, to be remembered in so very agreeable a manner by my old friends and protectors, gives me a heart felt joy which I cannot easily express to you."

The short narrative which I have now finished, however barren of incident, may convey a general idea of the genius and character of this illustrious man. Of the intellectual gifts and attainments by which he was so eminently distinguished ; of the originality and comprehensiveness of his views ; the extent, the variety, and the correctness of his information ; the inexhaustible fertility of his invention ; and the ornaments which his rich and beautiful imagination had borrowed from classical culture ; he has left behind him lasting monuments. To his private worth the most

hasty resolution, appears from the following letter to Mr. Hume, written by Mr. Smith in 1773, at a time when he was preparing himself for a journey to London, with a prospect of a pretty long absence from Scotland.

"My dear Friend,   "Edinburgh, 16 April, 1773.
"As I have left the care of all my literary papers to you, I must tell you, that except those which I carry along with me, there are none worth the publication, but a fragment of a great work, which contains a history of the astronomical systems that were succesively in fashion down to the time of Des Cartes. Whether that might not be published as a fragment of an intended juvenile work, I leave entirely to your judgment, though I begin to suspect myself that there is more refinement than solidity in some parts of it. This little work you will find in a thin folio paper book in my back room. All the other loose papers which you will find in that desk, or within the glass folding doors of a bureau which stands in my bed-room, together with about eighteen thin paper folio books, which you will likewise find within the same glass folding doors, I desire may be destroyed without any examination. Unless I die very suddenly, I shall take care that the papers I carry with me shall be carefully sent to you.
        "I ever am, my dear Friend, most faithfully yours,
                                    "ADAM SMITH."
"To David Hume, Esq., St. Andrew's Square."

certain of all testimonies may be found in that confidence, respect, and attachment, which followed him through all the various relations of life. The serenity and gaiety he enjoyed, under the pressure of his growing infirmities, and the warm interest he felt to the last, in every thing connected with the welfare of his friends, will be long remembered by a small circle, with whom, as long as his strength permitted, he regularly spent an evening in the week : and to whom the recollection of his worth still forms a pleasing, though melancholy bond of union.

The more delicate and characteristic features of his mind, it is perhaps impossible to trace. That there were many peculiarities both in his manners and in his intellectual habits, was manifest to the most superficial observer ; but although, to those who knew him, these peculiarities detracted nothing from the respect which his abilities commanded ; and although, to his intimate friends, they added an inexpressible charm to his conversation, while they displayed, in the most interesting light, the artless simplicity of his heart ; yet it would require a very skilful pencil to present them to the public eye. He was certainly not fitted for the general commerce of the world, or for the business of active life. The comprehensive speculations with which he had been occupied from his youth, and the variety of materials which his own invention continually supplied to his thoughts, rendered him habitually inattentive to familiar objects, and to common occurrences ; and he frequently exhibited instances of absence, which have scarcely been surpassed by the fancy of La Bruyere. Even in company, he was apt to be engrossed with his studies ; and appeared, at times, by the motion of his lips, as well as by his looks and gestures, to be in the fervour of composition. I have often, however, been struck, at the distance of years, with his accurate memory of the most trifling particulars ; and am inclined to believe, from this and some other circumstances, that he possessed a power, not perhaps uncommon among absent men. of recollecting, in consequence of subsequent efforts of reflection. many occurrences, which, at the time when they happened, did not seem to have sensibly attracted his notice.

To the defect now mentioned, it was probably owing, in part, that he did not fall in easily with the common dialogue of conversation, and that he was somewhat apt to convey his own ideas in the form of a lecture. When he did so, however, it never proceeded from a wish to engross the discourse, or to gratify his vanity. His own inclination disposed him so strongly to enjoy in silence the gaiety of those around him, that his friends were often led to concert little schemes, in order to engage him in the discussions most likely to interest him. Nor do I think I shall be accused of going too far, when I say, that he was scarcely ever known to start a new topic himself, or to appear unprepared upon those topics that were introduced by others. Indeed, his conversation was never more amusing than when he gave a loose to his genius, upon the very few branches of knowledge of which he only possessed the outlines.

The opinions he formed of men, upon a slight acquaintance, were frequently erroneous; but the tendency of his nature inclined him much more to blind partiality, than to ill-founded prejudice. The enlarged views of human affairs, on which his mind habitually dwelt, left him neither time nor inclination to study, in detail, the uninteresting peculiarities of ordinary characters; and accordingly, though intimately acquainted with the capacities of the intellect, and the workings of the heart, and accustomed, in his theories, to mark, with the most delicate hand, the nicest shades, both of genius and of the passions; yet, in judging of individuals, it sometimes happened that his estimates were, in a surprising degree, wide of the truth.

The opinions, too, which, in the thoughtlessness and confidence of his social hours, he was accustomed to hazard on books, and on questions of speculation, were not uniformly such as might have been expected from the superiority of his understanding, and the singular consistency of his philosophical principles. They were liable to be influenced by accidental circumstances, and by the humour of the moment; and when retailed by those who only saw him occasionally, suggested false and contradictory ideas of his real sentiments. On these, however, as on most other occasions, there was always much truth, as well as ingenuity, in his remarks; and if the different opinions which, at different times, he pronounced upon the same subject, had been all combined together, so as to modify and limit each other, they would probably have afforded materials for a decision, equally comprehensive and just. But, in the society of his friends, he had no disposition to form those qualified conclusions that we admire in his writings; and he generally contented himself with a bold and masterly sketch of the object, from the first point of view in which his temper, or his fancy, presented it. Something of the same kind might be remarked, when he attempted, in the flow of his spirits, to delineate those characters which, from long intimacy, he might have been supposed to understand thoroughly. The picture was always lively, and expressive; and commonly bore a strong and amusing resemblance to the original, when viewed under one particular aspect; but seldom, perhaps, conveyed a just and complete conception of it in all its dimensions and proportions. In a word, it was the fault of his unpremeditated judgments, to be too systematical, and too much in extremes.

But, in whatever way these trifling peculiarities in his manners may be explained, there can be no doubt, that they were intimately connected with the genuine artlessness of his mind. In this amiable quality, he often recalled to his friends the accounts that are given of good La Fontaine ; a quality which in him derived a peculiar grace from the singularity of its combination with those powers of reason and of eloquence, which, in his political and moral writings, have long engaged the admiration of Europe.

In his external form and appearance, there was nothing uncommon. When perfectly at ease, and when warmed with conversation, his gestures were animated, and not ungraceful ; and, in the society of those he loved, his features were often brightened with a smile of inexpressible benignity. In the company of strangers, his tendency to absence, and perhaps still more his consciousness of this tendency, rendered his manner somewhat embarrassed ;—an effect which was probably not a little heightened by those speculative ideas of propriety, which his recluse habits tended at once to perfect in his conception, and to diminish his power of realizing. He never sat for his picture ; but the medallion of Tassie conveys an exact idea of his profile, and of the general expression of his countenance.

His valuable library, together with the rest of his property, was bequeathed to his cousin Mr. David Douglas, Advocate. In the education of this young gentleman, he had employed much of his leisure ; and it was only two years before his death (at a time when he could ill spare the pleasure of his society), that he had sent him to study law at Glasgow, under the care of Mr. Millar ;—the strongest proof he could give of his disinterested zeal for the improvement of his friend, as well as of the esteem in which he held the abilities of that eminent Professor.

The executors of his will were Dr. Black and Dr. Hutton ; with whom he had long lived in habits of the most intimate and cordial friendship ; and who, to the many other testimonies which they had given him of their affection, added the mournful office of witnessing his last moments.

THE

THEORY OF MORAL SENTIMENTS.

Part First.

OF THE PROPRIETY OF ACTION,

CONSISTING OF THREE SECTIONS.

SECTION I.

CHAPTER I.

Of Sympathy.

How selfish soever man may be supposed, there are evidently some principles in his nature, which interest him in the fortune of others, and render their happiness necessary to him, though he derives nothing from it, except the pleasure of seeing it. Of this kind is pity or compassion, the emotion which we feel for the misery of others, when we either see it, or are made to conceive it in a very lively manner. That we often derive sorrow from the sorrow of others, is a matter of fact too obvious to require any instances to prove it; for this sentiment, like all the other original passions of human nature, is by no means confined to the virtuous and humane, though they perhaps may feel it with the most exquisite sensibility. The greatest ruffian, the most hardened violator of the laws of society, is not altogether without it.

As we have no immediate experience of what other men feel, we can form no idea of the manner in which they are affected, but by conceiving what we ourselves should feel in the like situation. Though our brother is upon the rack, as long as we ourselves are at our ease, our senses will never inform us of what he suffers. They never did, and never can, carry us beyond our own person, and it is by the imagination only that we can form any conception of what are his sensations. Neither can that faculty help us to this any other way, than by representing to us what would be our own, if we were in his case. It is the impressions of our own senses only, not those of his, which our imaginations copy. By the imagination we place ourselves in his situation, we conceive ourselves enduring all the same torments, we enter as it were into his body, and become in some measure the same person with him, and thence form some idea of his sensations, and even feel something which, though weaker in degree, is not altogether unlike them. His agonies, when they are thus brought home to ourselves, when we have thus adopted and made them our own, begin at last to affect us, and we then tremble and shudder at the thought of what he feels. For as to be in pain or distress of any kind excites the most excessive sorrow, so to conceive or to imagine that we are in it, excites some degree of the same emotion, in proportion to the vivacity or dulness of the conception.

That this is the source of our fellow-feeling for the misery of others, that it is by changing places in fancy with the sufferer, that we come either to conceive or to be affected by what he feels, may be demonstrated by many obvious observations, if it should not be thought sufficiently evident of itself. When we see a stroke aimed, and just ready to fall upon the leg or arm of another person, we naturally shrink and draw back our own leg or our own arm; and when it does fall, we feel it in some measure, and are hurt by it as well as the sufferer. The mob, when they are gazing at a dancer on the slack rope, naturally writhe and twist and balance their own bodies as they see him do, and as they feel that they themselves must do if in his situation. Persons of delicate fibres and a weak constitution of body complain, that in looking on the sores and ulcers which are exposed by beggars in the streets, they are apt to feel an itching or uneasy sensation in the corresponding part of their own bodies. The horror which they conceive at the misery of those wretches affects that particular part in themselves more than any other; because that horror arises from conceiving what they themselves would suffer, if they really were the wretches whom they are looking upon, and if that particular part in themselves was actually affected in the same miserable manner. The very force of this conception is sufficient, in their feeble frames, to produce that itching or uneasy sensation complained of. Men of the most robust make, observe that in looking upon sore eyes they often feel a very sensible soreness in their own, which proceeds from the same reason; that organ being in the strongest man more delicate than any other part of the body is in the weakest.

Neither is it those circumstances only, which create pain or sorrow, that call forth our fellow-feeling. Whatever is the passion which arises from any object in the person principally concerned, an analogous emotion springs up, at the thought of his situation, in the breast of every attentive spectator. Our joy for the deliverance of those heroes of tragedy or romance who interest us, is as sincere as our grief for their distress, and our fellow-feeling with their misery is not more real than that with their happiness. We enter into their gratitude towards those faithful friends who did not desert them in their difficulties; and we heartily go along with their resentment against those perfidious traitors who injured, abandoned, or deceived them. In every passion of which the mind of man is susceptible, the emotions of the bystander always correspond to what, by bringing the case home to himself, he imagines should be the sentiments of the sufferer.

Pity and compassion are words appropriated to signify our fellow-feeling with the sorrow of others. Sympathy, though its meaning was, perhaps, originally the same, may now, however, without much impropriety, be made use of to denote our fellow-feeling with any passion whatever.

Upon some occasions sympathy may seem to arise merely from the view of a certain emotion in another person. The passions, upon some occasions, may seem to be transfused from one man to another, instantaneously, and antecedent to any knowledge of what excited them in the person principally concerned. Grief and joy, for example, strongly expressed in the look and gestures of any person, at once affect the spectator with some degree of a like painful or agreeable emotion. A smiling face is, to everybody that sees it, a cheerful object; as a sorrowful countenance, on the other hand, is a melancholy one.

This, however, does not hold universally, or with regard to every passion. There are some passions of which the expressions excite no sort of sympathy, but, before we are acquainted with what gave occasion to them, serve rather to disgust and provoke us against them. The furious behaviour of an angry man is more likely to exasperate us against himself than against his enemies. As we are unacquainted with his provocation, we cannot bring his case home to ourselves, nor conceive any thing like the passions which it excites. But we plainly see what is the situation of those with whom he is angry, and to what violence they may be exposed from so enraged an adversary. We readily, therefore, sympathize with their fear or resentment, and are immediately disposed to take part against the man from whom they appear to be in danger.

If the very appearances of grief and joy inspire us with some degree of the like emotions, it is because they suggest to us the general idea of some good or bad fortune that has befallen the person in whom we observe them : and in these passions this is sufficient to have some little influence upon us. The effects of grief and joy terminate in the person who feels those emotions, of which the expressions do not, like those of resentment, suggest to us the idea of any other person for whom we are concerned, and whose interests are opposite to his. The general idea of good or bad fortune, therefore, creates some concern for the person who has met with it; but the general idea of provocation excites no sympathy with the anger of the man who has received it. Nature, it seems, teaches us to be more averse to enter into this passion, and, till informed of its cause, to be disposed rather to take part against it.

Even our sympathy with the grief or joy of another, before we are informed of the cause of either, is always extremely imperfect. General lamentations, which express nothing but the anguish of the sufferer, create rather a curiosity to enquire into his situation, along with some disposition to sympathize with him, than any actual sympathy that is very sensible. The first question which we ask is, What has befallen you? Till this be answered, though we are uneasy both from the vague idea of his misfortune, and still more from torturing ourselves with conjectures about what it may be, yet our fellow-feeling is not very considerable.

Sympathy, therefore, does not arise so much from the view of the passion, as from that of the situation which excites it. We sometimes feel for another, a passion of which he himself seems to be altogether incapable; because, when we put ourselves in his case, that passion arises in our breast from the imagination, though it does not in his from the reality. We blush for the impudence and rudeness of another, though he himself appears to have no sense of the impropriety of his own behaviour; because we cannot help feeling with what confusion we ourselves should be covered, had we behaved in so absurd a manner.

Of all the calamities to which the condition of mortality exposes mankind, the loss of reason appears, to those who have the least spark of humanity, by far the most dreadful ; and they behold that last stage of human wretchedness with deeper commiseration than any other. But the poor wretch, who is in it, laughs and sings, perhaps, and is altogether insensible to his own misery. The anguish which humanity feels, therefore, at the sight of such an object, cannot be the reflection of any sentiment of the sufferer. The compassion of the spectator must arise altogether from the consideration of what he himself would feel if he was reduced to the same unhappy situation, and, what perhaps is impossible, was at the same time able to regard it with his present reason and judgment.

What are the pangs of a mother, when she hears the moanings of her infant, that, during the agony of disease, cannot express what it feels ? In her idea of what it suffers, she joins, to its real helplessness, her own consciousness of that helplessness, and her own terrors for the unknown consequences of its disorder ; and out of all these, forms, for her own sorrow, the most complete image of misery and distress. The infant, however, feels only the uneasiness of the present instant, which can never be great. With regard to the future, it is perfectly secure, and in its thoughtlessness and want of foresight, possesses an antidote against fear and anxiety, the great tormentors of the human breast, from which reason and philosophy will in vain attempt to defend it, when it grows up to a man.

We sympathize even with the dead, and overlooking what is of real importance in their situation, that awful futurity which awaits them, we are chiefly affected by those circumstances which strike our senses, but can have no influence upon their happiness. It is miserable, we think, to be deprived of the light of the sun ; to be shut out from life and conversation ; to be laid in the cold grave, a prey to corruption and the reptiles of the earth ; to be no more thought of in this world, but to be obliterated, in a little time, from the affections, and almost from the memory, of their dearest friends and relations.   Surely, we imagine, we can never feel too much for those who have suffered so dreadful a calamity.   The tribute of our fellow-feeling seems doubly due to them now, when they are in danger of being forgot by every body; and, by the vain honours which we pay to their memory, we endeavour, for our own misery, artificially to keep alive our melancholy remembrance of their misfortune.   That our sympathy can afford them no consolation seems to be an addition to their calamity; and to think that all we can do is unavailing, and that, what alleviates all other distress, the regret, the love, and the lamentations of their friends, can yield no comfort to them, serves only to exasperate our sense of their misery.   The happiness of the dead, however, most assuredly is affected by none of these circumstances; nor is it the thought of these things which can ever disturb the profound security of their repose.   The idea of that dreary and endless melancholy, which the fancy naturally ascribes to their condition, arises altogether from our joining to the change which has been produced upon them, our own consciousness of that change; from our putting ourselves in their situation, and from our lodging, if I may be allowed to say so, our own living souls in their inanimated bodies, and thence conceiving what would be our emotions in this case.   It is from this very illusion of the imagination, that the foresight of our own dissolution is so terrible to us, and that the idea of those circumstances, which undoubtedly can give us no pain when we are dead, makes us miserable while we are alive. And from thence arises one of the most important principles in human nature, the dread of death—the great poison to the happiness, but the great restraint upon the injustice of mankind; which, while it afflicts and mortifies the individual, guards and protects the society.

CHAPTER II

Of the Pleasure of mutual Sympathy.

BUT whatever may be the cause of sympathy, or however it may be excited, nothing pleases us more than to observe in other men a fellow-feeling with all the emotions of our own breast ; nor are we ever so much shocked as by the appearance of the contrary. Those who are fond of deducing all our sentiments from certain refinements of self-love, think themselves at no loss to account, according to their own principles, both for this pleasure and this pain.   Man, say they, conscious of his own weakness, and of the need which he has for the assistance of others, rejoices whenever he observes that they adopt his own passions, because he is then assured of that assistance ; and grieves whenever he observes the contrary, because he is then assured of their opposition.   But both the pleasure and the pain are always felt so instantaneously, and often upon such frivolous occasions, that it seems evident that neither of them can be derived from any such self-interested consideration. A man is mortified when, after having endeavoured to divert the company, he looks round and sees that nobody laughs at his jests but himself.   On the contrary, the mirth of the company is highly agreeable to him, and he regards this correspondence of their sentiments with his own as the greatest applause.

Neither does his pleasure seem to arise altogether from the additional vivacity which his mirth may receive from sympathy with theirs, nor his pain from the disappointment he meets with when he misses this pleasure ; though both the one and the other, no doubt, do in some measure.

When we have read a book or poem so often that we can no longer find any amusement in reading it by ourselves, we can still take pleasure in reading it to a companion. To him it has all the graces of novelty; we enter into the surprise and admiration which it naturally excites in him, but which it is no longer capable of exciting in us; we consider all the ideas which it presents, rather in the light in which they appear to him, than in that in which they appear to ourselves, and we are amused by sympathy with his amusement, which thus enlivens our own. On the contrary, we should be vexed if he did not seem to be entertained with it, and we could no longer take any pleasure in reading it to him. It is the same case here. The mirth of the company, no doubt, enlivens our own mirth; and their silence, no doubt, disappoints us. But though this may contribute both to the pleasure which we derive from the one, and to the pain which we feel from the other, it is by no means the sole cause of either; and this correspondence of the sentiments of others with our own appears to be a cause of pleasure, and the want of it a cause of pain, which cannot be accounted for in this manner. The sympathy which my friends express with my joy, might indeed give me pleasure by enlivening that joy; but that which they express with my grief could give me none, if it served only to enliven that grief. Sympathy, however, enlivens joy and alleviates grief. It enlivens joy by presenting another source of satisfaction; and it alleviates grief by insinuating into the heart almost the only agreeable sensation which it is at that time capable of receiving.

It is to be observed accordingly, that we are still more anxious to communicate to our friends our disagreeable, than our agreeable passions; that we derive still more satisfaction from their sympathy with the former, than from that with the latter, and that we are still more shocked by the want of it.

How are the unfortunate relieved when they have found out a person to whom they can communicate the cause of their sorrow! Upon his sympathy they seem to disburden themselves of a part of their distress: he is not improperly said to share it with them. He not only feels a sorrow of the same kind with that which they feel, but, as if he had derived a part of it to himself; what he feels seems to alleviate the weight of what they feel. Yet, by relating their misfortunes, they in some measure renew their grief. They awaken in their memory the remembrance of those circumstances which occasion their affliction. Their tears accordingly flow faster than before, and they are apt to abandon themselves to all the weakness of sorrow. They take pleasure, however, in all this, and it is evident are sensibly relieved by it; because the sweetness of his sympathy more than compensates the bitterness of that sorrow, which, in order to excite this sympathy, they had thus enlivened and renewed. The cruelest insult, on the contrary, which can be offered to the unfortunate, is to appear to make light of their calamities. To seem not to be affected with the joy of our companions, is but want of politeness; but not to wear a serious countenance when they tell us their afflictions, is real and gross inhumanity.

Love is an agreeable, resentment a disagreeable passion: and accordingly we are not half so anxious that our friends should adopt our friendships, as that they should enter into our resentments. We can forgive them, though they seem to be little affected with the favours which we may have received, but lose all patience if they seem indifferent about the injuries which may have been done to us; nor are we half so angry with them for not entering into our gratitude, as for not sympathizing with our resentment. They can easily avoid being friends to our friends, but can hardly avoid being enemies to those with whom we are at variance. We seldom resent their being at enmity with the first, though, upon that account, we may sometimes affect to make an awkward quarrel with them ; but we quarrel with them in good earnest, if they live in friendship with the last. The agreeable passions of love and joy can satisfy and support the heart without any auxiliary pleasure. The bitter and painful emotions of grief and resentment more strongly require the healing consolation of sympathy.

As the person who is principally interested in any event is pleased with our sympathy, and hurt by the want of it, so we, too, seem to be pleased when we are able to sympathize with him, and to be hurt when we are unable to do so. We run not only to congratulate the successful, but to condole with the afflicted; and the pleasure which we find in the conversation of one, whom in all the passions of his heart we can entirely sympathize with, seems to do more than compensate the painfulness of that sorrow with which the view of his situation affects us. On the contrary, it is always disagreeable to feel that we cannot sympathize with him; and, instead of being pleased with this exemption from sympathetic pain, it hurts us to find that we cannot share his uneasiness. If we hear a person loudly lamenting his misfortunes, which, however, upon bringing the case home to ourselves, we feel, can produce no such violent effect upon us, we are shocked at his grief; and, because we cannot enter into it, call it pusillanimity and weakness. It gives us the spleen, on the other hand, to see another too happy, or too much elevated, as we call it, with any little piece of good fortune. We are disobliged even with his joy; and, because we cannot go along with it, call it levity and folly. We are even put out of humour if our companion laughs louder or longer at a joke than we think it deserves ; that is, than we feel that we ourselves could laugh at it.

CHAPTER III.

Of the manner in which we judge of the Propriety or Impropriety of the affections of other men, by their concord or dissonance with our own.

WHEN the original passions of the person principally concerned are in perfect concord with the sympathetic emotions of the spectator, they necessarily appear to this last just and proper, and suitable to their objects; and, on the contrary, when, upon bringing the case home to himself, he finds that they do not coincide with what he feels, they necessarily appear to him unjust and improper, and unsuitable to the causes which excite them. To approve of the passions of another, therefore, as suitable to their objects, is the same thing as to observe that we entirely sympathize with them; and not to approve of them as such, is the same thing as to observe that we do not entirely sympathize with them. The man who resents the injuries that have been done to me, and observes that I resent them precisely as he does, necessarily approves of my resentment. The man whose sympathy keeps time to my grief, cannot but admit the reasonableness of my sorrow. He who admires the same poem or the same picture, and admires them exactly as I do, must surely allow the justness of my admiration. He who laughs at the same joke, and laughs along with me, cannot well deny the propriety of my laughter. On the contrary, the person who, upon these different occasions, either feels no such emotion as that which I feel, or feels none that bears any proportion to mine, cannot avoid disapproving my sentiments, on account of their dissonance with his own. If my animosity goes beyond what the indignation of my friend can correspond to; if my grief

exceeds what his most tender compassion can go along
with; if my admiration is either too high or too low to tally
with his own; if I laugh loud and heartily when he only
smiles, or, on the contrary, only smile when he laughs loud
and heartily; in all these cases, as soon as he comes, from
considering the object, to observe how I am affected by it,
according as there is more or less disproportion between his
sentiments and mine, I must incur a greater or less degree
of his disapprobation: and, upon all occasions, his own sentiments are the standards and measures by which he judges
of mine.

To approve of another man's opinions is to adopt those
opinions, and to adopt them is to approve of them. If the
same arguments which convince you, convince me likewise,
I necessarily approve of your conviction; and if they do
not, I necessarily disapprove of it; neither can I possibly
conceive that I should do the one without the other. To
approve or disapprove, therefore, of the opinions of others
is acknowledged, by every body, to mean no more than to
observe their agreement or disagreement with our own.
But this is equally the case with regard to our approbation
or disapprobation of the sentiments or passions of others.

There are, indeed, some cases in which we seem to approve, without any sympathy or correspondence of sentiments; and in which, consequently, the sentiment of approbation would seem to be different from the perception of
this coincidence. A little attention, however, will convince
us, that even in these cases our approbation is ultimately
founded upon a sympathy or correspondence of this kind.
I shall give an instance in things of a very frivolous nature, because in them the judgments of mankind are less
apt to be perverted by wrong systems. We may often
approve of a jest, and think the laughter of the company
quite just and proper, though we ourselves do not laugh,

because, perhaps, we are in a grave humour, or happen to have our attention engaged with other objects. We have learned, however, from experience, what sort of pleasantry is upon most occasions capable of making us laugh, and we observe that this is one of that kind. We approve, therefore, of the laughter of the company, and feel that it is natural and suitable to its object; because, though in our present mood we cannot easily enter into it, we are sensible that upon most occasions we should very heartily join in it.

The same thing often happens with regard to all the other passions. A stranger passes by us in the street with all the marks of the deepest affliction; and we are immediately told that he has just received the news of the death of his father. It is impossible that, in this case, we should not approve of his grief. Yet it may often happen, without any defect of humanity on our part, that, so far from entering into the violence of his sorrow, we should scarce conceive the first movements of concern upon his account. Both he and his father, perhaps, are entirely unknown to us, or we happen to be employed about other things, and do not take time to picture out in our imagination the different circumstances of distress which must occur to him. We have learned, however, from experience, that such a misfortune naturally excites such a degree of sorrow; and we know that if we took time to consider his situation fully, and in all its parts, we should without doubt most sincerely sympathize with him. It is upon the consciousness of this conditional sympathy, that our approbation of his sorrow is founded, even in those cases in which that sympathy does not actually take place; and the general rules derived from our preceding experience of what our sentiments would commonly correspond with, correct, upon this, as upon many other occasions, the impropriety of our present emotions.

The sentiment or affection of the heart, from which any action proceeds, and upon which its whole virtue or vice must ultimately depend, may be considered under two different aspects, or in two different relations; first, in relation to the cause which excites it, or the motive which gives occasion to it; and, secondly, in relation to the end which it proposes, or the effect which it tends to produce.

n the suitableness or unsuitableness, in the proportion or disproportion, which the affection seems to bear to the cause or object which excites it, consists the propriety or impropriety, the decency or ungracefulness, of the consequent action.

In the beneficial or hurtful nature of the effects which the affection aims at, or tends to produce, consists the merit or demerit of the action, the qualities by which it is entitled to reward, or is deserving of punishment.

Philosophers have, of late years, considered chiefly the tendency of affections, and have given little attention to the relation which they stand in to the cause which excites them. In common life, however, when we judge of any person's conduct, and of the sentiments which directed it, we constantly consider them under both these aspects. When we blame in another man the excesses of love, of grief, of resentment, we not only consider the ruinous effects which they tend to produce, but the little occasion which was given for them. The merit of his favourite, we say, is not so great, his misfortune is not so dreadful, his provocation is not so extraordinary, as to justify so violent a passion. We should have indulged, we say, perhaps have approved of the violence of his emotion, had the cause been in any respect proportioned to it.

When we judge in this manner of any affection, as proportioned or disproportioned to the cause which excites it, it is scarce possible that we should make use of any other rule or canon but the correspondent affection in ourselves. If, upon bringing the case home to our own breast, we find that the sentiments which it gives occasion to coincide and tally with our own, we necessarily approve of them, as proportioned and suitable to their objects; if otherwise, we necessarily disapprove of them, as extravagant and out of proportion.

Every faculty in one man is the measure by which he judges of the like faculty in another. I judge of your sight by my sight, of your ear by my ear, of your reason by my reason, of your resentment by my resentment, of your love by my love. I neither have, nor can have, any other way of judging about them.

CHAPTER IV.

The same subject continued.

WE may judge of the propriety or impropriety of the sentiments of another person by their correspondence or disagreement with our own, upon two different occasions; either, first, when the objects which excite them are considered without any peculiar relation, either to ourselves or to the person whose sentiments we judge of; or, secondly, when they are considered as peculiarly affecting one or other of us.

1. With regard to those objects which are considered without any peculiar relation either to ourselves or to the person whose sentiments we judge of; wherever his sentiments entirely correspond with our own, we ascribe to him the qualities of taste and good judgment. The beauty of a plain, the greatness of a mountain, the ornaments of a building, the expression of a picture, the composition of a discourse, the conduct of a third person, the proportions of different quantities and numbers, the various appearances which the great machine of the universe is perpetually exhibiting, with the secret wheels and springs which produce them; all the general subjects of science and taste, are what we and our companions regard as having no peculiar relation to either of us. We both look at them from the same point of view, and we have no occasion for sympathy, or for that imaginary change of situations from which it arises, in order to produce, with regard to these, the most perfect harmony of sentiments and affections. If, notwithstanding, we are often differently affected, it arises either from the different degrees of attention which our different habits of

life allow us to give easily to the several parts of those complex objects, or from the different degrees of natural acuteness in the faculty of the mind to which they are addressed.

When the sentiments of our companion coincide with our own in things of this kind, which are obvious and easy, and in which, perhaps, we never found a single person who differed from us, though we, no doubt, must approve of them, yet he seems to deserve no praise or admiration on account of them. But when they not only coincide with our own, but lead and direct our own; when, in forming them, he appears to have attended to many things which we had overlooked, and to have adjusted them to all the various circumstances of their objects; we not only approve of them, but wonder and are surprised at their uncommon and unexpected acuteness and comprehensiveness, and he appears to deserve a very high degree of admiration and applause. For approbation heightened by wonder and surprise, constitutes the sentiment which is properly called admiration, and of which applause is the natural expression. The decision of the man who judges that exquisite beauty is preferable to the grossest deformity, or that twice two are equal to four, must certainly be approved of by all the world, but will not, surely, be much admired. It is the acute and delicate discernment of the man of taste, who distinguishes the minute, and scarce perceptible differences of beauty and deformity; it is the comprehensive accuracy of the experienced mathematician, who unravels with ease the most intricate and perplexed proportions; it is the great leader in science and taste, the man who directs and conducts our own sentiments, the extent and superior justness of whose talents astonish us with wonder and surprise, who excites our admiration, and seems to deserve our applause; and upon this foundation is grounded the greater part of the praise which is bestowed upon what are called the intellectual virtues.

The utility of these qualities, it may be thought, is what first recommends them to us ; and, no doubt, the consideration of this, when we come to attend to it, gives them a new value. Originally, however, we approve of another man's judgment, not as something useful, but as right, as accurate, as agreeable to truth and reality ; and it is evident we attribute those qualities to it for no other reason but because we find that it agrees with our own. Taste, in the same manner, is originally approved of, not as useful, but as just, as delicate, and as precisely suited to its object. The idea of the utility of all qualities of this kind is plainly an after-thought, and not what first recommends them to our approbation.

2. With regard to those objects, which affect in a particular manner either ourselves or the person whose sentiments we judge of, it is at once more difficult to preserve this harmony and correspondence, and, at the same time, vastly more important. My companion does not naturally look upon the misfortune that has befallen me, or the injury that has been done me, from the same point of view in which I consider them. They affect me much more nearly. We do not view them from the same station, as we do a picture, or a poem, or a system of philosophy ; and are therefore apt to be very differently affected by them. But I can much more easily overlook the want of this correspondence of sentiments with regard to such indifferent objects as concern neither me nor my companion, than with regard to what interests me so much as the misfortune that has befallen me, or the injury that has been done me. Though you despise that picture, or that poem, or even that system of philosophy which I admire, there is little danger of our quarrelling upon that account. Neither of us can reasonably be much interested about them. They ought all of them to be matters of great indifference to us both; so that, though our opinions may be opposite, our affections

may still be very nearly the same. But it is quite other-wise with regard to those objects by which either you or I are particularly affected. Though your judgments in matters of speculation, though your sentiments in matters of taste, are quite opposite to mine, I can easily overlook this opposition; and if I have any degree of temper, I may still find some entertainment in your conversation, even upon those very subjects. But if you have either no fellow-feeling for the misfortunes I have met with, or none that bears any proportion to the grief which distracts me; or if you have either no indignation at the injuries I have suffered, or none that bears any proportion to the resent-ment which transports me, we can no longer converse upon these subjects. We become intolerable to one another. I can neither support your company, nor you mine. You are confounded at my violence and passion, and I am en-raged at your cold insensibility and want of feeling.

In all such cases, that there may be some correspondence of sentiments between the spectator and the person princi-pally concerned, the spectator must, first of all, endeavour as much as he can to put himself in the situation of the other, and to bring home to himself every little circum-stance of distress which can possibly occur to the sufferer. He must adopt the whole case of his companion, with all its minutest incidents; and strive to render as perfect as possible that imaginary change of situation upon which his sympathy is founded.

After all this, however, the emotions of the spectator will still be very apt to fall short of the violence of what is felt by the sufferer. Mankind, though naturally sympathetic, never conceive, for what has befallen another, that degree of passion which naturally animates the person principally concerned. That imaginary change of situation, upon which their sympathy is founded, is but momentary. The

thought of their own safety, the thought that they themselves are not really the sufferers, continually intrudes itself upon them; and though it does not hinder them from
conceiving a passion somewhat analogous to what is felt
by the sufferer, hinders them from conceiving any thing
that approaches to the same degree of violence. The person principally concerned is sensible of this, and at the
same time passionately desires a more complete sympathy.
He longs for that relief which nothing can afford him but
the entire concord of the affections of the spectators with
his own. To see the emotions of their hearts in every respect beat time to his own, in the violent and disagreeable
passions, constitutes his sole consolation. But he can only
hope to obtain this by lowering his passion to that pitch,
in which the spectators are capable of going along with him.
He must flatten, if I may be allowed to say so, the sharp-
ness of its natural tone, in order to reduce it to harmony
and concord with the emotions of those who are about him.
What they feel will, indeed, always be in some respects
different from what he feels, and compassion can never be
exactly the same with original sorrow; because the secret
consciousness that the change of situations, from which the
sympathetic sentiment arises, is but imaginary, not only
lowers it in degree, but in some measure varies it in kind,
and gives it a quite different modification. These two
sentiments, however, may, it is evident, have such a correspondence with one another, as is sufficient for the harmony
of society. Though they will never be unisons, they may
be concords, and this is all that is wanted or required.

In order to produce this concord, as nature teaches the
spectators to assume the circumstances of the person principally concerned, so she teaches this last in some measure
to assume those of the spectators. As they are continually
placing themselves in his situation, and thence conceiving
emotions similar to what he feels; so he is as constantly

placing himself in theirs, and thence conceiving some degree of that coolness about his own fortune, with which he is sensible that they will view it. As they are constantly considering what they themselves would feel, if they actually were the sufferers, so he is constantly led to imagine in what manner he would be affected if he was only one of the spectators of his own situation. As their sympathy makes them look at it in some measure with his eyes, so his sympathy makes him look at it, in some measure, with theirs, especially when in their presence, and acting under their observation: and, as the reflected passion which he thus conceives is much weaker than the original one, it' necessarily abates the violence of what he felt before he came into their presence, before he began to recollect in what manner they would be affected by it, and to view his situation in this candid and impartial light.

The mind, therefore, is rarely so disturbed, but that the company of a friend will restore it to some degree of tranquillity and sedateness. The breast is, in some measure, calmed and composed the moment we come into his presence. We are immediately put in mind of the light in which he will view our situation, and we begin to view it ourselves in the same light; for the effect of sympathy is instantaneous. We expect less sympathy from a common acquaintance than from a friend; we cannot open to the former all those little circumstances which we can unfold to the latter; we assume, therefore, more tranquillity before him, and endeavour to fix our thoughts upon those general outlines of our situation which he is willing to consider. We expect still less sympathy from an assembly of strangers, and we assume, therefore, still more tranquillity before them, and always endeavour to bring down our passion to that pitch, which the particular company we are in may be expected to go along with. Nor is this only an assumed appearance; for if we are at all masters of ourselves, the presence of a mere acquaintance will really compose us, still more than that of a friend; and that of an assembly of strangers, still more than that of an acquaintance.

Society and conversation, therefore, are the most powerful remedies for restoring the mind to its tranquillity, if, at any time, it has unfortunately lost it; as well as the best preservatives of that equal and happy temper, which is so necessary to self-satisfaction and enjoyment. Men of retirement and speculation, who are apt to sit brooding at home over either grief or resentment, though they may often have more humanity, more generosity, and a nicer sense of honour, yet seldom possess that equality of temper which is so common among men of the world.

CHAPTER V.

Of the amiable and respectable Virtues.

Upon these two different efforts, upon that of the spectator to enter into the sentiments of the person principally concerned, and upon that of the person principally concerned, to bring down his emotions to what the spectator can go along with, are founded two different sets of virtues. The soft, the gentle, the amiable virtues, the virtues of candid condescension and indulgent humanity, are founded upon the one : the great, the awful, and respectable, the virtues of self-denial, of self-government, of that command of the passions which subjects all the movements of our nature to what our own dignity and honour, and the propriety of our own conduct, require, take their origin from the other.

How amiable does he appear to be, whose sympathetic heart seems to re-echo all the sentiments of those with whom he converses, who grieves for their calamities, who resents their injuries, and who rejoices at their good fortune? When we bring home to ourselves the situation of his companions, we enter into their gratitude, and feel what consolation they must derive from the tender sympathy of so affectionate a friend. And, for a contrary reason, how disagreeable does he appear to be, whose hard and obdurate heart feels for himself only, but is altogether insensible to the happiness or misery of others ! We enter, in this case too, into the pain which his presence must give to every mortal with whom he converses, to those especially with whom we are most apt to sympathize, the unfortunate and the injured.

On the other hand, what noble propriety and grace do we

feel in the conduct of those who, in their own case, exert that recollection and self-command which constitute the dignity of every passion, and which bring it down to what others can enter into ? We are disgusted with that clamorous grief, which, without any delicacy, calls upon our compassion with sighs and tears, and importunate lamentations. But we reverence that reserved, that silent and majestic sorrow, which discovers itself only in the swelling of the eyes, in the quivering of the lips and cheeks, and in the distant, but affecting, coldness of the whole behaviour. It imposes the like silence upon us. We regard it with respectful attention, and watch with anxious concern over our whole behaviour, lest by any impropriety we should disturb that concerted tranquillity, which it requires so great an effort to support.

The insolence and brutality of anger, in the same manner, when we indulge its fury without check or restraint, is, of all objects, the most detestable. But we admire that noble and generous resentment which governs its pursuit of the greatest injuries, not by the rage which they are apt to excite in the breast of the sufferer, but by the indignation which they naturally call forth in that of the impartial spectator; which allows no word, no gesture, to escape it beyond what this more equitable sentiment would dictate; which never, even in thought, attempts any greater vengeance, nor desires to inflict any greater punishment, than what every indifferent person would rejoice to see executed.

And hence it is, that to feel much for others, and little for ourselves, that to restrain our selfish, and to indulge our benevolent, affections, constitutes the perfection of human nature ; and can alone produce among mankind that harmony of sentiments and passions in which consists their whole grace and propriety. As to love our neighbour as we love ourselves is the great law of Christianity, so it is the great precept of nature to love ourselves only as we love our neighbour, or, what comes to the same thing, as our neighbour is capable of loving us.

As taste and good judgment, when they are considered as qualities which deserve praise and admiration, are supposed to imply a delicacy of sentiment and an acuteness of understanding not commonly to be met with; so the virtues of sensibility and self-command are not apprehended to consist in the ordinary, but in the uncommon degrees of those qualities. The amiable virtue of humanity requires, surely, a sensibility much beyond what is possessed by the rude vulgar of mankind. The great and exalted virtue of magnanimity undoubtedly demands much more than that degree of self-command, which the weakest of mortals is capable of exerting. As in the common degree of the intellectual qualities, there are no abilities; so in the common degree of the moral, there is no virtue. Virtue is excellence, something uncommonly great and beautiful, which rises far above what is vulgar and ordinary. The amiable virtues consist in that degree of sensibility which surprises by its exquisite and unexpected delicacy and tenderness. The awful and respectable, in that degree of self-command which astonishes by its amazing superiority over the most ungovernable passions of human nature.

There is, in this respect, a considerable difference between virtue and mere propriety; between those qualities and actions which deserve to be admired and celebrated, and those which simply deserve to be approved of. Upon many occasions, to act with the most perfect propriety, requires no more than that common and ordinary degree of sensibility or self-command which the most worthless of mankind are possessed of, and sometimes even that degree is not necessary. Thus, to give a very low instance, to eat when we are hungry, is certainly, upon ordinary occasions, perfectly right and proper, and cannot miss being approved of as such by every body. Nothing, however, could be more absurd than to say it was virtuous.

On the contrary, there may frequently be a considerable degree of virtue in those actions which fall short of the most perfect propriety; because they may still approach nearer to perfection than could well be expected upon occasions in which it was so extremely difficult to attain it: and this is very often the case upon those occasions which require the greatest exertions of self-command. There are some situations which bear so hard upon human nature, that the greatest degree of self-government, which can belong to so imperfect a creature as man, is not able to stifle, altogether, the voice of human weakness, or reduce the violence of the passions to that pitch of moderation, in which the impartial spectator can entirely enter into them. Though in those cases, therefore, the behaviour of the sufferer fall short of the most perfect propriety, it may still deserve some applause, and even, in a certain sense, may be denominated virtuous. It may still manifest an effort of generosity and magnanimity of which the greater part of men are incapable; and though it fails of absolute perfection, it may be a much nearer approximation towards perfection, than what, upon such trying occasions, is commonly either to be found or to be expected.

In cases of this kind, when we are determining the degree of blame or applause which seems due to any action, we very frequently make use of two different standards. The first is the idea of complete propriety and perfection, which, in those difficult situations, no human conduct ever did, or ever can, come up to; and in comparison with which the actions of all men must for ever appear blameable and imperfect. The second is the idea of that degree of proximity or distance from this complete perfection, which the

actions of the greater part of men commonly arrive at.
Whatever goes beyond this degree, how far soever it may
be removed from absolute perfection, seems to deserve applause ; and whatever falls short of it, to deserve blame.

It is in the same manner that we judge of the productions
of all the arts which address themselves to the imagination.
When a critic examines the work of any of the great masters in poetry or painting, he may sometimes examine it by
an idea of perfection, in his own mind, which neither that
nor any other human work will ever come up to ; and as
long as he compares it with this standard, he can see nothing in it but faults and imperfections.   But when he
comes to consider the rank which it ought to hold among
other works of the same kind, he necessarily compares it
with a very different standard, the common degree of excellence which is usually attained in this particular art;
and when he judges of it by this new measure, it may often
appear to deserve the highest applause, upon account of
its approaching much nearer to perfection than the greater
part of those works which can be brought into competition
with it.

SECTION II.

OF THE DEGREES OF THE DIFFERENT PASSIONS WHICH ARE CONSISTENT WITH PROPRIETY.

INTRODUCTION.

THE propriety of every passion excited by objects peculiarly related to ourselves, the pitch which the spectator can go along with, must lie, it is evident, in a certain mediocrity. If the passion is too high, or if it is too low, he cannot enter into it. Grief and resentment for private misfortunes and injuries may easily, for example, be too high, and in the greater part of mankind they are so. They may likewise, though this more rarely happens, be too low. We denominate the excess, weakness and fury: and we call the defect, stupidity, insensibility, and want of spirit. We can enter into neither of them, but are astonished and confounded to see them.

This mediocrity, however, in which the point of propriety consists, is different in different passions. It is high in some, and low in others. There are some passions which it is indecent to express very strongly, even upon those occasions in which it is acknowledged that we cannot avoid feeling them in the highest degree. And there are others of which the strongest expressions are upon many occasions extremely graceful, even though the passions themselves do not, perhaps, arise so necessarily. The first are those passions with which, for certain reasons, there is little or no sympathy : the second are those with which, for other reasons, there is the greatest.   And if we consider all the different passions of human nature, we shall find that they are regarded as decent or indecent, just in proportion as mankind are more or less disposed to sympathize with them.

CHAPTER I.

Of the Passions which take their origin from the Body.

1. It is indecent to express any strong degree of those passions which arise from a certain situation or disposition of the body; because the company, not being in the same disposition, cannot be expected to sympathize with them. Violent hunger, for example, though upon many occasions not only natural, but unavoidable, is always indecent; and to eat voraciously is universally regarded as a piece of ill manners. There is, however, some degree of sympathy, even with hunger. It is agreeable to see our companions eat with a good appetite, and all expressions of loathing are offensive. The disposition of body which is habitual to a man in health, makes his stomach easily keep time, if I may be allowed so coarse an expression, with the one, and not with the other. We can sympathize with the distress which excessive hunger occasions, when we read the description of it in the journal of a siege, or of a sea-voyage. We imagine ourselves in the situation of the sufferers, and thence readily conceive the grief, the fear, and consternation, which must necessarily distract them. We feel, ourselves, some degree of those passions, and therefore sympathize with them: but as we do not grow hungry by reading the description, we cannot properly, even in this case, be said to sympathize with their hunger.

It is the same case with the passion by which nature unites the two sexes. Though naturally the most furious of all the passions, all strong expressions of it are upon every occasion indecent, even between persons in whom its most complete indulgence is acknowledged by all laws, both human and divine, to be perfectly innocent. There seems, however, to be some degree of sympathy even with this passion. To talk to a woman as we should to a man is improper : it is expected that their company should inspire us with more gaiety, more pleasantry, and more attention ; and an entire insensibility to the fair sex renders a man contemptible in some measure even to the men.

Such is our aversion for all the appetites which take their origin from the body : all strong expressions of them are loathsome and disagreeable. According to some ancient philosophers, these are the passions which we share in common with the brutes, and which having no connection with the characteristical qualities of human nature, are upon that account beneath its dignity. But there are many other passions which we share in common with the brutes, such as resentment, natural affection, even gratitude, which do not, upon that account, appear to be so brutal. The true cause of the peculiar disgust which we conceive for the appetites of the body when we see them in other men, is, that we cannot enter into them. To the person himself who feels them, as soon as they are gratified, the object that excited them ceases to be agreeable : even its presence often becomes offensive to him ; he looks round to no purpose for the charm which transported him the moment before, and he can now as little enter into his own passion as another person. When we have dined, we order the covers to be removed; and we should treat in the same manner the objects of the most ardent and passionate desires, if they were the objects of no other passions but those which take their origin from the body.

In the command of those appetites of the body consists that virtue which is properly called temperance. To restrain them within those bounds, which regard to health and fortune prescribes, is the part of prudence. But to

confine them within those limits, which grace, which propriety, which delicacy, and modesty, require, is the office
of temperance.

2. It is for the same reason that to cry out with bodily
pain, how intolerable soever, appears always unmanly and
unbecoming. There is, however, a good deal of sympathy
even with bodily pain. If, as has already been observed,
I see a stroke aimed, and just ready to fall upon the leg or
arm of another person, I naturally shrink and draw back
my own leg or my own arm : and when it does fall, I feel
it in some measure, and am hurt by it as well as the sufferer. My hurt, however, is, no doubt, excessively slight,
and, upon that account, if he makes any violent outcry, as
I cannot go along with him, I never fail to despise him.
And this is the case of all the passions which take their
origin from the body : they excite either no sympathy at all,
or such a degree of it, as is altogether disproportioned to
the violence of what is felt by the sufferer.

It is quite otherwise with those passions which take
their origin from the imagination. The frame of my body
can be but little affected by the alterations which are
brought about upon that of my companion ; but my imagination is more ductile, and more readily assumes, if I may
say so, the shape and configuration of the imaginations of
those with whom I am familiar. A disappointment in
love, or ambition, will, upon this account, call forth more
sympathy than the greatest bodily evil. Those passions
arise altogether from the imagination. The person who
has lost his whole fortune, if he is in health, feels nothing
in his body. What he suffers is from the imagination
only, which represents to him the loss of his dignity, neglect from his friends, contempt from his enemies, dependence, want, and misery, coming fast upon him ; and we
sympathize with him more strongly upon this account, be-

cause our imaginations can more readily mould themselves
upon his imagination, than our bodies can mould themselves upon his body.

The loss of a leg may generally be regarded as a more
real calamity than the loss of a mistress. It would be a
ridiculous tragedy, however, of which the catastrophe was
to turn upon a loss of that kind. A misfortune of the other
kind, how frivolous soever it may appear to be, has given
occasion to many a fine one.

Nothing is so soon forgot as pain. The moment it is
gone, the whole agony of it is over, and the thought of it
can no longer give us any sort of disturbance. We ourselves cannot then enter into the anxiety and anguish
which we had before conceived. An unguarded word from
a friend will occasion a more durable uneasiness. The
agony which this creates is by no means over with the
word. What at first disturbs us is not the object of the
senses, but the idea of the imagination. As it is an idea,
therefore, which occasions our uneasiness, till time and
other accidents have in some measure effaced it from our
memory, the imagination continues to fret and rankle
within, from the thought of it.

Pain never calls forth any very lively sympathy, unless
it is accompanied with danger. We sympathize with the
fear, though not with the agony, of the sufferer. Fear,
however, is a passion derived altogether from the imagination, which represents, with an uncertainty and fluctuation
that increases our anxiety, not what we really feel, but what
we may hereafter possibly suffer. The gout or the tooth-
ache, though exquisitely painful, excite very little sympathy; more dangerous diseases, though accompanied with
very little pain, excite the highest.

Some people faint and grow sick at the sight of a chirurgical operation; and that bodily pain which is occasioned by tearing the flesh, seems, in them, to excite the most excessive sympathy. We conceive in a much more lively and distinct manner the pain which proceeds from an external cause, than we do that which arises from an internal disorder. I can scarce form an idea of the agonies of my neighbour when he is tortured with the gout, or the stone; but I have the clearest conception of what he must suffer from an incision, a wound, or a fracture. The chief cause, however, why such objects produce such violent effects upon us, is their novelty. One who has been witness to a dozen dissections, and as many amputations, sees, ever after, all operations of this kind with great indifference, and often with perfect insensibility. Though we have read, or seen represented, more than five hundred tragedies, we shall seldom feel so entire an abatement of our sensibility to the objects which they represent to us.

In some of the Greek tragedies there is an attempt to excite compassion, by the representation of the agonies of bodily pain. Philoctetes cries out and faints from the extremity of his sufferings. Hippolytus and Hercules are both introduced as expiring under the severest tortures, which it seems, even the fortitude of Hercules was incapable of supporting. In all these cases, however, it is not the pain which interests us, but some other circumstance. It is not the sore foot, but the solitude of Philoctetes which affects us, and diffuses over that charming tragedy, that romantic wildness, which is so agreeable to the imagination. The agonies of Hercules and Hippolytus are interesting only because we foresee that death is to be the consequence. If those heroes were to recover, we should think the representation of their sufferings perfectly ridiculous. What a tragedy would that be, of which the distress consisted in a colic! Yet no pain is more exquisite. These attempts

to excite compassion by the representation of bodily pain, may
be regarded as among the greatest breaches of decorum of
which the Greek theatre has set the example.

The little sympathy which we feel with bodily pain is
the foundation of the propriety of constancy and patience
in enduring it. The man who under the severest tortures,
allows no weakness to escape him, vents no groan, gives
way to no passion which we do not entirely enter into,
commands our highest admiration. His firmness enables
him to keep time with our indifference and insensibility.
We admire and entirely go along with the magnanimous
effort which he makes for this purpose. We approve of
his behaviour, and from our experience of the common
weakness of human nature, we are surprised, and wonder
how he should be able to act so as to deserve approbation.
Approbation mixed and animated by wonder and surprise,
constitutes the sentiment which is properly called admiration, of which applause is the natural expression, as has
already been observed.

CHAPTER II.

*Of those Passions which take their origin from a particular
turn or habit of the Imagination.*

EVEN of the passions derived from the imagination, those
which take their origin from a peculiar turn or habit it has
acquired, though they may be acknowledged to be perfectly
natural, are, however, but little sympathized with. The
imaginations of mankind, not having acquired that particular turn, cannot enter into them; and such passions,
though they may be allowed to be almost unavoidable in
some part of life, are always in some measure ridiculous.
This is the case with that strong attachment which naturally
grows up between two persons of different sexes, who have
long fixed their thoughts upon one another. Our imagination not having run in the same channel with that of the
lover, we cannot enter into the eagerness of his emotions.
If our friend has been injured, we readily sympathize with
his resentment, and grow angry with the very person with
whom he is angry. If he has received a benefit, we readily
enter into his gratitude, and have a very high sense of the
merit of his benefactor. But if he is in love, though we
may think his passion just as reasonable as any of the kind,
yet we never think ourselves bound to conceive a passion
of the same kind, and for the same person for whom he has
conceived it. The passion appears to every body, but the
man who feels it, entirely disproportioned to the value of
the object; and love, though it is pardoned in a certain age,
because we know it is natural, is always laughed at, because we cannot enter into it. All serious and strong expressions of it appear ridiculous to a third person; and
though a lover may be good company to his mistress, he is
so to nobody else. He himself is sensible of this; and as

long as he continues in his sober senses, endeavours to treat his own passion with railery and ridicule. It is the only style in which we care to hear of it; because it is the only style in which we ourselves are disposed to talk of it. We grow weary of the grave, pedantic, and long-sentenced love of Cowley and Petrarca, who never have done with exaggerating the violence of their attachments; but the gaiety of Ovid, and the gallantry of Horace, are always agreeable.

But though we feel no proper sympathy with an attachment of this kind, though we never approach even in imagination towards conceiving a passion for that particular person, yet as we either have conceived, or may be disposed to conceive, passions of the same kind, we readily enter into those high hopes of happiness which are proposed from its gratification, as well as into that exquisite distress which is feared from its disappointment. It interests us not as a passion, but as a situation that gives occasion to other passions which interest us; to hope, to fear, and to distress of every kind : in the same manner as in a description of a sea voyage, it is not the hunger which interests us, but the distress which that hunger occasions. Though we do not properly enter into the attachment of the lover, we readily go along with those expectations of romantic happiness which he derives from it. We feel how natural it is for the mind, in a certain situation, relaxed with indolence, and fatigued with the violence of desire, to long for serenity and quiet, to hope to find them in the gratification of that passion which distracts it, and to frame to itself the idea of that life of pastoral tranquillity and retirement which the elegant, the tender, and the passionate Tibullus takes so much pleasure in describing; a life like what the poets describe in the Fortunate islands, a life of friendship, liberty, and repose; free from labour, and from care, and from all the turbulent passions which attend them. Even scenes of this kind interest us most, when they are painted rather as what is hoped, than as what is enjoyed. The grossness of that passion, which mixes with, and is, perhaps, the foundation of love, disappears when its gratification is far off and at a distance; but renders the whole offensive, when described as what is immediately possessed. The happy passion, upon this account, interests us much less than the fearful and the melancholy. We tremble for whatever can disappoint such natural and agreeable hopes; and thus enter into all the anxiety, and concern, and distress, of the lover.

Hence it is, that, in some modern tragedies and romances, this passion appears so wonderfully interesting. It is not so much the love of Castalia and Monimia which attaches us in the Orphan, as the distress which that love occasions. The author who should introduce two lovers, in a scene of perfect security, expressing their mutual fondness for one another, would excite laughter, and not sympathy. If a scene of this kind is ever admitted into a tragedy, it is always, in some measure, improper, and is endured, not from any sympathy with the passion that is expressed in it, but from concern for the dangers and difficulties with which the audience foresee that its gratification is likely to be attended.

The reserve which the laws of society impose upon the fair sex, with regard to this weakness, renders it more peculiarly distressful in them, and, upon that very account, more deeply interesting. We are charmed with the love of Phædra, as it is expressed in the French tragedy of that name, notwithstanding all the extravagance and guilt which attend it. That very extravagance and guilt may be said, in some measure, to recommend it to us. Her fear, her shame, her remorse, her horror, her despair, become thereby more natural and interesting. All the secondary passions,

if I may be allowed to call them so, which arise from the
situation of love, become necessarily more furious and
violent; and it is with these secondary passions only that
we can properly be said to sympathize.

Of all the passions, however, which are so extravagantly
disproportioned to the value of their objects, love is the
only one that appears, even to the weakest minds, to have
any thing in it that is either graceful or agreeable.   In itself, first of all, though it may be ridiculous, it is not naturally odious; and though its consequences are often fatal
and dreadful, its intentions are seldom mischievous.   And
then, though there is little propriety in the passion itself,
there is a good deal in some of those which always accompany it.   There is in love a strong mixture of humanity,
generosity, kindness, friendship, esteem; passions with
which, of all others, for reasons which shall be explained
immediately, we have the greatest propensity to sympathize, even notwithstanding we are sensible that they are,
in some measure, excessive.   The sympathy which we feel
with them, renders the passion which they accompany less
disagreeable, and supports it in our imagination, notwithstanding all the vices which commonly go along with it;
though in the one sex it necessarily leads to the last ruin
and infamy; and though in the other, where it is apprehended to be least fatal, it is almost always attended with
an incapacity for labour, a neglect of duty, a contempt of
fame, and even of common reputation.   Notwithstanding
all this, the degree of sensibility and generosity with which
it is supposed to be accompanied, renders it to many the
object of vanity; and they are fond of appearing capable of
feeling what would do them no honour if they had really
felt it.

It is for a reason of the same kind, that a certain reserve
is necessary when we talk of our own friends, our own

studies, our own professions. All these are objects which we cannot expect should interest our companions in the same degree in which they interest us. And it is for want of this reserve, that the one half of mankind make bad company to the other. A philosopher is company to a philosopher only; the member of a club to his own little knot of companions.

CHAPTER III.

Of the unsocial Passions.

THERE is another set of passions, which, though derived from the imagination, yet before we can enter into them, or regard them as graceful or becoming, must always be brought down to a pitch much lower than that to which undisciplined nature would raise them. These are, hatred and resentment, with all their different modifications. With regard to all such passions, our sympathy is divided between the person who feels them and the person who is the object of them. The interests of these two are directly opposite. What our sympathy with the person who feels them would prompt us to wish for, our fellow-feeling with the other would lead us to fear. As they are both men, we are concerned for both; and our fear for what the one may suffer, damps our resentment for what the other has suffered. Our sympathy, therefore, with the man who has received the provocation, necessarily falls short of the passion which naturally animates him, not only upon account of those general causes which render all sympathetic passions inferior to the original ones, but upon account of that particular cause which is peculiar to itself, our opposite sympathy with another person. Before resentment, therefore, can become graceful and agreeable, it must be more humbled, and brought down below that pitch to which it would naturally rise, than almost any other passion.

Mankind, at the same time, have a very strong sense of the injuries that are done to another. The villain in a tragedy or romance, is as much the object of our indignation as the hero is that of our sympathy and affection. We detest Iago as much as we esteem Othello; and delight as

much in the punishment of the one, as we are grieved at
the distress of the other. But though mankind have so
strong a fellow-feeling with the injuries that are done to
their brethren, they do not always resent them the more
that the sufferer appears to resent them. Upon most occasions, the greater his patience, his mildness, his humanity,
provided it does not appear that he wants spirit, or that fear
was the motive of his forbearance, the higher the resentment against the person who injured him. The amiableness
of the character exasperates their sense of the atrocity of
the injury.

These passions, however, are regarded as necessary parts
of the character of human nature. A person becomes contemptible who tamely sits still and submits to insults, without attempting either to repel or to revenge them. We
cannot enter into his indifference and insensibility : we call
his behaviour mean-spiritedness, and are as really provoked
by it as by the insolence of his adversary. Even the mob are
enraged to see any man submit patiently to affronts and ill
usage. They desire to see this insolence resented, and
resented by the person who suffers from it. They cry
to him with fury to defend, or to revenge himself. If his
indignation rouses at last, they heartily applaud and sympathize with it. It enlivens their own indignation against
his enemy, whom they rejoice to see him attack in turn,
and are as really gratified by his revenge, provided it is not
immoderate, as if the injury had been done to themselves.

But though the utility of those passions to the individual,
by rendering it dangerous to insult or injure him, be acknowledged ; and though their utility to the public, as the
guardians of justice, and of the equality of its administration, be not less considerable, as shall be shewn hereafter ;
yet there is still something disagreeable in the passions
themselves, which makes the appearance of them in other

men the natural object of our aversion. The expression of anger towards any body present, if it exceeds a bare intimation that we are sensible of his ill usage, is regarded not only as an insult to that particular person, but as a rudeness to the whole company. Respect for them ought to have restrained us from giving way to so boisterous and offensive an emotion. It is the remote effects of these passions which are agreeable ; the immediate effects are mischief to the person against whom they are directed. But it is the immediate, and not the remote, effects of objects which render them agreeable or disagreeable to the imagination. A prison is certainly more useful to the public than a palace ; and the person who founds the one is generally directed by a much juster spirit of patriotism, than he who builds the other. But the immediate effects of a prison, the confinement of the wretches shut up in it, are disagreeable ; and the imagination either does not take time to trace out the remote ones, or sees them at too great a distance to be much affected by them. A prison, therefore, will always be a disagreeable object ; and the fitter it is for the purpose for which it was intended, it will be the more so. A palace, on the contrary, will always be agreeable ; yet its remote effects may often be inconvenient to the public. It may serve to promote luxury, and set the example of the dissolution of manners. Its immediate effects, however, the conveniency, the pleasure, and the gaiety of the people who live in it, being all agreeable, and suggesting to the imagination a thousand agreeable ideas, that faculty generally rests upon them, and seldom goes farther in tracing its more distant consequences. Trophies of the instruments of music or of agriculture, imitated in painting or in stucco, make a common and an agreeable ornament of our halls and dining-rooms. A trophy of the same kind, composed of the instruments of surgery, of dissecting and amputation knives, of saws for cutting the bones, of trepanning instruments, &c., would be absurd and shocking. Instruments of surgery, however, are always more finely polished, and generally more nicely adapted to the purposes for which they are intended, than instruments of agriculture. The remote effects of them too, the health of the patient, is agreeable; yet as the immediate effect of them is pain and suffering, the sight of them always displeases us. Instruments of war are agreeable, though their immediate effect may seem to be in the same manner pain and suffering. But then it is the pain and suffering of our enemies, with whom we have no sympathy. With regard to us, they are immediately connected with the agreeable ideas of courage, victory, and honour. They are themselves, therefore, supposed to make one of the noblest parts of dress, and the imitation of them one of the finest ornaments of architecture. It is the same case with the qualities of the mind. The ancient stoics were of opinion, that as the world was governed by the all-ruling providence of a wise, powerful, and good God, every single event ought to be regarded as making a necessary part of the plan of the universe, and as tending to promote the general order and happiness of the whole: that the vices and follies of mankind, therefore, made as necessary a part of this plan as their wisdom or their virtue; and by that eternal art which educes good from ill, were made to tend equally to the prosperity and perfection of the great system of nature. No speculation of this kind, however, how deeply soever it might be rooted in the mind, could diminish our natural abhorrence for vice, whose immediate effects are so destructive, and whose remote ones are too distant to be traced by the imagination.

It is the same case with those passions we have been just now considering. Their immediate effects are so disagreeable, that even when they are most justly provoked, there is still something about them which disgusts us. These, therefore, are the only passions of which the expressions, as I formerly observed, do not dispose and prepare us to sympathize with them, before we are informed of the cause which excites them. The plaintive voice of misery, when heard at a distance, will not allow us to be indifferent about the person from whom it comes. As soon as it strikes our ear, it interests us in his fortune, and, if continued, forces us almost involuntarily to fly to his assistance. The sight of a smiling countenance, in the same manner, elevates even the pensive into that gay and airy mood, which disposes him to sympathize with, and share, the joy which it expresses; and he feels his heart, which with thought and care was before that shrunk and depressed, instantly expanded and elated. But it is quite otherwise with the expressions of hatred and resentment. The hoarse, boisterous, and discordant voice of anger, when heard at a distance, inspires us either with fear or aversion. We do not fly towards it, as to one who cries out with pain and agony. Women, and men of weak nerves, tremble and are overcome with fear, though sensible that themselves are not the objects of the anger. They conceive fear, however, by putting themselves in the situation of the person who is so. Even those of stouter hearts are disturbed: not indeed enough to make them afraid, but enough to make them angry; for anger is the passion which they would feel in the situation of the other person. It is the same case with hatred. Mere expressions of spite inspire it against nobody, but the man who uses them. Both these passions are by nature the objects of our aversion. Their disagreeable and boisterous appearance never excites, never prepares, and often disturbs, our sympathy. Grief does not more powerfully engage and attract us to the person in whom we observe it, than these, while we are ignorant of their cause, disgust and detach us from him. It was, it seems, the intention of nature, that those rougher and more unamiable emotions, which drive men from one another, should be less easily and more rarely communicated.

When music imitates the modulations of grief or joy, it either actually inspires us with those passions, or at least puts us in the mood which disposes us to conceive them. But when it imitates the notes of anger, it inspires us with fear. Joy, grief, love, admiration, devotion, are all of them passions which are naturally musical. Their natural tones are all soft, clear, and melodious; and they naturally express themselves in periods which are distinguished by regular pauses, and which upon that account are easily adapted to the regular returns of the correspondent airs of a tune. The voice of anger, on the contrary, and of all the passions which are akin to it, is harsh and discordant. Its periods too are all irregular, sometimes very long, and sometimes very short, and distinguished by no regular pauses. It is with difficulty, therefore, that music can imitate any of those passions; and the music which does imitate them is not the most agreeable. A whole entertainment may consist, without any impropriety, of the imitation of the social and agreeable passions. It would be a strange entertainment which consisted altogether of the imitations of hatred and resentment.

If those passions are disagreeable to the spectator, they are not less so to the person who feels them. Hatred and anger are the greatest poison to the happiness of a good mind. There is, in the very feeling of those passions, something harsh, jarring, and convulsive, something that tears and distracts the breast, and is altogether destructive of that composure and tranquillity of mind which is so necessary to happiness, and which is best promoted by the contrary passions of gratitude and love. It is not the value of what they lose by the perfidy and ingratitude of those

they live with, which the generous and humane are most
apt to regret. Whatever they may have lost, they can generally be very happy without it. What most disturbs them
is the idea of perfidy and ingratitude exercised towards
themselves; and the discordant and disagreeable passions
which this excites, constitute, in their own opinion, the chief
part of the injury which they suffer.

How many things are requisite to render the gratification of resentment completely agreeable, and to make the
spectator thoroughly sympathize with our revenge? The
provocation must first of all be such that we should become
contemptible, and be exposed to perpetual insults, if we did
not, in some measure, resent it. Smaller offences are
always better neglected; nor is there any thing more despicable than that froward and captious humour which takes
fire upon every slight occasion of quarrel. We should
resent more from a sense of the propriety of resentment,
from a sense that mankind expect and require it of us, than
because we feel in ourselves the furies of that disagreeable
passion. There is no passion, of which the human mind is
capable, concerning whose justness we ought to be so
doubtful, concerning whose indulgence we ought so carefully to consult our natural sense of propriety, or so dili-
gently to consider what will be the sentiments of the cool
and impartial spectator. Magnanimity, or a regard to
maintain our own rank and dignity in society, is the only
motive which can ennoble the expressions of this disagreeable passion. This motive must characterize our whole
style and deportment. These must be plain, open, and
direct; determined without positiveness, and elevated without insolence; not only free from petulance and low scur-
rility, but generous, candid, and full of all proper regards,
even for the person who has offended us. It must appear,
in short, from our whole manner, without our labouring

affectedly to express it, that passion has not extinguished our humanity ; and that if we yield to the dictates of revenge, it is with reluctance, from necessity, and in consequence of great and repeated provocations. When resentment is guarded and qualified in this manner, it may be admitted to be even generous and noble.

CHAPTER IV.

Of the social Passions.

As it is a divided sympathy which renders the whole set of passions just now mentioned, upon most occasions, so ungraceful and disagreeable; so there is another set opposite to these which a redoubled sympathy renders almost always peculiarly agreeable and becoming. Generosity, humanity, kindness, compassion, mutual friendship and esteem, all the social and benevolent affections, when expressed in the countenance or behaviour, even towards those who are not peculiarly connected with ourselves, please the indifferent spectator upon almost every occasion. His sympathy with the person who feels those passions exactly coincides with his concern for the person who is the object of them. The interest, which, as a man, he is obliged to take in the happiness of this last, enlivens his fellow-feeling with the sentiments of the other, whose emotions are employed about the same object. We have always, therefore, the strongest disposition to sympathize with the benevolent affections. They appear in every respect agreeable to us. We enter into the satisfaction both of the person who feels them, and of the person who is the object of them. For as to be the object of hatred and indignation gives more pain than all the evil which a brave man can fear from his enemies; so there is a satisfaction in the consciousness of being beloved, which, to a person of delicacy and sensibility, is of more importance to happiness than all the advantage which he can expect to derive from it. What character is so detestable as that of one who takes pleasure in sowing dissension among friends, and turning their most tender love into mortal hatred? Yet wherein does the atrocity of this so much abhorred injury consist? Is it in depriving them of the frivolous good offices which, had their friendship continued, they might have expected from one another? It is in depriving them of that friendship itself, in robbing them of each other's affections, from which both derived so much satisfaction; it is in disturbing the harmony of their hearts, and putting an end to that happy commerce which had before subsisted between them. These affections, that harmony, this commerce, are felt, not only by the tender and the delicate, but by the rudest vulgar of mankind, to be of more importance to happiness than all the little services which could be expected to flow from them.

The sentiment of love is, in itself, agreeable to the person who feels it. It soothes and composes the breast, seems to favour the vital motions, and to promote the healthful state of the human constitution; and it is rendered still more delightful by the consciousness of the gratitude and satisfaction which it must excite in him who is the object of it. Their mutual regard renders them happy in one another, and sympathy with this mutual regard, makes them agreeable to every other person. With what pleasure do we look upon a family, through the whole of which reign mutual love and esteem, where the parents and children are companions for one another, without any other difference than what is made by respectful affection on the one side, and kind indulgence on the other; where freedom and fondness, mutual railery and mutual kindness, shew that no opposition of interest divides the brothers, nor any rivalship of favours sets the sisters at variance, and where every thing presents us with the idea of peace, cheerfulness, harmony, and contentment? On the contrary, how uneasy are we made when we go into a house in which jarring contention sets one half of those who dwell in it against the other; where, amidst affected smoothness and complaisance, suspicious looks and sudden starts of passion betray

the mutual jealousies which burn within them, and which
are every moment ready to burst out through all the restraints which the presence of the company imposes?

Those amiable passions, even when they are acknowledged to be excessive, are never regarded with aversion.
There is something agreeable even in the weakness of
friendship and humanity. The too tender mother and the
too indulgent father, the too generous and affectionate
friend, may sometimes, perhaps, on account of the softness
of their natures, be looked upon with a species of pity, in
which, however, there is a mixture of love, but can never
be regarded with hatred and aversion, nor even with contempt, unless by the most brutal and worthless of mankind.
It is always with concern, with sympathy, and kindness,
that we blame them for the extravagance of their attachment. There is a helplessness in the character of extreme
humanity which more than any thing interests our pity.
There is nothing in itself which renders it either ungraceful or disagreeable. We only regret that it is unfit for the
world, because the world is unworthy of it, and because it
must expose the person who is endowed with it as a prey
to the perfidy and ingratitude of insinuating falsehood, and
to a thousand pains and uneasinesses, which, of all men, he
the least deserves to feel, and which generally too he is, of
all men, the least capable of supporting. It is quite otherwise with hatred and resentment. Too violent a propensity
to those detestable passions, renders a person the object of
universal dread and abhorrence, who, like a wild beast,
ought, we think, to be hunted out of all civil society.

CHAPTER V.

Of the selfish Passions.

BESIDES those two opposite sets of passions, the social and unsocial, there is another which holds a sort of middle place between them; is never either so graceful as is sometimes the one set, nor is ever so odious as is sometimes the other. Grief and joy, when conceived upon account of our own private good or bad fortune, constitute this third set of passions. Even when excessive, they are never so disagreeable as excessive resentment, because no opposite sympathy can ever interest us against them; and when most suitable to their objects, they are never so agreeable as impartial humanity and just benevolence; because no double sympathy can ever interest us for them. There is, however, this difference between grief and joy, that we are generally most disposed to sympathize with small joys and great sorrows. The man who, by some sudden revolution of fortune, is lifted up all at once into a condition of life greatly above what he had formerly lived in, may be assured that the congratulations of his best friends are not all of them perfectly sincere. An upstart, though of the greatest merit, is generally disagreeable, and a sentiment of envy commonly prevents us from heartily sympathizing with his joy. If he has any judgment, he is sensible of this, and instead of appearing to be elated with his good fortune, he endeavours, as much as he can, to smother his joy, and keep down that elevation of mind with which his new circumstances naturally inspire him. He affects the same plainness of dress, and the same modesty of behaviour, which became him in his former station. He redoubles his attention to his old friends, and endeavours more than ever to be humble, assiduous, and complaisant. And this is the behaviour which in his situation we most approve of; because we expect, it seems, that he should have more sympathy with our envy and aversion to his happiness, than we have to his happiness. It is seldom that with all this he succeeds. We suspect the sincerity of his humility, and he grows weary of this constraint. In a little time, therefore, he generally leaves all his old friends behind him, some of the meanest of them excepted, who may, perhaps, condescend to become his dependants: nor does he always acquire any new ones; the pride of his new connections is as much affronted at finding him their equal, as that of his old ones had been by his becoming their superior: and it requires the most obstinate and persevering modesty to atone for this mortification to either. He generally grows weary too soon, and is provoked, by the sullen and suspicious pride of the one, and by the saucy contempt of the other, to treat the first with neglect, and the second with petulance, till at last he grows habitually insolent, and forfeits the esteem of all. If the chief part of human happiness arises from the consciousness of being beloved, as I believe it does, those sudden changes of fortune seldom contribute much to happiness. He is happiest who advances more gradually to greatness, whom the public destines to every step of his preferment long before he arrives at it, in whom, upon that account, when it comes, it can excite no extravagant joy, and with regard to whom it cannot reasonably create either any jealousy in those he overtakes, or any envy in those he leaves behind.

Mankind, however, more readily sympathize with those smaller joys which flow from less important causes. It is decent to be humble amidst great prosperity; but we can scarce express too much satisfaction in all the little occurrences of common life, in the company with which we spent the evening last night, in the entertainment that was

set before us, in what was said, and what was done, in all
the little incidents of the present conversation, and in all
those frivolous nothings which fill up the void of human
life. Nothing is more graceful than habitual cheerfulness,
which is always founded upon a peculiar relish for all the
little pleasures which common occurrences afford. We
readily sympathize with it : it inspires us with the same
joy, and makes every trifle turn up to us in the same agreeable aspect in which it presents itself to the person endowed with this happy disposition. Hence it is that youth, the
season of gaiety, so easily engages our affections. That
propensity to joy which seems even to animate the bloom,
and to sparkle from the eyes of youth and beauty, though
in a person of the same sex, exalts, even the aged, to a
more joyous mood than ordinary. They forget, for a time,
their infirmities, and abandon themselves to those agreeable
ideas and emotions to which they have long been strangers,
but which, when the presence of so much happiness recals
them to their breast, take their place there, like old acquaintance, from whom they are sorry to have ever been
parted, and whom they embrace more heartily upon account of this long separation.

It is quite otherwise with grief. Small vexations excite
no sympathy, but deep affliction calls forth the greatest.
The man who is made uneasy by every little disagreeable
incident; who is hurt if either the cook or the butler have
failed in the least article of their duty ; who feels every defect in the highest ceremonial of politeness, whether it be
shewn to himself or to any other person; who takes it
amiss that his intimate friend did not bid him good-mor-
row when they met in the forenoon, and that his brother
hummed a tune all the time he himself was telling a story ;
who is put out of humour by the badness of the weather
when in the country, by the badness of the roads when
upon a journey, and by the want of company, and dulness

of all public diversions, when in town; such a person, I say, though he should have some reason, will seldom meet with much sympathy. Joy is a pleasant emotion, and we gladly abandon ourselves to it upon the slightest occasion. We readily, therefore, sympathize with it in others, whenever we are not prejudiced by envy. But grief is painful, and the mind, even when it is our own misfortune, naturally resists and recoils from it. We would endeavour either not to conceive it at all, or to shake it off as soon as we have conceived it. Our aversion to grief will not, indeed, always hinder us from conceiving it in our own case upon very trifling occasions, but it constantly prevents us from sympathizing with it in others when excited by the like frivolous causes: for our sympathetic passions are always less irresistible than our original ones. There is, besides, a malice in mankind, which not only prevents all sympathy with little uneasinesses, but renders them in some measure diverting. Hence the delight which we all take in railery, and in the small vexation which we observe in our companion, when he is pushed, and urged, and teased upon all sides. Men of the most ordinary good breeding dissemble the pain which any little incident may give them; and those who are more thoroughly formed to society, turn, of their own accord, all such incidents into railery, as they know their companions will do for them. The habit which a man, who lives in the world, has acquired of considering how every thing that concerns himself will appear to others, makes those frivolous calamities turn up in the same ridiculous light to him, in which he knows they will certainly be considered by them.

Our sympathy, on the contrary, with deep distress, is very strong and very sincere. It is unnecessary to give an instance. We weep even at the feigned representation of a tragedy. If you labour, therefore, under any signal calamity; if by some extraordinary misfortune you are fallen into poverty, into diseases, into disgrace and disappoint-ment; even though your own fault may have been in part, the occasion, yet you may generally depend upon the sin-cerest sympathy of all your friends, and, as far as interest and honour will permit, upon their kindest assistance too. But if your misfortune is not of this dreadful kind, if you have only been a little baulked in your ambition, if you have only been jilted by your mistress, or are only hen-pecked by your wife, lay your account with the railery of all your acquaintance.

SECTION III.

OF THE EFFECTS OF PROSPERITY AND ADVERSITY
UPON THE JUDGMENT OF MANKIND WITH REGARD
TO THE PROPRIETY OF ACTION ; AND WHY IT IS
MORE EASY TO OBTAIN THEIR APPROBATION IN
THE ONE STATE THAN IN THE OTHER.

~~~~~~~~

CHAPTER I.

*That though our sympathy with sorrow is generally a more
lively sensation than our sympathy with joy, it commonly
falls much more short of the violence of what is naturally
felt by the person principally concerned.*

OUR sympathy with sorrow, though not more real, has
been more taken notice of than our sympathy with joy.
The word sympathy, in its most proper and primitive signification, denotes our fellow-feeling with the sufferings,
not that with the enjoyments, of others. A late ingenious
and subtile philosopher thought it necessary to prove, by
arguments, that we had a real sympathy with joy, and that
congratulation was a principle of human nature. Nobody,
I believe, ever thought it necessary to prove that compassion was such.

First of all, our sympathy with sorrow is, in some sense,
more universal, than that with joy. Though sorrow is excessive, we may still have some fellow-feeling with it.
What we feel does not, indeed, in this case, amount to that

complete sympathy, to that perfect harmony and correspondence of sentiments which constitutes approbation. We do not weep, and exclaim, and lament, with the sufferer. We are sensible, on the contrary, of his weakness, and of the extravagance of his passion, and yet often feel a very sensible concern upon his account. But if we do not entirely enter into, and go along with, the joy of another, we have no sort of regard or fellow-feeling for it. The man who skips and dances about with that intemperate and senseless joy which we cannot accompany him in, is the object of our contempt and indignation.

Pain, besides, whether of mind or body, is a more pungent sensation than pleasure, and our sympathy with pain, though it falls greatly short of what is naturally felt by the sufferer, is generally a more lively and distinct perception than our sympathy with pleasure, though this last often approaches more nearly, as I shall shew immediately, to the natural vivacity of the original passion.

Over and above all this, we often struggle to keep down our sympathy with the sorrow of others. Whenever we are not under the observation of the sufferer, we endeavour, for our own sake, to suppress it as much as we can, and we are not always successful. The opposition which we make to it, and the reluctance with which we yield to it, necessarily oblige us to take more particular notice of it. But we never have occasion to make this opposition to our sympathy with joy. If there is any envy in the case, we never feel the least propensity towards it; and if there is none, we give way to it without any reluctance. On the contrary, as we are always ashamed of our own envy, we often pretend, and sometimes really wish, to sympathize with the joy of others, when by that disagreeable sentiment we are disqualified from doing so. We are glad, we say, on account of our neighbour's good fortune, when in our hearts, perhaps, we are really sorry. We often feel a sympathy with sorrow when we would wish to be rid of it, and we often miss that with joy when we would be glad to have it. The obvious observation, therefore, which it naturally falls in our way to make, is, that our propensity to sympathize with sorrow must be very strong, and our inclination to sympathize with joy very weak.

Notwithstanding this prejudice, however, I will venture to affirm, that, when there is no envy in the case, our propensity to sympathize with joy is much stronger than our propensity to sympathize with sorrow; and that our fellow-feeling for the agreeable emotion approaches much more nearly to the vivacity of what is naturally felt by the persons principally concerned, than that which we conceive for the painful one.

We have some indulgence for that excessive grief which we cannot entirely go along with. We know what a prodigious effort is requisite before the sufferer can bring down his emotions to complete harmony and concord with those of the spectator. Though he fails, therefore, we easily pardon him. But we have no such indulgence for the intemperance of joy; because we are not conscious that any such vast effort is requisite to bring it down to what we can entirely enter into. The man who, under the greatest calamities, can command his sorrow, seems worthy of the highest admiration; but he who, in the fulness of prosperity, can in the same manner master his joy, seems hardly to deserve any praise. We are sensible that there is a much wider interval in the one case than in the other, between what is naturally felt by the person principally concerned, and what the spectator can entirely go along with.

What can be added to the happiness of the man who is in health, who is out of debt, and has a clear conscience?

To one in this situation all accessions of fortune may properly be said to be superfluous; and if he is much elevated upon account of them, it must be the effect of the most frivolous levity. This situation, however, may very well be called the natural and ordinary state of mankind. Notwithstanding the present misery and depravity of the world, so justly lamented, this really is the state of the greater part of men. The greater part of men, therefore, cannot find any great difficulty in elevating themselves to all the joy which any accession to this situation can well excite in their companion.

But though little can be added to this state, much may be taken from it. Though between this condition and the highest pitch of human prosperity, the interval is but a trifle; between it and the lowest depth of misery, the distance is immense and prodigious. Adversity, on this account, necessarily depresses the mind of the sufferer much more below its natural state, than prosperity can elevate him above it. The spectator, therefore, must find it much more difficult to sympathize entirely, and keep perfect time, with his sorrow, than thoroughly to enter into his joy, and must depart much further from his own natural and ordinary temper of mind in the one case than in the other. It is on this account, that though our sympathy with sorrow is often a more pungent sensation than our sympathy with joy, it always falls much short of the violence of what is naturally felt by the person principally concerned.

It is agreeable to sympathize with joy; and wherever envy does not oppose it, our heart abandons itself with satisfaction to the highest transports of that delightful sentiment. But it is painful to go along with grief, and we always enter into it with reluctance.* When we attend to

---

* It has been objected to me, that as I found the sentiment of approbation, which is always agreeable, upon sympathy, it is inconsistent with

the representation of a tragedy, we struggle against that sympathetic sorrow which the entertainment inspires as long as we can, and we give way to it at last only when we can no longer avoid it: we even then endeavour to cover our concern from the company. If we shed any tears, we carefully conceal them, and are afraid lest the spectators, not entering into this excessive tenderness, should regard it as effeminacy and weakness. The wretch whose misfortunes call upon our compassion feels with what reluctance we are likely to enter into his sorrow, and therefore proposes his grief to us with fear and hesitation : he even smothers the half of it, and is ashamed, upon account of this hard-heartedness of mankind, to give vent to the fulness of his affliction. It is otherwise with the man who riots in joy and success. Wherever envy does not interest us against him, he expects our completest sympathy. He does not fear, therefore, to announce himself with shouts of exultation, in full confidence that we are heartily disposed to go along with him.

Why should we be more ashamed to weep than to laugh before company ? We may often have as real occasion to do the one as to do the other : but we always feel that the spectators are more likely to go along with us in the agreeable than in the painful emotion. It is always miserable to complain, even when we are oppressed by the most dreadful calamities. But the triumph of victory is not

my system to admit any disagreeable sympathy. I answer, that in the sentiment of approbation there are two things to be taken notice of; first, the sympathetic passion of the spectator ; and, secondly, the emotion which arises from his observing the perfect coincidence between this sympathetic passion in himself, and the original passion in the person principally concerned. This last emotion, in which the sentiment of approbation properly consists, is always agreeable and delightful. The other may either be agreeable or disagreeable, according to the nature of the original passion, whose features it must always, in some measure, retain.

always ungraceful. Prudence, indeed, would often advise us to bear our prosperity with more moderation ; because prudence would teach us to avoid that envy which this very triumph is, more than any thing, apt to excite.

How hearty are the acclamations of the mob, who never bear any envy to their superiors, at a triumph or a public entry? And how sedate and moderate is commonly their grief at an execution? Our sorrow at a funeral generally amounts to no more than an affected gravity : but our mirth at a christening or a marriage is always from the heart and without any affectation. Upon these, and all such joyous occasions, our satisfaction, though not so durable, is often as lively as that of the persons principally concerned. Whenever we cordially congratulate our friends, which, however, to the disgrace of human nature, we do but seldom, their joy literally becomes our joy : we are, for the moment, as happy as they are : our heart swells and overflows with real pleasure : joy and complacency sparkle from our eyes, and animate every feature of our countenance and every gesture of our body.

But, on the contrary, when we condole with our friends in their afflictions, how little do we feel in comparison of what they feel? We sit down by them, we look at them, and while they relate to us the circumstances of their misfortune, we listen to them with gravity and attention. But while their narration is every moment interrupted by those natural bursts of passion which often seem almost to choke them in the midst of it, how far are the languid emotions of our hearts from keeping time to the transports of theirs? We may be sensible, at the same time, that their passion is natural, and no greater than what we ourselves might feel upon the like occasion. We may even inwardly reproach ourselves with our own want of sensibility, and perhaps, on that account, work ourselves up into an artificial sympathy,

which, however, when it is raised, is always the slightest
and most transitory imaginable; and generally, as soon as
we have left the room, vanishes, and is gone for ever. Nature, it seems, when she loaded us with our own sorrows,
thought that they were enough, and therefore did not command us to take any further share in those of others, than
what was necessary to prompt us to relieve them.

It is on account of this dull sensibility to the afflictions
of others, that magnanimity amidst great distress appears
always so divinely graceful. His behaviour is genteel and
agreeable who can maintain his cheerfulness amidst a
number of frivolous disasters. But he appears to be more
than mortal who can support, in the same manner, the most
dreadful calamities. We feel what an immense effort is requisite to silence those violent emotions which naturally agitate and distract those in his situation. We are amazed to
find that he can command himself so entirely. His firmness, at the same time, perfectly coincides with our insensibility. He makes no demand upon us for that more exquisite degree of sensibility which we find, and which we
are mortified to find, that we do not possess. There is the
most perfect correspondence between his sentiments and
ours, and on that account the most perfect propriety in his
behaviour. It is a propriety, too, which, from our experience of the usual weakness of human nature, we could not
reasonably have expected he should be able to maintain.
We wonder with surprise and astonishment at that strength
of mind which is capable of so noble and generous an effort.
The sentiment of complete sympathy and approbation,
mixed and animated with wonder and surprise, constitutes
what is properly called admiration, as has already been more
than once taken notice of. Cato, surrounded on all sides by
his enemies, unable to resist them, disdaining to submit to
them, and reduced by the proud maxims of that age to the
necessity of destroying himself, yet never shrinking from

his misfortunes, never supplicating with the lamentable voice of wretchedness those miserable sympathetic tears which we are always so unwilling to give, but, on the contrary, arming himself with manly fortitude, and the moment before he executes his fatal resolution, giving, with his usual tranquillity, all necessary orders for the safety of his friends ; appears to Seneca, that great preacher of insensibility, a spectacle which even the gods themselves might behold with pleasure and admiration.

Whenever we meet, in common life, with any examples of such heroic magnanimity, we are always extremely affected. We are more apt to weep and shed tears for such as, in this manner, seem to feel nothing for themselves, than for those who give way to all the weakness of sorrow: and in this particular case the sympathetic grief of the spectator appears to go beyond the original passion in the person principally concerned. The friends of Socrates all wept when he drank the last potion, while he himself expressed the gayest and most cheerful tranquillity. Upon all such occasions the spectator makes no effort, and has no occasion to make any, in order to conquer his sympathetic sorrow. He is under no fear that it will transport him to any thing that is extravagant and improper ; he is rather pleased with the sensibility of his own heart, and gives way to it with complaisance and self-approbation. He gladly indulges, therefore, the most melancholy views which can naturally occur to him concerning the calamity of his friend, for whom, perhaps, he never felt so exquisitely before the tender and tearful passion of love. But it is quite otherwise with the person principally concerned. He is obliged, as much as possible, to turn away his eyes from whatever is either naturally terrible or disagreeable in his situation. Too serious an attention to those circumstances, he fears, might make so violent an impression upon him, that he could no longer keep within the bounds of moderation, or render himself the object of the complete sympathy and approbation of the spectators. He fixes his thoughts, therefore, upon those only which are agreeable, the applause and admiration which he is about to deserve by the heroic magnanimity of his behaviour. To feel that he is capable of so noble and generous an effort, to feel that in this dreadful situation he can still act as he would desire to act, animates and transports him with joy, and enables him to support that triumphant gaiety which seems to exult in the victory he thus gains over his misfortunes.

On the contrary, he always appears, in some measure, mean and despicable, who is sunk in sorrow and dejection upon account of any calamity of his own. We cannot bring ourselves to feel for him what he feels for himself, and what, perhaps, we should feel for ourselves if in his situation. We therefore despise him; unjustly, perhaps, if any sentiment could be regarded as unjust, to which we are by nature irresistibly determined. The weakness of sorrow never appears in any respect agreeable, except when it arises from what we feel for others more than from what we feel for ourselves. A son, upon the death of an indulgent and respectable father, may give way to it without much blame. His sorrow is chiefly founded upon a sort of sympathy with his departed parent; and we readily enter into this humane emotion. But if he should indulge the same weakness upon account of any misfortune which affected himself only, he would no longer meet with any such indulgence. If he should be reduced to beggary and ruin, if he should be exposed to the most dreadful dangers, if he should even be led out to a public execution, and there shed one single tear upon the scaffold, he would disgrace himself for ever in the opinion of all the gallant and generous part of mankind. Their compassion for him, however, would be very strong, and very sincere; but as it would still fall short of this excessive weakness, they would have no pardon for the man who could thus expose himself in the eyes of the world. His behaviour would affect them with shame rather than with sorrow ; and the dishonour which he had thus brought upon himself would appear to them the most lamentable circumstance in his misfortune. How did it disgrace the memory of the intrepid Duke of Biron, who had so often braved death in the field, that he wept upon the scaffold, when he beheld the state to which he was fallen, and remembered the favour and the glory from which his own rashness had so unfortunately thrown him ?

CHAPTER II.

Of the origin of Ambition, and of the distinction of Ranks.

I⊤ is because mankind are disposed to sympathize more entirely with our joy than with our sorrow, that we make parade of our riches, and conceal our poverty. Nothing is so mortifying as to be obliged to expose our distress to the view of the public, and to feel, that though our situation is open to the eyes of all mankind, no mortal conceives for us the half of what we suffer. Nay, it is chiefly from this regard to the sentiments of mankind, that we pursue riches and avoid poverty. For to what purpose is all the toil and bustle of this world? what is the end of avarice and ambition, of the pursuit of wealth, of power, and pre-eminence? Is it to supply the necessities of nature? The wages of the meanest labourer can supply them. We see that they afford him food and clothing, the comfort of a house, and of a family. If we examine his economy with rigour, we should find that he spends a great part of them upon conveniences, which may be regarded as superfluities, and that, upon extraordinary occasions, he can give something even to vanity and distinction. What then is the cause of our aversion to his situation, and why should those who have been educated in the higher ranks of life, regard it as worse than death, to be reduced to live, even without labour, upon the same simple fare with him, to dwell under the same lowly roof, and to be clothed in the same humble attire? Do they imagine that their stomach is better, or their sleep sounder, in a palace than in a cottage? The contrary has been so often observed, and, indeed, is so very obvious, though it had never been observed, that there is nobody ignorant of it. From whence, then, arises that emulation which runs through all the different ranks of men, and what are the advantages which we propose by that great purpose of human life which we call bettering our condition? To be observed, to be attended to, to be taken notice of with sympathy, complacency, and approbation, are all the advan-tages which we can propose to derive from it. It is the vanity, not the ease, or the pleasure, which interests us. But vanity is always founded upon the belief of our being the object of attention and approbation. The rich man glories in his riches, because he feels that they naturally draw upon him the attention of the world, and that mankind are disposed to go along with him in all those agreeable emotions with which the advantages of his situation so readily inspire him. At the thought of this his heart seems to swell and dilate itself within him, and he is fonder of his wealth, upon this account, than for all the other advantages it procures him. The poor man, on the contrary, is ashamed of his poverty. He feels that it either places him out of the sight of mankind, or, that if they take any notice of him, they have, however, scarce any fellow-feeling with the misery and distress which he suffers. He is mortified upon both accounts ; for though to be overlooked, and to be dis-approved of, are things entirely different, yet as obscurity covers us from the day-light of honour and approbation, to feel that we are taken no notice of, necessarily damps the most agreeable hope, and disappoints the most ardent desire, of human nature. The poor man goes out and comes in unheeded, and when in the midst of a crowd is in the same obscurity as if shut up in his own hovel. Those humble cares and painful attentions which occupy those in his situa-tion, afford no amusement to the dissipated and the gay. They turn away their eyes from him, or if the extremity of his distress forces them to look at him, it is only to spurn so disagreeable an object from among them. The fortunate and the proud wonder at the insolence of human wretched-ness, that it should dare to present itself before them, and with the loathsome aspect of its misery presume to disturb the

serenity of their happiness. The man of rank and distinction, on the contrary, is observed by all the world. Every
body is eager to look at him, and to conceive, at least by
sympathy, that joy and exultation with which his circumstances naturally inspire him. His actions are the objects
of the public care. Scarce a word, scarce a gesture, can fall
from him that is altogether neglected. In a great assembly
he is the person upon whom all direct their eyes; it is upon
him that their passions seem all to wait with expectation,
in order to receive that movement and direction which he
shall impress upon them ; and if his behaviour is not altogether absurd, he has, every moment, an opportunity of
interesting mankind, and of rendering himself the object of
the observation and fellow-feeling of every body about him.
It is this, which, notwithstanding the restraint it imposes,
notwithstanding the loss of liberty with which it is attended,
renders greatness the object of envy, and compensates, in
the opinion of mankind, all that toil, all that anxiety, all
those mortifications, which must be undergone in the pursuit of it ; and what is of yet more consequence, all that
leisure, all that ease, all that careless security, which are
forfeited for ever by the acquisition.

When we consider the condition of the great, in those delusive colours in which the imagination is apt to paint it, it
seems to be almost the abstract idea of a perfect and happy
state. It is the very state which, in all our waking dreams
and idle reveries, we had sketched out to ourselves as the
final object of all our desires. We feel, therefore, a peculiar
sympathy with the satisfaction of those who are in it. We
favour all their inclinations, and forward all their wishes.
What pity, we think, that any thing should spoil and corrupt so agreeable a situation ! We could even wish them
immortal; and it seems hard to us, that death should at
last put an end to such perfect enjoyment. It is cruel, we
think, in nature to compel them from their exalted stations

to that humble, but hospitable, home, which she has provided for all her children. Great king, live for ever! is the compliment, which, after the manner of eastern adulation, we should readily make them, if experience did not teach us its absurdity. Every calamity that befals them, every injury that is done them, excites in the breast of the spectator ten times more compassion and resentment than he would have felt, had the same things happened to other men. It is the misfortunes of kings only which afford the proper subjects for tragedy. They resemble, in this respect, the misfortunes of lovers. Those two situations are the chief which interest us upon the theatre; because, in spite of all that reason and experience can tell us to the contrary, the prejudices of the imagination attach to these two states a happiness superior to any other. To disturb, or to put an end to, such perfect enjoyment, seems to be the most atrocious of all injuries. The traitor who conspires against the life of his monarch, is thought a greater monster than any other murderer. All the innocent blood that was shed in the civil wars, provoked less indignation than the death of Charles I. A stranger to human nature, who saw the indifference of men about the misery of their inferiors, and the regret and indignation which they feel for the misfortunes and sufferings of those above them, would be apt to imagine, that pain must be more agonizing, and the convulsions of death more terrible, to persons of higher rank than to those of meaner stations.

Upon this disposition of mankind to go along with all the passions of the rich and the powerful, is founded the distinction of ranks and the order of society. Our obsequiousness to our superiors more frequently arises from our admiration for the advantages of their situation, than from any private expectations of benefit from their good-will. Their benefits can extend but to a few; but their fortunes interest almost every body. We are eager to assist them in com-

pleting a system of happiness that approaches so near to
perfection ; and we desire to serve them for their own sake,
without any other recompence but the vanity or the honour
of obliging them. Neither is our deference to their inclinations founded chiefly, or altogether, upon a regard to the
utility of such submission, and to the order of society, which
is best supported by it. Even when the order of society
seems to require that we should oppose them, we can hardly
bring ourselves to do it. That kings are the servants of
the people, to be obeyed, resisted, deposed, or punished, as
the public conveniency may require, is the doctrine of
reason and philosophy ; but it is not the doctrine of nature. Nature would teach us to submit to them for their
own sake, to tremble and bow down before their exalted
station, to regard their smile as a reward sufficient to compensate any services, and to dread their displeasure, though
no other evil were to follow from it, as the severest of all
mortifications. To treat them in any respect as men, to
reason and dispute with them upon ordinary occasions, requires such resolution, that there are few men whose magnanimity can support them in it, unless they are likewise
assisted by familiarity and acquaintance. The strongest
motives, the most furious passions, fear, hatred, and resentment, are scarce sufficient to balance this natural disposition
to respect them : and their conduct must, either justly or
unjustly, have excited the highest degree of all those passions, before the bulk of the people can be brought to oppose
them with violence, or to desire to see them either punished
or deposed. Even when the people have been brought this
length, they are apt to relent every moment, and easily re-
lapse into their habitual state of deference to those to whom
they have been accustomed to look up as their natural
superiors. They cannot stand the mortification of their
monarch. Compassion soon takes the place of resentment,
they forget all past provocations, their old principles of
loyalty revive, and they run to re-establish the ruined authority of their old masters, with the same violence with

which they had opposed it. The death of Charles I. brought about the restoration of the royal family. Compassion for James II., when he was seized by the populace in making his escape on ship-board, had almost prevented the revolution, and made it go on more heavily than before.

Do the great seem insensible of the easy price at which they may acquire the public admiration; or do they seem to imagine that to them, as to other men, it must be the purchase either of sweat or of blood? By what important accomplishments is the young nobleman instructed to support the dignity of his rank, and to render himself worthy of that superiority over his fellow-citizens, to which the virtue of his ancestors had raised them? Is it by knowledge, by industry, by patience, by self-denial, or by virtue of any kind? As all his words, as all his motions are attended to, he learns an habitual regard to every circumstance of ordinary behaviour, and studies to perform all those small duties with the most exact propriety. As he is conscious how much he is observed, and how much mankind are disposed to favour all his inclinations, he acts, upon the most indifferent occasions, with that freedom and elevation which the thought of this naturally inspires. His air, his manner, his deportment, all mark that elegant and graceful sense of his own superiority, which those who are born to inferior stations can hardly ever arrive at. These are the arts by which he proposes to make mankind more easily submit to his authority, and to govern their inclinations according to his own pleasure; and in this he is seldom disappointed. These arts, supported by rank and pre-eminence, are, upon ordinary occasions, sufficient to govern the world. Louis XIV., during the greater part of his reign, was regarded, not only in France, but over all Europe, as the most perfect model of a great prince. But what were the talents and virtues by which he acquired this great reputation? Was it by the scrupulous and   flexible justice of all his undertak-

ings, by the immense dangers and difficulties with which
they were attended, or by the unwearied and unrelenting
application with which he pursued them? Was it by his
extensive knowledge, by his exquisite judgment, or by his
heroic valour? It was by none of these qualities. But he
was, first of all, the most powerful prince in Europe, and
consequently held the highest rank among kings; and
then, says his historian, " he surpassed all his courtiers in
the gracefulness of his shape, and the majestic beauty of
his features. The sound of his voice, noble and affecting,
gained those hearts which his presence intimidated. He
had a step and a deportment which could suit only him and
his rank, and which would have been ridiculous in any
other person. The embarrassment which he occasioned to
those who spoke to him, flattered that secret satisfaction
with which he felt his own superiority. The old officer,
who was confounded, and faultered in asking him a favour,
and not being able to conclude his discourse, said to him :
Sir, your majesty, I hope, will believe that I do not tremble
thus before your enemies : had no difficulty to obtain what
he demanded." These frivolous accomplishments, supported by his rank, and, no doubt too, by a degree of other
talents and virtues, which seems, however, not to have
been much above mediocrity, established this prince in the
esteem of his own age, and have drawn even from posterity
a good deal of respect for his memory. Compared with these,
in his own times, and in his own presence, no other virtue, it
seems, appeared to have any merit. Knowledge, industry,
valour, and beneficence, trembled, were abashed, and lost
all dignity, before them.

But it is not by accomplishments of this kind that the
man of inferior rank must hope to distinguish himself. Politeness is so much the virtue of the great, that it will do
little honour to any body but themselves. The coxcomb,
who imitates their manner, and affects to be eminent by the

superior propriety of his ordinary behaviour, is rewarded
with a double share of contempt for his folly and presumption. Why should the man, whom nobody thinks it worth
while to look at, be very anxious about the manner in
which he holds up his head, or disposes of his arms, while
he walks through a room? He is occupied surely with a
very superfluous attention, and with an attention too that
marks a sense of his own importance, which no other mortal
can go along with. The most perfect modesty and plainness, joined to as much negligence as is consistent with
the respect due to the company, ought to be the chief characteristics of the behaviour of a private man. If ever he
hopes to distinguish himself, it must be by more important
virtues. He must acquire dependants to balance the dependants of the great, and he has no other fund to pay them
from but the labour of his body and the activity of his
mind. He must cultivate these therefore : he must acquire
superior knowledge in his profession, and superior industry
in the exercise of it. He must be patient in labour, resolute in danger, and firm in distress. These talents he must
bring into public view, by the difficulty, importance, and,
at the same time, good judgment of his undertakings, and
by the severe and unrelenting application with which he
pursues them. Probity and prudence, generosity and frankness, must characterize his behaviour upon all ordinary
occasions ; and he must, at the same time, be forward to
engage in all those situations, in which it requires the
greatest talents and virtues to act with propriety, but in
which the greatest applause is to be acquired by those who
can acquit themselves with honour. With what impatience
does the man of spirit and ambition, who is depressed by
his situation, look round for some great opportunity to distinguish himself? No circumstances, which can afford this,
appear to him undesirable. He even looks forward with satisfaction to the prospect of foreign war, or civil dissension,
and, with secret transport and delight, sees through all the

confusion and bloodshed which attend them, the probability of those wished-for occasions presenting themselves, in
which he may draw upon himself the attention and admiration of mankind. The man of rank and distinction, on the
contrary, whose whole glory consists in the propriety of his
ordinary behaviour, who is contented with the humble renown which this can afford him, and has no talents to acquire any other, is unwilling to embarrass himself with what
can be attended either with difficulty or distress. To figure
at a ball is his great triumph, and to succeed in an intrigue
of gallantry, his highest exploit. He has an aversion to all
public confusions, not from the love of mankind, for the
great never look upon their inferiors as their fellow-crea
tures ; nor yet from want of courage, for in that he is seldom
defective ; but from a consciousness that he possesses none
of the virtues which are required in such situations, and
that the public attention will certainly be drawn away from
him by others. He may be willing to expose himself to
some little danger, and to make a campaign when it happens to be the fashion, but he shudders with horror at the
thought of any situation which demands the continual and
long exertion of patience, industry, fortitude, and application of thought. These virtues are hardly ever to be met
with in men who are born to those high stations. In all
governments accordingly, even in monarchies, the highest
offices are generally possessed, and the whole detail of the
administration conducted, by men who were educated in
the middle and inferior ranks of life, who have been carried
forward by their own industry and abilities, though loaded
with the jealousy, and opposed by the resentment, of all
those who were born their superiors, and to whom the great,
after having regarded them, first with contempt and afterwards with envy, are at last contented to truckle with the
same abject meanness with which they desire that the rest of
mankind should behave to themselves.

It is the loss of this easy empire over the affections of mankind which renders the fall from greatness so insupportable. When the family of the king of Macedon was led in triumph by Paulus Æmilius, their misfortunes, it is said, made them divide, with their conqueror, the attention of the Roman people. The sight of the royal children, whose tender age rendered them insensible of their situation, struck the spectators, amidst the public rejoicings and prosperity, with the tenderest sorrow and compassion. The king appeared next in the procession; and seemed like one confounded and astonished, and bereft of all sentiment, by the greatness of his calamities. His friends and ministers followed after him. As they moved along, they often cast their eyes upon their fallen sovereign, and always burst into tears at the sight; their whole behaviour demonstrating that they thought not of their own misfortunes, but were occupied entirely by the superior greatness of his. The generous Romans, on the contrary, beheld him with disdain and indignation, and regarded as unworthy of all compassion the man who could be so mean-spirited as to bear to live under such calamities. Yet what did those calamities amount to? According to the greater part of historians, he was to spend the remainder of his days, under the protection of a powerful and humane people, in a state which in itself should seem worthy of envy, a state of plenty, ease, leisure, and security, from which it was impossible for him, even by his own folly, to fall. But he was no longer to be surrounded by that admiring mob of fools, flatterers, and dependants, who had formerly been accustomed to attend upon all his motions. He was no longer to be gazed upon by multitudes, nor to have it in his power to render himself the object of their respect, their gratitude, their love, their admiration. The passions of nations were no longer to mould themselves upon his innations. This was that insupportable calamity which bereaved the king of all sentiment; which made his friends forget their own misfortunes; and which the Roman magnanimity could scarce conceive how any man could be so mean-spirited as to bear to survive.

"Love," says my Lord Rochefoucault, " is commonly succeeded by ambition, but ambition is hardly ever succeeded by love." That passion, when once it has got entire possession of the breast, will admit neither a rival nor a successor. To those who have been accustomed to the possession, or even to the hope, of public admiration, all other pleasures sicken and decay. Of all the discarded statesmen who, for their own ease, have studied to get the better of ambition, and to despise those honours which they could no longer arrive at, how few have been able to succeed? The greater part have spent their time in the most listless and insipid indolence, chagrined at the thoughts of their own insignificancy, incapable of being interested in the occupations of private life, without enjoyment, except when they talked of their former greatness, and without satisfaction, except when they were employed in some vain project to recover it. Are you in earnest resolved never to barter your liberty for the lordly servitude of a court, but to live free, fearless, and independent? There seems to be one way to continue in that virtuous resolution ; and perhaps but one. Never enter the place from whence so few have been able to return ; never come within the circle of ambition ; nor ever bring yourself into comparison with those masters of the earth who have already engrossed the attention of half mankind before you.

Of such mighty importance does it appear to be, in the imaginations of men, to stand in that situation which sets them most in the view of general sympathy and attention. And thus, place, that great object which divides the wives of aldermen, is the end of half the labours of human life ; and is the cause of all the tumult and bustle, all the rapine and injustice, which avarice and ambition have introduced into this world. People of sense, it is said, indeed despise place ·

that is, they despise sitting at the head of the table, and are indifferent who it is that is pointed out to the company by that frivolous circumstance, which the smallest advantage is capable of overbalancing. But rank, distinction, pre-eminence, no man despises, unless he is either raised very much above, or sunk very much below, the ordinary standard of human nature; unless he is either so confirmed in wisdom and real philosophy, as to be satisfied that, while the propriety of his conduct renders him the just object of appro-bation, it is of little consequence though he be neither attended to, nor approved of; or so habituated to the idea of his own meanness, so sunk in slothful and sottish indiffer-ence, as entirely to have forgot the desire, and almost the very wish, for superiority.

As to become the natural object of the joyous congratula-tions and sympathetic attentions of mankind is, in this manner, the circumstance which gives to prosperity all its dazzling splendour; so nothing darkens so much the gloom of adversity as to feel that our misfortunes are the objects, not of the fellow-feeling but of the contempt and aversion of our brethren. It is upon this account that the most dreadful calamities are not always those which it is most difficult to support. It is often more mortifying to appear in public under small disasters, than under great misfor-tunes. The first excite no sympathy; but the second, though they may excite none that approaches to the anguish of the sufferer, call forth, however, a very lively compassion. The sentiments of the spectators are, in this last case, less wide of those of the sufferer, and their imperfect fellow-feeling lends him some assistance in supporting his misery. Before a gay assembly, a gentleman would be more morti-fied to appear covered with filth and rags than with blood and wounds. This last situation would interest their pity; the other would provoke their laughter. The judge who orders a criminal to be set in the pillory, dishonours him more than if he had condemned him to the scaffold. The great prince, who, some years ago, caned a general officer at the head of his army, disgraced him irrecoverably. The punishment would have been much less, had he shot him through the body. By the laws of honour, to strike with a cane dishonours, to strike with a sword does not, for an obvious reason. Those slighter punishments, when inflicted on a gentleman, to whom dishonour is the greatest of all evils, come to be regarded among a humane and generous people as the most dreadful of any. With regard to persons of that rank, therefore, they are universally laid aside; and the law, while it takes their life upon many occasions, respects their honour upon almost all. To scourge a person of quality, or to set him in the pillory, upon account of any crime whatever, is a brutality of which no European government, except that of Russia, is capable.

A brave man is not rendered contemptible by being brought to the scaffold; he is, by being set in the pillory. His behaviour in the one situation may gain him universal esteem and admiration. No behaviour in the other can render him agreeable. The sympathy of the spectators supports him in the one case, and saves him from that shame, that consciousness, that his misery is felt by himself only, which is of all sentiments the most insupportable. There is no sympathy in the other; or, if there is any, it is not with his pain, which is a trifle, but with his consciousness of the want of sympathy with which this pain is attended. It is with his shame, not with his sorrow. Those who pity him, blush and hang down their heads for him. He droops in the same manner, and feels himself irrecoverably degraded by the punishment, though not by the crime. The man, on the contrary, who dies with resolution, as he is naturally regarded with the erect aspect of esteem and approbation, so he wears himself the same undaunted countenance; and, if the crime does not deprive him of the respect of others, the punishment never will. He has no suspicion that his situation is the object of contempt or derision to any body, and he can, with propriety, assume the air, not only of perfect serenity, but of triumph and exultation.

" Great dangers," says the Cardinal de Retz, " have their charms, because there is some glory to be got, even when we miscarry. But moderate dangers have nothing but what is horrible, because the loss of reputation always attends the want of success." His maxim has the same foundation with what we have been just now observing with regard to punishments.

Human virtue is superior to pain, to poverty, to danger, and to death ; nor does it even require its utmost efforts to despise them. But to have its misery exposed to insult and derision, to be led in triumph, to be set up for the hand of scorn to point at, is a situation in which its constancy is much more apt to fail. Compared with the contempt of mankind, all other external evils are easily supported.

CHAPTER III.

*Of the corruption of our moral sentiments, which is occasioned
by this disposition to admire the rich and the great, and to
despise or neglect persons of poor and mean condition.*

This disposition to admire, and almost to worship, the
rich and the powerful, and to despise, or, at least, to neglect, persons of poor and mean condition, though necessary
both to establish and to maintain the distinction of ranks
and the order of society, is, at the same time, the great and
most universal cause of the corruption of our moral sentiments.   That wealth and greatness are often regarded with
the respect and admiration which are due only to wisdom
and virtue ; and that the contempt, of which vice and folly
are the only proper objects, is often most unjustly bestowed
upon poverty and weakness, has been the complaint of
moralists in all ages.

We desire both to be respectable and to be respected.
We dread both to be contemptible and to be contemned.
But, upon coming into the world, we soon find that wisdom
and virtue are by no means the sole objects of respect ; nor
vice and folly, of contempt.   We frequently see the respectful attentions of the world more strongly directed towards
the rich and the great, than towards the wise and the virtuous.   We see frequently the vices and follies of the
powerful much less despised than the poverty and weakness
of the innocent.   To deserve, to acquire, and to enjoy, the
respect and admiration of mankind, are the great objects
of ambition and emulation.   Two different roads are presented to us, equally leading to the attainment of this so
much desired object ; the one, by the study of wisdom and
the practice of virtue ; the other, by the acquisition of

wealth and greatness. Two different characters are presented to our emulation; the one of proud ambition and
ostentatious avidity; the other, of humble modesty and
equitable justice. Two different models, two different pictures, are held out to us, according to which we may fashion
our own character and behaviour; the one more gaudy and
glittering in its colouring; the other more correct and more
exquisitely beautiful in its outline; the one forcing itself
upon the notice of every wandering eye; the other attract-
ing the attention of scarce any body but the most studious
and careful observer. They are the wise and the virtuous
chiefly, a select, though, I am afraid, but a small party, who
are the real and steady admirers of wisdom and virtue.
The great mob of mankind are the admirers and worshippers, and, what may seem more extraordinary, most frequently the disinterested admirers and worshippers, of
wealth and greatness.

The respect which we feel for wisdom and virtue is, no
doubt, different from that which we conceive for wealth
and greatness; and it requires no very nice discernment
to distinguish the difference. But, notwithstanding this
difference, those sentiments bear a very considerable resemblance to one another. In some particular features they
are no doubt different, but, in the general air of the countenance, they seem to be so very nearly the same, that inattentive observers are very apt to mistake the one for the
other.

In equal degrees of merit there is scarce any man who
does not respect more the rich and the great than the poor
and the humble. With most men the presumption and
vanity of the former are much more admired than the real
and solid merit of the latter. It is scarce agreeable to good
morals, or even to good language, perhaps, to say, that mere
wealth and greatness, abstracted from merit and virtue, de-

serve our respect. We must acknowledge, however, that they almost constantly obtain it; and they may, therefore, be considered as, in some respects, the natural objects of it. Those exalted stations may, no doubt, be completely degraded by vice and folly. But the vice and folly must be very great, before they can operate this complete degradation. The profligacy of a man of fashion is looked upon with much less contempt and aversion than that of a man of meaner condition. In the latter, a single transgression of the rules of temperance and propriety is commonly more resented than the constant and avowed contempt of them ever is in the former.

In the middling and inferior stations of life, the road to virtue and that to fortune, to such fortune, at least, as men in such stations can reasonably expect to acquire, are, happily, in most cases very nearly the same. In all the middling and inferior professions, real and solid professional abilities, joined to prudent, just, firm, and temperate conduct, can very seldom fail of success. Abilities will even sometimes prevail where the conduct is by no means correct. Either habitual imprudence, however, or injustice, or weakness, or profligacy, will always cloud, and sometimes depress altogether, the most splendid professional abilities. Men in the inferior and middling stations of life, besides, can never be great enough to be above the law, which must generally overawe them into some sort of respect for, at least, the more important rules of justice. The success of such people, too, almost always depends upon the favour and good opinion of their neighbours and equals ; and without a tolerably regular conduct, these can very seldom be obtained. The good old proverb, therefore, that honesty is the best policy, holds, in such situations, almost always perfectly true. In such situations, therefore, we may generally expect a considerable degree of virtue ; and, fortunately for the good morals of society, these are the situations of by far the greater part of mankind.

In the superior stations of life the case is unhappily not always the same. In the courts of princes, in the drawing-rooms of the great, where success and preferment depend, not upon the esteem of intelligent and well-informed equals, but upon the fanciful and foolish favour of ignorant, presumptuous, and proud superiors; flattery and falsehood too often prevail over merit and abilities. In such societies, the abilities to please are more regarded than the abilities to serve. In quiet and peaceable times, when the storm is at a distance, the prince, or great man, wishes only to be amused, and is even apt to fancy that he has scarce any occasion for the service of any body, or that those who amuse him are sufficiently able to serve him. The external graces, the frivolous accomplishments, of that impertinent and foolish thing called a man of fashion, are commonly more admired than the solid and masculine virtues of a warrior, a statesman, a philosopher, or a legislator. All the great and awful virtues, all the virtues which can fit, either for the council, the senate, or the field, are, by the insolent and insignificant flatterers, who commonly figure the most in such corrupted societies, held in the utmost contempt and derision. When the Duke of Sully was called upon by Louis XIII. to give his advice in some great emergency, he observed the favourites and courtiers whispering to one another, and smiling at his unfashionable appearance.—" Whenever your Majesty's father," said the old warrior and statesman, " did me the honour to consult me, he ordered the buffoons of the court to retire into the antechamber."

It is from our disposition to admire, and consequently to imitate, the rich and the great, that they are enabled to set, or to lead, what is called the fashion. Their dress is the fashionable dress ; the language of their conversation, the fashionable style ; their air and deportment, the fashionable behaviour. Even their vices and follies are fashionable ; and the greater part of men are proud to imitate and re- semble them in the very qualities which dishonour and de- grade them. Vain men often give themselves airs of a fashionable profligacy, which, in their hearts, they do not approve of, and of which, perhaps, they are really not guilty. They desire to be praised for what they themselves do not think praiseworthy, and are ashamed of unfashionable vir- tues, which they sometimes practise in secret, and for which they have secretly some degree of real veneration. There are hypocrites of wealth and greatness, as well as of religion and virtue ; and a vain man is as apt to pretend to be what he is not, in the one way, as a cunning man is in the other. He assumes the equipage and splendid way of living of his superiors, without considering, that whatever may be praise- worthy in any of these derives its whole merit and propriety from its suitableness to that situation and fortune which both require, and can easily support the expense. Many a poor man places his glory in being thought rich, without considering that the duties (if one may call such follies by so very venerable a name) which that reputation imposes upon him, must soon reduce him to beggary, and render his situation still more unlike that of those whom he admires and imitates, than it had been originally.

To attain to this envied situation, the candidates for for- tune too frequently abandon the paths of virtue ; for unhap- pily, the road which leads to the one and that which leads to the other, lie sometimes in very opposite directions. But the ambitious man flatters himself that, in the splendid situation to which he advances, he will have so many means of commanding the respect and admiration of mankind, and will be enabled to act with such superior propriety and grace, that the lustre of his future conduct will entirely

cover, or efface, the foulness of the steps by which he arrived at that elevation. In many governments the candidates for the highest stations are above the law; and, if
they can attain the object of their ambition, they have no
fear of being called to account for the means by which they
acquired it. They often endeavour, therefore, not only by
fraud and falsehood, the ordinary and vulgar arts of intrigue
and cabal, but sometimes by the perpetration of the most
enormous crimes, by murder and assassination, by rebellion
and civil war, to supplant and destroy those who oppose or
stand in the way of their greatness. They more frequently
miscarry than succeed; and commonly gain nothing but the
disgraceful punishment which is due to their crimes. But,
though they should be so lucky as to attain that wished-for
greatness, they are always most miserably disappointed in
the happiness which they expect to enjoy in it. It is not
ease or pleasure, but always honour, of one kind or another,
though frequently an honour very ill understood, that the
ambitious man really pursues. But the honour of his exalted station appears, both in his own eyes and in those of
other people, polluted and defiled by the baseness of the
means through which he rose to it. Though by the profusion of every liberal expense; though by excessive indulgence in every profligate pleasure, the wretched, but
usual, resource of ruined characters; though by the hurry
of public business, or by the prouder and more dazzling
tumult of war, he may endeavour to efface, both from his
own memory and from that of other people, the remembrance of what he has done; that remembrance never fails
to pursue him. He invokes in vain the dark and dismal
powers of forgetfulness and oblivion. He remembers himself what he has done, and that remembrance tells him
that other people must likewise remember it. Amidst
all the gaudy pomp of the most ostentatious greatness;
amidst the venal and vile adulation of the great and of the
learned; amidst the more innocent though more foolish,

acclamations of the common people; amidst all the pride of conquest and the triumph of successful war, he is still secretly pursued by the avenging furies of shame and remorse; and, while glory seems to surround him on all sides, he himself, in his own imagination, sees black and foul infamy fast pursuing him, and every moment ready to overtake him from behind. Even the great Cæsar, though he had the magnanimity to dismiss his guards, could not dismiss his suspicions. The remembrance of Pharsalia still haunted and pursued him. When, at the request of the senate, he had the generosity to pardon Marcellus, he told that assembly, that he was not unaware of the designs which were carrying on against his life; but that, as he had lived long enough both for nature and for glory, he was contented to die. and therefore despised all conspiracies. He had, perhaps, lived long enough for nature; but the man who felt himself the object of such deadly resentments from those whose favour he wished to gain, and whom he still wished to consider as his friends, had certainly lived too long for real glory; or for all the happiness which he could ever hope to enjoy in the love and esteem of his equals.

THE

THEORY OF MORAL SENTIMENTS.

Part Second.

OF MERIT AND DEMERIT;

OR,

THE OBJECTS OF REWARD AND PUNISHMENT;

CONSISTING OF THREE SECTIONS.

SECTION I.

OF THE SENSE OF MERIT AND DEMERIT.

INTRODUCTION.

THERE is another set of qualities ascribed to the actions and conduct of mankind, distinct from their propriety or impropriety, their decency or ungracefulness, and which are the objects of a distinct species of approbation and disapprobation. These are Merit and Demerit, the qualities of deserving reward, and of deserving punishment.

It has already been observed, that the sentiment or affection of the heart from which any action proceeds, and upon which its whole virtue or vice depends, may be considered under two different aspects, or in two different relations; first, in relation to the cause or object which excites it; and, secondly, in relation to the end which it proposes, or to the effect which it tends to produce: that upon the suitableness or unsuitableness, upon the proportion or disproportion, which the affection seems to bear to the cause or object which excites it, depends the propriety or impropriety, the decency or ungracefulness, of the consequent action; and that upon the beneficial or hurtful effects which the affection proposes or tends to produce depends the merit or demerit, the good or ill desert, of the action to which it gives occasion. Wherein consists our sense of the propriety or impropriety of actions, has been explained in the former part of this discourse. We come now to consider, wherein consists that of their good or ill desert.

CHAPTER I.

That whatever appears to be the proper object of gratitude, appears to deserve reward; and that, in the same manner, whatever appears to be the proper object of resentment, appears to deserve punishment.

To us, therefore, that action must appear to deserve reward, which appears to be the proper and approved object of that sentiment which most immediately and directly prompts us to reward, or to do good to, another. And in the same manner, that action must appear to deserve punishment, which appears to be the proper and approved object of that sentiment which most immediately and directly prompts us to punish, or to inflict evil upon, another.

The sentiment which most immediately and directly prompts us to reward, is gratitude; that which most immediately and directly prompts us to punish, is resentment.

To us, therefore, that action must appear to deserve reward, which appears to be the proper and approved object of gratitude; as, on the other hand, that action must appear to deserve punishment, which appears to be the proper and approved object of resentment.

To reward, is to recompence, to remunerate, to return good for good received. To punish, too, is to recompence, to remunerate, though in a different manner; it is to return evil for evil that has been done.

There are some other passions, besides gratitude and resentment, which interest us in the happiness or misery of others; but there are none which so directly excite us to be the instruments of either. The love and esteem which grow up upon acquaintance and habitual approbation, necessarily lead us to be pleased with the good fortune of the man who is the object of such agreeable emotions, and, consequently, to be willing to lend a hand to promote it. Our love, however, is fully satisfied, though his good fortune should be brought about without our assistance. All that this passion desires, is to see him happy, without regarding who was the author of his prosperity. But gratitude is not to be satisfied in this manner. If the person to whom we owe many obligations is made happy without our assistance, though it pleases our love, it does not content our gratitude. Till we have recompensed him, till we ourselves have been instrumental in promoting his happiness, we feel ourselves still loaded with that debt which his past services have laid upon us

The hatred and dislike, in the same manner, which grow upon habitual disapprobation, would often lead us to take a malicious pleasure in the misfortune of the man whose conduct and character excite so painful a passion. But though dislike and hatred harden us against all sympathy, and sometimes dispose us even to rejoice at the distress of another, yet, if there is no resentment in the case, if neither we nor our friends have received any great personal provocation, these passions would not naturally lead us to wish to be instrumental in bringing it about. Though we could fear no punishment in consequence of our having had some hand in it, we would rather that it should happen by other means. To one under the dominion of violent hatred it would be agreeable, perhaps, to hear, that the person whom he abhorred and detested was killed by some accident. But if he had the least spark of justice, which, though this passion is not very favourable to virtue, he might still have, it would hurt him excessively to have been himself, even without design, the occasion of this misfortune. Much more would the very thought of voluntarily contributing to it shock him beyond all measure. He would reject with horror even the imagination of so execrable a design; and if he could imagine himself capable of such an enormity, he would begin to regard himself in the same odious light in which he had considered the person who was the object of his dislike. But it is quite otherwise with resentment : if the person who had done us some great injury, who had murdered our father or our brother, for example, should soon afterwards die of a fever, or even be brought to the scaffold upon account of some other crime, though it might soothe our hatred, it would not fully gratify our resentment. Resentment would prompt us to desire, not only that he should be punished, but that he should be punished by our means, and upon account of that particular injury which he had done to us. Resentment cannot be fully gratified, unless the offender is not only made to grieve in his turn, but to grieve for that particular wrong which we have suffered from him. He must be made to repent and be sorry for this very action, that others, through fear of the like punishment, may be terrified from being guilty of the like offence. The natural gratification of this passion tends, of its own accord, to produce all the political ends of punishment; the correction of the criminal, and the example to the public.

Gratitude and resentment, therefore, are the sentiments which most immediately and directly prompt to reward and to punish. To us, therefore, he must appear to deserve reward, who appears to be the proper and approved object of gratitude ; and he to deserve punishment, who appears to be that of resentment.

CHAPTER II.

Of the proper Objects of Gratitude and Resentment.

To be the proper and approved object either of gratitude or resentment, can mean nothing but to be the object of that gratitude, and of that resentment, which naturally seems proper, and is approved of.

But these, as well as all the other passions of human nature, seem proper and are approved of, when the heart of every impartial spectator entirely sympathizes with them, when every indifferent bystander entirely enters into, and goes along with, them.

He, therefore, appears to deserve reward, who, to some person or persons, is the natural object of a gratitude which every human heart is disposed to beat time to, and thereby applaud : and he, on the other hand, appears to deserve punishment, who, in the same manner, is to some person or persons the natural object of a resentment which the breast of every reasonable man is ready to adopt and sympathize with. To us, surely, that action must appear to deserve reward which every body who knows of it would wish to reward, and therefore delights to see rewarded : and that action must as surely appear to deserve punishment which every body who hears of it is angry with, and upon that account rejoices to see punished.

1. As we sympathize with the joy of our companions when in prosperity, so we join with them in the complacency and satisfaction with which they naturally regard whatever is the cause of their good fortune. We enter into the love and affection which they conceive for it, and begin to

love it too.   We should be sorry for their sakes if it was
destroyed, or even if it was placed at too great a distance
from them, and out of the reach of their care and protection,
though they should lose nothing by its absence except the
pleasure of seeing it.   If it is man who has thus been the
fortunate instrument of the happiness of his brethren, this
is still more peculiarly the case.   When we see one man
assisted, protected, relieved, by another, our sympathy with
the joy of the person who receives the benefit serves only
to animate our fellow-feeling with his gratitude towards
him who bestows it.   When we look upon the person who
is the cause of his pleasure with the eyes with which we
imagine he must look upon him, his benefactor seems to
stand before us in the most engaging and amiable light.
We readily, therefore, sympathize with the grateful affection
which he conceives for a person to whom he has been so
much obliged; and consequently applaud the returns which
he is disposed to make for the good offices conferred upon
him.   As we entirely enter into the affection from which
these returns proceed, they necessarily seem every way proper and suitable to their object.

2. In the same manner, as we sympathize with the sorrow of our fellow-creature whenever we see his distress,
so we likewise enter into his abhorrence and aversion for
whatever has given occasion to it.   Our heart, as it adopts
and beats time to his grief, so is it likewise animated with
that spirit by which he endeavours to drive away or destroy
the cause of it.   The indolent and passive fellow-feeling
by which we accompany him in his sufferings, readily gives
way to that more vigorous and active sentiment by which
we go along with him in the effort he makes, either to repel them, or to gratify his aversion to what has given occasion to them.   This is still more peculiarly the case, when
it is man who has caused them.   When we see one man
oppressed or injured by another, the sympathy which we
feel with the distress of the sufferer seems to serve only to

animate our fellow-feeling with his resentment against the offender. We are rejoiced to see him attack his adversary in his turn, and are eager and ready to assist him whenever he exerts himself for defence, or even for vengeance, within a certain degree. If the injured should perish in the quarrel, we not only sympathize with the real resentment of his friends and relations, but with the imaginary resentment which in fancy we lend to the dead, who is no longer capable of feeling or any other human sentiment. But as we put ourselves in his situation, as we enter, as it were, into his body, and in our imaginations, in some measure, animate anew the deformed and mangled carcase of the slain, when we bring home in this manner his case to our own bosoms, we feel, upon this, as upon many other occasions, an emotion which the person principally concerned is incapable of feeling, and which yet we feel by an illusive sympathy with him. The sympathetic tears which we shed for that immense and irretrievable loss, which in our fancy he appears to have sustained, seem to be but a small part of the duty which we owe him. The injury which he has suffered demands, we think, a principal part of our attention. We feel that resentment which we imagine he ought to feel, and which he would feel if in his cold and lifeless body there remained any consciousness of what passes upon earth. His blood, we think, calls aloud for vengeance. The very ashes of the dead seem to be disturbed at the thought that his injuries are to pass unrevenged. The horrors which are supposed to haunt the bed of the murderer, the ghosts which, superstition imagines, rise from their graves to demand vengeance upon those who brought them to an untimely end, all take their origin from this natural sympathy with the imaginary resentment of the slain. And with regard, at least, to this most dreadful of all crimes, nature, antecedent to all reflections upon the utility of punishment, has in this manner stamped upon the human heart, in the strongest and most indelible characters, an immediate and instinctive approbation of the sacred and necessary law of retaliation.

CHAPTER III.

That where there is no approbation of the conduct of the person who confers the benefit, there is little sympathy with the gratitude of him who receives it: and that, on the contrary, where there is no disapprobation of the motives of the person who does the mischief, there is no sort of sympathy with the resentment of him who suffers it.

It is to be observed, however, that, how beneficial soever on the one hand, or how hurtful soever on the other, the actions or intentions of the person who acts may have been to the person who is, if I may say so, acted upon, yet if in the one case there appears to have been no propriety in the motives of the agent, if we cannot enter into the affections which influenced his conduct, we have little sympathy with the gratitude of the person who receives the benefit : or if, in the other case, there appears to have been no impropriety in the motives of the agent, if, on the contrary, the affections which influenced his conduct are such as we must necessarily enter into, we can have no sort of sympathy with the resentment of the person who suffers. Little gratitude seems due in the one case, and all sort of resentment seems unjust in the other. The one action seems to merit little reward, the other to deserve no punishment.

1. First, I say, that wherever we cannot sympathize with the affections of the agent, wherever there seems to be no propriety in the motives which influenced his conduct, we are less disposed to enter into the gratitude of the person who received the benefit of his actions. A very small return seems due to that foolish and profuse generosity which confers the greatest benefits from the most trivial motives, and gives an estate to a man merely because his name and sirname happen to be the same with those of the giver.

Such services do not seem to demand any propoitionable recompence. Our contempt for the folly of the agent hinders us from thoroughly entering into the gratitude of the person to whom the good office has been done. His benefactor seems unworthy of it. As when we place ourselves in the situation of the person obliged, we feel that we could conceive no great reverence for such a benefactor, we easily absolve him ·from a great deal of that submissive veneration and esteem which we should think due to a more respectable character; and provided he always treats his weak friend with kindness and humanity, we are willing to excuse him from many attentions and regards which we should demand to a worthier patron. Those princes who have heaped, with the greatest profusion, wealth, power, and honours, upon their favourites, have seldom excited that degree of attachment to their persons which has often been experienced by those who were more frugal of their favours. The well-natured, but injudicious, prodigality of James I. of Great Britain seems to have attached nobody to his person; and that prince, notwithstanding his social and harmless disposition, appears to have lived and died without a friend. The whole gentry and nobility of England exposed their lives and fortunes in the cause of his more frugal and distinguishing son, notwithstanding the coldness and distant severity of his ordinary deportment.

2. Secondly, I say, that wherever the conduct of the agent appears to have been entirely directed by motives and affections which we thoroughly enter into and approve of, we can have no sort of sympathy with the resentment of the sufferer, how great soever the mischief which may have been done to him. When two people quarrel, if we take part with, and entirely adopt, the resentment of one of them, it is impossible that we should enter into that of the other. Our sympathy with the person whose motives we go along with, and whom, therefore, we look upon as in the right,

cannot but harden us against all fellow-feeling with the other, whom we necessarily regard as in the wrong. Whatever this last, therefore, may have suffered, while it is no more than what we ourselves should have wished him to suffer, while it is no more than what our own sympathetic indignation would have prompted us to inflict upon him, it cannot either displease or provoke us. When an inhuman murderer is brought to the scaffold, though we have some compassion for his misery, we can have no sort of fellow-feeling with his resentment, if he should be so absurd as to express any against either his prosecutor or his judge. The natural tendency of their just indignation against so vile a criminal is indeed the most fatal and ruinous to him. But it is impossible that we should be displeased with the tendency of a sentiment, which, when we bring the case home to ourselves, we feel that we cannot avoid adopting.

CHAPTER IV.

Recapitulation of the foregoing Chapters.

1. WE do not, therefore, thoroughly and heartily sympathize with the gratitude of one man towards another, merely because this other has been the cause of his good fortune, unless he has been the cause of it from motives which we entirely go along with. Our heart must adopt the principles of the agent, and go along with all the affections which influenced his conduct, before it can entirely sympathize with, and beat time to, the gratitude of the person who has been benefited by his actions. If in the conduct of the benefactor there appears to have been no propriety, how beneficial soever its effects, it does not seem to demand, or necessarily to require, any proportionable recompence.

But when to the beneficent tendency of the action is joined the propriety of the affection from which it proceeds, when we entirely sympathize and go along with the motives of the agent, the love which we conceive for him upon his own account, enhances and enlivens our fellow-feeling with the gratitude of those who owe their prosperity to his good conduct. His actions seem then to demand, and, if I may say so, to call aloud for a proportionable recompence. We then entirely enter into that gratitude which prompts to bestow it. The benefactor seems then to be the proper object of reward, when we thus entirely sympathize with, and approve of, that sentiment which prompts to reward him. When we approve of, and go along with, the affection from which the action proceeds, we must necessarily approve of the action, and regard the person towards whom it is directed as its proper and suitable object.

2. In the same manner we cannot at all sympathize with the resentment of one man against another, merely because this other has been the cause of his misfortune, unless he has been the cause of it from motives which we cannot enter into. Before we can adopt the resentment of the sufferer, we must disapprove of the motives of the agent, and feel that our heart renounces all sympathy with the affections which influenced his conduct. If there appears to have been no impropriety in these, how fatal soever the tendency of the action which proceeds from them to those against whom it is directed, it does not seem to deserve any punishment, or to be the proper object of any resentment.

But when to the hurtfulness of the action is joined the impropriety of the affection from whence it proceeds, when our heart rejects with abhorrence all fellow-feeling with the motives of the agent, we then heartily and entirely sympathize with the resentment of the sufferer. Such actions seem then to deserve, and, if I may say so, to call aloud for, a proportionable punishment; and we entirely enter into, and thereby approve of, that resentment which prompts to inflict it. The offender necessarily seems then to be the proper object of punishment, when we thus entirely sympathize with, and thereby approve of, that sentiment which prompts to punish. In this case too, when we approve, and go along with, the affection from which the action proceeds, we must necessarily approve of the action, and regard the person against whom it is directed, as its proper and suitable object.

CHAPTER V.

The Analysis of the Sense of Merit and Demerit.

1. As our sense, therefore, of the propriety of conduct arises from what I shall call a direct sympathy with the affections and motives of the person who acts, so our sense of its merit arises from what I shall call an indirect sympathy with the gratitude of the person who is, if I may say so, acted upon.

As we cannot indeed enter thoroughly into the gratitude of the person who receives the benefit, unless we beforehand approve of the motives of the benefactor, so, upon this account, the sense of merit seems to be a compounded sentiment, and to be made up of two distinct emotions ; a direct sympathy with the sentiments of the agent, and an indirect sympathy with the gratitude of those who receive the benefit of his actions.

We may, upon many different occasions, plainly distinguish those two different emotions combining and uniting together in our sense of the good desert of a particular character or action. When we read in history concerning actions of proper and beneficent greatness of mind, how eagerly do we enter into such designs ? How much are we animated by that high-spirited generosity which directs them ? How keen are we for their success ? How grieved at their disappointment? In imagination we become the very person whose actions are represented to us : we transport ourselves in fancy to the scenes of those distant and forgotten adventures, and imagine ourselves acting the part of a Scipio or a Camillus, a Timoleon or an Aristides. So far our sentiments are founded upon the direct sympathy with the person

who acts. Nor is the indirect sympathy with those who receive the benefit of such actions less sensibly felt.   Whenever we place ourselves in the situation of these last, with
what warm and affectionate fellow-feeling do we enter into
their gratitude towards those who served them so essentially ?   We embrace, as it were, their benefactor along
with them.   Our heart readily sympathizes with the highest
transports of their grateful affection.   No honours, no rewards, we think, can be too great for them to bestow upon
him.   When they make this proper return for his services,
we heartily applaud and go along with them ; but are shocked beyond all measure, if by their conduct they appear to
have little sense of the obligations conferred upon them.
Our whole sense, in short, of the merit and good desert of
such actions, of the propriety and fitness of recompensing
them, and making the person who performed them rejoice
in his turn, arises from the sympathetic emotions of gratitude and love, with which, when we bring home to our own
breast the situation of those principally concerned, we feel
ourselves naturally transported towards the man who could
act with such proper and noble beneficence.

2. In the same manner as our sense of the impropriety
of conduct arises from a want of sympathy, or from a direct antipathy to the affections and motives of the agent,
so our sense of its demerit arises from what I shall here
too call an indirect sympathy with the resentment of the
sufferer.

As we cannot indeed enter into the resentment of the
sufferer, unless our heart beforehand disapproves the motives of the agent, and renounces all fellow-feeling with
them ; so upon this account the sense of demerit, as well
as that of merit, seems to be a compounded sentiment, and
to be made up of two distinct emotions ; a direct antipathy

to the sentiments of the agent, and an indirect sympathy with the resentment of the sufferer.

We may here too, upon many different occasions, plainly distinguish those two different emotions combining and uniting together in our sense of the ill-desert of a particular character or action. When we read in history concerning the perfidy and cruelty of a Borgia or a Nero, our heart rises up against the detestable sentiments which influenced their conduct, and renounces with horror and abomination all fellow-feeling with such execrable motives. So far our sentiments are founded upon the direct antipathy to the affections of the agent: and the indirect sympathy with the resentment of the sufferers is still more sensibly felt. When we bring home to ourselves the situation of the persons whom those scourges of mankind insulted, murdered, or betrayed, what indignation do we not feel against such insolent and inhuman oppressors of the earth? Our sympathy with the unavoidable distress of the innocent sufferers is not more real nor more lively, than our fellow-feeling with their just and natural resentment. The former sentiment only heightens the latter, and the idea of their distress serves only to inflame and blow up our animosity against those who occasioned it. When we think of the anguish of the sufferers, we take part with them more earnestly against their oppressors; we enter with more eagerness into all their schemes of vengeance, and feel ourselves every moment wreaking, in imagination, upon such violators of the laws of society, that punishment which our sympathetic indignation tells us is due to their crimes. Our sense of the horror and dreadful atrocity of such conduct, the delight which we take in hearing that it was properly punished, the indignation which we feel when it escapes this due retaliation, our whole sense and feeling, in short, of its ill desert, of the propriety and fitness of inflicting evil upon the person who is guilty of it, and of making him grieve in his turn, arises from the sympathetic indignation which naturally boils up in the breast of the spectator, whenever he thoroughly brings home to himself the case of the sufferer.*

* To ascribe in this manner our natural sense of the ill desert of human actions to a sympathy with the resentment of the sufferer, may seem, to the greater part of people, to be a degradation of that sentiment. Resentment is commonly regarded as so odious a passion, that they will be apt to think it impossible that so laudable a principle, as the sense of the ill desert of vice, should in any respect be founded upon it. They will be more willing, perhaps, to admit that our sense of the merit of good actions is founded upon a sympathy with the gratitude of the persons who receive the benefit of them; because gratitude, as well as all the other benevolent passions, is regarded as an amiable principle, which can take nothing from the worth of whatever is founded upon it. Gratitude and resentment, however, are, in every respect, it is evident, counterparts to one another; and if our sense of merit arises from a sympathy with the one, our sense of demerit can scarce miss to proceed from a fellow-feeling with the other.

Let it be considered, too, that resentment, though, in the degrees in which we too often see it, the most odious, perhaps, of all the passions, is not disapproved of when properly humbled, and entirely brought down to the level of the sympathetic indignation of the spectator. When we, who are the bystanders, feel that our own animosity entirely corresponds with that of the sufferer; when the resentment of this last does not in any respect go beyond our own; when no word, no gesture, escapes him that denotes an emotion more violent than what we can keep time to, and when he never aims at inflicting any punishment beyond what we should rejoice to see inflicted, or what we ourselves would upon this account, even desire to be the instruments of inflicting, it is impossible that we should not entirely approve of his sentiments. Our own emotion in this case must, in our eyes, undoubtedly justify his. And as experience teaches us how much the greater part of mankind are incapable of this moderation, and how great an effort must be made in order to bring down the rude and undisciplined impulse of resentment to this suitable temper, we cannot avoid conceiving a considerable degree of esteem and admiration for one who appears capable of exerting so much self-command over one of the most ungovernable passions of his nature. When indeed the animosity of the sufferer exceeds, as it almost always does, what we can go along with, as we cannot enter into it, we necessarily disapprove of it. We even disapprove of it more than we should of an equal excess of almost any other passion derived from the imagination. And this too violent resentment, instead of carrying us along with it, becomes itself the object of our resentment and indignation. We enter into the opposite resentment of the person who is the object of this unjust emotion, and who is in danger of suffering from it. Revenge, therefore, the excess of resentment, appears to be the most detestable of all the passions, and is the object of the horror and indignation of every body. And as in the way in which this passion commonly discovers itself among mankind, it is excessive a hundred times for once that it is moderate, we are very apt to consider it as altogether odious and detestable, because in its most ordinary appearances it is so. Nature, however, even in the present depraved state of mankind, does not seem to have dealt so unkindly with us, as to have endowed us with any principle which is wholly and in every respect evil, or which, in no degree and in no direction, can be the proper object of praise and approbation. Upon some occasions we are sensible that this passion, which is generally too strong, may likewise be too weak. We sometimes complain that a particular person shews too little spirit, and has too little sense of the injuries that have been done to him ; and we are as ready to despise him for the defect, as to hate him for the excess of this passion.

The inspired writers would not surely have talked so frequently or so strongly of the wrath and anger of God, if they had regarded every degree of those passions as vicious and evil, even in so weak and imperfect a creature as man.

Let it be considered, too, that the present inquiry is not concerning a matter of right, if I may say so, but concerning a matter of fact. We are not at present examining upon what principles a perfect being would approve of the punishment of bad actions ; but upon what principles so weak and imperfect a creature as man actually and in fact approves of it. The principles which I have just now mentioned, it is evident, have a very great effect upon his sentiments ; and it seems wisely ordered that it should be so. The very existence of society requires that unmerited and unprovoked malice should be restrained by proper punishments ; and, consequently, that to inflict those punishments should be regarded as a proper and laudable action. Though man, therefore, be naturally endowed with a desire of the welfare and preservation of society, yet the Author of nature has not entrusted it to his reason to find out that a certain application of punishments is the proper means of attaining this end ; but has endowed him with an immediate and instinctive approbation of that very application which is most proper to attain it. The economy of nature is in this respect exactly of a piece with what it is upon many other occasions. With regard to all those ends which, upon account of their peculiar importance, may be regarded, if such an expression is allowable, as the favourite ends of nature, she has constantly in this manner not only endowed mankind with an appetite for the end which she proposes, but likewise with an appetite for the means by which alone this end can be brought about, for their own sakes, and independent of their tendency to produce it. Thus self-preservation, and the propagation of the species, are the great ends which nature seems to have proposed in the formation of all animals. Mankind are endowed with a desire of those ends, and an aversion to the contrary ; with a love of life, and a dread of dissolution ; with a desire of the continuance and perpetuity of the species, and with an aversion to the thoughts of its entire extinction. But though we are in this manner endowed with a very strong desire of those ends, it has not been entrusted to the slow and un certain determinations of our reason, to find out the proper means of bringing them about. Nature has directed us to the greater part of these by original and immediate instincts. Hunger, thirst, the passion which unites the two sexes, the love of pleasure, and the dread of pain, prompt us to apply those means for their own sakes, and without any consideration of their tendency to those beneficent ends which the great Director of nature intended to produce by them.

Before I conclude this note, I must take notice of a difference between the approbation of propriety and that of merit or beneficence. Before we approve of the sentiments of any person as proper and suitable to their objects, we must not only be affected in the same manner as he is, but we must perceive this harmony and correspondence of sentiments between him and ourselves. Thus, though upon hearing of ·a misfortune that had befallen my friend, I should conceive precisely that degree of concern which he gives way to ; yet till I am informed of the manner in which he behaves, till I perceive the harmony between his emotions and mine, I cannot be said to approve of the sentiments which influence his behaviour. The approbation of propriety therefore requires, not only that we should entirely sympathize with the person who acts, but that we should perceive this perfect concord between his sentiments and our own. On the contrary, when I hear of a benefit that has been bestowed upon another person, let him who has received it be affected in what manner he pleases, if, by bringing his case home to myself, I feel gratitude arise in my own breast, I necessarily approve of the conduct of his benefactor, and regard it as meritorious, and the proper object of reward. Whether the person who has received the benefit conceives gratitude or not, cannot, it is evident, in any degree alter our sentiments with regard to the merit of him who has bestowed it. No actual correspondence of sentiments, therefore, is here required. It is sufficient that, if he was grateful, they would correspond ; and our sense of merit is often founded upon one of those illusive sympathies, by which, when we bring home to ourselves the case of another, we are often affected in a manner in which the person principally concerned is incapable of being affected.   There is a similar difference between our disapprobation of demerit and that of impropriety.

SECTION II.

OF JUSTICE AND BENEFICENCE.

CHAPTER I.

Comparison of those two Virtues.

ACTIONS of a beneficent tendency, which proceed from proper motives, seem alone to require a reward; because such alone are the approved objects of gratitude, or excite the sympathetic gratitude of the spectator.

Actions of a hurtful tendency, which proceed from improper motives, seem alone to deserve punishment; because such alone are the approved objects of resentment, or excite the sympathetic resentment of the spectator.

Beneficence is always free, it cannot be extorted by force, the mere want of it exposes to no punishment; because the mere want of beneficence tends to do no real positive evil. It may disappoint of the good which might reasonably have been expected, and upon that account it may justly excite dislike and disapprobation: it cannot, however, provoke any resentment which mankind will go along with. The man who does not recompense his benefactor, when he has it in his power, and when his benefactor needs his assistance, is, no doubt, guilty of the blackest ingratitude. The heart of every impartial spectator rejects all fellow-feeling with the selfishness of his motives, and he is the proper object of the highest disapprobation. But still he does no positive hurt to any body. He only does not do that good which in propriety he ought to have done. He is the object of hatred, a passion which is naturally excited by impropriety of sentiment and behaviour; not of resentment, a passion which is never properly called forth but by actions which tend to do real and positive hurt to some particular persons. His want of gratitude, therefore, cannot be punished. To oblige him by force to perform what in gratitude he ought to perform, and what every impartial spectator would approve of him for performing, would, if possible, be still more improper than his neglecting to perform it. His benefactor would dishonour himself if he attempted by violence to constrain him to gratitude, and it would be impertinent for any third person, who was not the superior of either, to intermeddle. But of all the duties of beneficence, those which gratitude recommends to us approach nearest to what is called a perfect and complete obligation. What friendship, what generosity, what charity, would prompt us to do with universal approbation, is still more free, and can still less be extorted by force than the duties of gratitude. We talk of the debt of gratitude, not of charity, or generosity, nor even of friendship, when friendship is mere esteem, and has not been enhanced and complicated with gratitude for good offices.

Resentment seems to have been given us by nature for defence, and for defence only. It is the safeguard of justice and the security of innocence. It prompts us to beat off the mischief which is attempted to be done to us, and to retaliate that which is already done, that the offender may be made to repent of his injustice, and that others, through fear of the like punishment, may be terrified from being guilty of the like offence. It must be reserved, therefore, for these purposes, nor can the spectator ever go along with it when it is exerted for any other. But the mere want of the beneficent virtues, though it may disappoint us of the good which might reasonably be expected, neither does, nor attempts to do, any mischief from which we can have occasion to defend ourselves.

There is, however, another virtue, of which the observance is not left to the freedom of our own wills, which may be extorted by force, and of which the violation exposes to resentment, and consequently to punishment. This virtue is justice : the violation of justice is injury : it does real and positive hurt to some particular persons, from motives which are naturally disapproved of. It is, therefore, the proper object of resentment, and of punishment, which is the natural consequence of resentment. As mankind go along with, and approve of, the violence employed to avenge the hurt which is done by injustice, so they much more go along with, and approve of, that which is employed to prevent and beat off the injury, and to restrain the offender from hurting his neighbours. The person himself who meditates an injustice is sensible of this, and feels that force may, with the utmost propriety, be made use of, both by the person whom he is about to injure, and by others, either to obstruct the execution of his crime, or to punish him when he has executed it. And upon this is founded that remarkable distinction between justice and all the other social virtues, which has of late been particularly insisted upon by an author of very great and original genius, that we feel ourselves to be under a stricter obligation to act according to justice, than agreeably to friendship, charity, or generosity; that the practice of these last-mentioned virtues seems to be left in some measure to our own choice, but that, somehow or other, we feel ourselves to be in a peculiar manner tied, bound, and obliged, to the observation of justice. We feel, that is to say, that force may, with the utmost propriety, and with the approbation of all mankind, be made use of to constrain us to observe the rules of the one, but not to follow the precepts of the other.

We must always, however, carefully distinguish what is only blameable, or the proper object of disapprobation, from what force may be employed either to punish or to prevent. That seems blameable which falls short of that ordinary degree of proper beneficence which experience teaches us to expect of every body ; and, on the contrary, that seems praiseworthy which goes beyond it. The ordinary degree itself seems neither blameable nor praiseworthy. A father, a son, a brother, who behaves to the corre spondent relation neither better nor worse than the greater part of men commonly do, seems properly to deserve neither praise nor blame. He who surprises us by extraordinary and unexpected, though still proper and suitable, kindness, or, on the contrary, by extraordinary and unexpected, as well as unsuitable, unkindness, seems praiseworthy in the one case, and blameable in the other.

Even the most ordinary degree of kindness or beneficence, however, cannot, among equals, be extorted by force. Among equals each individual is naturally, and antecedent to the institution of civil government, regarded as having a right both to defend himself from injuries, and to exact a certain degree of punishment for those which have been done to him. Every generous spectator not only approves of his conduct when he does this, but enters so far into his sentiments as often to be willing to assist him. When one man attacks, or robs, or attempts to murder, another, all the neighbours take the alarm, and think that they do right when they run, either to revenge the person who has been injured, or to defend him who is in danger of being so. But when a father fails in the ordinary degree of parental affection towards a son ; when a son seems to want that filial reverence which might be expected to his father; when brothers are without the usual degree of brotherly affection; when a man shuts his breast against compassion, and re- fuses to relieve the misery of his fellow-creatures, when he can with the greatest ease ; in all these cases, though every body blames the conduct, nobody imagines that those who might have reason, perhaps, to expect more kindness, have any right to extort it by force.   The sufferer can only complain, and the spectator can intermeddle no other way than by advice and persuasion.   Upon all such occasions, for equals to use force against one another, would be thought the highest degree of insolence and presumption.

A superior may, indeed, sometimes, with universal approbation, oblige those under his jurisdiction to behave, in this respect, with a certain degree of propriety to one another.   The laws of all civilized nations oblige parents to maintain their children, and children to maintain their parents, and impose upon men many other duties of beneficence.   The civil magistrate is entrusted with the power not only of preserving the public peace by restraining injustice, but of promoting the prosperity of the commonwealth, by establishing good discipline, and by discouraging every sort of vice and impropriety ; he may prescribe rules, therefore, which not only prohibit mutual injuries among fellow-citizens, but command mutual good offices to a certain degree.   When the sovereign commands what is merely indifferent, and what, antecedent to his orders, might have been omitted without any blame, it becomes not only blameable but punishable to disobey him.   When he commands, therefore, what, antecedent to any such order, could not have been omitted without the greatest blame, it surely becomes much more punishable to be wanting in obedience.   Of all the duties of a lawgiver, however, this, perhaps, is that which it requires the greatest delicacy and reserve to execute with propriety and judgment.   To neglect it altogether exposes the commonwealth to many gross disorders and shocking enormities, and to push it too far is destructive of all liberty, security, and justice.

Though the mere want of beneficence seems to merit no punishment from equals, the greater exertions of that virtue appear to deserve the highest reward. By being productive of the greatest good, they are the natural and approved objects of the liveliest gratitude. Though the breach of justice, on the contrary, exposes to punishment, the observance of the rules of that virtue seems scarce to deserve any reward. There is, no doubt, a propriety in the practice. of justice, and it merits, upon that account, all the approbation which is due to propriety. But as it does no real positive good, it is entitled to very little gratitude. Mere justice is, upon most occasions, but a negative virtue, and only hinders us from hurting our neighbour. The man who barely abstains from violating either the person or the estate, or the reputation, of his neighbours, has surely very little positive merit. He fulfils, however, all the rules of what is peculiarly called justice, and does every thing which his equals can with propriety force him to do, or which they can punish him for not doing. We may often fulfil all the rules of justice by sitting still and doing nothing.

As every man doth, so it shall be done to him, and retaliation seems to be the great law which is dictated to us by nature. Beneficence and generosity we think due to the generous and beneficent. Those whose hearts never open to the feelings of humanity, should, we think, be shut out in the same manner, from the affections of all their fellow-creatures, and be allowed to live in the midst of society, as in a great desert, where there is nobody to care for them, or to enquire after them. The violator of the laws of justice ought to be made to feel himself that evil which he has done to another ; and since no regard to the sufferings of his brethren is capable of restraining him, he ought to be overawed by the fear of his own. The man who is barely innocent, who only observes the laws of justice with regard to others, and merely abstains from hurting his neighbours, can merit only that his neighbours in their turn should respect his innocence, and that the same laws should be religiously observed with regard to him.

CHAPTER II.

Of the sense of Justice, of Remorse, and of the consciousness of Merit.

THERE can be no proper motive for hurting our neigh-bour, there can be no incitement to do evil to another which mankind will go along with, except just indignation for evil which that other has done to us. To disturb his happiness merely because it stands in the way of our own, to take from him what is of real use to him merely because it may be of equal or of more use to us, or to indulge, in this manner, at the expense of other people, the natural prefer-ence which every man has for his own happiness above that of other people, is what no impartial spectator can go along with. Every man is, no doubt, by nature, first and princi-pally recommended to his own care; and as he is fitter to take care of himself, than of any other person, it is fit and right that it should be so. Every man, therefore, is much more deeply interested in whatever immediately concerns himself, than in what concerns any other man : and to hear, perhaps, of the death of another person, with whom we have no particular connection, will give us less concern, will spoil our stomach, or break our rest, much less than a very insignificant disaster which has befallen ourselves. But though the ruin of our neighbour may affect us much less than a very small misfortune of our own, we must not ruin him to prevent that small misfortune, nor even to prevent our own ruin. We must here, as in all other cases, view ourselves not so much according to that light in which we may naturally appear to ourselves, as according to that in which we naturally appear to others. Though every man may, according to the proverb, be the whole world to him-

self, to the rest of mankind he is a most insignificant part
of it. Though his own happiness may be of more importance
to him than that of all the world besides, to every other
person it is of no more consequence than that of any other
man. Though it may be true, therefore, that every individual, in his own breast, naturally prefers himself to all
mankind, yet he dares not look mankind in the face, and
avow that he acts according to this principle. He feels
that in this preference they can never go along with him,
and that how natural soever it may be to him, it must
always appear excessive and extravagant to them. When
he views himself in the light in which he is conscious that
others will view him, he sees that to them he is but one of
the multitude, in no respect better than any other in it. If
he would act so as that the impartial spectator may enter
into the principles of his conduct, which is what of all things
he has the greatest desire to do, he must upon this, as upon
all other occasions, humble the arrogance of his self-love,
and bring it down to something which other men can go
along with. They will indulge it so far as to allow him to
be more anxious about, and to pursue with more earnest
assiduity, his own happiness than that of any other person.
Thus far, whenever they place themselves in his situation,
they will readily go along with him. In the race for wealth,
and honours, and preferments, he may run as hard as he
can, and strain every nerve and every muscle, in order to
outstrip all his competitors. But if he should justle, or
throw down any of them, the indulgence of the spectators
is entirely at an end. It is a violation of fair play, which
they cannot admit of. This man is to them, in every respect, as good as he : they do not enter into that self-love,
by which he prefers himself so much to this other, and cannot go along with the motive from which he hurt him.
They readily, therefore, sympathize with the natural resentment of the injured, and the offender becomes the object of
their hatred and indignation. He is sensible that he be-

comes so, and feels that those sentiments are ready to burst out from all sides against him.

As the greater and more irreparable the evil that is done, the resentment of the sufferer runs naturally the higher : so does likewise the sympathetic indignation of the spectator, as well as the sense of guilt in the agent. Death is the greatest evil which one man can inflict upon another, and excites the highest degree of resentment in those who are immediately connected with the slain. Murder, therefore, is the most atrocious of all crimes which affect individuals only, in the sight both of mankind and of the person who has committed it. To be deprived of that which we are possessed of, is a greater evil than to be disappointed of what we have only the expectation. Breach of property, therefore, theft and robbery, which take from us what we are possessed of, are greater crimes than breach of contract, which only disappoints us of what we expected. The most sacred laws of justice, therefore, those whose violation seems to call loudest for vengeance and punishment, are the laws which guard the life and person of our neighbour ; the next are those which guard his property and possessions ; and last of all come those which guard what are called his personal rights, or what is due to him from the promises of others.

The violator of the more sacred laws of justice can never reflect on the sentiments which mankind must entertain with regard to him, without feeling all the agonies of shame, and horror, and consternation. When his passion is gratified, and he begins coolly to reflect on his past conduct, he can enter into none of the motives which influenced it. They appear now as detestable to him as they did always to other people. By sympathizing with the hatred and abhorrence which other men must entertain for him, he becomes in some measure the object of his own hatred and

abhorrence.   The situation of the person, who suffered by
his injustice, now calls upon his pity.   He is grieved at the
thought of it; regrets the unhappy effects of his own conduct, and feels at the same time that they have rendered
him the proper object of the resentment and indignation of
mankind, and of what is the natural consequence of resentment, vengeance and punishment.   The thought of this
perpetually haunts him, and fills him with terror and amazement.   He dares no longer look society in the face, but
imagines himself, as it were, rejected, and thrown out from
the affections of all mankind.   He cannot hope for the consolation of sympathy in this his greatest and most dreadful
distress.   The remembrance of his crimes has shut out all
fellow-feeling with him from the hearts of his fellow-creatures.   The sentiments which they entertain with regard to
him, are the very thing which he is most afraid of.   Every
thing seems hostile, and he would be glad to fly to some
inhospitable desert, where he might never more behold the
face of a human creature, nor read in the countenance of
mankind the condemnation of his crimes.   But solitude is
still more dreadful than society.   His own thoughts can
present him with nothing but what is black, unfortunate,
and disastrous, the melancholy forebodings of incomprehensible misery and ruin.   The horror of solitude drives
him back into society, and he comes again into the presence
of mankind, astonished to appear before them loaded with
shame and distracted with fear, in order to supplicate some
little protection from the countenance of those very judges,
who he knows have already all unanimously condemned
him.   Such is the nature of that sentiment, which is properly called remorse; of all the sentiments which can enter
the human breast the most dreadful.   It is made up of
shame from the sense of the impropriety of past conduct; of grief for the effects of it; of pity for those who
suffer by it; and of the dread and terror of punishment
from the consciousness of the justly-provoked resentment
of all rational creatures.

The opposite behaviour naturally inspires the opposite sentiment. The man who, not from frivolous fancy, but from proper motives, has performed a generous action, when he looks forward to those whom he has served, feels himself to be the natural object of their love and gratitude, and, by sympathy with them, of the esteem and approbation of all mankind. And when he looks backward to the motive from which he acted, and surveys it in the light in which the indifferent spectator will survey it, he still continues to enter into it, and applauds himself by sympathy with the approbation of this supposed impartial judge. In both these points of view, his own conduct appears to him every way agreeable. His mind, at the thought of it, is filled with cheerfulness, serenity, and composure. He is in friendship and harmony with all mankind, and looks upon his fellow-creatures with confidence, and benevolent satisfaction, secure that he has rendered himself worthy of their most favourable regards. In the combination of all these sentiments, consists the consciousness of merit, or of deserved reward.

CHAPTER III.

Of the utility of this constitution of Nature.

IT is thus that man, who can subsist only in society, was fitted by nature to that situation for which he was made. All the members of human society stand in need of each other's assistance, and are likewise exposed to mutual injuries. Where the necessary assistance is reciprocally afforded from love, from gratitude, from friendship, and esteem, the society flourishes and is happy. All the different members of it are bound together by the agreeable bands of love and affection, and are, as it were, drawn to one common centre of mutual good offices.

But though the necessary assistance should not be afforded from such generous and disinterested motives, though among the different members of the society there should be no mutual love and affection, the society, though less happy and agreeable, will not necessarily be dissolved. Society may subsist among different men, as among different merchants, from a sense of its utility, without any mutual love or affection; and though no man in it should owe any obligation, or be bound in gratitude to any other, it may still be upheld by a mercenary exchange of good offices according to an agreed valuation.

Society, however, cannot subsist among those who are at all times ready to hurt and injure one another. The moment that injury begins, the moment that mutual resentment and animosity take place, all the bands of it are broken asunder, and the different members of which it consisted, are, as it were, dissipated and scattered abroad by the violence and opposition of their discordant affections.   If there is any society among robbers and murderers, they must at least, according to the trite observation, abstain from robbing and murdering one another.   Beneficence, therefore, is less essential to the existence of society than justice: Society may subsist, though not in the most comfortable state, without beneficencé; but the prevalence of injustice must utterly destroy it.

Though nature, therefore, exhorts mankind to acts of beneficence, by the pleasing consciousness of deserved reward, she has not thought it necessary to guard and enforce the practice of it by the terrors of merited punishment in case it should be neglected.   It is the ornament which embellishes, not the fcundation which supports the building, and which it was, therefore, sufficient to recommend, but by no means necessary to impose.   Justice, on the contrary, is the main pillar that upholds the whole edifice.   If it is removed, the great, the immense fabric of human society, that fabric which, to raise and support, seems, in this world, if I may say so, to have been the peculiar and darling care of nature, must in a moment crumble into atoms. In order to enforce the observation of justice, therefore, nature has implanted in the human breast that consciousness of ill desert, those terrors of merited punishment, which attend upon its violation, as the great safeguards of the association of mankind, to protect the weak, to curb the violent, and to chastise the guilty.   Men, though naturally sympathetic, feel so little for an another, withwhom they have no particular connection, in comparison of what they feel for themselves; the misery of one, who is merely their fellow-creature, is of so little importance to them in comparison even of a small conveniency of their own ; they have it so much in their power to hurt him, and may have so many temptations to do so, that if this principle did not stand up within them in his defence, and overawe them into a respect for his innocence, they would, like wild beasts, be at all times ready to fly upon him; and a man would enter an assembly of men as he enters a den of lions.

In every part of the universe we observe means adjusted with the nicest artifice to the ends which they are intended to produce; and in the mechanism of a plant, or animal body, admire how every thing is contrived for advancing the two great purposes of nature, the support of the individual, and the propagation of the species. But in these, and in all such objects, we still distinguish the efficient from the final cause of their several motions and organizations. The digestion of the food, the circulation of the blood, and the secretion of the several juices which are drawn from it, are operations all of them necessary for the great purposes of animal life. Yet we never endeavour to account for them from those purposes as from their efficient causes, nor imagine that the blood circulates, or that the food digests of its own accord, and with a view or intention to the purposes of circulation or digestion. The wheels of the watch are all admirably adjusted to the end for which it was made, the pointing of the hour. All their various motions conspire in the nicest manner to produce this effect. If they were endowed with a desire and intention to produce it, they could not do it better. Yet we never ascribe any such desire or intention to them, but to the watch-maker and we know that they are put into motion by a spring, which intends the effect it produces as little as they do. But though, in accounting for the operations of bodies, we never fail to distinguish in this manner the efficient from the final cause, in accounting for those of the mind, we are very apt to confound these two different things with one another. When by natural principles we are led to advance those ends which a refined and enlightened reason would recommend to us, we are very apt to impute to that reason, as to their efficient cause, the sentiments and actions by which we advance those ends, and to imagine that to be the wisdom of man, which in reality is the wisdom of God. Upon a superficial view, this cause seems sufficient to produce the effects which are ascribed to it; and the system of human nature seems to be more simple and agreeable, when all its different operations are in this manner deduced from a single principle.

As society cannot subsist unless the laws of justice are tolerably observed, as no social intercourse can take place among men who do not generally abstain from injuring one another; the consideration of this necessity, it has been thought, was the ground upon which we approved of the enforcement of the laws of justice, by the punishment of those who violated them. Man, it has been said, has a natural love for society, and desires that the union of mankind should be preserved for its own sake, and though he himself was to derive no benefit from it. The orderly and flourishing state of society is agreeable to him, and he takes delight in contemplating it. Its disorder and confusion, on the contrary, is the object of his aversion, and he is chagrined at whatever tends to produce it. He is sensible, too, that his own interest is connected with the prosperity of society, and that the happiness, perhaps the preservation of his existence, depends upon its preservation. Upon every account, therefore, he has an abhorrence at whatever can tend to destroy society, and is willing to make use of every means, which can hinder so hated and so dreadful an event. Injustice necessarily tends to destroy it. Every appearance of injustice, therefore, alarms him, and he runs, if I may say so, to stop the progress of what, if allowed to go on, would quickly put an end to every thing that is dear to him. If he cannot restrain it by gentle and fair means, he must bear it down by force and violence, and at any rate must put a stop to its further progress. Hence it is, they say, that he often approves of the

enforcement of the laws of justice, even by the capital punishment of those who violate them. The disturber of the
public peace is hereby removed out of the world, and others
are terrified by his fate from imitating his example.

Such is the account commonly given of our approbation
of the punishment of injustice. And so far this account is
undoubtedly true, that we frequently have occasion to confirm our natural sense of the propriety and fitness of punishment, by reflecting how necessary it is for preserving the
order of society. When the guilty is about to suffer that
just retaliation, which the natural indignation of mankind
tells them is due to his crimes ; when the insolence of his
injustice is broken and humbled by the terror of his approaching punishment; when he ceases to be an object of
fear, with the generous and humane he begins to be an object of pity. The thought of what he is about to suffer extinguishes their resentment for the sufferings of others to
which he has given occasion. They are disposed to pardon and forgive him, and to save him from that punishment,
which in all their cool hours they had considered as the re-
tribution due to such crimes. Here, therefore, they have
occasion to call to their assistance the consideration of the
general interest of society. They counterbalance the impulse of this weak and partial humanity, by the dictates of
a humanity that is more generous and comprehensive.
They reflect that mercy to the guilty is cruelty to the innocent, and oppose to the emotions of compassion which they
feel for a particular person, a more enlarged compassion
which they feel for mankind.

Sometimes, too, we have occasion to defend the propriety
of observing the general rules of justice, by the consideration of their necessity to the support of society. We frequently hear the young and the licentious ridiculing the most
sacred rules of morality, and professing, sometimes from the

corruption, but more frequently from the vanity of their hearts, the most abominable maxims of conduct. Our indignation rouses, and we are eager to refute and expose such detestable principles. But though it is their intrinsic hatefulness and detestableness which originally inflames us against them, we are unwilling to assign this as the sole reason why we condemn them, or to pretend that it is merely because we ourselves hate and detest them. The reason, we think, would not appear to be conclusive. Yet, why should it not; if we hate and detest them because they are the natural and proper objects of hatred and detestation? But when we are asked why we should not act in such or such a manner, the very question seems to suppose that, to those who ask it, this manner of acting does not appear to be for its own sake the natural and proper object of those sentiments. We must shew them, therefore, that it ought to be so for the sake of something else. Upon this account we generally cast about for other arguments, and the consideration which first occurs to us, is the disorder and confusion of society which would result from the universal prevalence of such practices. We seldom fail, therefore, to insist upon this topic.

But though it commonly requires no great discernment to see the destructive tendency of all licentious practices to the welfare of society, it is seldom this consideration which first animates us against them. All men, even the most stupid and unthinking, abhor fraud, perfidy, and injustice, and delight to see them punished. But few men have reflected upon the necessity of justice to the existence of society, how obvious soever that necessity may appear to be.

That it is not a regard to the preservation of society, which originally interests us in the punishment of crimes committed against individuals, may be demonstrated by many obvious considerations. The concern which we take in the fortune and happiness of individuals, does not, in common cases, arise from that which we take in the fortune and happiness of society. We are no more concerned for the destruction or loss of a single man, because this man is a member or part of society, and because we should be concerned for the destruction of society, than we are concerned for the loss of a single guinea, because this guinea is part of a thousand guineas, and because we should be concerned for the loss of the whole sum. In neither case does our regard for the individuals arise from our regard for the multitude; but in both cases our regard for the multitude is compounded and made up of the particular regards which we feel for the different individuals of which it is composed. As when a small sum is unjustly taken from us, we do not so much prosecute the injury from a regard to the preservation of our whole fortune, as from a regard to that particular sum which we have lost; so when a single man is injured, or destroyed, we demand the punishment of the wrong that has been done to him, not so much from a concern for the general interest of society, as from a concern for that very individual who has been injured. It is to be observed, however, that this concern does not necessarily include in it any degree of those exquisite sentiments which are commonly called love, esteem, and affection, and by which we distinguish our particular friends and acquaintance. The concern which is requisite for this, is no more than the general fellow-feeling which we have with every man, merely because he is our fellow-creature. We enter into the resentment even of an odious person, when he is injured by those to whom he has given no provocation. Our disapprobation of his ordinary character and conduct does not in this case altogether prevent our fellow-feeling with his natural indignation; though with those who are not either extremely candid, or who have not been accustomed to correct and regulate their natural sentiments by general rules, it is very apt to damp it.

Upon some occasions, indeed, we both punish and approve of punishment, merely from a view to the general interest of society, which, we imagine, cannot otherwise be secured Of this kind are all the punishments inflicted for breaches of what is called either civil police, or military discipline. Such crimes do not immediately or directly hurt any particular person; but their remote consequences, it is supposed, do produce, or might produce, either a considerable inconveniency, or a great disorder in the society. A sentinel, for example, who falls asleep upon his watch, suffers death by the laws of war, because such carelessness might endanger the whole army. This severity may, upon many occasions, appear necessary, and, for that reason, just and proper. When the preservation of an individual is inconsistent with the safety of a multitude, nothing can be more just than that the many should be preferred to the one. Yet this punishment, how necessary soever, always appears to be excessively severe. The natural atrocity of the crime seems to be so little, and the punishment so great, that it is with great difficulty that our heart can reconcile itself to it. Though such carelessness appears very blameable, yet the thought of this crime does not naturally excite any such resentment, as would prompt us to take such dreadful revenge. A man of humanity must recollect himself, must make an effort, and exert his whole firmness and resolution, before he can bring himself either to inflict it, or to go along with it when it is inflicted by others. It is not, however, in this manner, that he looks upon the just punishment of an ungrateful murderer or parricide. His heart, in this case, applauds with ardour, and even with transport, the just retaliation which seems due to such detestable crimes, and which, if, by any accident, they should happen to escape, he would be highly enraged and disappointed. The very different sentiments with which the spectator views those different punishments, is a proof that his approbation of the one is far from being founded upon the same principles with

that of the other.   He looks upon the sentinel as an unfortunate victim, who, indeed, must and ought to be devoted
to the safety of numbers, but whom still, in his heart, he
would be glad to save ; and he is only sorry that the interest
of the many should oppose it.   But if the murderer should
escape from punishment, it would excite his highest indignation, and he would call upon God to avenge, in another
world, that crime which the injustice of mankind had
neglected to chastise upon earth.

For it well deserves to be taken notice of, that we are so
far from imagining that injustice ought to be punished in
this life, merely on account of the order of society, which
cannot otherwise be maintained, that nature teaches us to
hope, and religion, we suppose, authorizes us to expect, that
it will be punished even in a life to come.   Our sense of its
ill desert pursues it, if I may say so, even beyond the grave,
though the example of its punishment there cannot serve to
deter the rest of mankind, who see it not, who know it not,
from being guilty of the like practices here.   The justice of
God, however, we think, still requires, that he should hereafter avenge the injuries of the widow and the fatherless,
who are here so often insulted with impunity.   In every
religion, and in every superstition that the world has ever
beheld, accordingly, there has been a Tartarus as well as an
Elysium; a place provided for the punishment of the wicked,
as well as one for the reward of the just.

SECTION III.

OF THE INFLUENCE OF FORTUNE UPON THE SENTI-
MENTS OF MANKIND, WITH REGARD TO THE MERIT
OR DEMERIT OF ACTIONS.

INTRODUCTION.

WHATEVER praise or blame can be due to any action,
must belong, either, first, to the intention or affection of the
heart, from which it proceeds; or, secondly, to the external
action or movement of the body, which this affection gives
occasion to; or, lastly, to the good or bad consequences,
which actually, and in fact, proceed from it. These three
different things constitute the whole nature and circumstances of the action, and must be the foundation of whatever quality can belong to it.

That the two last of these three circumstances cannot be
the foundation of any praise or blame, is abundantly evident;
nor has the contrary ever been asserted by any body. The
external action or movement of the body is often the same
in the most innocent and in the most blameable actions.
He who shoots a bird, and he who shoots a man, both of
them perform the same external movement: each of them
draws the trigger of a gun. The consequences which actually, and in fact, happen to proceed from any action, are, if
possible, still more indifferent either to praise or blame, than
even the external movement of the body. As they depend,
not upon the agent, but upon fortune, they cannot be the

proper foundation for any sentiment, of which his character
and conduct are the objects.

The only consequences for which he can be answerable,
or by which he can deserve either approbation or disapprobation of any kind, are those which were some way or other
intended, or those which, at least, shew some agreeable or
disagreeable quality in the intention of the heart, from which
he acted. To the intention or affection of the heart, therefore, to the propriety or impropriety, to the beneficence or
hurtfulness of the design, all praise or blame, all approbation
or disapprobation of any kind, which can justly be bestowed
upon any action, must ultimately belong.

When this maxim is thus proposed, in abstract and general
terms, there is nobody who does not agree to it. Its self-evi-
dent justice is acknowledged by all the world, and there is not
a dissenting voice among all mankind. Every body allows,
that how different soever the accidental, the unintended, and
unforeseen consequences of different actions, yet, if the intentions or affections from which they arose were, on the one
hand, equally proper and equally beneficent, or, on the other,
equally improper and equally malevolent, the merit or demerit of the actions is still the same, and the agent is equally
the suitable object either of gratitude or of resentment.

But how well soever we may seem to be persuaded of the
truth of this equitable maxim, when we consider it after this
manner, in abstract, yet when we come to particular cases,
the actual consequences which happen to proceed from any
action, have a very great effect upon our sentiments concerning its merit or demerit, and almost always either enhance
or diminish our sense of both. Scarce, in any one instance,
perhaps, will our sentiments be found, after examination, to
be entirely regulated by this rule, which we all acknowledge ought entirely to regulate them.

This irregularity of sentiment, which every body feels, which scarce any body is sufficiently aware of, and which nobody is willing to acknowledge, I proceed now to explain; and I shall consider, first, the cause which gives occasion to it, or the mechanism by which nature produces it; secondly, the extent of its influence; and, last of all, the end which it answers, or the purpose which the Author of nature seems to have intended by it.

CHAPTER I.

Of the Causes of this influence of Fortune.

THE causes of pain and pleasure, whatever they are, or however they operate, seem to be the objects, which, in all animals, immediately excite those two passions of gratitude and resentment. They are excited by inanimated, as well as by animated objects. We are angry, for a moment, even at the stone that hurts us. A child beats it, a dog barks at it, a choleric man is apt to curse it. The least reflection, indeed, corrects this sentiment, and we soon become sensible, that what has no feeling is a very improper object of revenge. When the mischief, however, is very great, the object which caused it becomes disagreeable to us ever after, and we take pleasure to burn or destroy it. We should treat, in this manner, the instrument which had accidentally been the cause of the death of a friend, and we should often think ourselves guilty of a sort of inhumanity, if we neglected to vent this absurd sort of vengeance upon it.

We conceive, in the same manner, a sort of gratitude for those inanimated objects which have been the causes of great or frequent pleasure to us. The sailor, who, as soon as he got ashore, should mend his fire with the plank upon which he had just escaped from a shipwreck, would seem to be guilty of an unnatural action. We should expect that he would rather preserve it with care and affection, as a monument that was, in some measure, dear to him. A man grows fond of a snuff-box, of a pen-knife, of a staff which he has long made use of, and conceives something like a real love and affection for them. If he breaks or loses them, he is vexed out of all proportion to the value of the damage. The house which we have long lived in, the tree whose verdure and shade we have long enjoyed, are both looked upon with a sort of respect that seems due to such benefactors. The decay of the one, or the ruin of the other, affects us with a kind of melancholy, though we should sustain no loss by it. The dryads and the lares of the ancients, a sort of genii of trees and houses, were probably first suggested by this sort of affection which the authors of those superstitions felt for such objects, and which seemed unreasonable, if there was nothing animated about them.

But, before any thing can be the proper object of gratitude or resentment, it must not only be the cause of pleasure or pain; it must likewise be capable of feeling them. Without this other quality, those passions cannot vent themselves with any sort of satisfaction upon it. As they are excited by the causes of pleasure and pain, so their gratification consists in retaliating those sensations upon what gave occasion to them; which it is to no purpose to attempt upon what has no sensibility. Animals, therefore, are less improper objects of gratitude and resentment than inanimated objects. The dog that bites, the ox that gores, are both of them punished. If they have been the causes of the death of any person, neither the public, nor the relations of the slain, can be satisfied, unless they are put to death in their turn : nor is this merely for the security of the living, but, in some measure, to revenge the injury of the dead. Those animals, on the contrary, that have been remarkably serviceable to their masters, become the objects of a very lively gratitude. We are shocked at the brutality of that officer, mentioned in the Turkish Spy, who stabbed the horse that had carried him across an arm of the sea, lest that animal should afterwards distinguish some other person by a similar adventure.

But, though animals are not only the causes of pleasure and pain, but are also capable of feeling those sensations they are still far from being complete and perfect objects either of gratitude or resentment; and those passions still feel, that there is something wanting to their entire gratification. What gratitude chiefly desires, is not only to make the benefactor feel pleasure in his turn, but to make him conscious that he meets with this reward on account of his past conduct, to make him pleased with that conduct, and to satisfy him that the person upon whom he bestowed his good offices was not unworthy of them. What most of all charms us in our benefactor, is the concord between his sentiments and our own, with regard to what interests us so nearly as the worth of our own character, and the esteem that is due to us. We are delighted to find a person who values us as we value ourselves, and distinguishes us from the rest of mankind, with an attention not unlike that with which we distinguish ourselves. To maintain in him these agreeable and flattering sentiments, is one of the chief ends proposed by the returns we are disposed to make to him. A generous mind often disdains the interested thought of extorting new favours from its benefactor, by what may be called the importunities of its gratitude. But to preserve and to increase his esteem, is an interest which the greatest mind does not think unworthy of its attention. And this is the foundation of what I formerly observed, that when we cannot enter into the motives of our benefactor, when his conduct and character appear unworthy of our approbation, let his services have been ever so great, our gratitude is always sensibly diminished. We are less flattered by the distinction; and to preserve the esteem of so weak, or so worthless a patron, seems to be an object which does not deserve to be pursued for its own sake.

The object, on the contrary, which resentment is chiefly intent upon, is not so much to make our enemy feel pain in his turn, as to make him conscious that he feels it upon account of his past conduct, to make him repent of that conduct, and to make him sensible, that the person whom he injured did not deserve to be treated in that manner. What chiefly enrages us against the man who injures or insults us, is the little account which he seems to make of us, the unreasonable preference which he gives to himself above us, and that absurd self-love, by which he seems to imagine, that other people may be sacrificed at any time, to his conveniency or his humour. The glaring impropriety of this conduct, the gross insolence and injustice which it seems to involve in it, often shock and exasperate us more than all the mischief which we have suffered. To bring him back to a more just sense of what is due to other people, to make him sensible of what he owes us, and of the wrong that he has done to us, is frequently the principal end proposed in our revenge, which is always imperfect when it cannot accomplish this. When our enemy appears to have done us no injury, when we are sensible that he acted quite properly, that, in his situation, we should have done the same thing, and that we deserved from him all the mischief we met with ; in that case, if we have the least spark either of candour or justice, we can entertain no sort of resentment.

Before any thing, therefore, can be the complete and proper object, either of gratitude or resentment, it must possess three different qualifications. First, it must be the cause of pleasure in the one case, and of pain in the other. Secondly, it must be capable of feeling those sensations. And, thirdly, it must not only have produced those sensations, but it must have produced them from design, and from a design that is approved of in the one case, and disapproved of in the other. It is by the first qualification that any object is capable of exciting those passions : it is by the second, that it is in any respect capable of gratifying them : the third qualification is not only necessary for their complete satisfaction, but, as it gives a pleasure or pain that is both exquisite and peculiar, it is likewise an additional exciting cause of those passions.

As what gives pleasure or pain, therefore, either in one way or another, is the sole exciting cause of gratitude and resentment; though the intentions of any person should be ever so proper and beneficent, on the one hand, or ever so improper and malevolent on the other; yet, if he has failed in producing either the good or the evil which he intended, as one of the exciting causes is wanting in both cases, less gratitude seems due to him in the one, and less resentment in the other. And, on the contrary, though in the intentions of any person, there was either no laudable degree of benevolence on the one hand, or no blameable degree of malice on the other; yet, if his actions should produce either great good or great evil, as one of the exciting causes takes place upon both these occasions, some gratitude is apt to arise towards him in the one, and some resentment in the other. A shadow of merit seems to fall upon him in the first, a shadow of demerit in the second. And, as the consequences of actions are altogether under the empire of fortune, hence arises her influence upon the sentiments of mankind with regard to merit and demerit.

CHAPTER II.

Of the Extent of this influence of Fortune.

THE effect of this influence of fortune, is, first, to diminish our sense of the merit or demerit of those actions which
arose from the most laudable or blameable intentions, when
they fail of producing their proposed effects : and, secondly,
to increase our sense of the merit or demerit of actions,
beyond what is due to the motives or affections from which
they proceed, when they accidentally give occasion either
to extraordinary pleasure or pain.

1. First, I say, though the intentions of any person should
be ever so proper and beneficent on the one hand, or ever
so improper or malevolent on the other, yet, if they fail
in producing their effects, his merit seems imperfect in the
one case, and his demerit imcomplete in the other.   Nor is
this irregularity of sentiment felt only by those who are
immediately affected by the consequences of any action.
It is felt, in some measure, even by the impartial spectator.
The man who solicits an office for another, without obtaining it, is regarded as his friend, and seems to deserve his
love and affection.   But the man who not only solicits, but
procures it, is more preculiarly considered as his patron and
benefactor, and is entitled to his respect and gratitude.
The person obliged, we are apt to think, may with some
justice, imagine himself on a level with the first : but we
cannot enter into his sentiments, if he does not feel himself
inferior to the second.   It is common indeed to say, that
we are equally obliged to the man who has endeavoured to
serve us, as to him who actually did so.   It is the speech
which we constantly make upon every unsuccessful attempt

of this kind; but which, like all other fine speeches, must
be understood with a grain of allowance. The sentiments
which a man of generosity entertains for the friend who
fails, may often indeed be nearly the same with those which
he conceives for him who succeeds : and the more generous
he is, the more nearly will those sentiments approach to an
exact level. With the truly generous, to be beloved, to be
esteemed by those whom they themselves think worthy of
esteem, gives more pleasure, and thereby excites more gratitude, than all the advantages which they can ever expect
from those sentiments. When they lose those advantages,
therefore, they seem to lose but a trifle, which is scarce worth
regarding. They still, however, lose something. Their pleasure, therefore, and consequently their gratitude, is not perfectly complete : and accordingly, if between the friend who
fails, and the friend who succeeds, all other circumstances are
equal, there will, even in the noblest and best mind, be some
little difference of affection in favour of him who succeeds.
Nay, so unjust are mankind in this respect, that though the intended benefit should be procured, yet if it is not procured
by the means of a particular benefactor, they are apt to
think that less gratitude is due to the man, who with the
best intentions in the world could do no more than help it
a little forward. As their gratitude is in this case divided
among the different persons who contributed to their pleasure, a smaller share of it seems due to any one. Such a
person, we hear men commonly say, intended no doubt to
serve us ; and we really believe exerted himself to the utmost of his abilities for that purpose. We are not, however, obliged to him for this benefit; since, had it not been
for the concurrence of others, all that he could have done
would never have brought it about. This consideration,
they imagine, should even in the eyes of the impartial spectator diminish the debt which they owe to him. The person
himself who has unsuccessfully endeavoured to confer a
benefit, has by no means the same dependency upon the
gratitude of the man whom he meant to oblige, nor the

same sense of his own merit towards him, which he would have had in the case of success.

Even the merit of talents and abilities which some accident has hindered from producing their effects, seems in some measure imperfect, even to those who are fully convinced of their capacity to produce them. The general who has been hindered by the envy of ministers from gaining some great advantage over the enemies of his country, regrets the loss of the opportunity for ever after. Nor is it only upon account of the public that he regrets it. He laments that he was hindered from performing an action which would have added a new lustre to his character in his own eyes, as well as in those of every other person. It satisfies neither himself nor others to reflect that the plan or design was all that depended on him: that no greater capacity was required to execute it than what was necessary to concert it: that he was allowed to be every way capable of executing it, and that had he been permitted to go on, success was infallible. He still did not execute it; and though he might deserve all the approbation which is due to a magnanimous and great design, he still wanted the actual merit of having performed a great action. To take the management of any affair of public concern from the man who has almost brought it to a conclusion, is regarded as the most invidious injustice. As he had done so much, he should, we think, have been allowed to acquire the complete merit of putting an end to it. It was objected to Pompey, that he came in upon the victories of Lucullus, and gathered those laurels which were due to the fortune and valour of another. The glory of Lucullus, it seems, was less complete even in the opinion of his own friends, when he was not permitted to finish that conquest which his conduct and courage had put in the power of almost any man to finish. It mortifies an architect when his plans are either not executed at all, or when they are so far altered as to spoil the effect of the

building.   The plan, however, is all that depends upon the
architect.   The whole of his genius is, to good judges, as
completely discovered in that as in the actual execution.
But a plan does not, even to the most intelligent, give the
same pleasure as a noble and magnificent building.   They
may discover as much both of taste and genius in the one
as in the other.   But their effects are still vastly different,
and the amusement derived from the first never approaches
to the wonder and admiration which are sometimes excited
by the second.   We may believe of many men, that their
talents are superior to those of Cæsar and Alexander;
and that in the same situations they would perform still
greater actions.   In the meantime, however, we do not behold them with that astonishment and admiration with which
those two heroes have been regarded in all ages and nations.
The calm judgments of the mind may approve of them more,
but they want the splendour of great actions to dazzle and
transport it.   The superiority of virtues and talents has not,
even upon those who acknowledge that superiority, the same
effect with the superiority of achievements.

As the merit of an unsuccessful attempt to do good seems
thus, in the eyes of ungrateful mankind, to be diminished
by the miscarriage, so does likewise the demerit of an unsuccessful attempt to do evil.   The design to commit a
crime, how clearly soever it may be proved, is scarce ever
punished with the same severity as the actual commission
of it.   The case of treason is perhaps the only exception.
That crime immediately affecting the being of the government itself, the government is naturally more jealous of it
than of any other.   In the punishment of treason, the sovereign resents the injuries which are immediately done to
himself: in the punishment of other crimes, he resents those
which are done to other men.   It is his own resentment
which he indulges in the one case : it is that of his subjects
which by sympathy he enters into in the other.   In the first

case, therefore, as he judges in his own cause, he is very
apt to be more violent and sanguinary in his punishments
than the impartial spectator can approve of. His resentment too rises here upon smaller occasions, and does not
always, as in other cases, wait for the perpetration of the
crime, or even for the attempt to commit it. A treasonable
concert, though nothing has been done, or even attempted
in consequence of it, nay, a treasonable conversation, is in
many countries punished in the same manner as the actual
commission of treason. With regard to all other crimes,
the mere design, upon which no attempt has followed, is
seldom punished at all, and is never punished severely. A
criminal design, and a criminal action, it may be said, indeed, do not necessarily suppose the same degree of depravity, and ought not therefore to be subjected to the
same punishment. We are capable, it may be said, of re-
solving, and even of taking measures to execute, many
things which, when it comes to the point, we feel ourselves
altogether incapable of executing. But this reason can
have no place when the design has been carried the length
of the last attempt. The man, however, who fires a pistol
at his enemy but misses him, is punished with death by the
laws of scarce any country. By the old law of Scotland,
though he should wound him, yet, unless death ensues
within a certain time, the assassin is not liable to the last
punishment. The resentment of mankind, however, runs
so high against this crime, their terror for the man who
shews himself capable of committing it, is so great, that the
mere attempt to commit it ought in all countries to be capital.
The attempt to commit smaller crimes is almost always
punished very lightly, and sometimes is not punished at all.
The thief, whose hand has been caught in his neighbour's
pocket before he had taken any thing out of it, is punished
with ignominy only. If he had got time to take away a
handkerchief, he would have been put to death. The
house-breaker, who has been found setting a ladder to his

neighbour's window, but had not got into it, is not exposed
to the capital punishment. The attempt to ravish is not punished as a rape. The attempt to seduce a married woman
is not punished at all, though seduction is punished severely.
Our resentment against the person who only attempted to
do a mischief, is seldom so strong as to bear us out in inflicting the same punishment upon him, which we should
have thought due if he had actually done it. In the one
case, the joy of our deliverance alleviates our sense of the
atrocity of his conduct; in the other, the grief of our misfortune increases it. His real demerit, however, is undoubtedly the same in both cases, since his intentions were
equally criminal; and there is in this respect, therefore, an
irregularity in the sentiments of all men, and a consequent
relaxation of discipline, in the laws of, I believe, all nations,
of the most civilized, as well as of the most barbarous. The
humanity of a civilized people disposes them either to dis-
pense with, or to mitigate punishments wherever their natural indignation is not goaded on by the consequences of
the crime. Barbarians, on the other hand, when no actual
consequence has happened from any action, are not apt to
be very delicate of inquisitive about the motives.

The person himself who, either from passion or from the
influence of bad company, has resolved, and perhaps taken
measures, to perpetrate some crime, but who has fortunately
been prevented by an accident which put it out of his power,
is sure, if he has any remains of conscience, to regard this
event all his life after as a great and signal deliverance.
He can never think of it without returning thanks to Heaven
for having been thus graciously pleased to save him from
the guilt in which he was just ready to plunge himself, and
to hinder him from rendering all the rest of his life a scene
of horror, remorse, and repentance. But though his hands
are innocent, he is conscious that his heart is equally guilty
as if he had actually executed what he was so fully resolved

upon. It gives great ease to his conscience, however, to consider that the crime was not executed, though he knows that the failure arose from no virtue in him. He still considers himself as less deserving of punishment and resentment; and this good fortune either diminishes, or takes away altogether, all sense of guilt. To remember how much he was resolved upon it, has no other effect than to make him regard his escape as the greater and more miraculous: for he still fancies that he has escaped, and he looks back upon the danger to which his peace of mind was exposed, with that terror, with which one who is in safety may sometimes remember the hazard he was in of falling over a precipice, and shudder with horror at the thought.

2. The second effect of this influence of fortune, is to increase our sense of the merit or demerit of actions beyond what is due to the motives or affection from which they proceed, when they happen to give occasion to extraordinary pleasure or pain. The agreeable or disagreeable effects of the action often throw a shadow of merit or demerit upon the agent, though in his intention there was nothing that deserved either praise or blame, or at least that deserved them in the degree in which we are apt to bestow them. Thus, even the messenger of bad news is disagreeable to us; and, on the contrary, we feel a sort of gratitude for the man who brings us good tidings. For a moment we look upon them both as the authors, the one of our good, the other of our bad fortune, and regard them in some measure as if they had really brought about the events which they only give an account of. The first author of our joy is naturally the object of a transitory gratitude: we embrace him with warmth and affection, and should be glad, during the instant of our prosperity, to reward him as for some signal service. By the custom of all courts, the officer who brings the news of a victory is entitled to considerable preferments, and the general always chooses one of his principal favourites

to go upon so agreeable an errand.   The first author of our sorrow is, on the contrary, just as naturally the object of a transitory resentment.   We can scarce avoid looking upon him with chagrin and uneasiness ; and the rude and brutal are apt to vent upon him that spleen which his intelligence gives occasion to.   Tigranes, King of Armenia, struck off the head of the man who brought him the first account of the approach of a formidable enemy.   To punish in this manner the author of bad tidings, seems barbarous and inhuman : yet, to reward the messenger of good news, is not disagreeable to us ; we think it suitable to the bounty of kings.   But why do we make this difference, since, if there is no fault in the one, neither is there any merit in the other ? It is because any sort of reason seems sufficient to authorize the exertion of the social and benevolent affections ; but it requires the most solid and substantial to make us enter into that of the unsocial and malevolent.

But though in general we are averse to enter into the unsocial and malevolent affections, though we lay it down for a rule that we ought never to approve of their gratification, unless so far as the malicious and unjust intention of the person against whom they are directed renders him their proper object ; yet, upon some occasions, we relax of this severity.   When the negligence of one man has occasioned some unintended damage to another, we generally enter so far into the resentment of the sufferer, as to approve of his inflicting a punishment upon the offender much beyond what the offence would have appeared to deserve, had no such unlucky consequence followed from it.

There is a degree of negligence, which would appear to deserve some chastisement though it should occasion no damage to any body.   Thus, if a person should throw a large stone over a wall into a public street without giving warning to those who might be passing by, and without regarding where it was likely to fall, he would undoubtedly deserve some chastisement. A very accurate police would punish so absurd an action, even though it had done no mischief. The person who has been guilty of it, shews an insolent contempt of the happiness and safety of others. There is real injustice in his conduct. He wantonly exposes his neighbour to what no man in his senses would choose to expose himself, and evidently wants that sense of what is due to his fellow-creatures, which is the basis of justice and of society. Gross negligence, therefore, is, in the law, said to be almost equal to malicious design.* When any unlucky consequences happen from such carelessness, the person who has been guilty of it is often punished as if he had really intended those consequences ; and his conduct, which was only thoughtless and insolent, and what deserved some chastisement, is considered as atrocious, and as liable to the severest punishment. Thus if, by the imprudent action above mentioned, he should accidentally kill a man, he is, by the laws of many countries, particularly by the old law of Scotland, liable to the last punishment. And though this is no doubt excessively severe, it is not altogether inconsistent with our natural sentiments. Our just indignation against the folly and inhumanity of his conduct is exasperated by our sympathy with the unfortunate sufferer. Nothing, however, would appear more shocking to our natural sense of equity, than to bring a man to the scaffold merely for having thrown a stone carelessly into the street without hurting any body. The folly and inhumanity of his conduct, however, would in this case be the same ; but still our sentiments would be very different. The consideration of this difference may satisfy us how much the indignation even of the spectator is apt to be animated by the actual consequences of the action. In cases of this kind there will, if I am not mistaken, be found a great de-

* Lata culpa prope dolum est.

gree of severity in the laws of almost all nations; as I have already observed that in those of an opposite kind there was a very general relaxation of discipline.

There is another degree of negligence which does not involve in it any sort of injustice. The person who is guilty of it treats his neighbour as he treats himself, means no harm to any body, and is far from entertaining any insolent contempt for the safety and happiness of others. He is not, however, so careful and circumspect in his conduct as he ought to be, and deserves upon this account some degree of blame and censure, but no sort of punishment. Yet if, by a negligence* of this kind, he should occasion some damage to another person, he is by the laws of, I believe, all countries, obliged to compensate it. And though this is no doubt a real punishment, and what no mortal would have thought of inflicting upon him, had it not been for the unlucky accident which his conduct gave occasion to; yet this decision of the law is approved of by the natural sentiments of all mankind. Nothing, we think, can be more just than that one man should not suffer by the carelessness of another; and that the damage occasioned by blameable negligence, should be made up by the person who was guilty of it.

There is another species of negligence,† which consists merely in a want of the most anxious timidity and circumspection with regard to all the possible consequences of our actions. The want of this painful attention, when no bad consequences follow from it, is so far from being regarded as blameable, that the contrary quality is rather considered as such. That timid circumspection which is afraid of every thing, is never regarded as a virtue, but as a quality which, more than any other, incapacitates for action and business. Yet when, from a want of this excessive care, a person

* Culpa levis.   † Culpa levissima.

happens to occasion some damage to another, he is often by the law obliged to compensate it. Thus, by the Aquilian law, the man, who not being able to manage a horse that had accidentally taken fright, should happen to ride down his neighbour's slave, is obliged to compensate the damage. When an accident of this kind happens, we are apt to think that he ought not to have rode such a horse, and to regard his attempting it as an unpardonable levity; though without this accident we should not only have made no such reflection, but should have regarded his refusing it as the effect of timid weakness, and of an anxiety about merely possible events, which it is to no purpose to be aware of. The person himself, who by an accident even of this kind has involuntarily hurt another, seems to have some sense of his own ill desert with regard to him. He naturally runs up to the sufferer to express his concern for what has happened, and to make every acknowledgment in his power. If he has any sensibility, he necessarily desires to compensate the damage, and to do every thing he can to appease that animal resentment, which he is sensible will be apt to arise in the breast of the sufferer. To make no apology, to offer no atonement, is regarded as the highest brutality. Yet why should he make an apology more than any other person? Why should he, since he was equally innocent with any other by-stander, be thus singled out from among all mankind, to make up for the bad fortune of another? This task would surely never be imposed upon him, did not even the impartial spectator feel some indulgence for what may be regarded as the unjust resentment of that other.

CHAPTER III.

Of the final cause of this Irregularity of Sentiments.

SUCH is the effect of the good or bad consequence of actions upon the sentiments both of the person who performs them, and of others ; and thus, fortune, which governs the world, has some influence where we should be least willing to allow her any, and directs in some measure the sentiments of mankind, with regard to the character and conduct both of themselves and others. That the world judges by the event, and not by the design, has been in all ages the complaint, and is the great discouragement of virtue. Every body agrees to the general maxim, that as the event does not depend on the agent, it ought to have no influence upon our sentiments, with regard to the merit or propriety of his conduct. But when we come to particulars, we find that our sentiments are scarce in any one instance exactly conformable to what this equitable maxim would direct. The happy or unprosperous event of any action, is not only apt to give us a good or bad opinion of the prudence with which it was conducted, but almost always too animates our gratitude or resentment, our sense of the merit or demerit of the design.

Nature, however, when she implanted the seeds of this irregularity in the human breast, seems, as upon all other occasions, to have intended the happiness and perfection of the species. If the hurtfulness of the design, if the malevolence of the affection, were alone the causes which excited our resentment, we should feel all the furies of that passion against any person in whose breast we suspected or believed such designs or affections were harboured, though they had never broken out into any actions. Sentiments, thoughts, intentions, would become the objects of punishment; and if the indignation of mankind run as high against them as against actions ; if the baseness of the thought which had given birth to no action, seemed in the eyes of the world as much to call aloud for vengeance as the baseness of the action, every court of judicature would become a real inquisition. There would be no safety for the most innocent and circumspect conduct. Bad wishes, bad views, bad designs, might still be suspected ; and while these excited the same indignation with bad conduct, while bad intentions were as much resented as bad actions, they would equally expose the person to punishment and resentment. Actions, therefore, which either produce actual evil, or attempt to produce it, and thereby put us in the immediate fear of it, are by the Author of nature rendered the only proper and approved objects of human punishment and resentment. Sentiments, designs, affections, though it is from these that according to cool reason human actions derive their whole merit or demerit, are placed by the great Judge of hearts beyond the limits of every human jurisdiction, and are reserved for the cognizance of his own unerring tribunal. That necessary rule of justice, therefore, that men in this life are liable to punishment for their actions only, not for their designs and intentions, is founded upon this salutary and useful irregularity in human sentiments concerning merit or demerit, which at first sight appears so absurd and unaccountable. But every part of nature, when attentively surveyed, equally demonstrates the providential care of its Author; and we may admire the wisdom and goodness of God even in the weakness and folly of men.

Nor is that irregularity of sentiments altogether without its utility, by which the merit of an unsuccessful attempt to serve, and much more that of mere good inclinations and kind wishes, appears to be imperfect. Man was made for action, and to promote by the exertion of his faculties such changes in the external circumstances both of himself and others, as may seem most favourable to the happiness of all. He must not be satisfied with indolent benevolence, nor fancy himself the friend of mankind, because in his heart he wishes well to the prosperity of the world. That he may call forth the whole vigour of his soul, and strain every nerve, in order to produce those ends which it is the purpose of his being to advance, Nature has taught him, that neither himself nor mankind can be fully satisfied with his conduct, nor bestow upon it the full measure of applause, unless he has actually produced them. He is made to know, that the praise of good intentions, without the merit of good offices, will be but of little avail to excite either the loudest acclamations of the world, or even the highest degree of self-applause. The man who has performed no single action of importance, but whose whole conversation and deportment express the justest, the noblest, and most generous sentiments, can be entitled to demand no very high reward, even though his inutility should be owing to nothing but the want of an opportunity to serve. We can still refuse it him without blame. We can still ask him, What have you done? What actual service can you produce, to entitle you to so great a recompence? We esteem you and love you; but we owe you nothing. To reward indeed that latent virtue which has been useless only for want of an opportunity to serve, to bestow upon it those honours and preferments, which, though in some measure it may be said to deserve them, it could not with propriety have insisted upon, is the effect of the most divine benevolence. To punish, on the contrary, for the affections of the heart only, where no crime has been committed, is the most insolent and barbarous tyranny. The benevolent affections seem to deserve most praise, when they do not wait till it becomes almost a crime for them not to exert themselves. The malevolent, on the contrary, can scarce be too tardy, too slow, or deliberate.

It is even of considerable importance that the evil which is done without design should be regarded as a misfortune to the doer as well as to the sufferer. Man is thereby taught to reverence the happiness of his brethren, to tremble lest he should, even unknowingly, do any thing that can hurt them, and to dread that animal resentment which, he feels, is ready to burst out against him, if he should, without design, be the unhappy instrument of their calamity. As, in the ancient heathen religion, that holy ground which had been consecrated to some god, was not to be trod upon but upon solemn and necessary occasions, and the man who had even ignorantly violated it, became piacular from that moment, and, until proper atonement should be made, incurred the vengeance of that powerful and invisible being to whom it had been set apart; so, by the wisdom of Nature, the happiness of every innocent man is, in the same manner, rendered holy, consecrated, and hedged round against the approach of every other man; not to be wantonly trod upon, not even to be, in any respect, ignorantly and involuntarily violated, without requiring some expiation, some atonement in proportion to the greatness of such undesigned violation. A man of humanity, who accidentally, and without the smallest degree of blameable negligence, has been the cause of the death of another man, feels himself piacular, though not guilty. During his whole life he considers this accident as one of the greatest misfortunes that could have befallen him. If the family of the slain is poor, and he himself in tolerable circumstances, he immediately takes them under his protection, and without any other merit, thinks them entitled to every degree of favour and kindness. If they are in better circumstances, he endeavours by every submission, by every expression of sorrow, by rendering them every good office which he can devise, or they accept of, to atone for what has happened, and to propitiate, as much as possible, their, perhaps natural, though no doubt most unjust resentment for the great, though involuntary, offence which he has given them.

The distress which an innocent person feels, who, by some accident, has been led to do something which, if it had been done with knowledge and design, would have justly exposed him to the deepest reproach, has given occasion to some of the finest and most interesting scenes both of the ancient and of the modern drama. It is this fallacious sense of guilt, if I may call it so, which constitutes the whole distress of Œdipus and Jocasta upon the Greek, of Monimia and Isabella upon the English, theatre. They are all of them in the highest degree piacular, though not one of them is in the smallest degree guilty.

Notwithstanding, however, all these seeming irregularities of sentiment, if man should unfortunately either give occasion to those evils which he did not intend, or fail in producing that good which he intended, Nature has not left his innocence altogether without consolation, nor his virtue altogether without reward. He then calls to his assistance that just and equitable maxim, that those events which did not depend upon our conduct, ought not to diminish the esteem that is due to us. He summons up his whole magnanimity and firmness of soul, and strives to regard himself, not in the light in which he at present appears, but in that in which he ought to appear, in which he would have appeared had his generous designs been crowned with success, and in which he would still appear, notwithstanding their miscarriage, if the sentiments of mankind were either altogether candid and equitable, or even perfectly consistent with themselves. The more candid and humane part of mankind entirely go along with the efforts which he thus makes to support himself in his own opinion. They exert their whole generosity and greatness of mind to correct in themselves this irregularity of human nature, and endeavour to regard his unfortunate magnanimity in the same light in which, had it been successful, they would, without any such generous exertion, have naturally been disposed to consider it.

THE

THEORY OF MORAL SENTIMENTS.

～～～～

Part Third.

OF THE FOUNDATION OF OUR JUDGMENTS

CONCERNING OUR

OWN SENTIMENTS AND CONDUCT, AND OF THE
SENSE OF DUTY.

CHAPTER I.

Of the Principle of Self-approbation and of Self-dis-approbation.

In the two foregoing parts of this discourse, I have chiefly considered the origin and foundation of our judgments concerning the sentiments and conduct of others. I come now to consider more particularly the origin of those concerning our own.

The principle by which we naturally either approve or disapprove of our own conduct, seems to be altogether the same with that by which we exercise the like judgments concerning the conduct of other people. We either approve or disapprove of the conduct of another man, according as we feel that, when we bring his case home to ourselves, we either can or cannot entirely sympathize with the sentiments and motives which directed it. And, in the same manner, we either approve or disapprove of our own conduct, according as we feel that, when we place ourselves in the situation of another man, and view it, as it were, with his eyes and from his station, we either can or cannot entirely enter into and sympathize with the sentiments and motives which influenced it. We can never survey our own sentiments and motives, we can never form any judgment concerning them, unless we remove ourselves, as it were, from our own natural station, and endeavour to view them as at a certain distance from us. But we can do this in no other way than by endeavouring to view them with the eyes of other people, or as other people are likely to view them. Whatever judgment we can form concerning them, accordingly, must always bear some secret reference, either to what are, or to what, upon a certain condition, would be, or to what, we imagine, ought to be the judgment of others. We endeavour to examine our own conduct as we imagine any other fair and impartial spectator would examine it. If, upon placing ourselves in his situation, we thoroughly enter into all the passions and motives which influenced it, we approve of it, by sympathy with the approbation of this supposed equitable judge. If otherwise, we enter into his disapprobation, and condemn it.

Were it possible that a human creature could grow up to manhood in some solitary place, without any communication with his own species, he could no more think of his own character, of the propriety or demerit of his own senti- ments and conduct, of the beauty or deformity of his own mind, than of the beauty or deformity of his own face. All these are objects which he cannot easily see, which naturally he does not look at, and with regard to which he is provided with no mirror which can present them to his view. Bring him into society, and he is immediately provided with the mirror which he wanted before. It is placed in the counte- nance and behaviour of those he lives with, which always mark when they enter into, and when they disapprove of his sentiments; and it is here that he first views the propriety and impropriety of his own passions, the beauty and defor- mity of his own mind. To a man who from his birth was a stranger to society, the objects of his passions, the external bodies which either pleased or hurt him, would occupy his whole attention. The passions themselves, the desires or aversions, the joys or sorrows, which those objects excited, though of all things the most immediately present to him, could scarce ever be the objects of his thoughts. The idea of them could never interest him so much as to call upon his attentive consideration. The consideration of his joy could in him excite no new joy, nor that of his sorrow any new sorrow, though the consideration of the causes of those passions might often excite both. Bring him into society, and all his own passions will immediately become the causes of new passions. He will observe that mankind approve of some of them, and are disgusted by others. He will be elevated in the one case, and cast down in the other; his desires and aversions, his joys and sorrows, will now often become the causes of new desires and new aversions, new joys and new sorrows: they will now, therefore, interest him deeply, and often call upon his most attentive consideration.

Our first ideas of personal beauty and deformity are drawn from the shape and appearance of others, not from our own. We soon become sensible, however, that others exercise the same criticism upon us. We are pleased when they approve of our figure, and are disobliged when they seem to be disgusted. We become anxious to know how far our appearance deserves either their blame or approbation. We examine our persons limb by limb, and by placing ourselves before a looking-glass, or by some such expedient, endeavour, as much as possible, to view ourselves at the distance and with the eyes of other people. If, after this examination, we are satisfied with our own appearance, we can more easily support the most disadvantageous judgments of others. If, on the contrary, we are sensible that we are the natural objects of distaste, every appearance of their disapprobation mortifies us beyond all measure. A man who is tolerably handsome, will allow you to laugh at any little irregularity in his person; but all such jokes are commonly unsupportable to one who is really deformed. It is evident, however, that we are anxious about our own beauty and deformity, only upon account of its effect upon others. If we had no connection with society, we should be altogether indifferent about either.

In the same manner our first moral criticisms are exercised upon the characters and conduct of other people; and we are all very forward to observe how each of these affects us. But we soon learn, that other people are equally frank with regard to our own. We become anxious to know how far we deserve their censure or applause, and whether to them we must necessarily appear those agreeable or disagreeable creatures which they represent us. We begin, upon this account, to examine our own passions and conduct, and to consider how these must appear to them, by considering how they would appear to us if in their situation. We suppose ourselves the spectators of our own behaviour, and endeavour to imagine what effect it would, in this light, produce upon us. This is the only looking-glass by which we can, in some measure, with the eyes of other people, scrutinize the propriety of our own conduct. If in this view it pleases us, we are tolerably satisfied. We can be more indifferent about the applause, and, in some measure, despise the censure of the world ; secure that, however misunderstood or misrepresented, we are the natural and proper objects of approbation. On the contrary, if we are doubtful about it, we are often, upon that very account, more anxious to gain their approbation, and, provided we have not already, as they say, shaken hands with infamy, we are altogether distracted at the thoughts of their censure, which then strikes us with double severity.

When I endeavour to examine my own conduct, when I endeavour to pass sentence upon it, and either to approve or condemn it, it is evident that, in all such cases, I divide myself, as it were, into two persons; and that I, the examiner and judge, represent a different character from that other I, the person whose conduct is examined into and judged of. The first is the spectator, whose sentiments with regard to my own conduct I endeavour to enter into, by placing myself in his situation, and by considering how it would appear to me, when seen from that particular point of view. The second is the agent, the person whom I properly call myself, and of whose conduct, under the character of a spectator, I was endeavouring to form some opinion. The first is the judge ; the second the person judged of. But that the judge should, in every respect, be the same with the person judged of, is as impossible as that the cause should, in every respect, be the same with the effect.

To be amiable and to be meritorious ; that is, to deserve love and to deserve reward, are the great characters of virtue ; and to be odious and punishable, of vice. But all these characters have an immediate reference· to the sentiments of others. Virtue is not said to be amiable, or to be meritorious, because it is the object of its own love, or of its own gratitude; but because it excites those sentiments in other men. The consciousness that it is the object of such favourable regards, is the source of that inward tranquillity and self-satisfaction with which it is naturally attended, as the suspicion of the contrary gives occasion to the torments of vice. What so great happiness as to be beloved, and to know that we deserve to be beloved? What so great misery as to be hated, and to know that we deserve to be hated?

CHAPTER II.

*Of the love of Praise, and of that of Praise-worthiness ; **and** of the dread of blame, and of that of Blame-worthiness.*

MAN naturally desires, not only to be loved, but to be lovely ; or to be that thing which is the natural and proper object of love.   He naturally dreads, not only to be hated, but to be hateful; or to be that thing which is the natural and proper object of hatred.   He desires not only praise, but praise-worthiness; or to be that thing which, though it should be praised by nobody, is, however, the natural and proper object of praise.   He dreads, not only blame, but blame-worthiness; or to be that thing which, though it should be blamed by nobody, is, however, the natural and proper object of blame.

The love of praise-worthiness is by no means derived altogether from the love of praise.   Those two principles, though they resemble one another, though they are connected, and often blended with one another, are yet, in many respects, distinct and independent of one another.

The love and admiration which we naturally conceive for those whose character and conduct we approve of, necessarily dispose us to desire to become ourselves the objects of the like agreeable sentiments, and to be as amiable and as admirable as those whom we love and admire the most. Emulation, the anxious desire that we ourselves should excel, is originally founded in our admiration of the excellence of others.   Neither can we be satisfied with being merely admired for what other people are admired.   We must at least believe ourselves to be admirable for what they are admirable. But, in order to attain this satisfaction, we must become the impartial spectators of our own character and conduct. We must endeavour to view them with the eyes of other people, or as other people are likely to view them. When seen in this light, if they appear to us as we wish, we are happy and contented. But it greatly confirms this happiness and contentment when we find that other people, viewing them with those very eyes with which we, in imagination only, were endeavouring to view them, see them precisely in the same light in which we ourselves had seen them. Their approbation necessarily confirms our own self-approbation. Their praise necessarily strengthens our own sense of our own praise-worthiness. In this case, so far is the love of praise-worthiness from being derived altogether from that of praise, that the love of praise seems, at least in a great measure, to be derived from that of praise-worthiness.

The most sincere praise can give little pleasure when it cannot be considered as some sort of proof of praise worthiness. It is by no means sufficient that, from ignorance or mistake, esteem and admiration should, in some way or other, be bestowed upon us. If we are conscious that we do not deserve to be so favourably thought of, and that if the truth were known, we should be regarded with very different sentiments, our satisfaction is far from being complete. The man who applauds us either for actions which we did not perform, or for motives which had no sort of influence upon our conduct, applauds not us, but another person. We can derive no sort of satisfaction from his praises. To us they should be more mortifying than any censure, and should perpetually call to our minds the most humbling of all reflections, the reflection of what we ought to be, but what we are not. A woman who paints could derive, one should imagine, but little vanity from the compliments that are paid to her complexion. These, we should expect, ought rather to put her in mind of the sentiments which her real complexion would excite, and mortify her the more by the contrast. To be pleased with such groundless applause is a proof of the most superficial levity and weakness. It is what is properly called vanity, and is the foundation of the most ridiculous and contemptible vices, the vices of affectation and common lying; follies which, if experience did not teach us how common they are, one should imagine the least spark of common sense would save us from. The foolish liar, who endeavours to excite the admiration of the company by the relation of adventures which never had any existence; the important coxcomb, who gives himself airs of rank and distinction which he well knows he has no just pretensions to; are both of them, no doubt, pleased with the applause which they fancy they meet with. But their vanity arises from so gross an illusion of the imagination, that it is difficult to conceive how any rational creature should be imposed upon by it. When they place themselves in the situation of those whom they fancy they have deceived, they are struck with the highest admiration for their own persons. They look upon themselves, not in that light in which, they know, they ought to appear to their companions, but in that which they believe their companions actuallylook upon them. Their superficial weakness and trivial folly hinder them from ever turning their eyes inwards, or from seeing themselves in that despicable point of view in which their own consciences must tell them that they would appear to every body, if the real truth should ever come to be known.

As ignorant and groundless praise can give no solid joy, no satisfaction that will bear any serious examination, so, on the contrary, it often gives real comfort to reflect, that though no praise should actually be bestowed upon us, our conduct, however, has been such as to deserve it, and has been in every respect suitable to those measures and rules by which praise and approbation are naturally and commonly bestowed. We are pleased, not only with praise, but with having done what is praiseworthy. We are pleased to think that we have rendered ourselves the natural objects of approbation, though no approbation should ever actually be bestowed upon us: and we are mortified to reflect that we have justly merited the blame of those we live with, though that sentiment should never actually be exerted against us. The man who is conscious to himself that he has exactly observed those measures of conduct which experience informs him are generally agreeable, reflects with satisfaction on the propriety of his own behaviour. When he views it in the light in which the impartial spectator would view it, he thoroughly enters into all the motives which influenced it. He looks back upon every part of it with pleasure and approbation, and though mankind should never be acquainted with what he has done, he regards himself, not so much according to the light in which they actually regard him, as according to that in which they would regard him if they were better informed. He anticipates the applause and admiration which, in this case, would be bestowed upon him; and he applauds and admires himself by sympathy with sentiments, which do not indeed actually take place, but which the ignorance of the public alone hinders from taking place, which he knows are the natural and ordinary effects of such conduct, which his imagination strongly connects with it, and which he has acquired a habit of conceiving as something that naturally and in propriety ought to follow from it. Men have voluntarily thrown away life to acquire after death a renown which they could no longer enjoy. Their imagination, in the meantime, anticipated that fame which was in future times to be bestowed upon them. Those applauses which they were never to hear rung in their ears; the thoughts of that admiration, whose effects they were never to feel, played about their hearts, banished from their

breasts the strongest of all natural fears, and transported
them to perform actions which seem almost beyond the reach
of human nature. But in point of reality there is surely no
great difference between that approbation which is not to
be bestowed till we can no longer enjoy it, and that which,
indeed, is never to be bestowed, but which would be bestowed, if the world was ever made to understand properly
the real circumstances of our behaviour. If the one often
produces such violent effects, we cannot wonder that the
other should always be highly regarded.

Nature, when she formed man for society, endowed him
with an original desire to please, and an original aversion
to offend his brethren. She taught him to feel pleasure in
their favourable, and pain in their unfavourable regard.
She rendered their approbation most flattering and most
agreeable to him for its own sake ; and their disapprobation
most mortifying and most offensive.

But this desire of the approbation, and this aversion
to the disapprobation of his brethren, would not alone
have rendered him fit for that society for which he was
made. Nature, accordingly, has endowed him, not only
with a desire of being approved of, but with a desire of
being what ought to be approved of; or of being what he
himself approves of in other men. The first desire could
only have made him wish to appear to be fit for society.
The second was necessary in order to render him anxious
to be really fit. The first could only have prompted him
to the affectation of virtue, and to the concealment of vice.
The second was necessary in order to inspire him with the
real love of virtue, and with the real abhorrence of vice.
In every well-informed mind this second desire seems to
be the strongest of the two. It is only the weakest and
most superficial of mankind who can be much delighted
with that praise which they themselves know to be alto-

gether unmerited. A weak man may sometimes be pleased with it, but a wise man rejects it upon all occasions. But, though a wise man feels little pleasure from praise where he knows there is no praiseworthiness, he often feels the highest in doing what he knows to be praiseworthy, though he knows equally well that no praise is ever to be bestowed upon it. To obtain the approbation of mankind, where no approbation is due, can never be an object of any importance to him. To obtain that approbation where it is really due, may sometimes be an object of no great importance to him. But to be that thing which deserves approbation, must always be an object of the highest.

To desire, or even to accept of praise, where no praise is due, can be the effect only of the most contemptible vanity. To desire it where it is really due, is to desire no more than that a most essential act of justice should be done to us. The love of just fame, of true glory, even for its own sake, and independent of any advantage which he can derive from it, is not unworthy even of a wise man. He sometimes, however, neglects, and even despises it; and he is never more apt to do so than when he has the most perfect assurance of the perfect propriety of every part of his own conduct. His self-approbation, in this case, stands in need of no confirmation from the approbation of other men. It is alone sufficient, and he is contented with it. This self-approbation, if not the only, is at least the principal object, about which he can or ought to be anxious. The love of it is the love of virtue.

As the love and admiration which we naturally conceive for some characters dispose us to wish to become ourselves the proper objects of such agreeable sentiments; so the hatred and contempt which we as naturally conceive for others, dispose us, perhaps still more strongly, to dread the very thought of resembling them in any respect. Neither is it, in this case too, so much the thought of being hated and despised that we are afraid of, as that of being hateful and despicable. We dread the thought of doing any thing which can render us the just and proper objects of the hatred and contempt of our fellow-creatures; even though we had the most perfect security that those sentiments were never actually to be exerted against us. The man who has broken through all those measures of conduct which can alone render him agreeable to mankind, though he should have the most perfect assurance that what he had done was for ever to be concealed from every human eye, it is all to no purpose. When he looks back upon it, and views it in the light in which the impartial spectator would view it, he finds that he can enter into none of the motives which influenced it. He is abashed and confounded at the thoughts of it, and necessarily feels a very high degree of that shame which he would be exposed to, if his actions should ever come to be generally known. His imagination, in this case, too, anticipates the contempt and derision from which nothing saves him but the ignorance of those he lives with. He still feels that he is the natural object of these sentiments, and still trembles at the thought of what he would suffer, if they were ever actually exerted against him. But if what he had been guilty of was not merely one of those improprieties which are the objects of simple disapprobation, but one of those enormous crimes which excite detestation and resentment, he could never think of it as long as he had any sensibility left, without feeling all the agony of horror and remorse; and though he could be assured that no man was ever to know it, and could even bring himself to believe that there was no God to revenge it, he would still feel enough of both these sentiments to embitter the whole of his life: he would still regard himself as the natural object of the hatred and indignation of all his fellow-creatures; and if his heart was not grown callous by the habit of crimes, he could not think without terror and astonishment even of the manner in which mankind would look upon him, of what would be the expression of their countenance and of their eyes, if the dreadful truth should ever come to be known. These natural pangs of an affrighted conscience are the demons, the avenging furies, which, in this life, haunt the guilty, which allow them neither quiet nor repose, which often drive them to despair and distraction, from which no assurance of secrecy can protect them, from which no principle of irreligion can entirely deliver them, and from which nothing can free them but the vilest and most abject of all states, a complete insensibility to honour and infamy, to vice and virtue. Men of the most detestable characters, who, in the execution of the most dreadful crimes, had taken their measures so coolly as to avoid even the suspicion of guilt, have sometimes been driven, by the horror of their situation, to discover, of their own accord, what no human sagacity could ever have investigated. By acknowledging their guilt, by submitting themselves to the resentment of their offended fellow-citizens, and, by thus satiating that vengeance, of which they were sensible that they had become the proper objects, they hoped by their death to reconcile themselves, at least in their own imagination, to the natural sentiments of mankind; to be able to consider themselves as less worthy of hatred and resentment; to atone, in some measure, for their crimes, and, by thus becoming the objects, rather of compassion than of horror, if possible to die in peace, and with the forgiveness of all their fellow-creatures. Compared to what they felt before the discovery, even the thought of this, it seems, was happiness.

In such cases, the horror of blameworthiness seems, even in persons who cannot be suspected of any extraordinary delicacy or sensibility of character, completely to conquer the dread of blame. In order to allay that horror, in order to pacify, in some degree, the remorse of their own consciences, they voluntarily submitted themselves both to the reproach and to the punishment which they knew were due to their crimes, but which, at the same time, they might easily have avoided.

They are the most frivolous and superficial of mankind only who can be much delighted with that praise which they themselves know to be altogether unmerited. Unmerited reproach, however, is frequently capable of mortifying very severely even men of more than ordinary constancy. Men of the most ordinary constancy, indeed, easily learn to despise those foolish tales which are so frequently circulated in society, and which, from their own absurdity and falsehood, never fail to die away in the course of a few weeks, or of a few days. But an innocent man, though of a more than ordinary constancy, is often, not only shocked, but most severely mortified by the serious, though false, imputation of a crime; especially when that imputation happens unfortunately to be supported by some circumstances which give it an air of probability. He is humbled to find that any body should think so meanly of his character as to suppose him capable of being guilty of it. Though perfectly conscious of his own innocence, the very imputation seems often, even in his own imagination, to throw a shadow of disgrace and dishonour upon his character. His just indignation, too, at so very gross an injury, which, however, it may frequently be improper, and sometimes even impossible to revenge, is itself a very painful sensation. There is no greater tormentor of the human breast than violent resentment which cannot be gratified. An innocent man, brought to the scaffold by the false imputation of an infamous or odious crime, suffers the most cruel misfortune which it is possible for innocence to suffer. The agony of his mind may, in this case, frequently be greater than that of those who suffer for the like crimes, of which they have been actually guilty. Profligate criminals, such as common thieves and highwaymen, have frequently little sense of the baseness of their own conduct,

and consequently no remorse. Without troubling themselves about the justice or injustice of the punishment, they
have always been accustomed to look upon the gibbet as a
lot very likely to fall to them.   When it does fall to them,
therefore, they consider themselves only as not quite so lucky
as some of their companions, and submit to their fortune,
without any other uneasiness than what may arise from the
fear of death ; a fear which, even by such worthless wretches,
we frequently see, can be so easily, and so very completely
conquered.   The innocent man, on the contrary, over and
above the uneasiness which this fear may occasion, is tormented by his own indignation at the injustice which has
been done to him.   He is struck with horror at the thoughts
of the infamy which the punishment may shed upon his
memory, and foresees, with the most exquisite anguish, that
he is hereafter to be remembered by his dearest friends and
relations, not with regret and affection, but with shame, and
even with horror for his supposed disgraceful conduct : and
the shades of death appear to close round him with a darker
and more melancholy gloom than naturally belongs to them·
Such fatal accidents, for the tranquillity of mankind, it is to
be hoped, happen very rarely in any country ; but they happen
sometimes in all countries, even in those where justice is, in
general, very well administered.   The unfortunate Calas, a
man of much more than ordinary constancy (broken upon the
wheel and burnt at Tholouse for the supposed murder of his
own son, of which he was perfectly innocent), seemed, with
his last breath, to deprecate, not so much the cruelty of the
punishment as the disgrace which the imputation might bring
upon his memory.   After he had been broken, and was just
going to be thrown into the fire, the monk who attended the
execution, exhorted him to confess the crime for which he had
been condemned.   My father, said Calas, can you yourself bring yourself to believe that I am guilty ?

To persons in such unfortunate circumstances, that humble

philosophy which confines its views to this life, can afford,
perhaps, but little consolation. Every thing that could render either life or death respectable is taken from them. They
are condemned to death and to everlasting infamy. Religion
can alone afford them any effectual comfort. She alone can
tell them, that it is of little importance what man may think
of their conduct, while the all-seeing Judge of the world approves of it. She alone can present to them the view of
another world; a world of more candour, humanity, and
justice, than the present; where their innocence is in due
time to be declared, and their virtue to be finally rewarded:
and the same great principle which can alone strike terror
into triumphant vice, affords the only effectual consolation
to disgraced and insulted innocence.

In smaller offences, as well as in greater crimes, it frequently happens that a person of sensibility is much more
hurt by the unjust imputation than the real criminal is by
the actual guilt. A woman of gallantry laughs even at the
well-founded surmises which are circulated concerning her
conduct. The worst-founded surmise of the same kind is
a mortal stab to an innocent virgin. The person who is deliberately guilty of a disgraceful action, we may lay it down,
I believe, as a general rule, can seldom have much sense of
the disgrace; and the person who is habitually guilty of it,
can scarce ever have any.

When every man, even of middling understanding, so
readily despises unmerited applause, how it comes to pass
that unmerited reproach should often be capable of mortifying so severely men of the soundest and best judgment, may
perhaps deserve some consideration.

Pain, I have already had occasion to observe, is, in
almost all cases, a more pungent sensation than the opposite
and correspondent pleasure. The one almost always

depresses us much more below the ordinary, or what may be called the natural state of our happiness, than the other ever raises us above it. A man of sensibility is apt to be more humiliated by just censure than he is ever elavated by just applause. Unmerited applause a wise man rejects with contempt upon all occasions ; but he often feels very severely the injustice of unmerited censure. By suffering himself to be applauded for what he has not performed, by assuming a merit which does not belong to him, he feels that he is guilty of a mean falsehood, and deserves, not the admiration, but the contempt, of those very persons who, by mistake, had been led to admire him. It may, perhaps, give him some well-founded pleasure to find that he has been, by many people, thought capable of performing what he did not perform. But, though he may be obliged to his friends for their good opinion, he would think himself guilty of the greatest baseness if he did not immediately undeceive them. It gives him little pleasure to look upon himself in the light in which other people actually look upon him, when he is conscious that, if they knew the truth, they would look upon him in a very different light. A weak man, however, is often much delighted with viewing himself in this false and delusive light. He assumes the merit of every laudable action that is ascribed to him, and pretends to that of many which nobody ever thought of ascribing to him. He pretends to have done what he never did, to have written what another wrote, to have invented what another discovered ; and is led into all the miserable vices of plagiarism and common lying. But though no man of middling good sense can derive much pleasure from the imputation of a laudable action which he never performed, yet a wise man may suffer great pain from the serious imputation of a crime which he never committed. Nature, in this case, has rendered the pain not only more pungent than the opposite and correspondent pleasure, but she has rendered it so in a much greater than the ordinary degree. A denial rids a man at once of the foolish and ridiculous pleasure ; but it will not always rid him of the pain. When he refuses the merit which is ascribed to him, nobody doubts his veracity. It may be doubted when he denies the crime which he is accused of. He is at once enraged at the falsehood of the imputation, and mortified to find that any credit should be given to it. He feels that his character is not sufficient to protect him. He feels that his brethren, far from looking upon him in that light in which he anxiously desires to be viewed by them, think him capable of being guilty of what he is accused of. He knows perfectly that he has not been guilty : he knows perfectly what he has done ; but, perhaps, scarce any man can know perfectly what he himself is capable of doing. What the peculiar constitution of his own mind may or may not admit of, is, perhaps, more or less a matter of doubt to every man. The trust and good opinion of his friends and neighbours tend more than any thing to relieve him from this most disagreeable doubt ; their distrust and unfavourable opinion, to increase it. He may think himself very confident that their unfavourable judgment is wrong : but this confidence can seldom be so great as to hinder that judgment from making some impression upon him ; and the greater his sensibility, the greater his delicacy, the greater his worth, in short, this impression is likely to be the greater.

The agreement or disagreement both of the sentiments and judgments of other people with our own, is, in all cases, it must be observed, of more or less importance to us, exactly in proportion as we ourselves are more or less uncertain about the propriety of our own sentiments, about the accuracy of our own judgments.

A man of sensibility may sometimes feel great uneasiness lest he should have yielded too much even to what may be called an honourable passion ; to his just indignation, perhaps, at the injury which may have been done either to himself or to his friend. He is anxiously afraid lest, meaning only to act with spirit, and to do justice, he may, from the too great vehemence of his emotion, have done a real injury to some other person; who, though not innocent, may not have been altogether so guilty as he at first apprehended. The opinion of other people becomes, in this case, of the utmost importance to him. Their approbation is the most healing balsam; their disapprobation, the bitterest and most tormenting poison that can be poured into his uneasy mind. When he is perfectly satisfied with every part of his own conduct, the judgment of other people is often of less importance to him.

There are some very noble and beautiful arts, in which the degree of excellence can be determined only by a certain nicety of taste, of which the decisions, however, appear always, in some measure, uncertain. There are others, in which the success admits, either of clear demonstration, or very satisfactory proof. Among the candidates for excellence in those different arts, the anxiety about the public opinion is always much greater in the former than in the latter.

The beauty of poetry is a matter of such nicety, that a young beginner can scarce ever be certain that he has attained it. Nothing delights him so much, therefore, as the favourable judgments of his friends and of the public; and nothing mortifies him so severely as the contrary. The one establishes, the other shakes, the good opinion which he is anxious to entertain concerning his own performances. Experience and success may in time give him a little more confidence in his own judgment. He is at all times, however, liable to be most severely mortified by the unfavourable judgments of the public. Racine was so disgusted by the indifferent success of his Phædra, the finest tragedy, perhaps, that is extant in any language, that, though in the vigour of his life, and at the height of his abilities, he resolved to write no more for the stage. That great poet used frequently to tell his son, that the most paltry and impertinent criticism had always given him more pain than the highest and justest eulogy had ever given him pleasure. The extreme sensibility of Voltaire to the slightest censure of the same kind is well known to every body. The Dunciad of Mr Pope is an everlasting monument of how much the most correct, as well as the most elegant and harmonious of all the English poets, had been hurt by the criticisms of the lowest and most contemptible authors. Gray (who joins to the sublimity of Milton the elegance and harmony of Pope, and to whom nothing is wanting to render him, perhaps, the first poet in the English language, but to have written a little more), is said to have been so much hurt by a foolish and impertinent parody of two of his finest odes, that he never afterwards attempted any considerable work. Those men of letters who value themselves upon what is called fine writing in prose, approach somewhat to the sensibility of poets.

Mathematicians, on the contrary, who may have the most perfect assurance both of the truth and of the importance of their discoveries, are frequently very indifferent about the reception which they may meet with from the public. The two greatest mathematicians that I ever have had the honour to be known to, and, I believe, the two greatest that have lived in my time, Dr Robert Simpson of Glasgow, and Dr Matthew Stewart of Edinburgh, never seemed to feel even the slightest uneasiness from the neglect with which the ignorance of the public received some of their most valuable works. The great work of Sir Isaac Newton, his Mathematical Principles of Natural Philosophy, I have been told, was for several years neglected by the public. The tranquillity of that great man, it is probable, never suf-

fered, upon that account, the interruption of a single quar
ter of an hour. Natural philosophers, in their independency
upon the public opinion, approach nearly to mathematicians,
and, in their judgments concerning the merit of their own
discoveries and observations, enjoy some degree of the same
security and tranquillity.

The morals of those different classes of men of letters
are, perhaps, sometimes somewhat affected by this very
great difference in their situation with regard to the
public.

Mathematicians and natural philosophers, from their independency upon the public opinion, have little temptation
to form themselves into factions and cabals, either for the
support of their own reputation, or for the depression of
that of their rivals. They are almost always men of the
most amiable simplicity of manners, who live in good har--
mony with one another, are the friends of one another's reputation, enter into no intrigue in order to secure the public
applause, but are pleased when their works are approved of,
without being either much vexed or very angry when they
are neglected.

It is not always the same case with poets, or with those
who value themselves upon what is called fine writing.
They are very apt to divide themselves into a sort of literary
factions; each cabal being often avowedly, and almost always
secretly, the mortal enemy of the reputation of every other,
and employing all the mean arts of intrigue and solicitation
to pre-occupy the public opinion in favour of the works of
its own members, and against those of its enemies and
rivals. In France, Despreaux and Racine did not think it
below them to set themselves at the head of a literary
cabal, in order to depress the reputation, first of Quinault
and Perrault, and afterwards of Fontenelle and La Motte,

and even to treat the good La Fontaine with a species of
most disrespectful kindness.   In England, the amiable Mr
Addison did not think it unworthy of his gentle and modest
character to set himself at the head of a little cabal of the
same kind, in order to keep down the rising reputation of
Mr Pope.   Mr Fontenelle, in writing the lives and characters of the members of the academy of sciences, a society
of mathematicians and natural philosophers, has frequent
opportunities of celebrating the amiable simplicity of their
manners ; a quality which, he observes, was so universal
among them as to be characteristical rather of that whole
class of men of letters than of any individual.   Mr
D'Alembert, in writing the lives and characters of the
members of the French Academy, a society of poets and
fine writers, or of those who are supposed to be such, seems
not to have had such frequent opportunities of making any
remark of this kind, and nowhere pretends to represent this
amiable quality as characteristical of that class of men of
letters whom he celebrates.

Our uncertainty concerning our own merit, and our
anxiety to think favourably of it, should together naturally
enough make us desirous to know the opinion of other people concerning it ; to be more than ordinarily elevated when
that opinion is favourable, and to be more than ordinarily
mortified when it is otherwise : but they should not make
us desirous either of obtaining the favourable, or of avoiding
the unfavourable opinion, by intrigue and cabal.   When a
man has bribed all the judges, the most unanimous decision
of the court, though it may gain him his law-suit, cannot
give him any assurance that he was in the right : and had
he carried on his law-suit merely to satisfy himself that he
was in the right, he never would have bribed the judges.
But though he wished to find himself in the right, he wished
likewise to gain his law-suit ; and therefore he bribed the
judges.   If praise were of no consequence to us, but as a

proof of our own praiseworthiness, we never should endeavour to obtain it by unfair means. But though to wise men it is, at least in doubtful cases, of principal consequence upon this account, it is likewise of some consequence upon its own account; and therefore (we cannot, indeed, upon such occasions, call them wise men, but) men very much above the common level have sometimes attempted both to obtain praise and to avoid blame by very unfair means.

Praise and blame express what actually are; praiseworthiness and blameworthiness what naturally ought to be the sentiments of other people with regard to our character and conduct. The love of praise is the desire of obtaining the favourable sentiments of our brethren. The love of praiseworthiness is the desire of rendering ourselves the proper objects of those sentiments. So far those two principles resemble and are akin to one another. The like affinity and resemblance take place between the dread of blame and that of blameworthiness.

The man who desires to do, or who actually does, a praiseworthy action, may likewise desire the praise which is due to it, and sometimes, perhaps, more than is due to it. The two principles are in this case blended together. How far his conduct may have been influenced by the one, and how far by the other, may frequently be unknown even to himself. It must almost always be so to other people. They who are disposed to lessen the merit of his conduct, impute it chiefly or altogether to the mere love of praise, or to what they call mere vanity. They who are disposed to think more favourably of it, impute it chiefly or altogether to the love of praiseworthiness; to the love of what is really honourable and noble in human conduct; to the desire not merely of obtaining, but of deserving, the approbation and applause of his brethren. The imagination of the spectator throws upon it either the one colour or the other, according either to his habits of thinking, or to the favour or dislike which he may bear to the person whose conduct he is considering.

Some splenetic philosophers, in judging of human nature, have done as peevish individuals are apt to do in judging of the conduct of one another, and have imputed to the love of praise, or to what they call vanity, every action which ought to be ascribed to that of praiseworthiness. I shall hereafter have occasion to give an account of some of their systems, and shall not at present stop to examine them.

Very few men can be satisfied with their own private consciousness that they have attained those qualities, or performed those actions, which they admire and think praiseworthy in other people; unless it is at the same time generally acknowledged that they possess the one, or have performed the other; or, in other words, unless they have actually obtained that praise which they think due both to the one and to the other. In this respect, however, men differ considerably from one another. Some seem indifferent about the praise, when, in their own minds, they are perfectly satisfied that they have attained the praiseworthiness. Others appear much less anxious about the praiseworthiness than about the praise.

No man can be completely or even tolerably satisfied with having avoided every thing blameworthy in his conduct; unless he has likewise avoided the blame or the reproach. A wise man may frequently neglect praise, even when he has best deserved it; but, in all matters of serious consequence, he will most carefully endeavour so to regulate his conduct as to avoid, not only blameworthiness, but, as much as possible, every probable imputation of blame. He will never, indeed, avoid blame by doing any thing which he judges blameworthy; by omitting any part of his duty, or by neglecting any opportunity of doing any thing which he judges to be really and greatly praisewor-thy. But, with these modifications, he will most anxiously and carefully avoid it. To shew much anxiety about praise, even for praiseworthy actions, is seldom a mark of great wisdom, but generally of some degree of weakness. But, in being anxious to avoid the shadow of blame or reproach, there may be no weakness, but frequently the most praise-worthy prudence.

"Many people," says Cicero, "despise glory, who are yet most severely mortified by unjust reproach; and that most inconsistently." This inconsistency, however, seems to be founded in the unalterable principles of human nature.

The all-wise Author of Nature has, in this manner, taught man to respect the sentiments and judgments of his brethren; to be more or less pleased when they approve of his con-duct, and to be more or less hurt when they disapprove of it. He has made man, if I may say so, the immediate judge of mankind; and has in this respect, as in many others, created him after his own image, and appointed him his vicegerent upon earth, to superintend the behaviour of his brethren. They are taught by nature to acknowledge that power and jurisdiction which has thus been conferred upon him, to be more or less humbled and mortified when they have incurred his censure, and to be more or less elated when they have obtained his applause.

But though man has, in this manner, been rendered the immediate judge of mankind, he has been rendered so only in the first instance; and an appeal lies from his sentence to a much higher tribunal, to the tribunal of their own con-sciences, to that of the supposed impartial and well-inform-ed spectator, to that of the man within the breast, the great judge and arbiter of their conduct. The jurisdictions of those two tribunals are founded upon principles which, though in some respects resembling and akin, are, however, in reality different and distinct. The jurisdiction of the man without is founded altogether in the desire of actual praise, and in the aversion to actual blame. The jurisdiction of the man within is founded altogether in the desire of praiseworthiness, and in the aversion to blameworthiness; in the desire of possessing those qualities, and performing those actions, which we love and admire in other people; and in the dread of possessing those qualities, and performing those actions, which we hate and despise in other people. If the man without should applaud us, either for actions which we have not performed, or for motives which had no influence upon us; the man within can immediately humble that pride and elevation of mind which such groundless acclamations might otherwise occasion, by telling us, that as we know that we do not deserve them, we render ourselves despicable by accepting them. If, on the contrary, the man without should reproach us, either for actions which we never performed, or for motives which had no influence upon those which we may have performed; the man within may immediately correct this false judgment, and assure us, that we are by no means the proper objects of that censure which has so unjustly been bestowed upon us. But in this, and in some other cases, the man within seems sometimes, as it were, astonished and confounded by the vehemence and clamour of the man without. The violence and loudness with which blame is sometimes poured out upon us, seems to stupify and benumb our natural sense of praiseworthiness and blameworthiness; and the judgments of the man within, though not, perhaps, absolutely altered or perverted, are, however, so much shaken in the steadiness and firmness of their decision, that their natural effect, in securing the tranquillity of the mind, is frequently, in a great measure, destroyed. We scarce dare to absolve ourselves, when all our brethren appear loudly to condemn us. The supposed impartial spectator of our conduct seems to give his opinion in our favour with fear and hesitation; when that of all the real spectators, when that of all those with whose eyes and from whose station he endeavours to consider it, is unanimously and violently against us. In such cases, this demigod within the breast appears, like the demigods of the poets, though partly of immortal, yet partly too of mortal extraction. When his judgments are steadily and firmly directed by the sense of praiseworthiness and blameworthiness, he seems to act suitably to his divine extraction: but when he suffers himself to be astonished and confounded by the judgments of ignorant and weak man, he discovers his connection with mortality, and appears to act suitably rather to the human than to the divine part of his origin.

In such cases, the only effectual consolation of humbled and afflicted man lies in an appeal to a still higher tribunal, to that of the all-seeing Judge of the world, whose eye can never be deceived, and whose judgments can never be perverted. A firm confidence in the unerring rectitude of this great tribunal, before which his innocence is in due time to be declared, and his virtue to be finally rewarded, can alone support him under the weakness and despondency of his own mind, under the perturbation and astonishment of the man within the breast, whom nature has set up as, in this life, the great guardian, not only of his innocence but of his tranquillity. Our happiness in this life is thus, upon many occasions, dependent upon the humble hope and expectation of a life to come; a hope and expectation deeply rooted in human nature, which can alone support its lofty ideas of its own dignity, can alone illumine the dreary prospect of its continually approaching mortality, and maintain its cheerfulness under all the heaviest calamities to which, from the disorders of this life, it may sometimes be exposed. That there is a world to come, where exact justice will be done to every man; where every man

will be ranked with those who, in the moral and intellectual
qualities, are really his equals; where the owner of those
humble talents and virtues which, from being depressed by
fortune, had, in this life, no opportunity of displaying themselves; which were unknown, not only to the public, but
which he himself could scarce be sure that he possessed,
and for which even the man within the breast could scarce
venture to afford him any distinct and clear testimony;
where that modest, silent, and unknown merit will be placed
upon a level, and sometimes above those who, in this world,
had enjoyed the highest reputation, and who, from the
advantage of their situation, had been enabled to perform
the most splendid and dazzling actions; is a doctrine, in
every respect so venerable, so comfortable to the weakness,
so flattering to the grandeur of human nature, that the
virtuous man who has the misfortune to doubt of it, cannot
possibly avoid wishing most earnestly and anxiously to believe it.   It could never have been exposed to the derision
of the scoffer, had not the distribution of rewards and
punishments, which some of its most zealous assertors have
taught us was to be made in that world to come, been too
frequently in direct opposition to all our moral sentiments.

That the assiduous courtier is often more favoured than
the faithful and active servant; that attendance and adulation are often shorter and surer roads to preferment than
merit or service; and that a campaign at Versailles
or St James's is often worth two either in Germany or
Flanders, is a complaint which we have all heard from
many a venerable but discontented old officer.   But what
is considered as the greatest reproach even to the weakness
of earthly sovereigns, has been ascribed, as an act of justice,
to divine perfection; and the duties of devotion, the public
and private worship of the Deity, have been represented,
even by men of virtue and abilities, as the sole virtues
which can either entitle to reward, or exempt from punish-

ment, in the life to come. They were the virtues, perhaps,
most suitable to their station, and in which they themselves
chiefly excelled; and we are all naturally disposed to overrate
the excellencies of our own characters. In the discourse
which the eloquent and philosophical Massillon pronounced,
on giving his benediction to the standards of the regiment of
Catinat, there is the following address to the officers :—
" What is most deplorable in your situation, gentlemen,
is, that in a life hard and painful, in which the services
and the duties sometimes go beyond the rigour and severity
of the most austere cloisters ; you suffer always in vain for
the life to come, and frequently even for this life. Alas !
the solitary monk in his cell, obliged to mortify the flesh
and to subject it to the spirit, is supported by the hope of
an assured recompence, and by the secret unction of that
grace which softens the yoke of the Lord. But you, on
the bed of death, can you dare to represent to him your
fatigues and the daily hardships of your employment ? can
you dare to solicit him for any recompence ? and in all the
exertions that you have made, in all the violences that you
have done to yourselves, what is there that he ought to
place to his own account ? The best days of your life,
however, have been sacrificed to your profession, and ten
years' service has more worn out your body, than would,
perhaps, have done a whole life of repentance and mortification. Alas ! my brother, one single day of those sufferings,
consecrated to the Lord, would, perhaps, have obtained
you an eternal happiness. One single action, painful to nature, and offered up to Him, would, perhaps, have secured
to you the inheritance of the saints. And you have done
all this, and in vain, for this world."

To compare, in this manner, the futile mortifications of
a monastery, to the ennobling hardships and hazards of
war ; to suppose that one day, or one hour, employed in
the former should, in the eye of the great Judge of the

world, have more merit than a whole life spent honourably in the latter, is surely contrary to all our moral sentiments; to all the principles by which nature has taught us to regulate our contempt or admiration. It is this spirit, however, which, while it has reserved the celestial regions for monks and friars, or for those whose conduct and conversation resembled those of monks and friars, has condemned to the infernal all the heroes, all the statesmen and lawgivers, all the poets and philosophers of former ages; all those who have invented, improved, or excelled in the arts which contribute to the subsistence, to the conveniency, or to the ornament of human life; all the great protectors, instructors, and benefactors of mankind; all those to whom our natural sense of praiseworthiness forces us to ascribe the highest merit and most exalted virtue. Can we wonder that so strange an application of this most respectable doctrine should sometimes have exposed it to contempt and derision? with those at least who had themselves, perhaps, no great taste or turn for the devout and contemplative virtues?*

* See Voltaire.

Vous y grillez sage et docte Platon,
Divin Homere, eloquent Ciceron, &c.

CHAPTER III.

Of the Influence and Authority of Conscience.

BUT though the approbation of his own conscience can scarce, upon some extraordinary occasions, content the weakness of man ; though the testimony of the supposed impartial spectator of the great inmate of the breast cannot always alone support him ; yet the influence and authority of this principle is, upon all occasions, very great ; and it is only by consulting this judge within that we can ever see what relates to ourselves in its proper shape and dimensions ; or that we can ever make any proper comparison between our own interests and those of other people.

As to the eye of the body, objects appear great or small, not so much according to their real dimensions as according to the nearness or distance of their situation ; so do they likewise to what may be called the natural eye of the mind : and we remedy the defects of both these organs pretty much in the same manner. In my present situation, an immense landscape of lawns and woods, and distant mountains, seems to do no more than cover the little window which I write by, and to be out of all proportion less than the chamber in which I am sitting. I can form a just comparison between those great objects and the little objects around me, in no other way than by transporting myself, at least in fancy, to a different station, from whence I can survey both at nearly equal distances, and thereby form some judgment of their real proportions. Habit and experience have taught me to do this so easily and so readily, that I am scarce sensible that I do it ; and a man must be, in some measure, acquainted with the philosophy of vision, before he can be thoroughly convinced how little those distant objects would appear to the eye, if the imagination, from a knowledge of their real magnitudes, did not swell and dilate them.

In the same manner, to the selfish and original passions of human nature, the loss or gain of a very small interest of our own appears to be of vastly more importance, excites a much more passionate joy or sorrow, a much more ardent desire or aversion, than the greatest concern of another with whom we have no particular connection. His interests, as long as they are surveyed from his station, can never be put into the balance with our own, can never restrain us from doing whatever may tend to promote our own, how ruinous soever to him. Before we can make any proper comparison of those opposite interests, we must change our position. We must view them, neither from our own place nor yet from his, neither with our own eyes nor yet with his, but from the place and with the eyes of a third person, who has no particular connection with either, and who judges with impartiality between us. Here, too, habit and experience have taught us to do this so easily and so readily, that we are scarce sensible that we do it; and it requires, in this case, too, some degree of reflection, and even of philosophy, to convince us, how little interest we should take in the greatest concerns of our neighbour, how little we should be affected by whatever relates to him, if the sense of propriety and justice did not correct the otherwise natural inequality of our sentiments.

Let us suppose that the great empire of China, with all its myriads of inhabitants, was suddenly swallowed up by an earthquake, and let us consider how a man of humanity in Europe, who had no sort of connection with that part of the world, would be affected upon receiving intelligence of this dreadful calamity. He would, I imagine, first of all express very strongly his sorrow for the misfortune of that

unhappy people, he would make many melancholy reflections upon the precariousness of human life, and the vanity
of all the labours of man, which could thus be annihilated
in a moment. He would, too, perhaps, if he was a man of
speculation, enter into many reasonings concerning the
effects which this disaster might produce upon the commerce of Europe, and the trade and business of the world
in general. And when all this fine philosophy was over,
when all these humane sentiments had been once fairly expressed, he would pursue his business or his pleasure, take
his repose or his diversion, with the same ease and tranquillity as if no such accident had happened. The most
frivolous disaster which could befall himself would occasion
a more real disturbance. If he was to lose his little finger
to morrow, he would not sleep to-night; but, provided he
never saw them, he will snore with the most profound security over the ruin of a hundred millions of his brethren,
and the destruction of that immense multitude seems plainly
an object less interesting to him than this paltry misfortune
of his own. To prevent, therefore, this paltry misfortune
to himself, would a man of humanity be willing to sacrifice
the lives of a hundred millions of his brethren, provided he
had never seen them? Human nature startles with horror
at the thought, and the world, in its greatest depravity and
corruption, never produced such a villain as could be capable of entertaining it. But what makes this difference?
when our passive feelings are almost always so sordid and
so selfish, how comes it that our active principles should
often be so generous and so noble? When we are always
so much more deeply affected by whatever concerns ourselves than by whatever concerns other men; what is it
which prompts the generous upon all occasions, and the
mean upon many, to sacrifice their own interests to the
greater interests of others? It is not the soft power of
humanity, it is not that feeble spark of benevolence which
Nature has lighted up in the human heart, that is thus cap-

able of counteracting the strongest impluses of self-love.
It is a stronger power, a more forcible motive, which exerts
itself upon such occasions. It is reason, principle, conscience,
the inhabitant of the breast, the man within, the great judge
and arbiter of our conduct. It is he who, whenever we
are about to act so as to affect the happiness of others, calls
to us, with a voice capable of astonishing the most pre
sumptuous of our passions, that we are but one of the multitude, in no respect better than any other in it; and that
when we prefer ourselves so shamefully and so blindly to
others, we become the proper objects of resentment, abhorrence, and execration. It is from him only that we learn
the real littleness of ourselves, and of whatever relates to
ourselves, and the natural misrepresentations of self-love can
be corrected only by the eye of this impartial spectator. It
is he who shews us the propriety of generosity and the deformity of injustice; the propriety of resigning the greatest
interests of our own for the yet greater interests of others;
and the deformity of doing the smallest injury to another in
order to obtain the greatest benefit to ourselves. It is not
the love of our neighbour, it is not the love of mankind,
which upon many occasions prompts us to the practice of
those divine virtues. It is a stronger love, a more powerful affection, which generally takes place upon such occasions; the love of what is honourable and noble, of the grandeur, and dignity, and superiority of our own characters.

When the happiness or misery of others depends in any
respect upon our conduct, we dare not, as self-love might
suggest to us, prefer the interest of one to that of many.
The man within immediately calls to us, that we value
ourselves too much and other people too little, and that,
by doing so, we render ourselves the proper object of the
contempt and indignation of our brethren. Neither is this
sentiment confined to men of extraordinary magnanimity
and virtue. It is deeply impressed upon every tolerably

good soldier, who feels that he would become the scorn of his companions if he could be supposed capable of shrinking from danger, or of hesitating either to expose or to throw away his life when the good of the service required it

One individual must never prefer himself so much even to any other individual as to hurt or injure that other in order to benefit himself, though the benefit to the one should be much greater than the hurt or injury to the other. The poor man must neither defraud nor steal from the rich, though the acquisition might be much more beneficial to the one than the loss could be hurtful to the other. The man within immediately calls to him in this case, too, that he is no better than his neighbour, and that by his unjust preference, he renders himself the proper obiect of the contempt and indignation of mankind, as well as of the punishment which that contempt and indignation must naturally dispose them to inflict, for having thus violated one of those sacred rules, upon the tolerable observation of which depend the whole security and peace of human society. There is no commonly honest man who does not more dread the inward disgrace of such an action, the indelible stain which it would for ever stamp upon his own mind, than the greatest external calamity which, without any fault of his own, could possibly befall him ; and who does not inwardly feel the truth of that great stoical maxim, that for one man to deprive another unjustly of any thing, or unjustly to promote his own advantage by the loss or disadvantage of another, is more contrary to nature than death, than poverty, than pain, than all the misfortunes which can affect him, either in his body, or in his external circumstances.

When the happiness or misery of others, indeed, in no respect depends upon our conduct, when our interests are altogether separated and detached from theirs, so that there is neither connection nor competition between them, we do

not always think it so necessary to restrain, either our natural, and, perhaps, improper anxiety about our own affairs.
or our natural, and, perhaps, equally improper indifference
about those of other men.   The most vulgar education
teaches us to act, upon all important occasions, with some
sort of impartiality between ourselves and others, and even
the ordinary commerce of the world is capable of adjust-
ing our active principles to some degree of propriety.   But
it is the most artificial and refined education only, it has
been said, which can correct the inequalities of our passive
feelings ; and we must for this purpose, it has been pretended, have recourse to the severest, as well as to the
profoundest, philosophy.

Two different sets of philosophers have attempted to teach
us this hardest of all the lessons of morality.   One set
have laboured to increase our sensibility to the interests of
others ; another, to diminish that to our own.   The first
would have us feel for others as we naturally feel for ourselves.   The second would have us feel for ourselves as we
naturally feel for others.   Both, perhaps, have carried their
doctrines a good deal beyond the just standard of nature
and propriety.

The first are those whining and melancholy moralists
who are perpetually reproaching us with our happiness,
while so many of our brethren are in misery,* who regard
as impious the natural joy of prosperity, which does not
think of the many wretches that are at every instant
labouring under all sorts of calamities, in the langour of
poverty, in the agony of disease, in the horrors of death,
under the insults and oppression of their enemies.   Commiseration for those miseries which we never saw, which we

---

* See Thomson's Seasons, Winter :
      "Ah ! little think the gay licentious proud," &c.
See also Pascal.

never heard of, but which we may be assured are at all times infesting such numbers of our fellow-creatures, ought, they think, to damp the pleasures of the fortunate, and to render a certain melancholy dejection habitual to all men. But, first of all, this extreme sympathy with misfortunes which we know nothing about seems altogether absurd and unreasonable. Take the whole earth at an average, for one man who suffers pain or misery, you will find twenty in prosperity and joy, or at least in tolerable circumstances. No reason, surely, can be assigned why we should rather weep with the one than rejoice with the twenty. This artificial commiseration, besides, is not only absurd, but seems altogether unattainable ; and those who affect this character have commonly nothing but a certain affected and sentimental sadness, which, without reaching the heart, serves only to render the countenance and conversation impertinently dismal and disagreeable. And, last of all, this disposition of mind, though it could be attained, would be perfectly useless, and could serve no other purpose than to render miserable the person who possessed it. Whatever interest we take in the fortune of those with whom we have no acquaintance or connection, and who are placed altogether out of the sphere of our activity, can produce only anxiety to ourselves, without any manner of advantage to them. To what purpose should we trouble ourselves about the world in the moon ? All men, even those at the greatest distance, are no doubt entitled to our good wishes, and our good wishes we naturally give them. But if, notwithstanding, they should be unfortunate, to give ourselves any anxiety upon that account seems to be no part of our duty. That we should be but little interested, therefore, in the fortune of those whom we can neither serve nor hurt, and who are in every respect so very remote from us, seems wisely ordered by Nature ; and if it were possible to alter in this respect the original constitution of our frame, we could yet gain nothing by the change.

It is never objected to us that we have too little fellow-feeling with the joy of success. Wherever envy does not prevent it, the favour which we bear to prosperity is rather apt to be too great; and the same moralists who blame us for want of sufficient sympathy with the miserable, reproach us for the levity with which we are too apt to admire and almost to worship the fortunate, the powerful, and the rich.

Among the moralists who endeavour to correct the natural inequality of our passive feelings by diminishing our sensibility to what peculiarly concerns ourselves, we may count all the ancient sects of philosophers; but, particularly, the ancient Stoics. Man, according to the Stoics, ought to regard himself, not as something separated and detached, but as a citizen of the world, a member of the vast commonwealth of nature. To the interest of this great community he ought at all times to be willing that his own little interest should be sacrificed. Whatever concerns himself ought to affect him no more than whatever concerns any other equally important part of this immense system. We should view ourselves, not in the light in which our own selfish passions are apt to place us, but in the light in which any other citizen of the world would view us. What befalls ourselves we should regard as what befalls our neighbour, or, what comes to the same thing, as our neighbour regards what befalls us. "When our neighbour," says Epictetus, "loses his wife, or his son, there is nobody who is not sensible that this is a human calamity, a natural event altogether according to the ordinary course of things; but, when the same thing happens to ourselves, then we cry out, as if we had suffered the most dreadful misfortune. We ought, however, to remember how we were affected when this accident happened to another, and such as we were in his case, such ought we to be in our own."

Those private misfortunes, for which our feelings are apt to go beyond the bounds of propriety, are of two different kinds. They are either such as affect us only indirectly, by affecting, in the first place, some other persons who are particularly dear to us; such as our parents, our children, our brothers and sisters, our intimate friends; or they are such as affect ourselves immediately and directly, either in our body, in our fortune, or in our reputation; such as pain, sickness, approaching death, poverty, disgrace, &c.

In misfortunes of the first kind, our emotions may, no doubt, go very much beyond what exact propriety will admit of; but they may likewise fall short of it, and they frequently do so. The man who should feel no more for the death or distress of his own father or son than for those of any other man's father or son, would appear neither a good son nor a good father. Such unnatural indifference, far from exciting our applause, would incur our highest disapprobation. Of those domestic affections, however, some are most apt to offend by their excess, and others by their defect. Nature, for the wisest purposes, has rendered in most men, perhaps in all men, parental tenderness a much stronger affection than filial piety. The continuance and propagation of the species depend altogether upon the former, and not upon the latter. In ordinary cases, the existence and preservation of the child depend altogether upon the care of the parents. Those of the parents seldom depend upon that of the child. Nature, therefore, has rendered the former affection so strong, that it generally requires not to be excited, but to be moderated; and moralists seldom endeavour to teach us how to indulge, but generally how to restrain our fondness, our excessive attachment, the unjust preference which we are disposed to give to our own children above those of other people. They exhort us, on the contrary, to an affectionate attention to our parents, and to make a proper return to them in their old age for the kindness which they had shewn to us in our infancy and youth. In the Decalogue we are commanded to honour our fathers and mothers. No mention is made of the love of our children. Nature had sufficiently prepared us for the performance of this latter duty. Men are seldom accused of affecting to be fonder of their children than they really are. They have sometimes been suspected of displaying their piety to their parents with too much ostentation. The ostentatious sorrow of widows has, for a like reason, been suspected of insincerity. We should respect, could we believe it sincere, even the excess of such kind affections; and though we might not perfectly approve, we should not severely condemn it. That it appears praiseworthy, at least in the eyes of those who affect it, the very affectation is a proof.

Even the excess of those kind affections which are most apt to offend by their excess, though it may appear blameable, never appears odious. We blame the excessive fondness and anxiety of a parent, as something which may, in the end, prove hurtful to the child, and which, in the meantime, is excessively inconvenient to the parent; but we easily pardon it, and never regard it with hatred and detestation. But the defect of this usually excessive affection appears always peculiarly odious. The man who appears to feel nothing for his own children, but who treats them upon all occasions with unmerited severity and harshness, seems of all brutes the most detestable. The sense of propriety, so far from requiring us to eradicate altogether that extraordinary sensibility, which we naturally feel for the misfortunes of our nearest connections, is always much more offended by the defect than it ever is by the excess of that sensibility. The stoical apathy is, in such cases, never agreeable, and all the metaphysical sophisms by which it is supported can seldom serve any other purpose than to blow up the hard insensibility of a coxcomb to ten times its native impertinence.

The poets and romance writers, who best paint the refinements and delicacies of love and friendship, and of all other private and domestic affections, Racine and Voltaire, Richardson, Marivaux, and Riccoboni, are, in such cases, much better instructors than Zeno, Chrysippus, or Epictetus.

That moderated sensibility to the misfortunes of others, which does not disqualify us for the performance of any duty—the melancholy and affectionate remembrance of our departed friends—*the pang*, as Gray says, *to secret sorrow dear*—are by no means undelicious sensations. Though they outwardly wear the features of pain and grief, they are all inwardly stamped with the ennobling characters of virtue and self-approbation.

It is otherwise in the misfortunes which affect ourselves immediately and directly, either in our body, in our fortune, or in our reputation. The sense of propriety is much more apt to be offended by the excess than by the defect of our sensibility, and there are but very few cases in which we can approach too near to the stoical apathy and indifference.

That we have very little fellow-feeling with any of the passions which take their origin from the body, has already been observed. That pain which is occasioned by an evident cause, such as the cutting or tearing of the flesh, is, perhaps, the affection of the body with which the spectator feels the most lively sympathy. The approaching death of his neighbour, too, seldom fails to affect him a good deal. In both cases, however, he feels so very little in comparison of what the person principally concerned feels, that the latter can scarce ever offend the former by appearing to suffer with too much ease.

The mere want of fortune, mere poverty, excites little compassion. Its complaints are too apt to be the objects rather of contempt than of fellow-feeling. We despise a beggar; and, though his importunities may extort an alms from us, he is scarce ever the object of any serious commiseration. The fall from riches to poverty, as it commonly occasions the most real distress to the sufferer, so it seldom fails to excite the most sincere commiseration in the spectator. Though in the present state of society this misfortune can seldom happen without some misconduct, and some very considerable misconduct, too, in the sufferer, yet he is almost always so much pitied, that he is scarce ever allowed to fall into the lowest state of poverty; but, by the means of his friends, frequently by the indulgence of those very creditors who have much reason to complain of his imprudence, is almost always supported in some degree of decent, though humble, mediocrity. To persons under such misfortunes we could, perhaps, easily pardon some degree of weakness; but, at the same time, they who carry the firmest countenance, who accommodate themselves with the greatest ease to their new situation, who seem to feel no humiliation from the change, but to rest their rank in the society, not upon their fortune, but upon their character and conduct, are always the most approved of, and never fail to command our highest and most affectionate admiration.

As, of all the external misfortunes which can affect an innocent man immediately and directly, the undeserved loss of reputation is certainly the greatest; so a considerable degree of sensibility to whatever can bring on so great a calamity does not always appear ungraceful or disagreeable. We often esteem a young man the more when he resents, though with some degree of violence, any unjust reproach that may have been thrown upon his character or his honour. The affliction of an innocent young lady, on account of the groundless surmises which may have been circulated concerning her conduct, appears often perfectly amiable. Persons of an advanced age, whom long experience of the folly and injustice of the world has taught to pay little regard either to its censure or to its applause, neglect and despise obloquy, and do not even deign to honour its futile authors with any serious resentment. This indifference, which is founded altogether on a firm confidence in their own well-tried and well-established characters, would be disagreeable in young people, who neither can nor ought to have any such confidence. It might in them be supposed to forebode in their advancing years a most improper insensibility to real honour and infamy.

In all other private misfortunes which affect ourselves immediately and directly, we can very seldom offend by appearing to be too little affected. We frequently remember our sensibility to the misfortunes of others with pleasure and satisfaction. We can seldom remember that to our own, without some degree of shame and humiliation.

If we examine the different shades and gradations of weakness and self-command, as we meet with them in common life, we shall very easily satisfy ourselves that this control of our passive feelings must be acquired, not from the abstruse syllogisms of a quibbling dialectic, but from that great discipline which Nature has established for the acquisition of this and of every other virtue ; a regard to the sentiments of the real or supposed spectator of our conduct.

A very young child has no self-command ; but, whatever are its emotions, whether fear, or grief, or anger, it endeavours always, by the violence of its outcries, to alarm, as much as it can, the attention of its nurse, or of its parents. While it remains under the custody of such partial protectors, its anger is the first, and, perhaps, the only passion which it is taught to moderate. By noise and threatening they are, for their own ease, often obliged to frighten it into good temper; and the passion which incites it to attack, is restrained by that which teaches it to attend to its own safety. When it is old enough to go to school, or to mix with its equals, it soon finds that they have no such indulgent partiality. It naturally wishes to gain their favour, and to avoid their hatred or contempt. Regard even to its own safety teaches it to do so ; and it soon finds that it can do so in no other way than by moderating, not only its anger, but all its other passions, to the degree which its playfellows and companions are likely to be pleased with. It thus enters into the great school of self-command ; it studies to be more and more master of itself ; and begins to exercise over its own feelings a discipline which the practice of the longest life is very seldom sufficient to bring to complete perfection.

In all private misfortunes, in pain, in sickness, in sorrow, the weakest man, when his friend, and still more when a stranger visits him, is immediately impressed with the view in which they are likely to look upon his situation. Their view calls off his attention from his own view ; and his breast is, in some measure, becalmed the moment they come into his presence. This effect is produced instantaneously, and, as it were, mechanically ; but, with a weak man, it is not of long continuance. His own view of his situation immediately recurs upon him. He abandons himself, as before, to sighs, and tears, and lamentations ; and endeavours, like a child that has not yet gone to school, to produce some sort of harmony between his own grief and the compassion of the spectator, not by moderating the former, but by importunately calling upon the latter.

With a man of a little more firmness, the effect is somewhat more permanent. He endeavours, as much as he can, to fix his attention upon the view which the company are likely to take of his situation. He feels, at the same time, the esteem and approbation which they naturally conceive for him when he thus preserves his tranquillity ; and, though under the pressure of some recent and great calamity, appears to feel for himself no more than what they really feel for him. He approves and applauds himself by sympathy with their approbation, and the pleasure which he derives from this sentiment supports and enables him more easily to continue this generous effort. In most cases he avoids mentioning his own misfortune ; and his company, if they are tolerably well bred, are careful to say nothing which can put him in mind of it. He endeavours to entertain them, in his usual way, upon indifferent subjects, or, if he feels himself strong enough to venture to mention his misfortune, he endeavours to talk of it as he thinks they are capable of talking of it, and even to feel it no further than they are capable of feeling it. If he has not, however, been well inured to the hard discipline of self-command, he soon grows weary of this restraint. A long visit fatigues him ; and, towards the end of it, he is constantly in danger of doing, what he never fails to do the moment it is over, of abandoning himself to all the weakness of excessive sorrow. Modern good manners, which are extremely indulgent to human weakness, forbid for some time the visits of strangers to persons under great family distress, and permit those only of the nearest relations and most intimate friends. The presence of the latter, it is thought, will impose less restraint than that of the former ; and the sufferers can more easily accommodate themselves to the feelings of those from whom they have reason to expect a more indulgent sympathy. Secret enemies, who fancy that they are not known to be such, are frequently fond of making those charitable visits as early as the most intimate friends. The weakest man in the world, in this case, endeavours to support his manly countenance, and, from indignation and contempt of their malice, to behave with as much gaiety and ease as he can.

The man of real constancy and firmness, the wise and just man who has been thoroughly bred in the great school of self-command, in the bustle and business of the world, exposed, perhaps, to the violence and injustice of faction, and to the hardships and hazards of war, maintains this control of his passive feelings upon all occasions; and whether in solitude or in society, wears nearly the same countenance, and is affected very nearly in the same manner. In success and in disappointment, in prosperity and in adversity, before friends and before enemies, he has often been under the necessity of supporting this manhood. He has never dared to forget for one moment the judgment which the impartial spectator would pass upon his sentiments and conduct. He has never dared to suffer the man within the breast to be absent one moment from his attention. With the eyes of this great inmate he has always been accustomed to regard whatever relates to himself. This habit has become perfectly familiar to him: he has been in the constant practice, and, indeed, under the constant necessity, of modelling, or of endeavouring to model, not only his outward conduct and behaviour, but, as much as he can, even his inward sentiments and feelings, according to those of this awful and respectable judge. He does not merely affect the sentiments of the impartial spectator; he really adopts them. He almost identifies himself with, he almost becomes himself that impartial spectator, and scarce even feels but as that great arbiter of his conduct directs him to feel.

The degree of the self-approbation with which every man upon such occasions surveys his own conduct, is higher or lower, exactly in proportion to the degree of self-command which is necessary in order to obtain that self-approbation. Where little self-command is necessary, little self-approbation is due. The man who has only scratched his finger cannot much applaud himself, though he should immediately appear to have forgot this paltry misfortune. The man who has lost his leg by a cannon shot, and who, the moment after, speaks and acts with his usual coolness and tranquillity, as he exerts a much higher degree of self-command, so he naturally feels a much higher degree of self-approbation. With most men, upon such an accident, their own natural view of their own misfortune would force itself upon them with such a vivacity and strength of colouring, as would entirely efface all thought of every other view. They would feel nothing, they could attend to nothing, but their own pain and their own fear ; and not only the judgment of the ideal man within the breast, but that of the real spectators who might happen to be present, would be entirely overlooked and disregarded.

The reward which Nature bestows upon good behaviour under misfortune is thus exactly proportioned to the degree of that good behaviour. The only compensation she could possibly make for the bitterness of pain and distress is thus, too, in equal degrees of good behaviour, exactly proportioned to the degree of that pain and distress. In proportion to the degree of the self-command which is necessary in order to conquer our natural sensibility, the pleasure and pride of the conquest are so much the greater; and this pleasure and pride are so great that no man can be altogether unhappy who completely enjoys them. Misery and wretchedness can never enter the breast in which dwells complete self-satisfaction ; and though it may be too much, perhaps, to say with the Stoics, that, under such an accident as that above mentioned, the happiness of a wise man is in every respect equal to what it could have been under any other circumstances ; yet it must be acknowledged, at least, that this complete enjoyment of his own self-applause, though it may not altogether extinguish, must certainly very much alleviate his sense of his own sufferings.

In such paroxysms of distress, if I may be allowed to call them so, the wisest and firmest man, in order to preserve his equanimity, is obliged, I imagine, to make a considerable, and even a painful exertion.   His own natural feeling of his own distress, his own natural view of his own situation, presses hard upon him, and he cannot, without a very great effort, fix his attention upon that of the impartial spectator. Both views present themselves to him at the same time. His sense of honour, his regard to his own dignity, directs him to fix his whole attention upon the one view.   His natural, his untaught and undisciplined feelings, are continually calling it off to the other.   He does not, in this case, perfectly identify himself with the ideal man within the breast, he does not become himself the impartial spectator of his own conduct.   The different views of both characters exist in his mind separate and distinct from one another, and each directing him to a behaviour different from that to which the other directs him.   When he follows that view which honour and dignity point out to him, Nature does not, indeed, leave him without a recompense.   He enjoys his own complete self-approbation, and the applause of every candid and impartial spectator.   By her unalterable laws, however, he still suffers; and the recompense which she bestows, though very considerable, is not sufficient completely to compensate the sufferings which those laws inflict.   Neither is it fit that it should.   If it did completely compensate them, he could, from self-interest, have no motive for avoiding an accident which must necessarily diminish his utility both to himself and to society; and Nature, from her parental care of both, meant that he should anxiously avoid all such accidents.   He suffers, therefore, and though, in the agony of the paroxysm, he maintains not only the manhood of his countenance but the sedateness and sobriety of his judgment, it requires his utmost and most fatiguing exertions to do so.

By the constitution of human nature, however, agony can never be permanent; and if he survives the paroxysm, he soon comes, without any effort, to enjoy his ordinary tranquillity. A man with a wooden leg suffers, no doubt, and foresees that he must continue to suffer during the remainder of his life, a very considerable inconveniency. He soon comes to view it, however, exactly as every impartial spectator views it, as an inconveniency under which he can enjoy all the ordinary pleasures both of solitude and of society. He soon identifies himself with the ideal man within the breast; he soon becomes himself the impartial spectator of his own situation. He no longer weeps, he no longer laments, he no longer grieves over it, as a weak man may sometimes do in the beginning. The view of the impartial spectator becomes so perfectly habitual to him, that, without any effort, without any exertion, he never thinks of surveying his misfortune in any other view.

The never-failing certainty with which all men, sooner or later, accommodate themselves to whatever becomes their permanent situation, may, perhaps, induce us to think that the Stoics were, at least, thus far very nearly in the right; that, between one permanent situation and another, there was, with regard to real happiness, no essential difference : or that, if there were any difference, it was no more than just sufficient to render some of them the objects of simple choice or preference, but not of any earnest or anxious desire ; and others, of simple rejection, as being fit to be set aside or avoided, but not of any earnest or anxious aversion. Happiness consists in tranquillity and enjoyment. Without tranquillity there can be no enjoyment; and where there is perfect tranquillity there is scarce anything which is not capable of amusing. But in every permanent situation, where there is no expectation of change, the mind of every man, in a longer or shorter time, returns to its natural and usual state of tranquillity. In prosperity, after a certain time, it falls back to that state; in adversity, after a certain time, it rises up to it. In the confinement and solitude of the Bastile, after a certain time, the fashionable and frivolous Count de Lauzun recovered tranquillity enough to be capable of amusing himself with feeding a spider. A mind better furnished would, perhaps, have both sooner recovered its tranquillity, and sooner found, in its own thoughts, a much better amusement.

The great source of both the misery and disorders of human life seems to arise from overrating the difference between one permanent situation and another. Avarice overrates the difference between poverty and riches: ambition, that between a private and a public station: vainglory, that between obscurity and extensive reputation. The person under the influence of any of those extravagant passions is not only miserable in his actual situation, but is often disposed to disturb the peace of society in order to arrive at that which he so foolishly admires. The slightest observation, however, might satisfy him, that, in all the ordinary situations of human life, a well-disposed mind may be equally calm, equally cheerful, and equally contented. Some of those situations may, no doubt, deserve to be preferred to others; but none of them can deserve to be pursued with that passionate ardour which drives us to violate the rules either of prudence or of justice; or to corrupt the future tranquillity of our minds, either by shame from the remembrance of our own folly, or by remorse from the horror of our own injustice. Wherever prudence does not direct, wherever justice does not permit, the attempt to change our situation, the man who does attempt it, plays at the most unequal of all games of hazard, and stakes every thing against scarce any thing. What the favourite of the King of Epirus said to his master, may be applied to men in all the ordinary situations of human life. When the king had recounted to him, in their proper order, all the conquests which he proposed to make, and had come to the last of them—" And what does your Majesty propose to do then?" said the favourite.—" I propose then," said the King, "to enjoy myself with my friends, and endeavour to be good company over a bottle."—" And what hinders your Majesty from doing so now?" replied the favourite. In the most glittering and exalted situation that our idle fancy can hold out to us, the pleasures from which we propose to derive our real happi-- ness are almost always the same with those which, in our actual though humble station, we have at all times at hand and in our power. Except the frivolous pleasures of vanity and superiority, we may find, in the most humble station, where there is only personal liberty, every other which the most exalted can afford; and the pleasures of vanity and superiority are seldom consistent with perfect tranquillity, the principle and foundation of all real and satisfactory enjoyment. Neither is it always certain that, in the splen- did situation which we aim at, those real and satisfactory pleasures can be enjoyed with the same security as in the humble one which we are so very eager to abandon. Exa- mine the records of history, recollect what has happened within the circle of your own experience, consider with attention what has been the conduct of almost all the greatly unfortunate, either in private or public life, whom you may have either read of, or heard of, or remember, and you will find that the misfortunes of by far the greater part of them have arisen from their not knowing when they were well, when it was proper for them to sit still and to be contented. The inscription upon the tombstone of the man who had endeavoured to mend a tolerable constitution by taking physic—" *I was well, I wished to be better ; here I am,*" may generally be applied with great justness to the distress of disappointed avarice and ambition.

It may be thought a singular, but I believe it to be a just observation, that, in the misfortunes which admit of some remedy, the greater part of men do not either so readily or so universally recover their natural and usual tranquillity, as in those which plainly admit of none. In misfortunes of the latter kind, it is chiefly in what may be called the paroxysm, or in the first attack, that we can discover any sensible difference between the sentiments and behaviour of the wise and those of the weak man. In the end, time, the great and universal comforter, gradually composes the weak man to the same degree of tranquillity which a regard to his own dignity and manhood teaches the wise man to assume in the beginning. The case of the man with the wooden leg is an obvious example of this. In the irreparable misfortunes occasioned by the death of children, or of friends and relations, even a wise man may for some time indulge himself in some degree of moderated sorrow. An affectionate, but weak woman, is often upon such occasions almost perfectly distracted. Time, however, in a longer or shorter period, never fails to compose the weakest woman to the same degree of tranbuillity as the strongest man. In all the irreparable calamities which affect himself im- mediately and directly, a wise man endeavours, from the beginning, to anticipate and to enjoy beforehand, that tran- quillity which he foresees the course of a few months or a few years will certainly restore to him in the end.

In the misfortunes for which the nature of things admits, or seems to admit, of a remedy, but in which the means of applying that remedy are not within the reach of the suf- ferer, his vain and fruitless attempts to restore himself to his former situation, his continual anxiety for their success, his repeated disappointments upon their miscarriage, are what chiefly hinder him from resuming his natural tran- quillity, and frequently render miserable, during the whole of his life, a man to whom a greater misfortune, but which plainly admitted of no remedy, would not have given a fortnight's disturbance. In the fall from royal favour to disgrace, from power to insignificancy, from riches to poverty, from liberty to confinement, from strong health to some lingering, chronical, and, perhaps, incurable disease; the man who struggles the least, who most easily and readily acquiesces in the fortune which has fallen to him, very soon recovers his usual and natural tranquillity, and surveys the most disagreeable circumstances of his actual situation in the same light, or, perhaps, in a much less unfavourable light, than that in which the most indifferent spectator is disposed to survey them. Faction, intrigue, and cabal, disturb the quiet of the unfortunate statesman Extravagant projects, visions of gold mines, interrupt the repose of the ruined bankrupt. The prisoner, who is continually plotting to escape from his confinement, cannot enjoy that careless security which even a prison can afford him. The medicines of the physician are often the greatest torment of the incurable patient. The monk who, in order to comfort Johanna of Castile upon the death of her husband Philip, told her of a king, who, fourteen years after his decease, had been restored to life again by the prayers of his afflicted queen, was not likely by his legendary tale to restore sedateness to the distempered mind of that unhappy princess. She endeavoured to repeat the same experiment in hopes of the same success; resisted for a long time the burial of her husband, soon after raised his body from the grave, attended it almost constantly herself, and watched, with all the impatient anxiety of frantic expectation, the happy moment when her wishes were to be gratified by the revival of her beloved Philip.*

Our sensibility to the feelings of others, so far from being inconsistent with the manhood of self-command, is the very principle upon which that manhood is founded. The very same principle or instinct which, in the misfortune of our

* See Robertson's Charles V., vol. ii. pp. 14 and 15, first edition.

neighbour, prompts us to compassionate his sorrow, in our own misfortune, prompts us to restrain the abject and miserable lamentations of our own sorrow. The same principle or instinct which, in his prosperity and success, prompts us to congratulate his joy, in our own prosperity and success, prompts us to restrain the levity and intemperance of our own joy. In both cases, the propriety of our own sentiments and feelings seems to be exactly in proportion to the vivacity and force with which we enter into and conceive his sentiments and feelings.

The man of the most perfect virtue, the man whom we naturally love and revere the most, is he who joins, to the most perfect command of his own original and selfish feelings, the most exquisite sensibility both to the original and sympathetic feelings of others. The man who, to all the soft, the amiable, and the gentle virtues, joins all the great, the awful, and the respectable, must surely be the natural and proper object of our highest love and admiration.

The person best fitted by nature for acquiring the former of those two sets of virtues, is likewise necessarily best fitted for acquiring the latter. The man who feels the most for the joys and sorrows of others, is best fitted for acquiring the most complete control of his own joys and sorrows. The man of the most exquisite humanity is naturally the most capable of acquiring the highest degree of self-command. He may not, however, always have acquired it; and it very frequently happens that he has not. He may have lived too much in ease and tranquillity. He may have never been exposed to the violence of faction, or to the hardships and hazards of war. He may have never experienced the insolence of his superiors, the jealous and malignant envy of his equals, or the pilfering injustice of his inferiors. When in an advanced age some accidental change of fortune exposes him to all these, they all make too great an impression upon him. He has the disposition which fits him for acquiring the most perfect self-command, but he has never had the opportunity of acquiring it. Exercise and practice have been wanting ; and without these no habit can ever be tolerably established. Hardships, dangers, injuries, misfortunes, are the only masters under whom we can learn the exercise of this virtue. But these are all masters to whom nobody willingly puts himself to school.

The situations in which the gentle virtue of humanity can be most happily cultivated, are by no means the same with those which are best fitted for forming the austere virtue of self-command. The man who is himself at ease can best attend to the distress of others. The man who is himself exposed to hardships is most immediately called upon to attend to, and to control his own feelings. In the mild sunshine of undisturbed tranquillity, in the calm retirement of undissipated and philosophical leisure, the soft virtue of humanity flourishes the most, and is capable of the highest improvement. But, in such situations, the greatest and noblest exertions of self-command have little exercise. Under the boisterous and stormy sky of war and faction, of public tumult and confusion, the sturdy severity of self-command prospers the most, and can be the most successfully cultivated. But, in such situations, the strongest suggestions of humanity must frequently be stifled or neglected ; and every such neglect necessarily tends to weaken the principle of humanity. As it may frequently be the duty of a soldier not to take, so it may sometimes be his duty not to give quarter ; and the humanity of the man who has been several times under the necessity of submitting to this disagreeable duty, can scarce fail to suffer a considerable diminution. For his own ease, he is too apt to learn to make light of the misfortunes which he is so often under the necessity of occasioning ; and the situations which call forth the noblest exertions of self-command, by imposing the necessity of violating sometimes the property, and sometimes the life of our neighbour, always tend to diminish, and too often to extinguish altogether, that sacred regard to both, which is the foundation of justice and humanity. It is upon this account that we so frequently find in the world men of great humanity who have little self-command, but who are indolent and irresolute, and easily disheartened, either by difficulty or danger, from the most honourable pursuits; and, on the contrary, men of the most perfect self-command, whom no difficulty can discourage, no danger appal, and who are at all times ready for the most daring and desperate enter·prizes, but who, at the same time, seem to be hardened against all sense either of justice or humanity.

In solitude, we are apt to feel too strongly whatever relates to ourselves: we are apt to overrate the good offices we may have done, and the injuries we may have suffered: we are apt to be too much elated by our own good, and too much dejected by our own bad fortune. The conversation of a friend brings us to a better, that of a stranger to a still better temper. The man within the breast, the abstract and ideal spectator of our sentiments and conduct, requires often to be awakened and put in mind of his duty, by the presence of the real spectator: and it is always from that spectator, from whom we can expect the least sympathy and indulgence, that we are likely to learn the most complete lesson of self-command.

Are you in adversity? Do not mourn in the darkness of solitude, do not regulate your sorrow according to the indulgent sympathy of your intimate friends; return, as soon as possible, to the daylight of the world and of society. Live with strangers, with those who know nothing, or care nothing about your misfortune; do not even shun the company of enemies; but give yourself the pleasure of mortifying their malignant joy, by making them feel how little you are affected by your calamity, and how much you are above it.

Are you in prosperity ? Do not confine the enjoyment of your good fortune to your own house, to the company of your own friends, perhaps of your flatterers, of those who build upon your fortune the hopes of mending their own; frequent those who are independent of you, who can value you only for your character and conduct, and not for your fortune. Neither seek nor shun, neither intrude yourself into, nor run away from, the society of those who were once your superiors, and who may be hurt at finding you their equal, or, perhaps, even their superior. The impertinence of their pride may, perhaps, render their company too disagreeable : but if it should not, be assured that it is the best company you can possibly keep ; and if by the simplicity of your unassuming demeanour you can gain their favour and kindness, you may rest satisfied that you are modest enough, and that your head has been in no respect turned by your good fortune.

The propriety of our moral sentiments is never so apt to be corrupted as when the indulgent and partial spectator is at hand, while the indifferent and impartial one is at a great distance.

Of the conduct of one independent nation towards another, neutral nations are the only indifferent and impartial spectators. But they are placed at so great a distance that they are almost quite 'out of sight. When two nations are at variance, the citizen of each pays little regard to the sentiments which foreign nations may entertain concerning his conduct. His whole ambition is to obtain the approbation of his own fellow-citizens ; and as they are all animated by the same hostile passions which animate himself, he can

never please them so much as by enraging and offending
their enemies. The partial spectator is at hand : the impartial one at a great distance. In war and negotiation,
therefore, the laws of justice are very seldom observed.
Truth and fair dealing are almost totally disregarded.
Treaties are violated; and the violation, if some advantage
is gained by it, sheds scarce any dishonour upon the violator.
The ambassador who dupes the minister of a foreign nation
is admired and applauded. The just man who disdains
either to take or to give any advantage, but who would
think it less dishonourable to give than to take one—the
man who in all private transactions would be the most beloved and the most esteemed, in those public transactions
is regarded as a fool and an idiot, who does not understand
his business, and he incurs always the contempt, and sometimes even the detestation, of his fellow-citizens. In war,
not only what are called the laws of nations are frequently
violated, without bringing (among his own fellow-citizens,
whose judgments he only regards) any considerable dishonour upon the violator; but those laws themselves are,
the greater part of them, laid down with very little regard
to the plainest and most obvious rules of justice. That the
innocent, though they may have some connection or dependency upon the guilty (which, perhaps, they themselves
cannot help), should not upon that account suffer or be
punished for the guilty, is one of the plainest and most
obvious rules of justice. In the most unjust war, however,
it is commonly the sovereign or the rulers only who are
guilty. The subjects are almost always perfectly innocent.
Whenever it suits the conveniency of a public enemy, however, the goods of the peaceable citizens are seized both at
land and at sea; their lands are laid waste, their houses are
burnt, and they themselves, if they presume to make any
resistance, are murdered or led into captivity ; and all this
in the most perfect conformity to what are called the laws
of nations.

The animosity of hostile factions, whether civil or ecclesiastical, is often still more furious than that of hostile nations, and their conduct towards one another is often still more atrocious. What may be called the laws of faction have often been laid down by grave authors with still less regard to the rules of justice than what are called the laws of nations. The most ferocious patriot never stated it as a serious question, whether faith ought to be kept with public enemies.—Whether faith ought to be kept with rebels; whether faith ought to be kept with heretics ; are questions which have been often furiously agitated by celebrated doctors, both civil and ecclesiastical. It is needless to observe, I presume, that both rebels and heretics are those unlucky persons, who, when things have come to a certain degree of violence, have the misfortune to be of the weaker party. In a nation distracted by faction, there are, no doubt, always a few, though commonly but a very few, who preserve their judgment untainted by the general contagion. They seldom amount to more than here and there a solitary individual, without any influence, excluded by his own candour from the confidence of either party, and who, though he may be one of the wisest, is necessarily upon that very account one of the most insignificant men in the society. All such people are held in contempt and derision, frequently in detestation, by the furious zealots of both parties. A true party-man hates and despises candour ; and, in reality, there is no vice which could so effectually disqualify him for the trade of a party-man as that single virtue. The real, revered, and impartial spectator, therefore, is upon no occasion at a greater distance than amidst the violence and rage of contending parties. To them it may be said, that such a spectator scarce exists anywhere in the universe. Even to the great Judge of the universe they impute all their own prejudices, and often view that divine Being as animated by all their own vindictive and implacable passions. Of all the corrupters of moral sentiments, therefore, faction and fanaticism have always been by far the greatest.

Concerning the subject of self-command, I shall only observe further, that our admiration for the man who, under the heaviest and most unexpected misfortunes, continues to behave with fortitude and firmness, always supposes that his sensibility to those misfortunes is very great, and such as it requires a very great effort to conquer or command. The man who was altogether insensible to bodily pain, could deserve no applause from enduring the torture with the most perfect patience and equanimity. The man who had been created without the natural fear of death, could claim no merit from preserving his coolness and presence of mind in the midst of the most dreadful dangers. It is one of the extravagancies of Seneca, that the Stoical wise man was, in this respect, superior even to a god; that the security of the god was altogether the benefit of nature, which had exempted him from suffering; but that the security of the wise man was his own benefit, and derived altogether from himself and from his own exertions.

The sensibility of some men, however, to some of the objects which immediately affect themselves, is sometimes so strong as to render all self-command impossible. No sense of honour can control the fears of the man who is weak enough to faint, or to fall into convulsions, upon the approach of danger. Whether such weakness of nerves, as it has been called, may not by gradual exercise and proper discipline admit of some cure, may perhaps be doubtful. It seems certain that it ought never to be trusted or employed.

CHAPTER IV.

Of the Nature of Self-deceit, and of the Origin and Use of general Rules.

In order to pervert the rectitude of our own judgments concerning the propriety of our own conduct, it is not always necessary that the real and impartial spectator should be at a great distance. When he is at hand, when he is present, the violence and injustice of our own selfish passions are sometimes sufficient to induce the man within the breast to make a report very different from what the real circumstances of the case are capable of authorizing.

There are two different occasions upon which we examine our own conduct, and endeavour to view it in the light in which the impartial spectator would view it: first, when we are about to act; and, secondly, after we have acted. Our views are apt to be very partial in both cases; but they are apt to be most partial when it is of most importance that they should be otherwise.

When we are about to act, the eagerness of passion will seldom allow us to consider what we are doing with the candour of an indifferent person. The violent emotions which at that time agitate us, discolour our views of things, even when we are endeavouring to place ourselves in the situation of another, and to regard the objects that interest us in the light in which they will naturally appear to him. The fury of our own passions constantly calls us back to our own place, where every thing appears magnified and misrepresented by self-love. Of the manner in which those objects would appear to another, of the view which he would

take of them, we can obtain, if I may say so, but instantaneous glimpses, which vanish in a moment, and which, even
while they last, are not altogether just.   We cannot even
for that moment divest ourselves entirely of the heat and
keenness with which our peculiar situation inspires us, nor
consider what we are about to do with the complete impartiality of an equitable judge.   The passions, upon this
account, as Father Malebranche says, all justify themselves,
and seem reasonable and proportioned to their objects as
long as we continue to feel them.

When the action is over, indeed, and the passions which
prompted it have subsided, we can enter more coolly into
the sentiments of the indifferent spectator.   What before
interested us is now become almost as indifferent to us as it
always was to him, and we can now examine our own conduct
with his candour and impartiality.   The man of to-day is
no longer agitated by the same passions which distracted
the man of yesterday : and when the paroxysm of emotion,
in the same manner as when the paroxysm of distress, is
fairly over, we can identify ourselves, as it were, with the
ideal man within the breast, and, in our own character,
view, as in the one case our own situation, so in the other
our own conduct, with the severe eyes of the most impartial
spectator.   But our judgments now are often of little importance in comparison of what they were before, and can
frequently produce nothing but vain regret and unavailing
repentance, without always securing us from the like errors in time to come.   It is seldom, however, that they are
quite candid even in this case.   The opinion which we entertain of our own character depends entirely on our judgment concerning our past conduct.   It is so disagreeable
to think ill of ourselves, that we often purposely turn away
our view from those circumstances which might render that
judgment unfavourable.   He is a bold surgeon, they say,
whose hand does not tremble when he performs an opera-

tion upon his own person ; and he is often equally bold who
does not hesitate to pull off the mysterious veil of self-de-
lusion which covers from his view the deformities of his
own conduct. Rather than see our own behaviour under
so disagreeable an aspect, we too often, foolishly and weakly,
endeavour to exasperate anew those unjust passions which
had formerly misled us ; we endeavour by artifice to awaken our old hatreds, and irritate afresh our almost forgotten
resentments: we even exert ourselves for this miserable
purpose, and thus persevere in injustice, merely because we
once were unjust, and because we are ashamed and afraid
to see that we were so.

So partial are the views of mankind with regard to the
propriety of their own conduct, both at the time of action
and after it ; and so difficult is it for them to view it in the
light in which any indifferent spectator would consider
it. But if it was by a peculiar faculty, such as the
moral sense is supposed to be, that they judged of their
own conduct, if they were endued with a particular power
of perception, which distinguished the beauty or deformity of passions and affections; as their own passions
would be more immediately exposed to the view of this
faculty, it would judge with more accuracy concerning them
than concerning those of other men, of which it had only a
more distant prospect.

This self-deceit, this fatal weakness of mankind, is the
source of half the disorders of human life. If we saw
ourselves in the light in which others see us, or in which
they would see us if they knew all, a reformation would
generally be unavoidable. We could not otherwise endure
the sight.

Nature, however, has not left this weakness, which is of
so much importance altogether without a remedy ; nor has

she abandoned us entirely to the delusions of self-love
Our continual observations upon the conduct of others insensibly lead us to form to ourselves certain general rules
concerning what is fit and proper either to be done or to be
avoided. Some of their actions shock all our natural sentiments. We hear every body about us express the like
detestation against them. This still further confirms, and
even exasperates, our natural sense of their deformity. It
satisfies us that we view them in the proper light, when we
see other people view them in the same light. We resolve never to be guilty of the like, nor ever, upon any account, to render ourselves in this manner the objects of
universal disapprobation. We thus naturally lay down to
ourselves a general rule, that all such actions are to be
avoided, as tending to render us odious, contemptible, or
punishable,—the objects of all those sentiments for which we
have the greatest dread and aversion. Other actions, on
the contrary, call forth our approbation, and we hear every
body around us express the same favourable opinion concerning them. Every body is eager to honour and reward
them. They excite all those sentiments for which we have
by nature the strongest desire ; the love, the gratitude, the
admiration, of mankind. We become ambitious of performing the like; and thus naturally lay down to ourselves a
rule of another kind, that every opportunity of acting in
this manner is carefully to be sought after.

It is thus that the general rules of morality are formed.
They are ultimately founded upon experience of what, in
particular instances, our moral faculties, our natural sense
of merit and propriety, approve or disapprove of. We do
not originally approve or condemn particular actions,
because, upon examination, they appear to be agreeable or
inconsistent with a certain general rule. The general rule,
on the contrary, is formed by finding from experience that
all actions of a certain kind, or circumstanced in a certain

manner, are approved or disapproved of. To the man who first saw an inhuman murder committed from avarice, envy, or unjust resentment, and upon one, too, that loved and trusted the murderer; who beheld the last agonies of the dying person; who heard him with his expiring breath complain more of the perfidy and ingratitude of his false friend than of the violence which had. been done to him; there could be no occasion, in order to conceive how horrible such an action was, that he should reflect, that one of the most sacred rules of conduct was what prohibited the taking away the life of an innocent person, that this was a plain violation of that rule, and, consequently, a very blameable action. His detestation of this crime, it is evident, would arise instantaneously and antecedent to his having formed to himself any such general rule. The general rule, on the contrary, which he might afterwards form, would be founded upon the detestation which he felt necessarily arise in his own breast, at the thought of this and every other particular action of the same kind.

When we read in history or romance the account of actions either of generosity or of baseness, the admiration which we conceive for the one, and the contempt which we feel for the other, neither of them arise from reflecting that there are certain general rules which declare all actions of the one kind admirable, and all actions of the other contemptible. Those general rules, on the contrary, are all formed from the experience we have had of the effects which actions of all different kinds naturally produce upon us.

An amiable action, a respectable action, an horrid action, are all of them actions which naturally excite for the person who performs them, the love, the respect, or the horror of the spectator. The general rules which determine what actions are, and what are not, the objects of each of those sentiments, can be formed no other way than by observing what actions actually and in fact excite them.

When these general rules, indeed, have been formed when they are universally acknowledged and established by the concurring sentiments of mankind, we frequently appeal to them as to the standards of judgment, in debating concerning the degree of praise or blame that is due to certain actions of a complicated and dubious nature. They are upon these occasions commonly cited as the ultimate foundations of what is just and unjust in human conduct; and this circumstance seems to have misled several very eminent authors, to draw up their systems in such a manner as if they had supposed that the original judgments of mankind with regard to right and wrong were formed like the decisions of a court of judicatory, by considering first the general rule, and then, secondly, whether the particular action under consideration fell properly within its comprehension.

Those general rules of conduct, when they have been fixed in our mind by habitual reflection, are of great use in correcting the misrepresentations of self-love concerning what is fit and proper to be done in our particular situation. The man of furious resentment, if he was to listen to the dictates of that passion, would, perhaps, regard the death of his enemy as but a small compensation for the wrong he imagines he has received, which, however, may be no more than a very slight provocation. But his observations upon the conduct of others have taught him how horrible all such sanguinary revenges appear. Unless his education has been very singular, he has laid it down to himself as an inviolable rule, to abstain from them upon all occasions. This rule preserves its authority with him, and renders him incapable of being guilty of such a violence. Yet the fury of his own temper may be such, that had this been the first time in which he considered such an action, he would undoubtedly have determined it to be quite just and proper, and what every impartial spectator would approve of. But that reverence for the rule which past experience has impressed upon him, checks the impetuosity of his passion, and helps him to correct the too partial views which self-love might otherwise suggest of what was proper to be done in his situation. If he should allow himself to be so far transported by passion as to violate this rule, yet, even in this case, he cannot throw off altogether the awe and respect with which he has been accustomed to regard it. At the very time of acting, at the moment in which passion mounts the highest, he hesitates and trembles at the thought of what he is about to do : he is secretly conscious to himself that he is breaking through those measures of conduct which, in all his cool hours, he had resolved never to infringe, which he had never seen infringed by others without the highest disapprobation, and the infringement of which, his own mind forebodes, must soon render him the object of the same disagreeable sentiments. Before he can take the last fatal resolution, he is tormented with all the agonies of doubt and uncertainty ; he is terrified at the thought of violating so sacred a rule, and at the same time is urged and goaded on by the fury of his desires to violate it. He changes his purpose every moment ; sometimes he resolves to adhere to his principle, and not indulge a passion which may corrupt the remaining part of his life with the horrors of shame and repentance ; and a momentary calm takes possession of his breast, from the prospect of that security and tranquillity which he will enjoy when he thus determines not to expose himself to the hazard of a contrary conduct. But immediately the passion rouses anew, and with fresh fury drives him on to commit what he had the instant before resolved to abstain from. Wearied and distracted with those continual irresolutions, he at length, from a sort of despair, makes the last fatal and irrecoverable step ; but with that terror and amazement with which one flying from an enemy throws himself over a precipice, where he is sure of meeting with more certain destruction than from any thing that pursues him from behind. Such are his sentiments even at the time of acting; though he is then, no doubt, less sensible of the impropriety of his own conduct than afterwards, when his passion being gratified and palled, he begins to view what he has done in the light in which others are apt to view it; and actually feels, what he had only foreseen very imperfectly before, the stings of remorse and repentance begin to agitate and torment him.

CHAPTER V.

Of the Influence and Authority of the general Rules of Morality, and that they are justly regarded as the Laws of the Deity.

THE regard to those general rules of conduct is what is properly called a sense of duty, a principle of the greatest consequence in human life, and the only principle by which the bulk of mankind are capable of directing their actions. Many men behave very decently, and through the whole of their lives avoid any considerable degree of blame, who yet, perhaps, never felt the sentiment upon the propriety of which we found our approbation of their conduct, but acted merely from a regard to what they saw were the established rules of behaviour. The man who has received great benefits from another person, may, by the natural coldness of his temper, feel but a very small degree of the sentiment of gratitude. If he has been virtuously educated, however, he will often have been made to observe how odious those actions appear which denote a want of this sentiment, and how amiable the contrary. Though his heart, therefore, is not warmed with any grateful affection, he will strive to act as if it was, and will endeavour to pay all those regards and attentions to his patron which the liveliest gratitude could suggest. He will visit him regularly; he will behave to him respectfully; he will never talk of him but with expressions of the highest esteem, and of the many obligations which he owes to him. And, what is more, he will carefully embrace every opportunity of making a proper return for past services. He may do all this, too, without any hypocrisy or blameable dissimulation, without any selfish inten-

tion of obtaining new favours, and without any design of
imposing either upon his benefactor or the public. The
motive of his actions may be no other than a reverence for
the established rule of duty, a serious and earnest desire of
acting, in every respect, according to the law of gratitude.
A wife, in the same manner, may sometimes not feel that
tender regard for her husband which is suitable to the relation that subsists between them. If she has been virtuously educated, however, she will endeavour to act as if
she felt it, to be careful, officious, faithful, and sincere, and
to be deficient in none of those attentions which the sentiment of conjugal affection could have prompted her to perform. Such a friend, and such a wife, are neither of them,
undoubtedly, the very best of their kinds; and though both
of them may have the most serious and earnest desire to
fulfil every part of their duty, yet they will fail in many
nice and delicate regards, they will miss many opportunities
of obliging, which they could never have overlooked if they
had possessed the sentiment that is proper to their situation.
Though not the very first of their kinds, however, they are
perhaps the second; and if the regard to the general rules
of conduct has been very strongly impressed upon them,
neither of them will fail in any very essential part of their
duty. None but those of the happiest mould are capable of
suiting, with exact justness, their sentiments and behaviour
to the smallest difference of situation, and of acting upon
all occasions with the most delicate and accurate propriety.
The coarse clay of which the bulk of mankind are formed,
cannot be wrought up to such perfection. There is scarce
any man, however, who by discipline, education, and example, may not be so impressed with a regard to general
rules, as to act upon almost every occasion with tolerable
decency, and through the whole of his life to avoid any
considerable degree of blame.

Without this sacred regard to general rules, there is no

man whose conduct can be much depended upon It is
this which constitutes the most essential difference between
a man of principle and honour and a worthless fellow. The
one adheres, on all occasions, steadily and resolutely to his
maxims, and preserves, through the whole of his life, one
even tenor of conduct. The other acts variously and
accidentally, as humour, inclination, or interest, chance to
be uppermost. Nay, such are the inequalities of humour
to which all men are subject, that without this principle,
the man who, in all his cool hours, had the most delicate
sensibility to the propriety of conduct, might often be led
to act absurdly upon the most frivolous occasions, and when
it was scarce possible to assign any serious motive for his
behaving in this manner. Your friend makes you a visit
when you happen to be in a humour which makes it disagreeable to receive him ; in your present mood his civility is very apt to appear an impertinent intrusion ; and
if you were to give way to the views of things which at
this time occur, though civil in your temper, you would
behave to him with coldness and contempt. What renders
you incapable of such a rudeness is nothing but a regard
to the general rules of civility and hospitality, which prohibit it. That habitual reverence which your former experience has taught you for these, enables you to act, upon
all such occasions, with nearly equal propriety, and hinders
those inequalities of temper, to which all men are subject,
from influencing your conduct in any very sensible degree.
But if without regard to these general rules, even the duties
of politeness, which are so easily observed, and which one
can scarce have any serious motive to violate, would yet
be so frequently violated, what would become of the duties
of justice, of truth, of chastity, of fidelity, which it is often
so difficult to observe, and which there may be so many
strong motives to violate ? But upon the tolerable observance of these duties depends the very existence of human
society, which would crumble into nothing if mankind were

not generally impressed with a reverence for those important rules of conduct.

This reverence is still further enhanced by an opinion which is first impressed by nature, and afterwards confirmed by reasoning and philosophy, that those important rules of morality are the commands and laws of the Deity, who will finally reward the obedient, and punish the transgressors of their duty.

This opinion or apprehension, I say, seems first to be impressed by nature.   Men are naturally led to ascribe to those mysterious beings, whatever they are, which happen in any country to be the objects of religious fear, all their own sentiments and passions.   They have no other, they can conceive no other, to ascribe to them.   Those unknown intelligences which they imagine but see not, must necessarily be formed with some sort of resemblance to those intelligences of which they have experience.   During the ignorance and darkness of pagan superstition, mankind seem to have formed the ideas of their divinities with so little delicacy, that they ascribed to them, indiscriminately, all the passions of human nature, those not excepted which do the least honour to our species, such as lust, hunger, avarice, envy, revenge.   They could not fail, therefore, to ascribe to those beings, for the excellence of whose nature they still conceived the highest admiration, those sentiments and qualities which are the great ornaments of humanity, and which seem to raise it to a resemblance of divine perfection, the love of virtue and beneficence, and the abhorrence of vice and injustice.   The man who was injured called upon Jupiter to be witness of the wrong that was done to him, and could not doubt but that divine being would behold it with the same indignation which would animate the meanest of mankind, who looked on when injustice was committed.   The man who did the injury felt

himself to be the proper object of the detestation and resentment of mankind; and his natural fears led him to impute the same sentiments to those awful beings, whose
presence he could not avoid, and whose power he could not
resist. These natural hopes, and fears, and suspicions, were
propagated by sympathy, and confirmed by education; and
the gods were universally represented and believed to be
the rewarders of humanity and mercy, and the avengers of
perfidy and injustice. And thus religion, even in its rudest
form, gave a sanction to the rules of morality, long before
the age of artificial reasoning and philosophy. That the
terrors of religion should thus enforce the natural sense of
duty, was of too much importance to the happiness of mankind for nature to leave it dependent upon the slowness
and uncertainty of philosophical researches.

These researches, however, when they came to take place,
confirmed those original anticipations of nature. Upon
whatever we suppose that our moral faculties are founded,
whether upon a certain modification of reason, upon an
original instinct, called a moral sense, or upon some other
principle of our nature, it cannot be doubted that they were
given us for the direction of our conduct in this life. They
carry along with them the most evident badges of this
authority, which denote that they were set up within us to
be the supreme arbiters of all our actions, to superintend
all our senses, passions, and appetites, and to judge how
far each of them was either to be indulged or restrained.
Our moral faculties are by no means, as some have pretended, upon a level in this respect with the other faculties
and appetites of our nature, endowed with no more right to
restrain these last, than these last are to restrain them. No
other faculty or principle of action judges of any other.
Love does not judge of resentment, nor resentment of love.
Those two passions may be opposite to one another, but
cannot, with any propriety, be said to approve or disap-

prove of one another.   But it is the peculiar office of those
faculties now under our consideration to judge, to bestow censure or applause upon all the other principles of our nature.
They may be considered as a sort of senses, of which those
principles are the objects.   Every sense is supreme over
its own objects.   There is no appeal from the eye with
regard to the beauty of colours, nor from the ear with regard to the harmony of sounds, nor from the taste with
regard to the agreeableness of flavours.   Each of those
senses judges in the last resort of its own objects.   Whatever gratifies the taste is sweet, whatever pleases the eye
is beautiful, whatever soothes the ear is harmonious.   The
very essence of each of those qualities consists in its being
fitted to please the sense to which it is addressed.   It belongs to our moral faculties, in the same manner, to determine when the ear ought to be soothed, when the eye ought
to be indulged, when the taste ought to be gratified, when
and how far every other principle of our nature ought either
to be indulged or restrained.   What is agreeable to our
moral faculties, is fit, and right, and proper to be done ; the
contrary, wrong, unfit, and improper.   The sentiments
which they approve of are graceful and becoming ; the contrary, ungraceful and unbecoming.   The very words, right,
wrong, fit, improper, graceful, unbecoming, mean only what
pleases or displeases those faculties.

Since these, therefore, were plainly intended to be the
governing principles of human nature, the rules which they
prescribe are to be regarded as the commands and laws of
the Deity, promulgated by those vicegerents which he has
thus set up within us.   All general rules are commonly denominated laws : thus the general rules which bodies observe in
the communication of motion, are called the laws of motion·
But those general rules which our moral faculties observe in
approving or condemning whatever sentiment or action is
subjected to their examination, may much more justly be

denominated such. They have a much greater resemblance to what are properly called laws, those general rules which the sovereign lays down to direct the conduct of his subjects. Like them they are rules to direct the free actions of men: they are prescribed most surely by a lawful superior, and are attended too with the sanction of rewards and punishments. Those vicegerents of God within us never fail to punish the violation of them by the torments of inward shame and self-condemnation; and, on the contrary, always reward obedience with tranquillity of mind, with contentment, and self-satisfaction.

There are innumerable other considerations which serve to confirm the same conclusion. The happiness of mankind, as well as of all other rational creatures, seems to have been the original purpose intended by the Author of Nature when he brought them into existence. No other end seems worthy of that supreme wisdom and divine benignity which we necessarily ascribe to him; and this opinion, which we are led to by the abstract consideration of his infinite perfections, is still more confirmed by the examination of the works of Nature, which seem all intended to promote happiness, and to guard against misery. But, by acting according to the dictates of our moral faculties, we necessarily pursue the most effectual means for promoting the happiness of mankind, and may therefore be said, in some sense, to co-operate with the Deity, and to advance, as far as in our power, the plan of providence. By acting otherwise, on the contrary, we seem to obstruct, in some measure, the scheme which the Author of Nature has established for the happiness and perfection of the world, and to declare ourselves, if I may say so, in some measure the enemies of God. Hence we are naturally encouraged to hope for his extraordinary favour and reward in the one case, and to dread his vengeance and punishment in the other.

There are besides many other reasons, and many other natural principles, which all tend to confirm and inculcate the same salutary doctrine. If we consider the general rules by which external prosperity and adversity are commonly distributed in this life, we shall find, that notwithstanding the disorder in which all things appear to be in this world, yet even here every virtue naturally meets with its proper reward, with the recompence which is most fit to encourage and promote it; and this too so surely, that it requires a very extraordinary concurrence of circumstances entirely to disapoint it. What is the reward most proper for encouraging industry, prudence, and circumspection?—Success in every sort of business. And is it possible that in the whole of life these virtues should fail of attaining it?—Wealth and external honours are their proper recompence, and the recompence which they can seldom fail of acquiring. What reward is most proper for promoting the practice of truth, justice, and humanity?—The confidence, the esteem, and love of those we live with. Humanity does not desire to be great, but to be beloved. It is not in being rich that truth and justice would rejoice, but in being trusted and believed, recompences which those virtues must almost always acquire. By some very extraordinary and unlucky circumstance, a good man may come to be suspected of a crime of which he was altogether incapable, and upon that account be most unjustly exposed for the remaining part of his life to the horror and aversion of mankind. By an accident of this kind he may be said to lose his all, notwithstanding his integrity and justice; in the same manner as a cautious man, notwithstanding his utmost circumspection, may be ruined by an earthquake or an inundation. Accidents of the first kind, however, are perhaps still more rare, and still more contrary to the common course of things, than those of the second; and it still remains true, that the practice of truth, justice, and humanity, is a certain and almost infallible method of acquiring what those virtues chiefly aim at, the confidence and love of those we live with. A person may be very easily misrepresented with regard to a particular action ; but it is scarce possible that he should be so with regard to the general tenor of his conduct. An innocent man may be believed to have done wrong—this, however, will rarely happen. On the contrary, the established opinion of the innocence of his manners will often lead us to absolve him where he has really been in the fault, notwithstanding very strong presumptions. A knave, in the same manner, may escape censure, or even meet with applause, for a particular knavery, in which his conduct is not understood. But no man was ever habitually such, without being almost universally known to be so, and without being even frequently suspected of guilt, when he was in reality perfectly innocent. And so far as vice and virtue can be either punished or rewarded by the sentiments and opinions of mankind, they both, according to the common course of things, meet even here with something more than exact and impartial justice.

But though the general rules by which prosperity and adversity are commonly distributed, when considered in this cool and philosophical light, appear to be perfectly suited to the situation of mankind in this life, yet they are by no means suited to some of our natural sentiments. Our natural love and admiration for some virtues is such, that we should wish to bestow on them all sorts of honours and rewards, even those which we must acknowledge to be the proper recompences of other qualities, with which those virtues are not always accompanied. Our detestation, on the contrary, for some vices is such, that we should desire to heap upon them every sort of disgrace and disaster, those not excepted which are the natural consequences of very different qualities. Magnanimity, generosity, and justice, command so high a degree of admiration, that we desire to see them crowned with wealth, and power, and honours of every kind, the natural consequences of prudence, industry, and application; qualities with which those virtues are not inseparably connected. Fraud, falsehood, brutality, and violence, on the other hand, excite in every human breast such scorn and abhorrence, that our indignation rouses to see them possess those advantages which they may in some sense be said to have merited, by the diligence and industry with which they are sometimes attended. The industrious knave cultivates the soil; the indolent good man leaves it un cultivated. Who ought to reap the harvest? Who starve, and who live in plenty? The natural course of things decides it in favour of the knave: the natural sentiments of mankind in favour of the man of virtue. Man judges that the good qualities of the one are greatly over-recompensed by those advantages which they tend to procure him, and that the omissions of the other are by far too severely punished by the distress which they naturally bring upon him; and human laws, the consequences of human sentiments, forfeit the life and the estate of the industrious and cautious traitor, and reward, by extraordinary recompences, the fidelity and public spirit of the improvident and careless good citizen. Thus man is by nature directed to correct, in some measure, that distribution of things which she herself would otherwise have made. The rules which for this purpose she prompts him to follow, are different from those which she herself observes. She bestows upon every virtue, and upon every vice, that precise reward or punishment which is best fitted to encourage the one, or to restrain the other. She is directed by this sole consideration, and pays little regard to the different degrees of merit and demerit which they may seem to possess in the sentiments and passions of man. Man, on the contrary, pays regard to this only, and would endeavour to render the state of every virtue precisely proportioned to that degree of love and esteem, and of every vice to that degree of contempt and abhorrence, which he himself conceives for it. The rules which she follows are fit for her, those which he follows for him : but both are calculated to promote the same great end, the order of the world, and the perfection and happiness of human nature.

But though man is thus employed to alter that distribution of things which natural events would make, if left to themselves; though like the gods of the poets he is perpetually interposing, by extraordinary means, in favour of virtue and in opposition to vice, and, like them, endeavours to turn away the arrow that is aimed at the head of the righteous, but to accelerate the sword of destruction that is lifted up against the wicked ; yet he is by no means able to render the fortune of either quite suitable to his own sentiments and wishes. The natural course of things cannot be entirely controlled by the impotent endeavours of man : the current is too rapid and too strong for him to stop it ; and though the rules which direct it appear to have been established for the wisest and best purposes, they sometimes produce effects which shock all his natural sentiments That a great combination of men should prevail over a small one; that those who engage in an enterprize with forethought and all necessary preparation, should prevail over such as oppose them without any; and that every end should be acquired by those means only which nature has established for acquiring it, seems to be a rule not only necessary and unavoidable in itself, but even useful and proper for rousing the industry and attention of mankind. Yet when, in consequence of this rule, violence and artifice prevail over sincerity and justice, what indignation does it not excite in the breast of every human spectator ? What sorrow and compassion for the sufferings of the innocent, and what furious resentment against the success of the oppressor ? We are equally grieved and enraged at the wrong that is done, but often find it altogether out of our power to redress it. When we thus despair of finding any force upon earth which can check the triumph of injustice, we naturally appeal to heaven, and hope that the great Author of our nature will himself execute hereafter, what all the principles which he has given us for the direction of our conduct prompt us to attempt even here; that he will complete the plan which he himself has thus taught us to begin; and will, in a life to come, render to every one according to the works which he has performed in this world. And thus we are led to the belief of a future state, not only by the weaknesses, by the hopes and fears of human nature, but by the noblest and best principles which belong to it, by the love of virtue, and by the abhorrence of vice and injustice.

" Does it suit the greatness of God," says the eloquent and philosophical Bishop of Clermont, with that passionate and exaggerating force of imagination which seems sometimes to exceed the bounds of decorum; " does it suit the greatness of God to leave the world which he has created in so universal a disorder? To see the wicked prevail almost always over the just; the innocent dethroned by the usurper; the father become the victim of the ambition of an unnatural son; the husband expiring under the stroke of a barbarous and faithless wife? From the height of his greatness ought God to behold those melancholy events as a fantastical amusement, without taking any share in them? Because he is great, should he be weak, or unjust, or barbarous? Because men are little, ought they to be allowed either to be dissolute without punishment, or virtuous without reward? O God! if this is the character of your supreme being; if it is you whom we adore under such dreadful ideas; I can no longer acknowledge you for my father, for my protector, for the comforter of my sorrow, the support of my weakness, the rewarder of my fidelity. You would then be no more than an indolent and fantastical tyrant, who sacrifices mankind to his insolent vanity, and who has brought them out of nothing, only to make them serve for the sport of his leisure and of his caprice."

When the general rules which determine the merit and demerit of actions come thus to be regarded as the laws of an all-powerful being, who watches over our conduct, and who, in a life to come, will reward the observance and punish the breach of them—they necessarily acquire a new sacredness from this consideration. That our regard to the will of the Deity ought to be the supreme rule of our conduct, can be doubted of by nobody who believes his existence. The very thought of disobedience appears to involve in it the most shocking impropriety. How vain, how absurd would it be for man, either to oppose or to neglect the commands that were laid upon him by infinite wisdom and infinite power! How unnatural, how impiously ungrateful not to reverence the precepts that were prescribed to him by the infinite goodness of his Creator, even though no punishment was to follow their violation! The sense of propriety, too, is here well supported by the strongest motives of self-interest. The idea that, however we may escape the observation of man or be placed above the reach of human punishment, yet we are always acting under the eye and exposed to the punishment of God, the great avenger of injustice, is a motive capable of restraining the most headstrong passions, with those at least who, by constant reflection, have rendered it familiar to them.

It is in this manner that religion enforces the natural sense of duty : and hence it is that mankind are generally disposed to place great confidence in the probity of those who seem deeply impressed with religious sentiments. Such persons, they imagine, act under an additional tie, besides those which regulate the conduct of other men. The regard to the propriety of action, as well as to reputation ; the regard to the applause of his own breast, as well

as to that of others; are motives which, they suppose, have
the same influence over the religious man as over the man
of the world.   But the former lies under another restraint,
and never acts deliberately but as in the presence of that
great Superior who is finally to recompense him according to his deeds.   A greater trust is reposed, upon this account, in the regularity and exactness of his conduct.   And
wherever the natural principles of religion are not corrupted by the factious and party zeal of some worthless cabal;
wherever the first duty which it requires is to fulfil all the
obligations of morality; wherever men are not taught to regard frivolous observances as more immediate duties of religion than acts of justice and beneficence; and to imagine,
that by sacrifices, and ceremonies, and vain supplications,
they can bargain with the Deity for fraud, and perfidy, and
violence, the world undoubtedly judges right in this respect, and justly places a double confidence in the rectitude of the religious man's behaviour.

CHAPTER VI.

In what cases the Sense of Duty ought to be the sole Principle of our Conduct; and in what cases it ought to concur with other Motives.

RELIGION affords such strong motives to the practice of virtue, and guards us by such powerful restraints from the temptations of vice, that many have been led to suppose that religious principles were the sole laudable motives of action. "We ought neither," they say, "to reward from gratitude, nor punish from resentment; we ought neither to protect the helplessness of our children, nor afford support to the infirmities of our parents, from natural affection. All affections for particular objects ought to be extinguished in our breast, and one great affection take the place of all others, the love of the Deity, the desire of rendering ourselves agreeable to him, and of directing our conduct in every respect according to his will. We ought not to be grateful from gratitude, we ought not to be charitable from humanity, we ought not to be public-spirited from the love of our country, nor generous and just from the love of mankind. The sole principle and motive of our conduct in the performance of all those different duties, ought to be a sense that God has commanded us to perform them." I shall not at present take time to examine this opinion particularly; I shall only observe, that we should not have expected to have found it entertained by any sect, who professed themselves of a religion in which, as it is the first precept to love the Lord our God with all our heart, with all our soul, and with all our strength, so it is the second to love our neighbour as we love ourselves; and we love ourselves surely for our own sakes, and not merely because we are commanded to do so. That the sense of duty should be the sole principle of our conduct, is nowhere the precept of Christianity ; but that it should be the ruling and the governing one, as philosophy, and as, indeed, common sense, directs. It may be a question, however, in what cases our actions ought to arise chiefly or entirely from a sense of duty, or from a regard to general rules ; and in what cases some other sentiment or affection ought to concur, and have a principal influence.

The decision of this question, which cannot, perhaps, be given with any very great accuracy, will depend upon two different circumstances ; first, upon the natural agreeableness or deformity of the sentiment or affection which would prompt us to any action independent of all regard to general rules ; and, secondly, upon the precision and exactness, or the looseness and inaccuracy, of the general rules themselves.

I. First, I say, it will depend upon the natural agreeableness or deformity of the affection itself, how far our actions ought to arise from it, or entirely proceed from a regard to the general rule.

All those graceful and admired actions to which the benevolent affections would prompt us, ought to proceed as much from the passions themselves as from any regard to the general rules of conduct. A benefactor thinks himself but ill requited if the person upon whom he has bestowed his good offices repays them merely from a cold sense of duty, and without any affection to his person. A husband is dissatisfied with the most obedient wife, when he imagines her conduct is animated by no other principle besides her regard to what the relation she stands in requires. Though a son should fail in none of the offices of filial duty, yet if he wants that affectionate reverence which it so well becomes him to feel, the parent may justly complain of his indifference. Nor could a son be quite satisfied with a parent who, though he performed all the duties of his situation, had nothing of that fatherly fondness which might have been expected from him. With regard to all such benevolent and social affections, it is agreeable to see the sense of duty employed rather to restrain than to enliven them, rather to hinder us from doing too much, than to prompt us to do what we ought. It gives us pleasure to see a father obliged to check his own fondness, a friend obliged to set bounds to his natural generosity, a person who has received a benefit, obliged to restrain the too sanguine gratitude of his own temper.

The contrary maxim takes place with regard to the malevolent and unsocial passions. We ought to reward from the gratitude and generosity of our own hearts, without any reluctance, and without being obliged to reflect how great the propriety of rewarding; but we ought always to punish with reluctance, and more from a sense of the propriety of punishing than from any savage disposition to revenge. Nothing is more graceful than the behaviour of the man who appears to resent the greatest injuries, more from a sense that they deserve, and are the proper objects of resentment, than from feeling himself the furies of that disagreeable passion; who, like a judge, considers only the general rule, which determines what vengeance is due for each particular offence; who, in executing that rule, feels less for what himself has suffered, than for what the offender is about to suffer; who, though in wrath, remembers mercy, and is disposed to interpret the rule in the most gentle and favourable manner, and to allow all the alleviations which the most candid humanity could, consistently with good sense, admit of.

As the selfish passions, according to what has formerly been observed, hold in other respects a sort of middle place between the social and unsocial affections, so do they

likewise in this. The pursuit of the objects of private interest, in all common, little, and ordinary cases, ought to
flow rather from a regard to the general rules which prescribe such conduct, than from any passion for the objects
themselves; but upon more important and extraordinary
occasions, we should be awkward, insipid, and ungraceful,
if the objects themselves did not appear to animate us with
a considerable degree of passion. To be anxious, or to be
laying a plot either to gain or to save a single shilling,
would degrade the most vulgar tradesman in the opinion of
all his neighbours. Let his circumstances be ever so mean,
no attention to any such small matters, for the sake of the
things themselves, must appear in his conduct. His situation may require the most severe economy and the most
exact assiduity : but each particular exertion of that economy and assiduity must proceed, not so much from a regard
for that particular saving or gain, as for the general rule
which to him prescribes, with the utmost rigour, such a
tenor of conduct. His parsimony to-day must not arise
from a desire of the particular threepence which he will
save by it, nor his attendance in his shop from a passion for
the particular tenpence which he will acquire by it : both
the one and the other ought to proceed solely from a regard
to the general rule, which prescribes, with the most unrelenting severity, this plan of conduct to all persons in his
way of life. In this consists the difference between the
character of a miser and that of a person of exact economy
and assiduity. The one is anxious about small matters for
their own sake ; the other attends to them only in consequence of the scheme of life which he has laid down to
himself.

It is quite otherwise with regard to the more extraordinary and important objects of self-interest. A person appears mean-spirited, who does not pursue these with some
degree of earnestness for their own sake. We should de-

spise a prince who was not anxious about conquering or defending a province. We should have little respect for a private gentleman who did not exert himself to gain an estate, or even a considerable office, when he could acquire them without either meanness or injustice. A member of Parliament who shews no keenness about his own election, is abandoned by his friends as altogether unworthy of their attachment. Even a tradesman is thought a poor-spirited fellow among his neighbours, who does not bestir himself to get what they call an extraordinary job, or some uncommon advantage. This spirit and keenness constitutes the difference between the man of enterprise and the man of dull regularity. Those great objects of self-interest, of which the loss or acquisition quite changes the rank of the person, are the objects of the passion properly called ambition ; a passion which, when it keeps within the bounds of prudence and justice, is always admired in the world, and has even sometimes a certain irregular greatness, which dazzles the imagination when it passes the limits of both these virtues, and is not only unjust but extravagant. Hence the general admiration for heroes and conquerors, and even for statesmen, whose projects have been very daring and extensive, though altogether devoid of justice ; such as those of the cardinals of Richelieu and of Retz. The objects of avarice and ambition differ only in their greatness. A miser is as furious about a halfpenny as a man of ambition about the conquest of a kingdom.

II. Secondly, I say it will depend partly upon the precision and exactness, or the looseness and inaccuracy of the general rules themselves, how far our conduct ought to proceed entirely from a regard to them.

The general rules of almost all the virtues, the general rules which determine what are the offices of prudence, of charity, of generosity, of gratitude, of friendship, are in many respects loose and inaccurate, admit of many exceptions, and require so many modifications, that it is scarce possible to regulate our conduct entirely by a regard to them.   The common proverbial maxims of prudence, being founded in universal experience, are perhaps the best general rules which can be given about it.   To affect, however, a very strict and literal adherence to them, would evidently be the most absurd and ridiculous pedantry.   Of all the virtues I have just now mentioned, gratitude is that, perhaps, of which the rules are the most precise, and admit of the fewest exceptions.   That as soon as we can we should make a return of equal, and, if possible, of superior value to the services we have received, would seem to be a pretty plain rule, and one which admitted of scarce any exceptions. Upon the most superficial examination, however, this rule will appear to be in the highest degree loose and inaccurate, and to admit of ten thousand exceptions.   If your benefactor attended you in your sickness, ought you to attend him in his ? or can you fulfil the obligation of gratitude by making a return of a different kind ?   If you ought to attend him, how long ought you to attend him ?   The same time which he attended you, or longer, and how much longer ?   If your friend lent you money in your distress, ought you to lend him money in his ?   How much ought you to lend him ?   When ought you to lend him ?   Now, or to-morrow, or next month ?   And for how long a time ? It is evident, that no general rule can be laid down by which a precise answer can, in all cases, be given to any of these questions.   The difference between his character and yours, between his circumstances and yours, may be such, that you may be perfectly grateful, and justly refuse to lend him a halfpenny : and, on the contrary, you may be willing to lend, or even to give him ten times the sum which he lent you, and yet justly be accused of the blackest ingratitude, and of not having fulfilled the hundredth part of the obligation you lie under.   As the duties of gratitude, however, are perhaps the most sacred of all those which the beneficent virtues prescribe to us, so the general rules which determine them are, as I said before, the most accurate. Those which ascertain the actions required by friendship, humanity, hospitality, generosity, are still more vague and indeterminate.

There is, however, one virtue, of which the general rules determine, with the greatest exactness, every external action which it requires. This virtue is Justice. The rules of justice are accurate in the highest degree, and admit of no exceptions or modifications but such as may be ascertained as accurately as the rules themselves, and which generally, indeed, flow from the very same principles with them. If I owe a man ten pounds, justice requires that I should precisely pay him ten pounds, either at the time agreed upon, or when he demands it. What I ought to perform, how much I ought to perform, when and where I ought to perform it, the whole nature and circumstances of the action prescribed, are all of them precisely fixed and determined. Though it may be awkward and pedantic, therefore, to affect too strict an adherence to the common rules of prudence or generosity, there is no pedantry in sticking fast by the rules of justice. On the contrary, the most sacred regard is due to them; and the actions which this virtue requires are never so properly performed as when the chief motive for performing them is a reverential and religious regard to those general rules which require them. In the practice of the other virtues, our conduct should rather be directed by a certain idea of propriety, by a certain taste for a particular tenor of conduct, than by any regard to a precise maxim or rule; and we should consider the end and foundation of the rule more than the rule itself. But it is otherwise with regard to justice: the man who in that refines the least, and adheres with the most obstinate stedfastness to the general rules themselves, is the most com-

mendable, and the most to be depended upon. Though
the end of the rules of justice be to hinder us from hurting
our neighbour, it may frequently be a crime to violate them,
though we could pretend, with some pretext of reason, that
this particular violation could do no hurt. A man often
becomes a villain the moment he begins, even in his own
heart, to chicane in this manner. The moment he thinks
of departing from the most staunch and positive adherence
to what those inviolable precepts prescribe to him, he is no
longer to be trusted, and no man can say what degree of
guilt he may not arrive at. The thief imagines he does no
evil when he steals from the rich, what he supposes they
may easily want, and what possibly they may never even
know has been stolen from them. The adulterer imagines
he does no evil when he corrupts the wife of his friend,
provided he covers his intrigue from the suspicion of the
husband, and does not disturb the peace of the family.
When once we begin to give way to such refinements,
there is no enormity so gross of which we may not be
capable.

The rules of justice may be compared to the rules of
grammar; the rules of the other virtues to the rules which
critics lay down for the attainment of what is sublime and
elegant in composition. The one are precise, accurate,
and indispensable. The other are loose, vague, and indeterminate, and present us rather with a general idea of
the perfection we ought to aim at, than afford us any certain and infallible directions for acquiring it. A man may
learn to write grammatically by rule, with the most absolute
infallibility; and so, perhaps, he may be taught to act justly.
But there are no rules whose observance will infallibly lead
us to the attainment of elegance or sublimity in writing:
though there are some which may help us, in some measure, to correct and ascertain the vague ideas which we
might otherwise have entertained of those perfections. And

there are no rules by the knowledge of which we can infallibly be taught to act upon all occasions with prudence,
with just magnanimity, or proper beneficence : though there
are some which may enable us to correct and ascertain, in
several respects, the imperfect ideas which we might otherwise have entertained of those virtues.

It may sometimes happen, that with the most serious
and earnest desire of acting so as to deserve approbation,
we may mistake the proper rules of conduct, and thus be
misled by that very principle which ought to direct us.
It is in vain to expect that in this case mankind should
entirely approve of our behaviour. They cannot enter into
that absurd idea of duty which influenced us, nor go along
with any of the actions which follow from it. There is still,
however, something respectable in the character and behaviour of one who is thus betrayed into vice, by a wrong
sense of duty, or by what is called an erroneous conscience.
How fatally soever he may be misled by it, he is still, with
the generous and humane, more the object of commiseration
than of hatred or resentment. They lament the weakness
of human nature, which exposes us to such unhappy delusions, even while we are most sincerely labouring after
perfection, and endeavouring to act according to the best
principle which can possibly direct us. False notions of
religion are almost the only causes which can occasion any
very gross perversion of our natural sentiments in this
way ; and that principle which gives the greatest authority
to the rules of duty, is alone capable of distorting our ideas
of them in any considerable degree. In all other cases
common sense is sufficient to direct us, if not to the most
exquisite propriety of conduct, yet to something which is
not very far from it ; and provided we are desirous in earnest to do well, our behaviour will always, upon the whole,
be praiseworthy. That to obey the will of the Deity is
the first rule of duty, all men are agreed. But concerning

the particular commandments which that will may impose upon us, they differ widely from one another. In this, therefore, the greatest mutual forbearance and toleration is due; and though the defence of society requires that crimes should be punished, from whatever motives they proceed, yet a good man will always punish them with reluctance, when they evidently proceed from false notions of religious duty. He will never feel against those who commit them that indignation which he feels against other criminals, but will rather regret, and sometimes even admire, their unfortunate firmness and magnanimity, at the very time that he punishes their crime. In the tragedy of Mahomet, one of the finest of Mr Voltaire's, it is well represented what ought to be our sentiments for crimes which proceed from such motives. In that tragedy, two young people of different sexes, of the most innocent and virtuous dispositions, and without any other weakness except what endears them the more to us, a mutual fondness for one another, are instigated by the strongest motives of a false religion, to commit a horrid murder, that shocks all the principles of human nature. A venerable old man, who had expressed the most tender affection for them both, for whom, notwithstanding he was the avowed enemy of their religion, they had both conceived the highest reverence and esteem, and who was in reality their father, though they did not know him to be such, is pointed out to them as a sacrifice which God had expressly required at their hands, and they are commanded to kill him. While they are about executing this crime, they are tortured with all the agonies which can arise from the struggle between the idea of the indispensableness of religious duty on the one side, and compassion, gratitude, reverence for the age and love for the humanity and virtue of the person whom they are going to destroy, on the other. The representation of this exhibits one of the most interesting, and perhaps the most instructive, spectacles that was ever introduced upon any theatre. The sense of duty, however, at last prevails over all the amiable weaknesses of human nature. They execute the crime imposed upon them; but immediately discover their error, and the fraud which had deceived them, and are distracted with horror, remorse, and resentment. Such as are our sentiments for the unhappy Seid and Palmira, such ought we to feel for every person who is in this manner misled by religion, when we are sure that it is really religion that misleads him, and not the pretence of it, which is made a cover to some of the worst of human passions.

As a person may act wrong by following a wrong sense of duty, so nature may sometimes prevail, and lead him to act right in opposition to it. We cannot in this case be displeased to see that motive prevail, which we think ought to prevail, though the person himself is so weak as to think otherwise. As his conduct, however, is the effect of weakness, not principle, we are far from bestowing upon it any thing that approaches to complete approbation. A bigotted Roman Catholic, who, during the massacre of St Bartholomew, had been so overcome by compassion, as to save some unhappy Protestants whom he thought it his duty to destroy, would not seem to be entitled to that high applause which we should have bestowed upon him, had he exerted the same generosity with complete self-approbation. We might be pleased with the humanity of his temper, but we should still regard him with a sort of pity, which is altogether inconsistent with the admiration that is due to perfect virtue. It is the same case with all the other passions. We do not dislike to see them exert themselves properly, even when a false notion of duty would direct the person to restrain them. A very devout quaker, who upon being struck upon one cheek, instead of turning up the other, should so far forget his literal interpretation of our Saviour's precept, as to bestow some good discipline upon the brute that insulted him, would not be disagreeable to us. We should laugh, and be diverted with his spirit, and rather like him the better for it.   But we should by no means regard him with that respect and esteem which would seem due to one who, upon a like occasion, had acted properly from a just sense of what was proper to be done. No action can properly be called virtuous, which is not accompanied with the sentiment of self-approbation.

THE

THEORY OF MORAL SENTIMENTS.

Part Fourth.

OF THE EFFECT OF UTILITY UPON THE SENTIMENT OF APPROBATION.

CONSISTING OF ONE SECTION.

CHAPTER I.

*Of the Beauty which the Appearance of Utility bestows upon
all the Productions of Art, and of the extensive Influence of
this Species of Beauty.*

THAT utility is one of the principal sources of beauty, has
been observed by every body who has considered with any
attention what constitutes the nature of beauty. The conveniency of a house gives pleasure to the spectator as well
as its regularity ; and he is as much hurt when he observes
the contrary defect, as when he sees the correspondent win-
dows of different forms, or the door not placed exactly in
the middle of the building. That the fitness of any system
or machine to produce the end for which it was intended,
bestows a certain propriety and beauty upon the whole, and
renders the very thought and contemplation of it agreeable,
is so very obvious, that nobody has overlooked it.

The cause, too, why utility pleases, has of late been assigned
by an ingenious and agreeable philosopher, who joins the
greatest depth of thought to the greatest elegance of expression, and possesses the singular and happy talent of treating
the abstrusest subjects not only with the most perfect perspicuity but with the most lively eloquence. The utility
of any object, according to him, pleases the master by perpetually suggesting to him the pleasure or conveniency
which it is fitted to promote. Every time he looks at it,
he is put in mind of this pleasure ; and the object in this
manner becomes a source of perpetual satisfaction and enjoyment. The spectator enters by sympathy into the sentiments of the master, and necessarily views the object

under the same agreeable aspect. When we visit the palaces of the great, we cannot help conceiving the satisfaction
we should enjoy if we ourselves were the masters, and were
possessed of so much artful and ingenuously contrived accommodation. A similar account is given why the appearance of inconveniency should render any object disagreeable both to the owner and to the spectator.

But that this fitness, this happy contrivance of any production of art, should often be more valued than the very
end for which it was intended; and that the exact adjustment of the means for attaining any conveniency or pleasure
should frequently be more regarded than that very conveniency or pleasure, in the attainment of which their whole
merit would seem to consist, has not, so far as I know, been
yet taken notice of by any body. That this, however, is
very frequently the case, may be observed in a thousand
instances, both in the most frivolous and in the most important concerns of human life.

When a person comes into his chamber and finds the
chairs all standing in the middle of the room, he is angry
with his servant, and rather than see them continue in that
disorder, perhaps takes the trouble himself to set them all
in their places with their backs to the wall. The whole
propriety of this new situation arises from its superior conveniency in leaving the floor free and disengaged. To attain this conveniency he voluntarily puts himself to more
trouble than all he could have suffered from the want of it;
since nothing was more easy than to have set himself down
upon one of them, which is probably what he does when
his labour is over. What he wanted therefore, it seems,
was not so much this conveniency, as that arrangement of
things which promotes it. Yet it is this conveniency which
ultimately recommends that arrangement, and bestows upon
it the whole of its propriety and beauty.

A watch, in the same manner, that falls behind above two minutes in a day, is despised by one curious in watches. He sells it perhaps for a couple of guineas, and purchases another at fifty, which will not lose above a minute in a fortnight. The sole use of watches, however, is to tell us what o'clock it is, and to hinder us from breaking any engagement, or suffering any other inconveniency by our ignorance in that particular point. But the person so nice with regard to this machine will not always be found either more scrupulously punctual than other men, or more anxiously concerned upon any other account to know precisely what time of day it is. What interests him is not so much the attainment of this piece of knowledge, as the perfection of the machine which serves to attain it.

How many people ruin themselves by laying out money on trinkets of frivolous utility? What pleases these lovers of toys, is not so much the utility as the aptness of the machines which are fitted to promote it. All their pockets are stuffed with little conveniencies. They contrive new pockets, unknown in the clothes of other people, in order to carry a greater number. They walk about loaded with a multitude of baubles, in weight, and sometimes in value, not inferior to an ordinary Jew's-box, some of which may sometimes be of some little use, but all of which might at all times be very well spared, and of which the whole utility is certainly not worth the fatigue of bearing the burden.

Nor is it only with regard to such frivolous objects that our conduct is influenced by this principle; it is often the secret motive of the most serious and important pursuits of both private and public life.

The poor man's son, whom heaven in its anger has visited with ambition, when he begins to look around him, admires the condition of the rich. He finds the cottage of his

father too small for his accommodation, and fancies he should
be lodged more at his ease in a palace. He is displeased
with being obliged to walk afoot, or to endure the fatigue
of riding on horseback. He sees his superiors carried about
in machines, and imagines that in one of these he could tra-
vel with less inconveniency. He feels himself naturally
indolent, and willing to serve himself with his own hands
as little as possible; and judges that a numerous retinue
of servants would save him from a great deal of trouble.
He thinks if he had attained all these, he would sit still con-
tentedly, and be quiet, enjoying himself in the thought of
the happiness and tranquillity of his situation. He is enchant-
ed with the distant idea of this felicity. It appears in his
fancy like the life of some superior rank of beings, and, in
order to arrive at it, he devotes himself for ever to the pursuit of wealth and greatness. To obtain the conveniencies
which these afford, he submits in the first year, nay, in the
first month of his appli cation, to more fatigue of body and
more uneasiness of mind, than he could have suffered
through the whole of his life from the want of them. He
studies to distinguish himself in some laborious profession.
With the most unrelenting industry he labours night and
day to acquire talents superior to all his competitors. He
endeavours next to bring those talents into public view, and
with equal assiduity solicits every opportunity of employment. For this purpose he makes his court to all mankind;
he serves those whom he hates, and is obsequious to those
whom he despises. Through the whole of his life he pursues the idea of a certain artificial and elegant repose which
he may never arrive at, for which he sacrifices a real tranquillity that is at all times in his power, and which, if in the
extremity of old age he should at last attain to it, he will
find to be in no respect preferable to that humble security
and contentment which he had abandoned for it. It is then,
in the last dregs of life, his body wasted with toil and diseases, his mind galled and ruffled by the memory of a thou-

sand injuries and disappointments which he imagines he has met with from the injustice of his enemies, or from the perfidy and ingratitude of his friends, that he begins at last to find that wealth and greatness are mere trinkets of frivolous utility, no more adapted for procuring ease of body or tranquillity of mind, than the tweezer-cases of the lover of toys; and like them, too, more troublesome to the person who carries them about with him than all the advantages they can afford him are commodious. There is no other real difference between them, except that the conveniencies of the one are somewhat more observable than those of the other. The palaces, the gardens, the equipage, the retinue of the great, are objects of which the obvious conveniency strikes every body. They do not require that their masters should point out to us wherein consists their utility. Of our own accord we readily enter into it, and by sympathy enjoy, and thereby applaud the satisfaction which they are fitted to afford him. But the curiosity of a toothpick, of an earpicker, of a machine for cutting the nails, or of any other trinket of the same kind, is not so obvious. Their conveniency may perhaps be equally great, but it is not so striking, and we do not so readily enter into the satisfaction of the man who possesses them. They are therefore less reasonable subjects of vanity than the magnificence of wealth and greatness ; and in this consists the sole advantage of these last. They more effectually gratify that love of distinction so natural to man. To one who was to live alone in a desolate island, it might be a matter of doubt perhaps, whether a palace, or a collection of such small conveniencies as are commonly contained in a tweezer-case, would contribute most to his happiness and enjoyment. If he is to live in society, indeed, there can be no comparison, because in this, as in all other cases, we constantly pay more regard to the sentiments of the spectator than to those of the person principally concerned, and consider rather how his situation will appear to other people than how it will appear to him-

self. If we examine, however, why the spectator distinguishes with such admiration the condition of the rich and
the great, we shall find that it is not so much upon account
of the superior ease or pleasure which they are supposed to
enjoy, as of the numberless artificial and elegant contrivances for promoting this ease or pleasure. He does not
even imagine that they are really happier than other
people; but he imagines that they possess more means of
happiness. And it is the ingenious and artful adjustment
of those means to the end for which they were intended,
that is the principal source of his admiration. But in the
langour of disease and the weariness of old age, the pleasures of the vain and empty distinctions of greatness disappear. To one in this situation they are no longer capable
of recommending those toilsome pursuits in which they had
formerly engaged him. In his heart he curses ambition,
and vainly regrets the ease and the indolence of youth, pleasures which are fled for ever, and which he has foolishly
sacrificed for what, when he has got it, can afford him no
real satisfaction. In this miserable aspect does greatness appear to every man when reduced, either by spleen or disease,
to observe with attention his own situation, and to consider
what it is that is really wanting to his happiness. Power
and riches appear then to be, what they are, enormous and
operose machines contrived to produce a few trifling conveniencies to the body, consisting of springs the most nice
and delicate, which must be kept in order with the most
anxious attention, and which, in spite of all our care, are
ready every moment to burst into pieces, and to crush in their
ruins their unfortunate possessor. They are immense fabrics
which it requires the labour of a life to raise, which threaten
every moment to overwhelm the person that dwells in them,
and which, while they stand, though they may save him
from some smaller inconveniencies, can protect him from
none of the severer inclemencies of the season. They keep
off the summer shower, not the winter storm, but leave him

always as much, and sometimes more, exposed than before to anxiety, to fear, and to sorrow; to diseases, to danger, and to death.

But though this splenetic philosophy, which in time of sickness or low spirits is familiar to every man, thus entirely depreciates those great objects of human desire, when in better health and in better humour, we never fail to regard them under a more agreeable aspect. Our imagination, which in pain and sorrow seems to be confined and cooped up within our own persons, in times of ease and prosperity expands itself to every thing around us. We are then charmed with the beauty of that accommodation which reigns in the palaces and economy of the great; and admire how every thing is adapted to promote their ease, to prevent their wants, to gratify their wishes, and to amuse and entertain their most frivolous desires. If we consider the real satisfaction which all these things are capable of affording, by itself and separated from the beauty of that arrangement which is fitted to promote it, it will always appear in the highest degree contemptible and trifling. But we rarely view it in this abstract and philosophical light. We naturally confound it in our imagination with the order, the regular and harmonious movement of the system, the machine or economy by means of which it is produced. The pleasures of wealth and greatness, when considered in this complex view, strike the imagination as something grand, and beautiful, and noble, of which the attainment is well worth all the toil and anxiety which we are so apt to bestow upon it.

And it is well that nature imposes upon us in this manner. It is this deception which rouses and keeps in continual motion the industry of mankind. It is this which first prompted them to cultivate the ground, to build houses, to found cities and commonwealths, and to invent and improve all the sciences and arts, which ennoble and embellish human life; which have entirely changed the whole face of the globe, have turned the rude forests of nature into agreeable and fertile plains, and made the trackless and barren ocean a new fund of subsistence, and the great high road of communication to the different nations of the earth. The earth, by these labours of mankind, has been obliged to redouble her natural fertility, and to maintain a greater multitude of inhabitants. It is to no purpose that the proud and unfeeling landlord views his extensive fields, and without a thought for the wants of his brethren, in imagination consumes himself the whole harvest that grows upon them. The homely and vulgar proverb, that the eye is larger than the belly, never was more fully verified than with regard to him. The capacity of his stomach bears no proportion to the immensity of his desires, and will receive no more than that of the meanest peasant. The rest he is obliged to distribute among those who prepare, in the nicest manner, that little which he himself makes use of, among those who fit up the palace in which this little is to be consumed, among those who provide and keep in order all the different baubles and trinkets which are employed in the economy of greatness; all of whom thus derive from his luxury and caprice that share of the necessaries of life which they would in vain have expected from his humanity or his justice. The produce of the soil maintains at all times nearly that number of inhabitants which it is capable of maintaining. The rich only select from the heap what is most precious and agreeable. They consume little more than the poor; and in spite of their natural selfishness and rapacity, though they mean only their own conveniency, though the sole end which they propose from the labours of all the thousands whom they employ be the gratification of their own vain and insatiable desires, they divide with the poor the produce of all their improvements. They are led by an invisible hand to make nearly the same distribution of the necessaries of life which would have been made had the earth been divided into equal portions among all its inhabitants; and thus, without intending it, without knowing it, advance the interest of the society, and afford means to the multiplication of the species. When providence divided the earth among a few lordly masters, it neither forgot nor abandoned those who seemed to have been left out in the partition. These last, too, enjoy their share of all that it produces. In what constitutes the real happiness of human life, they are in no respect inferior to those who would seem so much above them. In ease of body and peace of mind, all the different ranks of life are nearly upon a level, and the beggar, who suns himself by the side of the highway, possesses that security which kings are fighting for.

The same principle, the same love of system, the same regard to the beauty of order, of art and contrivance, frequently serves to recommend those institutions which tend to promote the public welfare. When a patriot exerts himself for the improvement of any part of the public police, his conduct does not always arise from pure sympathy with the happiness of those who are to reap the benefit of it. It is not commonly from a fellow-feeling with carriers and waggoners that a public-spirited man encourages the mending of high roads. When the Legislature establishes premiums and other encouragements to advance the linen or woollen manufactures, its conduct seldom proceeds from pure sympathy with the wearer of cheap or fine cloth, and much less from that with the manufacturer or merchant. The perfection of police, the extension of trade and manufactures, are noble and magnificent objects. The contemplation of them pleases us, and we are interested in whatever can tend to advance them. They make part of the great system of government, and the wheels of the political machine seem to move with more harmony and ease by means of them. We take pleasure in beholding the per-

fection of so beautiful and so grand a system, and we are
uneasy till we remove any obstruction that can in the least
disturb or encumber the regularity of its motions. All
constitutions of government, however, are valued only in
proportion as they tend to promote the happiness of those
who live under them. This is their sole use and end
From a certain spirit of system, however, from a certain
love of art and contrivance, we sometimes seem to value
the means more than the end, and to be eager to promote
the happiness of our fellow-creatures, rather from a view
to perfect and improve a certain beautiful and orderly
system than from any immediate sense or feeling of what
they either suffer or enjoy. There have been men of the
greatest public spirit, who have shewn themselves in other
respects not very sensible to the feelings of humanity.
And, on the contrary, there have been men of the greatest
humanity, who seem to have been entirely devoid of public
spirit. Every man may find in the circle of his acquaintance instances both of the one kind and the other. Who
had ever less humanity or more public spirit than the
celebrated legislator of Muscovy? The social and well-natured James the First of Great Britain seems, on the contrary, to have had scarce any passion, either for the glory
or the interest of his country. Would you awaken the industry of the man who seems almost dead to ambition, it
will often be to no purpose to describe to him the happiness of the rich and the great; to tell him that they are
generally sheltered from the sun and the rain, that they are
seldom hungry, that they are seldom cold, and that they
are rarely exposed to weariness, or to want of any kind.
The most eloquent exhortation of this kind will have
little effect upon him. If you would hope to succeed,
you must describe to him the conveniency and arrangement of the different apartments in their palaces; you
must explain to him the propriety of their equipages, and
point out to him the number, the order, and the different

offices of all their attendants.   If any thing is capable of
making impression upon him, this will.   Yet all these things
tend only to keep off the sun and the rain, to save them
from hunger and cold, from want and weariness.   In the
same manner, if you would implant public virtue in the
breast of him who seems heedless of the interest of his
country, it will often be to no purpose to tell him what
superior advantages the subjects of a well-governed state
enjoy; that they are better lodged, that they are better
clothed, that they are better fed.   These considerations will
commonly make no great impression.   You will be more
likely to persuade, if you describe the great system of
public police which procures these advantages,—if you explain the connections and dependencies of its several parts,
their mutual subordination to one another, and their general
subserviency to the happiness of the society ; if you shew
how this system might be introduced into his own country,
what it is that hinders it from taking place there at present,
how those obstructions might be removed, and all the
several wheels of the machine of government be made to
move with more harmony and smoothness, without grating
upon one another, or mutually retarding one another's
motions.   It is scarce possible that a man should listen to
a discourse of this kind, and not feel himself animated to
some degree of public spirit.   He will, at least for the moment, feel some desire to remove those obstructions, and to
put into motion so beautiful and so orderly a machine.
Nothing tends so much to promote public spirit as the study
of politics,—of the several systems of civil government, their
advantages and disadvantages,—of the constitution of our
own country, its situation, and interest with regard to foreign
nations, its commerce, its defence, the disadvantages it
labours under, the dangers to which it may be exposed,
how to remove the one, and how to guard against the other.
Upon this account political disquisitions, if just, and reasonable, and practicable, are of all the works of speculation the

most useful. Even the weakest and the worst of them are not altogether without their utility. They serve at least to animate the public passions of men, and rouse them to seek out the means of promoting the happiness of the society.

CHAPTER II.

Of the Beauty which the appearance of Utility bestows upon the Characters and Actions of Men ; and how far the Perception of this Beauty may be regarded as one of the original Principles of approbation.

THE characters of men, as well as the contrivances of art, or the institutions of civil government, may be fitted either to promote or to disturb the happiness both of the individual and of the society. The prudent, the equitable, the active, resolute, and sober character promises prosperity and satisfaction, both to the person himself and to every one connected with him. The rash, the insolent, the slothful, effeminate, and voluptuous, on the contrary, forebodes ruin to the individual, and misfortune to all who have any thing to do with him. The first turn of mind has at least all the beauty which can belong to the most perfect machine that was ever invented for promoting the most agreeable purpose : and the second, all the deformity of the most awkward and clumsy contrivance. What institution of government could tend so much to promote the happiness of mankind as the general prevalence of wisdom and virtue ? All government is but an imperfect remedy for the deficiency of these. Whatever beauty, therefore, can belong to civil government upon account of its utility, must in a far superior degree belong to these. On the contrary, what civil policy can be so ruinous and destructive as the vices of men ? The fatal effects of bad government arise from nothing, but that it does not sufficiently guard against the mischiefs which human wickedness gives occasion to.

This beauty and deformity which characters appear to derive from their usefulness or inconveniency, are apt to

strike in a peculiar manner those who consider, in an abstract and philosophical light, the actions and conduct of
mankind.   When a philosopher goes to examine why humanity is approved of or cruelty condemned, he does not
always form to himself, in a very clear and distinct man
ner, the conception of any one particular action either of
cruelty or of humanity, but is commonly contented with
the vague and indeterminate idea which the general names
of those qualities suggest to him.   But it is in particular
instances only that the propriety or impropriety, the merit
or demerit, of actions is very obvious and discernible. It is
only when particular examples are given that we perceive
distinctly either the concord or disagreement between our
own affections and those of the agent, or feel a social gratitude arise towards him in the one case, or a sympathetic
resentment in the other.   When we consider virtue and vice
in an abstract and general manner, the qualities by which
they excite these several sentiments seem in a great measure
to disappear, and the sentiments themselves become less
obvious and discernible.   On the contrary, the happy effects
of the one, and the fatal consequences of the other, seem
then to rise up to the view, and, as it were, to stand out
and distinguish themselves from all the other qualities of
either.

The same ingenious and agreeable author who first explained why utility pleases, has been so struck with this
view of things, as to resolve our whole approbation of virtue
into a perception of this species of beauty which results
from the appearance of utility.   No qualities of the mind,
he observes, are approved of as virtuous, but such as are
useful or agreeable either to the person himself or to others;
and no qualities are disapproved of as vicious, but such as
have a contrary tendency.   And Nature, indeed, seems to
have so happily adjusted our sentiments of approbation and
disapprobation, to the conveniency both of the individual

and of the society, that after the strictest examination it will
be found, I believe, that this is universally the case.   But
still I affirm, that it is not the view of this utility or hurtfulness which is either the first or principal source of our
approbation and disapprobation.   These sentiments are, no
doubt, enhanced and enlivened by the perception of tho
beauty or deformity which results from this utility or hurtfulness.   But still, I say, they are originally and essentially
different from this perception.

For, first of all, it seems impossible that the approbation
of virtue should be a sentiment of the same kind with that
by which we approve of a convenient and well-contrived
building ; or, that we should have no other reason for
praising a man than that for which we commend a chest of
drawers.

And, secondly, it will be found upon examination, that
the usefulness of any disposition of mind is seldom the first
ground of our approbation ; and that the sentiment of approbation always involves in it a sense of propriety quite
distinct from the perception of utility.   We may observe
this with regard to all the qualities which are approved of
as virtuous, both those which, according to this system, are
originally valued as useful to ourselves, as well as those
which are esteemed on account of their usefulness to
others.

The qualities most useful to ourselves are, first of all,
superior reason and understanding, by which we are capable
of discerning the remote consequences of all our actions,
and of foreseeing the advantage or detriment which is likely
to result from them ; and, secondly, self-command, by which
we are enabled to abstain from present pleasure or to endure
present pain, in order to obtain a greater pleasure or to avoid
a greater pain in some future time.   In the union of those

two qualities consists the virtue of prudence, of all the virtues that which is most useful to the individual.

With regard to the first of those qualities, it has been observed on a former occasion, that superior reason and understanding are originally approved of as just, and right, and accurate, and not merely as useful or advantageous. It is in the abstruser sciences, particularly in the higher parts of mathematics, that the greatest and most admired exertions of human reason have been displayed. But the utility of those sciences, either to the individual or to the public, is not very obvious, and to prove it, requires a discussion which is not always very easily comprehended. It was not, therefore, their utility which first recommended them to the public admiration. This quality was but little insisted upon, till it became necessary to make some reply to the reproaches of those, who, having themselves no taste for such sublime discoveries, endeavour to depreciate them as useless.

That self-command, in the same manner, by which we restrain our present appetites, in order to gratify them more fully upon another occasion, is approved of as much under the aspect of propriety as under that of utility. When we act in this manner, the sentiments which influence our conduct seem exactly to coincide with those of the spectator. The spectator does not feel the solicitations of our present appetites. To him the pleasure which we are to enjoy a week hence, or a year hence, is just as interesting as that which we are to enjoy this moment. When for the sake of the present, therefore, we sacrifice the future, our conduct appears to him absurd and extravagant in the highest degree, and he cannot enter into the principles which influence it. On the contrary, when we abstain from present pleasure, in order to secure greater pleasure to come; when we act as if the remote object interested us as much as that which immediately presses upon the senses, as our affections exactly correspond with his own, he cannot fail to approve of our behaviour; and as he knows from experience how few are capable of this self-command, he looks upon our conduct with a considerable degree of wonder and admiration. Hence arises that eminent esteem with which all men naturally regard a steady perseverance in the practice of frugality, industry, and application, though directed to no other purpose than the acquisition of fortune. The resolute firmness of the person who acts in this manner, and in order to obtain a great though remote advantage, not only gives up all present pleasures, but endures the greatest labour both of mind and body, necessarily commands our approbation. That view of his interest and happiness which appears to regulate his conduct, exactly tallies with the idea which we naturally form of it. There is the most perfect correspondence between his sentiments and our own, and at the same time, from our experience of the common weakness of human nature, it is a correspondence which we could not reasonably have expected. We not only approve, therefore, but in some measure admire his conduct, and think it worthy of a considerable degree of applause. It is the consciousness of this merited approbation and esteem which is alone capable of supporting the agent in this tenor of conduct. The pleasure which we are to enjoy ten years hence interests us so little in comparison with that which we may enjoy to-day; the passion which the first excites is naturally so weak in comparison with that violent emotion which the second is apt to give occasion to, that the one could never be any balance to the other, unless it was supported by the sense of propriety, by the consciousness that we merited the esteem and approbation of every body by acting in the one way, and that we became the proper objects of their contempt and derision by behaving in the other.

Humanity, justice, gen rosity, and public spirit, are the

qualities most useful to others.　Wherein consists the propriety of humanity and justice has been explained upon a former occasion, where it was shewn how much our esteem and approbation of those qualities depended upon the concord between the affections of the agent and those of the spectators.

The propriety of generosity and public spirit is founded upon the same principle with that of justice.　Generosity is different from humanity.　Those two qualities, which at first sight seem so nearly allied, do not always belong to the same person.　Humanity is the virtue of a woman, generosity of a man.　The fair sex, who have commonly much more tenderness than ours, have seldom so much generosity.　That women rarely make considerable donations is an observation of the civil law.*　Humanity consists merely in the exquisite fellow-feeling which the spectator entertains with the sentiments of the persons principally concerned, so as to grieve for their sufferings, to resent their injuries, and to rejoice at their good fortune.　The most humane actions require no self-denial, no self-command, no great exertion of the sense of propriety.　They consist only in doing what this exquisite sympathy would of its own accord prompt us to do.　But it is otherwise with generosity.　We never are generous except when in some respect we prefer some other person to ourselves, and sacrifice some great and important interest of our own to an equal interest of a friend or of a superior.　The man who gives up his pretensions to an office that was the great object of his ambition, because he imagines that the services of another are better entitled to it ; the man who exposes his life to defend that of his friend, which he judges to be of more importance, neither of them act from humanity, or because they feel more exquisitely what concerns that other person than what concerns themselves.　They both

* Raro mulieres donare solent.

consider those opposite interests, not in the light in which they naturally appear to themselves, but in that in which they appear to others. To every bystander, the success or preservation of this other person may justly be more interesting than their own; but it cannot be so to themselves. When to the interest of this other person, therefore, they sacrifice their own, they accommodate themselves to the sentiments of the spectator, and by an effort of magnanimity act according to those views of things which they feel must naturally occur to any third person. The soldier who throws away his life in order to defend that of his officer, would perhaps be but little affected by the death of that officer if it should happen without any fault of his own; and a very small disaster which had befallen himself might excite a much more lively sorrow. But when he endeavours to act so as to deserve applause, and to make the impartial spectator enter into the principles of his conduct, he feels that to every body but himself his own life is a trifle compared with that of his officer, and that when he sacrifices the one to the other, he acts quite properly and agreeably to what would be the natural apprehensions of every impartial bystander.

It is the same case with the greater exertions of public spirit. When a young officer exposes his life to acquire some inconsiderable addition to the dominions of his sovereign, it is not because the acquisition of the new territory is to himself an object more desirable than the preservation of his own life. To him his own life is of infinitely more value than the conquest of a whole kingdom for the state which he serves. But when he compares those two objects with one another, he does not view them in the light in which they naturally appear to himself, but in that in which they appear to the nation he fights for. To them the success of the war is of the highest importance—the life of a private person of scarce any consequence. When he puts himself in their situation, he immediately feels that he cannot be too prodigal of his blood, if by shedding it he can promote so valuable a purpose. In thus thwarting, from a sense of duty and propriety, the strongest of all natural propensities, consists the heroism of his conduct. There is many an honest Englishman, who in his private station would be more seriously disturbed by the loss of a guinea than by the national loss of Minorca, who yet, had it been in his power to defend that fortress, would have sacrificed his life a thousand times rather than, through his fault, have let it fall into the hands of the enemy. When the first Brutus led forth his own sons to a capital punishment, because they had conspired against the rising liberty of Rome, he sacrificed what, if he had consulted his own breast only, would appear to be the stronger to the weaker affection. Brutus ought naturally to have felt much more for the death of his own sons than for all that probably Rome could have suffered from the want of so great an example. But he viewed them, not with the eyes of a father, but with those of a Roman citizen. He entered so thoroughly into the sentiments of this last character, that he paid no regard to that tie by which he himself was connected with them ; and to a Roman citizen, the sons even of Brutus seemed contemptible when put into the balance with the smallest interest of Rome. In these and in all other cases of this kind, our admiration is not so much founded upon the utility as upon the unexpected, and on that account the great, the noble, and exalted propriety of such actions. This utility, when we come to view it, bestows upon them undoubtedly a new beauty, and upon that account still further recommends them to our approbation. This beauty, however, is chiefly perceived by men of reflection and speculation, and is by no means the quality which first recommends such actions to the natural sentiments of the bulk of mankind.

It is to be observed, that so far as the sentiment of ap-

probation arises from the perception of this beauty of utility, it has no reference of any kind to the sentiments of
others. If it was possible, therefore, that a person should
grow up to manhood without any communication with
society, his own actions might, notwithstanding, be agreeable or disagreeable to him on account of their tendency
to his happiness or disadvantage. He might perceive
a beauty of this kind in prudence, temperance, and good
conduct, and a deformity in the opposite behaviour; he
might view his own temper and character with that sort
of satisfaction with which we consider a well-contrived
machine in the one case; or with that sort of distaste
and dissatisfaction with which we regard a very awkward
and clumsy contrivance in the other. As these perceptions, however, are merely a matter of taste, and have all the
feebleness and delicacy of that species of perceptions upon
the justness of which what is properly called taste is founded,
they probably would not be much attended to by one in his
solitary and miserable condition. Even though they should
occur to him, they would by no means have the same effect
upon him, antecedent to his connection with society, which
they would have in consequence of that connection. He
would not be cast down with inward shame at the thought
of this deformity; nor would he be elevated with secret
triumph of mind from the consciousness of the contrary
beauty. He would not exult from the notion of deserving
reward in the one case, nor tremble from the suspicion of
meriting punishment in the other. All such sentiments suppose the idea of some other being, who is the natural judge
of the person that feels them; and it is only by sympathy
with the decisions of this arbiter of his conduct, that he can
conceive either the triumph of self-applause or the shame
of self-condemnation.

THE

THEORY OF MORAL SENTIMENTS.

~~~~~~~~~~~~~~

Part Fifth.

OF THE

INFLUENCE OF CUSTOM AND FASHION

UPON THE

SENTIMENTS OF MORAL APPROBATION AND DISAPPROBATION.

CONSISTING OF ONE SECTION.

CHAPTER I.

Of the Influence of Custom and Fashion upon our notions of Beauty and Deformity.

THERE are other principles besides those already enumerated, which have a considerable influence upon the moral sentiments of mankind, and are the chief causes of the many irregular and discordant opinions which prevail in different ages and nations concerning what is blameable or praiseworthy. These principles are custom and fashion, principles which extend their dominion over our judgments concerning beauty of every kind.

When two objects have frequently been seen together, the imagination acquires a habit of passing easily from the one to the other. If the first appear, we lay our account that the second is to follow. Of their own accord they put us in mind of one another, and the attention glides easily along them. Though, independent of custom, there should be no real beauty in their union, yet when custom has thus connected them together, we feel an impropriety in their separation. The one we think is awkward when it appears without its usual companion. We miss something which we expected to find, and the habitual arrangement of our ideas is disturbed by the disappointment. A suit of clothes, for example, seems to want something if they are without the most insignificant ornament which usually accompanies them, and we find a meanness or awkwardness in the absence even of a haunch button. When there is any natural propriety in the union, custom increases our sense of it, and makes a different arrangement appear still more disagreeable than it would otherwise seem to be. Those who have

been accustomed to see things in a good taste, are more
disgusted by whatever is clumsy or awkward. Where the
conjunction is improper, custom either diminishes, or takes
away altogether, our sense of the impropriety. Those who
have been accustomed to slovenly disorder lose all sense of
neatness or elegance. The modes of furniture or dress
which seem ridiculous to strangers, give no offence to the
people who are used to them.

Fashion is different from custom, or rather is a particular
species of it. That is not the fashion which every body
wears, but which those wear who are of a high rank or
character. The graceful, the easy, and commanding man
ners of the great, joined to the usual richness and magnificence of their dress, give a grace to the very form which
they happen to bestow upon it. As long as they continue
to use this form, it is connected in our imaginations with
the idea of something that is genteel and magnificent, and
though in itself it should be indifferent, it seems, on account
of this relation, to have something about it that is genteel
and magnificent too. As soon as they drop it, it loses all
the grace which it had appeared to possess before, and being now used only by the inferior ranks of people, seems to
have something of their meanness and awkwardness.

Dress and furniture are allowed by all the world to be
entirely under the dominion of custom and fashion. The
influence of those principles, however, is by no means confined to so narrow a sphere, but extends itself to whatever
is in any respect the object of taste,—to music, to poetry, to
architecture. The modes of dress and furniture are con
tinually changing; and that fashion appearing ridiculous
to-day which was admired five years ago, we are experi-
mentally convinced that it owed its vogue chiefly or entirely
to custom and fashion. Clothes and furniture are not made
of very durable materials. A well-fancied coat is done in

a twelvemonth, and cannot continue longer to propagate, as the fashion, that form according to which it was made. The modes of furniture change less rapidly than those of dress; because furniture is commonly more durable. In five or six years, however, it generally undergoes an entire revolution, and every man in his own time sees the fashion in this respect change many different ways. The productions of the other arts are much more lasting, and, when happily imagined, may continue to propagate the fashion of their make for a much longer time. A well-contrived building may endure many centuries; a beautiful air may be delivered down, by a sort of tradition, through many successive generations; a well-written poem may last as long as the world; and all of them continue for ages together to give the vogue to that particular style, to that particular taste or manner, according to which each of them was composed. Few men have an opportunity of seeing in their own times the fashion in any of these arts change very considerably. Few men have so much experience and acquaintance with the different modes which have obtained in remote ages and nations, as to be thoroughly reconciled to them, or to judge with impartiality between them and what takes place in their own age and country. Few men, therefore, are willing to allow, that custom or fashion have much influence upon their judgments concerning what is beautiful, or otherwise, in the productions of any of those arts; but imagine that all the rules which they think ought to be observed in each of them are founded upon reason and nature, not upon habit or prejudice. A very little attention, however, may convince them of the contrary, and satisfy them that the influence of custom and fashion over dress and furniture is not more absolute than over architecture, poetry, and music.

Can any reason, for example, be assigned why the Doric capital should be appropriated to a pillar, whose height is equal to eight diameters; the Ionic volute to one of nine; and the Corinthian foliage to one of ten? The propriety of each of those appropriations can be founded upon nothing but habit and custom. The eye having been used to see a particular proportion connected with a particular ornament, would be offended if they were not joined together. Each of the five orders has its peculiar ornaments, which cannot be changed for any other, without giving offence to all those who know anything of the rules of architecture. According to some architects, indeed, such is the exquisite judgment with which the ancients have assigned to each order its proper ornaments, that no others can be found which are equally suitable. It seems, however, a little difficult to be conceived that these forms, though no doubt extremely agreeable, should be the only forms which can suit those proportions, or that there should not be five hundred others, which, antecedent to established custom, would have fitted them equally well. When custom, however, has established particular rules of building, provided they are not absolutely unreasonable, it is absurd to think of altering them for others which are only equally good, or even for others which, in point of elegance and beauty, have naturally some little advantage over them. A man would be ridiculous who should appear in public with a suit of clothes quite different from those which are commonly worn, though the new dress should in itself be ever so graceful or convenient. And there seems to be an absurdity of the same kind in ornamenting a house after a quite different manner from that which custom and fashion have prescribed; though the new ornaments should in themselves be somewhat superior to the common ones.

According to the ancient rhetoricians, a certain measure or verse was by nature appropriated to each particular species of writing, as being naturally expressive of that character, sentiment, or passion which ought to predominate

in it.   One verse, they said, was fit for grave, and another
for gay works, which could not, they thought, be inter-
changed without the greatest impropriety.   The experience
of modern times, however, seems to contradict this principle,
though in itself it would appear to be extremely probable.
What is the burlesque verse in English is the heroic verse
in French.   The tragedies of Racine and the Henriad of
Voltaire are nearly in the same verse with,

> " Let me have your advice in a weighty affair."

The burlesque verse in French, on the contrary, is pretty
much the same with the heroic verse of ten syllables in
English.   Custom has made the one nation associate the
ideas of gravity, sublimity, and seriousness, to that measure
which the other has connected with whatever is gay, flip-
pant, and ludicrous.   Nothing would appear more absurd
in English than a tragedy written in the Alexandrine verses
of the French ; or in French, than a work of the same kind
in verses of ten syllables.

An eminent artist will bring about a considerable change
in the established modes of each of those arts, and introduce a new fashion of writing, music, or architecture.   As
the dress of an agreeable man of high rank recommends it
self, and how peculiar and fantastical soever, comes soon
to be admired and imitated ; so the excellencies of an
eminent master recommend his peculiarities, and his manner becomes the fashionable style in the art which he
practises.   The taste of the Italians in music and architecture has, within these fifty years, undergone a considerable
change, from imitating the peculiarities of some 'eminent
masters in each of those arts.   Seneca is accused by Quin-
tilian of having corrupted the taste of the Romans, and of
having introduced a frivolous prettiness in the room of
majestic reason and masculine eloquence.   Sallust and Ta-
citus have by others been charged with the same accusa-

tion, though in a different manner. They gave reputation, it is pretended, to a style which, though in the highest degree concise, elegant, expressive, and even poetical, wanted, however, ease, simplicity, and nature, and was evidently the production of the most laboured and studied affectation. How many great qualities must that writer possess who can thus render his very faults agreeable? After the praise of refining the taste of a nation, the highest eulogy, perhaps, which can be bestowed upon any author, is to say that he corrupted it. In our own language, Mr Pope and Dr Swift have each of them introduced a manner different from what was practised before into all works that are written in rhyme, the one in long verses, the other in short. The quaintness of Butler has given place to the plainness of Swift. The rambling freedom of Dryden, and the correct, but often tedious and prosaic languor of Addison, are no longer the objects of imitation, but all long verses are now written after the manner of the nervous precision of Mr Pope.

Neither is it only over the productions of the arts that custom and fashion exert their dominion. They influence our judgments in the same manner with regard to the beauty of natural objects. What various and opposite forms are deemed beautiful in different species of things! The proportions which are admired in one animal are altogether different from those which are esteemed in another. Every class of things has its own peculiar conformation, which is approved of, and has a beauty of its own, distinct from that of every other species. It is upon this account that a learned Jesuit, Father Buffier, has determined that the beauty of every object consists in that form and colour, which is most usual among things of that particular sort to which it belongs. Thus in the human form the beauty of each feature lies in a certain middle, equally removed from a variety of other forms that are ugly. A beautiful nose, for example, is one that is neither very long nor very short, neither very straight nor very crooked, but a sort of middle among all those extremes, and less different from any one of them than all of them are from one another. It is the form which Nature seems to have aimed at in them all, which, however, she deviates from in a great variety of ways, and very seldom hits exactly ; but to which all those deviations still bear a very strong resemblance. When a number of drawings are made after one pattern, though they may all miss it in some respects, yet they will all resemble it more than they resemble one another; the general character of the pattern will run through them all; the most singular and odd will be those which are most wide of it; and though very few will copy it exactly, yet the most accurate delineations will bear a greater resemblance to the most careless, than the careless ones will bear to one another. In the same manner, in each species of creatures, what is most beautiful bears the strongest characters of the general fabric of the species, and has the strongest resemblance to the greater part of the individuals with which it is classed. Monsters, on the contrary, or what is perfectly deformed, are always most singular and odd, and have the least resemblance to the generality of that species to which they belong. And thus the beauty of each species, though in one sense the rarest of all things, because few individuals hit this middle form exactly, yet in another is the most common, because all the deviations from it resemble it more than they resemble one another. The most customary form therefore is, in each species of things, according to him, the most beautiful. And hence it is that a certain practice and experience in contemplating each species of objects is requisite, before we can judge of its beauty, or know wherein the middle and most usual form consists. The nicest judgment concerning the beauty of the human species will not help us to judge of that of flowers or horses, or any other species of things. It is for the same

reason that in different climates, and where different customs and ways of living take place, as the generality of any
species receives a different conformation from those circumstances, so different ideas of its beauty prevail. The beauty
of a Moorish is not exactly the same with that of an English horse. What different ideas are formed in different
nations concerning the beauty of the human shape and
countenance! A fair complexion is a shocking deformity
upon the coast of Guinea. Thick lips and a flat nose are
a beauty. In some nations long ears that hang down
upon the shoulders are the objects of universal admiration. In China, if a lady's foot is so large as to be fit to
walk upon, she is regarded as a monster of ugliness.
Some of the savage nations in North America tie four
boards round the heads of their children, and thus squeeze
them, while the bones are tender and gristly, into a form
that is almost perfectly square. Europeans are astonished
at the absurd barbarity of this practice, to which some mis-
sionaries have imputed the singular stupidity of those nations among whom it prevails. But when they condemn
those savages, they do not reflect that the ladies in Europe
had, till within these very few years, been endeavouring for
near a century past to squeeze the beautiful roundness of
their natural shape into a square form of the same kind.
And that, notwithstanding the many distortions and diseases which this practice was known to occasion, custom
had rendered it agreeable among some of the most civilized
nations which perhaps the world ever beheld.

Such is the system of this learned and ingenious father,
concerning the nature of beauty; of which the whole charm,
according to him, would thus seem to arise from its falling
in with the habits which custom had impressed upon the
imagination, with regard to things of each particular kind.
I cannot, however, be induced to believe that our sense
even of external beauty is founded altogether on custom.

The utility of any form, its fitness for the useful purposes for which it was intended, evidently recommends it, and renders it agreeable to us, independent of custom. Certain colours are more agreeable than others, and give more delight to the eye the first time it ever beholds them. A smooth surface is more agreeable than a rough one. Variety is more pleasing than a tedious undiversified uniformity. Connected variety, in which each new appearance seems to be introduced by what went before it, and in which all the adjoining parts seem to have some natural relation to one another, is more agreeable than a disjointed and disorderly assemblage of unconnected objects. But though I cannot admit that custom is the sole principle of beauty, yet I can so far allow the truth of this ingenious system, as to grant that there is scarce any one external form so beautiful as to please, if quite contrary to custom, and unlike whatever we have been used to in that particular species of things ; or so deformed as not to be agreeable, if custom uniformly supports it, and habituates us to see it in every single individual of the kind.

CHAPTER II.

Of the Influence of Custom and Fashion upon Moral Senti-
ments.

SINCE our sentiments concerning beauty of every kind
are so much influenced by custom and fashion, it cannot be
expected that those concerning the beauty of conduct
should be entirely exempted from the dominion of those
principles. Their influence here, however, seems to be
much less than it is everywhere else. There is, perhaps,
no form of external objects, how absurd and fantastical soever, to which custom will not reconcile us, or which fashion
will not render even agreeable. But the characters and
conduct of a Nero, or a Claudius, are what no custom will
ever reconcile us to, what no fashion will ever render
agreeable; but the one will always be the object of dread
and hatred—the other of scorn and derision. The principles
of the imagination, upon which our sense of beauty depends,
are of a very nice and delicate nature, and may easily be
altered by habit and education; but the sentiments of moral
approbation and disapprobation are founded on the strongest
and most vigorous passions of human nature; and though
they may be somewhat warpt, cannot be entirely perverted.

But though the influence of custom and fashion upon
moral sentiments is not altogether so great, it is, however,
perfectly similar to what it is everywhere else. When custom and fashion coincide with the natural principles of right
and wrong, they heighten the delicacy of our sentiments, and
increase our abhorrence for everything which approaches
to evil. Those who have been educated in what is really

good company, not in what is commonly called such, who have been accustomed to see nothing in the persons whom they esteemed and lived with, but justice, modesty, humanity, and good order, are more shocked with whatever seems to be inconsistent with the rules which those virtues prescribe. Those, on the contrary, who have had the misfortune to be brought up amidst violence, licentiousness, falsehood, and injustice, lose though not all sense of the impropriety of such conduct, yet all sense of its dreadful enormity, or of the vengeance and punishment due to it. They have been familiarized with it from their infancy, custom has rendered it habitual to them, and they are very apt to regard it as what is called the way of the world, something which either may, or must be practised, to hinder us from being the dupes of our own integrity.

Fashion, too, will sometimes give reputation to a certain degree of disorder, and, on the contrary, discountenance qualities which deserve esteem. In the reign of Charles II. a degree of licentiousness was deemed the characteristic of a liberal education. It was connected, according to the notions of those times, with generosity, sincerity, magnanimity, loyalty, and proved that the person who acted in this manner was a gentleman and not a puritan. Severity of manners and regularity of conduct, on the other hand, were altogether unfashionable, and were connected, in the imagination of that age, with cant, cunning, hypocrisy, and low manners. To superficial minds the vices of the great seem at all times agreeable. They connect them, not only with the splendour of fortune, but with many superior virtues which they ascribe to their superiors; with the spirit of freedom and independency, with frankness, generosity, humanity, and politeness. The virtues of the inferior ranks of people, on the contrary, their parsimonious frugality, their painful industry, and rigid adherence to rules, seem to them mean and disagreeable. They connect them both with the meanness of the station to which those qualities commonly belong, and with many great vices which, they suppose, usually accompany them—such as an abject, cowardly, ill-natured, lying, pilfering disposition.

The objects with which men in the different professions and states of life are conversant being very different, and habituating them to very different passions, naturally form in them very different characters and manners. We expect in each rank and profession a degree of those manners which, experience has taught us, belonged to it. But as in each species of things we are particularly pleased with the middle confirmation, which, in every part and feature, agrees most exactly with the general standard which nature seems to have established for things of that kind; so in each rank, or, if I may say so, in each species of men, we are particularly pleased, if they have neither too much nor too little of the character which usually accompanies their particular condition and situation. A man, we say, should look like his trade and profession; yet the pedantry of every profession is disagreeable. The different periods of life have, for the same reason, different manners assigned to them. We expect in old age that gravity and sedateness which its infirmities, its long experience, and its worn-out sensibility seem to render both natural and respectable; and we lay our account to find in youth that sensibility, that gaiety and sprightly vivacity, which experience teaches us to expect from the lively impressions that all interesting objects are apt to make upon the tender and unpractised senses of that early period of life. Each of those two ages, however, may easily have too much of these peculiarities which belong to it. The flirting levity of youth, and the immoveable insensibility of old age, are equally disagreeable. The young, according to the common saying, are most agreeable when in their behaviour there is something of the manners of the old; and the old, when they retain something of the gaiety of the young. Either of them, however, may easily have too much of the manners of the other. The extreme coldness and dull formality which are pardoned in old age, make youth ridiculous. The levity, the carelessness, and the vanity, which are indulged in youth, render old age contemptible.

The peculiar character and manners which we are led by custom to appropriate to each rank and profession, have sometimes, perhaps, a propriety independent of custom, and are what we should approve of for their own sakes, if we took into consideration all the different circumstances which naturally affect those in each different state of life. The propriety of a person's behaviour depends not upon its suitableness to any one circumstance of his situation, but to all the circumstances which, when we bring his case home to ourselves, we feel should naturally call upon his attention. If he appears to be so much occupied by any one of them as entirely to neglect the rest, we disapprove of his conduct as something which we cannot entirely go along with, because not properly adjusted to all the circumstances of his situation : yet, perhaps, the emotion he expresses for the object which principally interests him does not exceed what we should entirely sympathize with and approve of in one whose attention was not required by any other thing. A parent in private life might, upon the loss of an only son, express without blame a degree of grief and tenderness which would be unpardonable in a general at the head of an army, when glory and the public safety demanded so great a part of his attention. As different objects ought, upon common occasions, to occupy the attention of men of different professions, so different passions ought naturally to become habitual to them ; and when we bring home to ourselves their situation in this particular respect, we must be sensible that every occurrence should naturally affect them more or less, according as the emotion which it excites coincides or disagrees with the fixed habit and temper of their minds. We cannot expect the same sensibility to the gay pleasures and amusements of life in a clergyman which we lay our account with in an officer. The man whose peculiar occupation is to keep the world in mind of that awful futurity which awaits them, who is to announce what may be the fatal consequences of every deviation from the rules of duty, and who is himself to set the example of the most exact conformity, seems to be the messenger of tidings which cannot, in propriety, be delivered either with levity or indifference. His mind is supposed to be continually occupied with what is too grand and solemn to leave any room for the impressions of those frivolous objects which fill up the attention of the dissipated and the gay. We readily feel, therefore, that independent of custom, there is a propriety in the manners which custom has allotted to this profession, and that nothing can be more suitable to the character of a clergyman than that grave, that austere and abstracted severity which we are habituated to expect in his behaviour. These reflections are so very obvious, that there is scarce any man so inconsiderate as not at some time to have made them, and to have accounted to himself in this manner for his approbation of the usual character of this order.

The foundation of the customary character of some other professions is not so obvious, and our approbation of it is founded entirely in habit, without being either confirmed or enlivened by any reflections of this kind. We are led by custom, for example, to annex the character of gaiety, levity, and sprightly freedom, as well as of some degree of dissipation, to the military profession. Yet if we were to consider what mood or tone of temper would be most suitable to this situation, we should be apt to determine, perhaps, that the most serious and thoughtful turn of mind would best become those whose lives are continually ex-

posed to uncommon danger, and who should, therefore, be
more constantly occupied with the thoughts of death and
its consequences than other men.   It is this very circumstance, however, which is not improbably the occasion why
the contrary turn of mind prevails so much among men of
this profession.   It requires so great an effort to conquer
the fear of death, when we survey it with steadiness and
attention, that those who are constantly exposed to it find
it easier to turn away their thoughts from it altogether, to
wrap themselves up in careless security and indifference,
and to plunge themselves, for this purpose, into every sort
of amusement and dissipation.   A camp is not the element
of a thoughtful or a melancholy man : persons of that cast,
indeed, are often abundantly determined, and are capable,
by a great effort, of going on with inflexible resolution to
the most unavoidable death.   But to be exposed to continual,
though less imminent danger, to be obliged to exert, for a
long time, a degree of this effort, exhausts and depresses the
mind, and renders it incapable of all happiness and enjoyment.   The gay and careless, who have occasion to make
no effort at all, who fairly resolve never to look before
them, but to lose, in continual pleasures and amusements,
all anxiety about their situation, more easily support such
circumstances.   Whenever, by any peculiar circumstances,
an officer has no reason to lay his account with being exposed to any uncommon danger, he is very apt to lose the
gaiety and dissipated thoughtlessness of his character.   The
captain of a city-guard is commonly as sober, careful, and
penurious an animal as the rest of his fellow-citizens.   A
long peace is, for the same reason, very apt to diminish the
difference between the civil and the military character.   The
ordinary situation, however, of men of this profession,
renders gaiety and a degree of dissipation so much their
usual character, and custom has, in our imagination, so
strongly connected this character with this state of life, that

we are very apt to despise any man whose peculiar humour
or situation renders him incapable of acquiring it. We
laugh at the grave and careful faces of a city-guard, which
so little resemble those of their profession: they themselves
seem often to be ashamed of the regularity of their own
manners, and, not to be out of the fashion of their trade,
are fond of affecting that levity which is by no means natural to them. Whatever is the deportment which we have
been accustomed to see in a respectable order of men, it
comes to be so associated in our imagination with that order,
that whenever we see the one we lay our account that we
are to meet with the other, and when disappointed, miss
something which we expected to find. We are embarrassed,
and put to a stand, and know not how to address ourselves
to a character which plainly affects to be of a different
species from those with which we should have been disposed
to class it.

The different situations of different ages and countries
are apt, in the same manner, to give different characters to
the generality of those who live in them, and their sentiments concerning the particular degree of each quality that
is either blameable or praiseworthy, vary according to that
degree which is usual in their own country and in their
own times. That degree of politeness which would be
highly esteemed, perhaps would be thought effeminate
adulation, in Russia, would be regarded as rudeness and
barbarism at the court of France. That degree of order
and frugality which, in a Polish nobleman, would be considered as excessive parsimony, would be regarded as extravagance in a citizen of Amsterdam. Every age and
country look upon that degree of each quality which is
commonly to be met with in those who are esteemed, among
themselves, as the golden mean of that particular talent or
virtue ; and as this varies according as their different cir-

cumstances render different qualities more or less habitual to them, their sentiments, concerning the exact propriety of character and behaviour, vary accordingly.

Among civilized nations, the virtues which are founded upon humanity are more cultivated than those which are founded upon self-denial and the command of the passions. Among rude and barbarous nations it is quite otherwise— the virtues of self-denial are more cultivated than those of humanity. The general security and happiness which prevail in ages of civility and politeness, afford little exercise to the contempt of danger, to patience in enduring labour, hunger, and pain. Poverty may easily be avoided, and the contempt of it, therefore, almost ceases to be a virtue. The abstinence from pleasure becomes less necessary, and the mind is more at liberty to unbend itself, and to indulge its natural inclinations in all those particular respects.

Among savages and barbarians it is quite otherwise. Every savage undergoes a sort of Spartan discipline, and, by the necessity of his situation, is inured to every sort of hardship. He is in continual danger: he is often exposed to the greatest extremities of hunger, and frequently dies of pure want. His circumstances not only habituate him to every sort of distress, but teach him to give way to none of the passions which that distress is apt to excite. He can expect from his countrymen no sympathy or indulgence for such weakness. Before we can feel much for others, we must in some measure be at ease ourselves. If our own misery pinches us very severely, we have no leisure to attend to that of our neighbour: and all savages are too much occupied with their own wants and necessities to give much attention to those of another person. A savage, therefore, whatever be the nature of his distress, expects no sympathy from those about him, and disdains upon that account to expose himself, by allowing the least weakness to escape him. His passions, how furious and violent soever, are never permitted to disturb the serenity of his countenance, or the composure of his conduct and behaviour. The savages in North America, we are told, assume upon all occasions the greatest indifference, and would think themselves degraded if they should ever appear in any respect to be overcome either by love, or grief, or resentment. Their magnanimity and self-command in this respect are almost beyond the conception of Europeans. In a country in which all men are upon a level with regard to rank and fortune, it might be expected that the mutual inclinations of the two parties should be the only thing considered in marriages, and should be indulged without any sort of control. This, however, is the country in which all marriages, without exception, are made up by the parents, and in which a young man would think himself disgraced for ever if he shewed the least preference of one woman above another, or did not express the most complete indifference both about the time when and the person to whom he was to be married. The weakness of love, which is so much indulged in ages of humanity and politeness, is regarded among savages as the most unpardonable effeminacy. Even after the marriage, the two parties seem to be ashamed of a connection which is founded upon so sordid a necessity. They do not live together: they see one another by stealth only: they both continue to dwell in the houses of their respective fathers, and the open cohabitation of the two sexes, which is permitted without blame in all other countries, is here considered as the most indecent and unmanly sensuality. Nor is it only over this agreeable passion that they exert this absolute self-command. They often bear, in the sight of all their countrymen, with injuries, reproach, and the grossest insults, with the appearance of the greatest insensibility, and without expressing the smallest resentment. When a savage is made prisoner of war, and receives, as is usual, the sen-

tence of death from his conquerors, he hears it without expressing any emotion, and afterwards submits to the most
dreadful torments, without ever bemoaning himself, or discovering any other passion but contempt of his enemies.
While he is hung by the shoulders over a slow fire, he
derides his tormentors, and tells them with how much more
ingenuity he himself had tormented such of their countrymen as had fallen into his hands. After he has been scorch-
ed and burnt, and lacerated in all the most tender and
sensible parts of his body for several hours together, he is
often allowed, in order to prolong his misery, a short respite,
and is taken down from the stake; he employs this interval
in talking upon all indifferent subjects, inquires after the
news of the country, and seems indifferent about nothing
but his own situation. The spectators express the same
insensibility; the sight of so horrible an object seems to
make no impression upon them; they scarce look at the
prisoner, except when they lend a hand to torment him.
At other times they smoke tobacco, and amuse themselves
with any common object, as if no such matter was going
on. Every savage is said to prepare himself, from his
earliest youth, for this dreadful end: he composes for this
purpose what they call the song of death, a song which he
is to sing when he has fallen into the hands of his enemies,
and is expiring under the tortures which they inflict upon
him. It consists of insults upon his tormentors, and expresses the highest contempt of death and pain. He sings
this song upon all extraordinary occasions; when he goes
out to war, when he meets his enemies in the field, or whenever he has a mind to shew that he has familiarized his
imagination to the most dreadful misfortunes, and that no
human event can daunt his resolution or alter his purpose.
The same contempt of death and torture prevails among all
other savage nations. There is not a negro from the coast
of Africa who does not, in this respect, possess a degree of
magnanimity which the soul of his sordid master is too

often scarce capable of conceiving. Fortune never exerted more cruelly her empire over mankind than when she subjected those nations of heroes to the refuse of the gaols of Europe, to wretches who possess the virtues neither of the countries which they come from, nor of those which they go to, and whose levity, brutality, and baseness, so justly expose them to the contempt of the vanquished.

This heroic and unconquerable firmness, which the custom and education of his country demand of every savage, is not required of those who are brought up to live in civilized societies. If these last complain when they are in pain, if they grieve when they are in distress, if they allow themselves either to be overcome by love, or to be discomposed by anger, they are easily pardoned. Such weaknesses are not apprehended to affect the essential parts of their character. As long as they do not allow themselves to be transported to do any thing contrary to justice or humanity, they lose but little reputation, though the serenity of their countenance, or the composure of their discourse and behaviour, should be somewhat ruffled and disturbed. A humane and polished people, who have more sensibility to the passions of others, can more readily enter into an animated and passionate behaviour, and can more easily pardon some little excess. The person principally concerned is sensible of this; and being assured of the equity of his judges, indulges himself in stronger expressions of passion, and is less afraid of exposing himself to their contempt by the violence of his emotions. We can venture to express more emotion in the presence of a friend than in that of a stranger, because we expect more indulgence from the one than from the other. And in the same manner the rules of decorum among civilized nations admit of a more animated behaviour than is approved of among barbarians. The first converse together with the openness of friends; the second, with the reserve of strangers. The emotion and vivacity

with which the French and the Italians, the two most polished nations upon the Continent, express themselves on
occasions that are at all interesting, surprise at first those
strangers who happen to be travelling among them, and
who, having been educated among a people of duller sensibility, cannot enter into this passionate behaviour, of which
they have never seen any example in their own country. A
young French nobleman will weep, in the presence of the
whole court, upon being refused a regiment. An Italian,
says the Abbot Dû Bos, expresses more emotion on being
condemned in a fine of twenty shillings than an Englishman
on receiving the sentence of death. Cicero, in the times of
the highest Roman politeness, could, without degrading
himself, weep, with all the bitterness of sorrow, in the
sight of the whole senate and the whole people—as it is
evident he must have done in the end of almost every ora-
tion. The orators of the earlier and ruder ages of Rome
could not probably, consistent with the manners of the times,
have expressed themselves with so much emotion. It
would have been regarded, I suppose, as a violation of nature and propriety in the Scipios, in the Leliuses, and in
the elder Cato, to have exposed so much tenderness to the
view of the public. Those ancient warriors could express
themselves with order, gravity, and good judgment, but
are said to have been strangers to that sublime and passionate eloquence which was first introduced into Rome, not
many years before the birth of Cicero, by the two Gracchi,
by Crassus, and by Sulpitius. This animated eloquence,
which has been long practised with or without success both
in France and Italy, is but just beginning to be introduced
into England. So wide is the difference between the degrees of self-command which are required in civilized
and in barbarous nations, and by such different standards
do they judge of the propriety of behaviour.

This difference gives occasion to many others that are

not less essential. A polished people being accustomed to give way, in some measure, to the movements of nature, become frank, open, and sincere. Barbarians, on the contrary, being obliged to smother and conceal the appearance of every passion, necessarily acquire the habits of falsehood and dissimulation. It is observed by all those who have been conversant with savage nations, whether in Asia, Africa, or America, that they are all equally impenetrable, and that, when they have a mind to conceal the truth, no examination is capable of drawing it from them. They cannot be trepanned by the most artful questions. The torture itself is incapable of making them confess any thing which they have no mind to tell. The passions of a savage, too, though they never express themselves by any outward emotion, but lie concealed in the breast of the sufferer, are, notwithstanding, all mounted to the highest pitch of fury. Though he seldom shews any symptoms of anger, yet his vengeance, when he comes to give way to it, is always sanguinary and dreadful. The least affront drives him to despair. His countenance and discourse, indeed, are still sober and composed, and express nothing but the most perfect tranquillity of mind ; but his actions are often the most furious and violent. Among the North Americans it is not uncommon for persons of the tenderest age and more fearful sex, to drown themselves upon receiving only a slight reprimand from their mothers, and this too without expressing any passion, or saying any thing, except " *you shall no longer have a daughter.*" In civilized nations, the passions of men are not commonly so furious or so desperate. They are often clamorous and noisy, but are seldom very hurtful, and seem frequently to aim at no other satisfaction but that of convincing the spectator that they are in the right to be so much moved, and of procuring his sympathy and approbation.

All these effects of custom and fashion, however, upon

the moral sentiments of mankind, are inconsiderable in comparison of those which they give occasion to in some other cases; and it is not concerning the general style of character and behaviour that those principles produce the greatest perversion of judgment, but concerning the propriety or impropriety of particular usages.

The different manners which custom teaches us to approve of in the different professions and states of life, do not concern things of the greatest importance. We expect truth and justice from an old man as well as from a young, from a clergyman as well as from an officer; and it is in matters of small moment only that we look for the distinguishing marks of their respective characters. With regard to these, too, there is often some unobserved circumstance, which, if it was attended to, would shew us, that, independent of custom, there was a propriety in the character which custom had taught us to allot to each profession. We cannot complain, therefore, in this case, that the perversion of natural sentiment is very great. Though the manners of different nations require different degrees of the same quality in the character which they think worthy of esteem, yet the worst that can be said to happen even here is, that the duties of one virtue are sometimes extended so as to encroach a little upon the precincts of some other. The rustic hospitality that is in fashion among the Poles encroaches, perhaps, a little upon economy and good order; and the frugality that is esteemed in Holland, upon generosity and good-fellowship. The hardiness demanded of savages diminishes their humanity; and, perhaps, the delicate sensibility required in civilized nations sometimes destroys the masculine firmness of the character. In general the style of manners which takes place in any nation may commonly, upon the whole, be said to be that which is most suitable to its situation. Hardiness is the character most suitable to the cir-

cumstances of a savage; sensibility to those of one who
lives in a very civilized society. Even here, therefore, we
cannot complain that the moral sentiments of men are very
grossly perverted.

It is not, therefore, in the general style of conduct or
behaviour that custom authorizes the widest departure from
what is the natural propriety of action. With regard to
particular usages, its influence is often much more destructive of good morals, and it is capable of establishing, as
lawful and blameless, particular actions, which shock the
plainest principles of right and wrong.

Can there be greater barbarity, for example, than to hurt
an infant?—its helplessness, its innocence, its amiableness,
call forth the compassion even of an enemy, and not to
spare that tender age is regarded as the most furious effort
of an enraged and cruel conqueror What then should we
imagine must be the heart of a parent who could injure that
weakness which even a furious enemy is afraid to violate?
Yet the exposition, that is, the murder of new-born infants,
was a practice allowed of in almost all the states of Greece,
even among the polite and civilized Athenians; and whenever the circumstances of the parent rendered it inconvenient to bring up the child, to abandon it to hunger, or to
wild beasts, was regarded without blame or censure. This
practice had, probably, begun in times of the most savage
barbarity. The imaginations of men had been first made
familiar with it in that earliest period of society, and the
uniform continuance of the custom had hindered them afterwards from perceiving its enormity. We find at this day
that this practice prevails among all savage nations; and
in that rudest and lowest state of society it is undoubtedly
more pardonable than in any other. The extreme indigence
of a savage is often such that he himself is frequently ex-

posed to the greatest extremity of hunger; he often dies of pure want; and it is frequently impossible for him to support both himself and his child. We cannot wonder, therefore, that in this case he should abandon it. One who, in flying from an enemy whom it was impossible to resist, should throw down his infant because it retarded his flight, would surely be excusable; since, by attempting to save it, he could only hope for the consolation of dying with it. That in this state of society, therefore, a parent should be allowed to judge whether he can bring up his child ought not to surprise us so greatly. In the latter ages of Greece, however, the same thing was permitted from views of remote interest or conveniency, which could by no means excuse it. Uninterrupted custom had by this time so thoroughly authorized the practice, that not only the loose maxims of the world tolerated this barbarous prerogative, but even the doctrine of philosophers, which ought to have been more just and accurate, was led away by the established custom; and upon this, as upon many other occasions, instead of censuring, supported the horrible abuse by far-fetched considerations of public utility. Aristotle talks of it as of what the magistrate ought, upon many occasions, to encourage. The humane Plato is of the same opinion, and, with all that love of mankind which seems to animate all his writings, nowhere marks this practice with disapprobation. When custom can give sanction to so dreadful a violation of humanity, we may well imagine that there is scarce any particular practice so gross which it cannot authorize. Such a thing, we hear men every day saying, is commonly done, and they seem to think this a sufficient apology for what, in itself, is the most unjust and unreasonable conduct.

There is an obvious reason why custom should never pervert our sentiments with regard to the general style and

character of conduct and behaviour, in the same degree as
with regard to the propriety or unlawfulness of particular
usages.   There never can be any such custom. No society
could subsist a moment, in which the usual strain of men's
conduct and behaviour was of a piece with the horrible
practice I have just now mentioned.

THE

THEORY OF MORAL SENTIMENTS.

Part Sixth.

OF THE CHARACTER OF VIRTUE.

CONSISTING OF THREE SECTIONS.

INTRODUCTION.

WHEN we consider the character of any individual, we naturally view it under two different aspects; first, as it may affect his own happiness; and secondly, as it may affect that of other people.

SECTION I.

THE preservation and healthful state of the body seem
to be the objects which nature first recommends to the care
of every individual. The appetites of hunger and thirst,
the agreeable or disagreeable sensations of pleasure and
pain, of heat and cold, &c. may be considered as lessons
delivered by the voice of Nature herself, directing him what
he ought to choose, and what he ought to avoid, for this
purpose. The first lessons which he is taught by those
to whom his childhood is entrusted, tend, the greater part
of them, to the *same* purpose. Their principal object is to
teach him how to keep out of harm's way.

As he grows up, he soon learns that some care and foresight are necessary for providing the means of gratifying
those natural appetites, of procuring pleasure and avoiding
pain, of procuring the agreeable and avoiding the disagreeable temperature of heat and cold. In the proper direction
of this care and foresight consists the art of preserving and
increasing what is called his external fortune.

Though it is in order to supply the necessities and conveniences of the body that the advantages of external fortune are originally recommended to us, yet we cannot live
long in the world without perceiving that the respect of
our equals, our credit and rank in the society we live in,
depend very much upon the degree in which we possess,
or are supposed to possess, those advantages. The desire

of becoming the proper objects of this respect, of deserving and obtaining this credit and rank among our equals, is perhaps the strongest of all our desires; and our anxiety to obtain the advantages of fortune is, accordingly, much more excited and irritated by this desire than by that of supplying all the necessities and conveniences of the body, which are always very easily supplied.

Our rank and credit among our equals, too, depend very much upon what, perhaps, a virtuous man would wish them to depend entirely,—our character and conduct, or upon the confidence, esteem, and good-will, which these naturally excite in the people we live with.

The care of the health, of the fortune, of the rank and reputation of the individual, the objects upon which his comfort and happiness in this life are supposed principally to depend, is considered as the proper business of that virtue which is commonly called prudence.

We suffer more, it has already been observed, when we fall from a better to a worse situation, than we ever enjoy when we rise from a worse to a better. Security, therefore, is the first and the principal object of prudence. It is averse to expose our health, our fortune, our rank, or reputation, to any sort of hazard. It is rather cautious than enterprising, and more anxious to preserve the advantages which we already possess than forward to prompt us to the acquisition of still greater advantages. The methods of improving our fortune, which it principally recommends to us, are those which expose to no loss or hazard; real knowledge and skill in our trade or profession, assiduity and industry in the exercise of it, frugality, and even some degree of parsimony, in all our expenses.

The prudent man always studies seriously and earnestly

to understand whatever he professes to understand, and not merely to persuade other people that he understands it; and though his talents may not always be very brilliant, they are always perfectly genuine. He neither endeavours to impose upon you by the cunning devices of an artful impostor, nor by the arrogant airs of an assuming pedant, nor by the confident assertions of a superficial and impudent pretender : he is not ostentatious even of the abilities which he really possesses. His conversation is simple and modest, and he is averse to all the quackish arts by which other people so frequently thrust themselves into public notice and reputation. For reputation in his profession he is naturally disposed to rely a good deal upon the solidity of his knowledge and abilities ; and he does not always think of cultivating the favour of those little clubs and cabals, who, in the superior arts and sciences, so often erect themselves into the supreme judges of merit ; and who make it their business to celebrate the talents and virtues of one another, and to decry whatever can come into competition with them. If he ever connects himself with any society of this kind, it is merely in self-defence, not with a view to impose upon the public, but to hinder the public from being imposed upon, to his disadvantage, by the clamours, the whispers, or the intrigues, either of that particular society or of some other of the same kind.

The prudent man is always sincere, and feels horror at the very thought of exposing himself to the disgrace which attends upon the detection of falsehood. But though always sincere, he is not always frank and open ; and though he never tells any thing but the truth, he does not always think himself bound, when not properly called upon, to tell the whole truth. As he is cautious in his actions, so he is reserved in his speech, and never rashly or unnecessarily obtrudes his opinion concerning either things or persons.

The prudent man, though not always distinguished by the most exquisite sensibility, is always very capable of friendship. But his friendship is not that ardent and passionate but too often transitory affection, which appears so delicious to the generosity of youth and inexperience. It is a sedate, but steady and faithful attachment to a few well-tried and well-chosen companions; in the choice of whom he is not guided by the giddy admiration of shining accomplishments, but by the sober esteem of modesty, discretion, and good conduct. But though capable of friendship, he is not always much disposed to general sociality. He rarely frequents, and more rarely figures in, those convivial societies which are distinguished for the jollity and gaiety of their conversation. Their way of life might too often interfere with the regularity of his temperance, might interrupt the steadiness of his industry, or break in upon the strictness of his frugality.

But though his conversation may not always be very sprightly or diverting, it is always perfectly inoffensive. He hates the thought of being guilty of any petulance or rudeness: he never assumes impertinently over any body, and, upon all common occasions, is willing to place himself rather below than above his equals. Both in his conduct and conversation he is an exact observer of decency, and respects, with an almost religious scrupulosity, all the established decorums and ceremonials of society. And in this respect he sets a much better example than has frequently been done by men of much more splendid talents and virtues—who in all ages, from that of Socrates and Aristippus down to that of Dr Swift and Voltaire, and from that of Philip and Alexander the Great down to that of the great Czar Peter of Moscovy, have too often distinguished themselves by the most improper and even insolent contempt of all the ordinary decorums of life and conversation, and who have thereby set the most pernicious example to those who wish

to resemble them, and who too often content themselves
with imitating their follies without even attempting to attain their perfections.

In the steadiness of his industry and frugality, in his
steadily sacrificing the ease and enjoyment of the present
moment for the probable expectation of the still greater
ease and enjoyment of a more distant but more lasting
period of time, the prudent man is always both supported
and rewarded by the entire approbation of the impartial
spectator, and of the representative of the impartial spectator, the man within the breast.   The impartial spectator
does not feel himself worn out by the present labour of
those whose conduct he surveys; nor does he feel himself
solicited by the importunate calls of their present appetites.
To him their present, and what is likely to be their future
situation, are very nearly the same : he sees them nearly
at the same distance, and is affected by them very nearly
in the same manner : he knows, however, that to the persons principally concerned they are very far from being
the same, and that they naturally affect *them* in a very different manner.   He cannot, therefore, but approve, and
even applaud, that proper exertion of self-command which
enables them to act as if their present and their future
situation affected them nearly in the same manner in which
they affect him.

The man who lives within his income is naturally contented with his situation, which, by continual, though small
accumulations, is growing better and better every day.
He is enabled gradually to relax, both in the rigour of his
parsimony and in the severity of his application; and he
feels with double satisfaction this gradual increase of ease
and enjoyment, from having felt before the hardship which
attended the want of them.   He has no anxiety to change
so comfortable a situation, and does not go in quest of new

enterprises and adventures, which might endanger, but could not well increase, the secure tranquillity which he actually enjoys. If he enters into any new projects or enterprises, they are likely to be well concerted and well prepared. He can never be hurried or driven into them by any necessity, but has always time and leisure to deliberate soberly and coolly concerning what are likely to be their consequences.

The prudent man is not willing to subject himself to any responsibility which his duty does not impose upon him. He is not a bustler in business where he has no concern ; is not a meddler in other people's affairs ; is not a professed counsellor or adviser, who obtrudes his advice where nobody is asking it : he confines himself, as much as his duty will permit, to his own affairs, and has no taste for that foolish importance which many people wish to derive from appearing to have some influence in the management of those of other people : he is averse to enter into any party disputes, hates faction, and is not always very forward to listen to the voice even of noble and great ambition. When distinctly called upon, he will not decline the service of his country ; but he will not cabal in order to force himself into it, and would be much better pleased that the public business were well managed by some other person, than that he himself should have the trouble, and incur the responsibility, of managing it. In the bottom of his heart he would prefer the undisturbed enjoyment of secure tranquillity, not only to all the vain splendour of successful ambition, but to the real and solid glory of performing the greatest and most magnanimous actions.

Prudence, in short, when directed merely to the care of the health, of the fortune, and of the rank and reputation of the individual, though it is regarded as a most respectable, and even, in some degree, as an amiable and agreeable quality, yet it never is considered as one either of the most endearing or of the most ennobling of the virtues. It commands a certain cold esteem, but seems not entitled to any very ardent love or admiration.

Wise and judicious conduct, when directed to greater and nobler purposes than the care of the health, the fortune, the rank, and reputation, of the individual, is frequently and very properly called Prudence. We talk of the prudence of the great general, of the great statesman, of the great legislator. Prudence is, in all these cases, combined with many greater and more splendid virtues; with valour, with extensive and strong benevolence, with a sacred regard to the rules of justice, and all these supported by a proper degree of self-command. This superior prudence, when carried to the highest degree of perfection, necessarily supposes the art, the talent, and the habit or disposition of acting with the most perfect propriety in every possible circumstance and situation. It necessarily supposes the utmost perfection of all the intellectual and of all the moral virtues. It is the best head joined to the best heart. It is the most perfect wisdom combined with the most perfect virtue. It constitutes very nearly the character of the Academical or Peripatetic sage, as the inferior prudence does that of the Epicurean.

Mere imprudence, or the mere want of the capacity to take care of one's self, is, with the generous and humane, the object of compassion; with those of less delicate sentiments, of neglect, or, at worst, of contempt, but never of hatred or indignation. When combined with other vices, however, it aggravates in the highest degree the infamy and disgrace which would otherwise attend them. The artful knave, whose dexterity and address exempt him, though not from strong suspicions yet from punishment or distinct detection, is too often received in the world with an indulgence which he by no means deserves. The awkward and foolish one, who, for want of this dexterity and address, is convicted and brought to punishment, is the object of universal hatred, contempt, and derision. In countries where great crimes frequently pass unpunished, the most atrocious actions become almost familiar, and cease to impress the people with that horror which is universally felt in countries where an exact administration of justice takes place. The injustice is the same in both countries; but the imprudence is often very different. In the latter, great crimes are evidently great follies. In the former, they are not always considered as such. In Italy, during the greater part of the sixteenth century, assassinations, murders, and even murders under trust, seem to have been almost familiar among the superior ranks of people. Cæsar Borgia invited four of the little princes in his neighbourhood, who all possessed little sovereignties, and commanded little armies of their own, to a friendly conference at Senigaglia, where, as soon as they arrived, he put them all to death. This infamous action, though certainly not approved of even in that age of crimes, seems to have contributed very little to the discredit, and not in the least to the ruin, of the perpetrator. That ruin happened a few years after, from causes altogether disconnected with this crime. Machiavel—not indeed a man of the nicest morality even for his own times—was resident, as minister from the republic of Florence, at the court of Cæsar Borgia, when this crime was committed. He gives a very particular account of it, and in that pure, elegant, and simple language which distinguishes all his writings: he talks of it very coolly; is pleased with the address with which Cæsar Borgia conducted it; has much contempt for the dupery and weakness of the sufferers; but no compassion for their miserable and untimely death; and no sort of indignation at the cruelty and falsehood of their murderer. The violence and injustice of great conquerors are often regarded with foolish wonder

and admiration; those of petty thieves, robbers, and murderers, with contempt, hatred, and even horror, upon all
occasions.   The former, though they are a hundred times
more mischievous and destructive, yet, when successful,
they often pass for deeds of the most heroic magnanimity.
The latter are always viewed with hatred and aversion, as
the follies as well as the crimes of the lowest and most
worthless of mankind.   The injustice of the former is certainly, at least, as great as that of the latter; but the folly
and imprudence are not near so great.   A wicked and
worthless man of parts often goes through the world with
much more credit than he deserves.   A wicked and worthless fool appears always of all mortals the most hateful,
as well as the most contemptible.   As prudence, combined
with other virtues, constitutes the noblest, so imprudence,
combined with other vices, constitutes the vilest, of all
characters.

SECTION II.

OF THE CHARACTER OF THE INDIVIDUAL, SO FAR AS IT CAN AFFECT THE HAPPINESS OF OTHER PEOPLE.

INTRODUCTION.

THE character of every individual, so far as it can affect the happiness of other people, must do so by its disposition either to hurt or to benefit them.

Proper resentment for injustice attempted, or actually committed, is the only motive which, in the eyes of the impartial spectator, can justify our hurting or disturbing, in any respect, the happiness of our neighbour. To do so from any other motive is itself a violation of the laws of justice, which force ought to be employed either to restrain or to punish. The wisdom of every state or commonwealth endeavours, as well as it can, to employ the force of the society to restrain those who are subject to its authority from hurting or disturbing the happiness of one another. The rules which it establishes for this purpose constitute the civil and criminal law of each particular state or country. The principles upon which those rules either are or ought to be founded, are the subject of a particular science, of all sciences by far the most important, but hitherto, perhaps, the least cultivated—that of natural jurisprudence; concerning which it belongs not to our present subject to enter into any detail. A sacred and religious regard not to hurt or distu:b, in any respect, the happiness of our neighbour,

even in those cases where no law can properly protect him,
constitutes the character of the perfectly innocent and just
man; a character which, when carried to a certain delicacy
of attention, is always highly respectable and even venerable for its own sake, and can scarce ever fail to be accompanied with many other virtues—with great feeling for other
people, with great humanity and great benevolence. It is
a character sufficiently understood, and requires no further
explanation. In the present section I shall only endeavour
to explain the foundation of that order which Nature seems
to have traced out for the distribution of our good offices,
or for the direction and employment of our very limited
powers of beneficence; first, towards individuals; and,
secondly, towards societies.

The same unerring wisdom, it will be found, which regu-
lates every other part of her conduct, directs, in this respect
too, the order of her recommendations; which are always
stronger or weaker in proportion as our beneficence is more
or less necessary, or can be more or less useful.

CHAPTER I.

*Of the Order in which Individuals are recommended by Nature
to our care and attention.*

EVERY man, as the Stoics used to say, is first and principally recommended to his own care ; and every man is
certainly, in every respect, fitter and abler to take care of
himself than of any other person. Every man feels his own
pleasures and his own pains more sensibly than those of
other people. The former are the original sensations—the
latter the reflected or sympathetic images of those sensations. The former may be said to be the substance—the
latter the shadow.

After himself, the members of his own family, those who
usually live in the same house with him, his parents, his
children, his brothers and sisters, are naturally the objects
of his warmest affections. They are naturally and usually
the persons upon whose happiness or misery his conduct
must have the greatest influence. He is more habituated
to sympathize with them : he knows better how every thing
is likely to affect them, and his sympathy with them is more
precise and determinate than it can be with the greater
part of other people. It approaches nearer, in short, to
what he feels for himself.

This sympathy, too, and the affections which are founded
on it, are by nature more strongly directed towards his children than towards his parents, and his tenderness for the former seems generally a more active principle than his reverence and gratitude towards the latter. In the natural state of
things, it has already been observed, the existence of the child
for some time after it comes into the world, depends altogether

upon the care of the parent; that of the parent does not
naturally depend upon the care of the child. In the eye
of nature, it would seem, a child is a more important object than an old man, and excites a much more lively, as
well as a much more universal sympathy. It ought to do so.
Every thing may be expected, or at least hoped, from the
child. In ordinary cases, very little can be either expected
or hoped from the old man. The weakness of childhood
interests the affections of the most brutal and hard-heart-
ed. It is only to the virtuous and humane that the infirmities of old age are not the objects of contempt and aversion. In ordinary cases an old man dies without being much
regretted by any body. Scarce a child can die without
rending asunder the heart of somebody.

The earliest friendships, the friendships which are naturally contracted when the heart is most susceptible of that
feeling, are those among brothers and sisters. Their good
agreement, while they remain in the same family, is necessary for its tranquillity and happiness. They are capable of
giving more pleasure or pain to one another than to the
greater part of other people. Their situation renders their
mutual sympathy of the utmost importance to their common
happiness; and, by the wisdom of nature, the same situation, by obliging them to accommodate to one another, renders that sympathy more habitual, and thereby more lively,
more distinct, and more determinate.

The children of brothers and sisters are naturally connected by the friendship which, after separating into different families, continues to take place between their parents.
Their good agreement improves the enjoyment of that friendship—their discord would disturb it. As they seldom live
in the same family, however, though of more importance to
one another than to the greater part of other people, they
are of much less than brothers and sisters. As their mutual

sympathy is less necessary, so it is less habitual, and, therefore, proportionably weaker.

The children of cousins, being still less connected, are of still less importance to one another ; and the affection gradually diminishes as the relation grows more and more remote.

What is called affection is in reality nothing but habitual sympathy. Our concern in the happiness or misery of those who are the objects of what we call our affections ; our desire to promote the one and to prevent the other, are either the actual feeling of that habitual sympathy, or the necessary consequences of that feeling. Relations being usually placed in situations which naturally create this habitual sympathy, it is expected that a suitable degree of affection should take place among them. We generally find that it actually does take place ;—we therefore naturally expect that it should ; and we are, upon that account, more shocked when upon any occasion we find that it does not. The general rule is established, that persons related to one another in a certain degree ought always to be affected towards one another in a certain manner, and that there is always the highest impropriety, and sometimes even a sort of impiety, in their being affected in a different manner. A parent without parental tenderness, a child devoid of all filial reverence, appear monsters, the objects, not of hatred only, but of horror.

Though in a particular instance the circumstances which usually produce those natural affections, as they are called, may by some accident not have taken place, yet respect for the general rule will frequently, in some measure, supply their place, and produce something which, though not altogether the same, may bear, however, a very considerable resemblance to those affections. A father is apt to be less

attached to a child who, by some accident, has been separated from him in its infancy, and who does not return to
him till it is grown up to manhood. The father is apt to
feel less paternal tenderness for the child; the child less
filial reverence for the father. Brothers and sisters, when
they have been educated in distant countries, are apt to
feel a similar diminution of affection. With the dutiful
and the virtuous, however, respect for the general rule will
frequently produce something which, though by no means
the same, yet may very much resemble those natural affections. Even during the separation, the father and the child,
the brothers or the sisters, are by no means indifferent to
one another. They all consider one another as persons to
and from whom certain affections are due, and they live in
the hopes of being some time or another in a situation to
enjoy that friendship which ought naturally to have taken
place among persons so nearly connected. Till they meet,
the absent son, the absent brother, are frequently the favourite son, the favourite brother. They have never offended,
or, if they have, it is so long ago that the offence is forgotten as some childish trick not worth the remembering.
Every account they have heard of one another, if conveyed
by people of any tolerable good nature, has been in the
highest degree flattering and favourable. The absent
son, the absent brother, is not like other ordinary sons
and brothers, but an all-perfect son, an all-perfect brother;
and the most romantic hopes are entertained of the
happiness to be enjoyed in the friendship and conversation of such persons. When they meet, it is often with
so strong a disposition to conceive that habitual sympathy
which constitutes the family affection, that they are very apt
to fancy they have actually conceived it, and to behave to
one another as if they had. Time and experience, however,
I am afraid, too frequently undeceive them. Upon a more
familiar acquaintance, they frequently discover in one another
habits, humours, and inclinations, different from what they

expected, to which, from want of habitual sympathy, from want of the real principle and foundation of what is properly called family affection, they cannot now easily accommodate themselves. They have never lived in the situation which almost necessarily forces that easy accommodation, and, though they may now be sincerely desirous to assume it, they have really become incapable of doing so. Their familiar conversation and intercourse soon become less pleasing to them, and, upon that account, less frequent. They may continue to live with one another in the mutual exchange of all essential good offices, and with every other external appearance of decent regard. But that cordial satisfaction, that delicious sympathy, that confidential openness and ease, which naturally take place in the conversation of those who have lived long and familiarly with one another, it seldom happens that they can completely enjoy.

It is only, however, with the dutiful and the virtuous that the general rule has even this slender authority. With the dissipated, the profligate, and the vain, it is entirely disregarded. They are so far from respecting it, that they seldom talk of it but with the most indecent derision ; and an early and long separation of this kind never fails to estrange them most completely from one another. With such persons respect for the general rule can at best produce only a cold and affected civility (a very slender semblance of real regard) ; and even this, the slightest offence, the smallest opposition of interest, commonly puts an end to altogether.

The education of boys at distant great schools, of young men at distant colleges, of young ladies in distant nunneries and boarding-schools, seems in the higher ranks of life to have hurt most essentially the domestic morals, and consequently the domestic happiness, both of France and

England. Do you wish to educate your children to be dutiful to their parents, to be kind and affectionate to their brothers and sisters? put them under the necessity of being dutiful children, of being kind affectionate brothers and sisters : educate them in your own house. From their parents' house they may, with propriety and advantage, go out every day to attend public schools; but let their dwelling be always at home. Respect for you must always impose a very useful restraint upon their conduct; and respect for them may frequently impose no useless restraint upon your own. Surely no acquirement which can possibly be derived from what is called a public education can make any sort of compensation for what is almost certainly and necessarily lost by it. Domestic education is the institution of nature—public education the contrivance of man. It is surely unnecessary to say which is likely to be the wisest.

In some tragedies and romances we meet with many beautiful and interesting scenes, founded upon what is called the force of blood, or upon the wonderful affection which near relations are supposed to conceive for one another, even before they know that they have any such connection. This force of blood, however, I am afraid, exists nowhere but in tragedies and romances. Even in tragedies and romances it is never supposed to take place between any relations but those who are naturally bred up in the same house; between parents and children, between brothers and sisters. To imagine any such mysterious affection between cousins— or even between aunts or uncles, and nephews or nieces— would be too ridiculous.

In pastoral countries, and in all countries where the authority of law is not alone sufficient to give perfect security to every member of the state, all the different branches of the same family commonly choose to live in the neigh-

bourhood of one another. Their association is frequently
necessary for their common defence. They are all, from the
highest to the lowest, of more or less importance to one another. Their concord strengthens their necessary association—their discord always weakens, and might destroy it.
They have more intercourse with one another than with the
members of any other tribe. The remotest members of the
same tribe claim some connexion with one another ; and,
where all other circumstances are equal, expect to be treated with more distinguished attention than is due to those
who have no such pretensions. It is not many years ago
that, in the Highlands of Scotland, the chieftain used to consider the poorest man of his clan as his cousin and relation.
The same extensive regard to kindred is said to take place
among the Tartars, the Arabs, the Turkomans, and, I believe, among all other nations who are nearly in the same
state of society in which the Scots Highlanders were about
the beginning of the present century.

In commercial countries, where the authority of law is
always perfectly sufficient to protect the meanest man in
the state, the descendants of the same family, having no such
motive for keeping together, naturally separate and disperse,
as interest or inclination may direct. They soon cease to
be of importance to one another ; and, in a few generations,
not only lose all care about one another, but all remembrance
of their common origin, and of the connection which took
place among their ancestors. Regard for remote relations
becomes in every country less and less, according as this
state of civilization has been longer and more completely
established. It has been longer and more completely established in England than in Scotland ; and remote relations
are, accordingly, more considered in the latter country than
in the former, though in this respect the difference between
the two countries is growing less and less every day. Great
lords, indeed, are in every country proud of remembering

and acknowledging their connection with one another, however remote. The remembrance of such illustrious relations
flatters not a little the family pride of them all; and it is
neither from affection, nor from any thing which resembles
affection, but from the most frivolous and childish of all
vanities, that this remembrance is so carefully kept up.
Should some more humble, though, perhaps, much nearer,
kinsman presume to put such great men in mind of his
relation to their family, they seldom fail to tell him that
they are bad genealogists, and miserably ill-informed concerning their own family history. It is not in that order, I
am afraid, that we are to expect any extraordinary extension
of what is called natural affection.

I consider what is called natural affection as more the
effect of the moral than of the supposed physical connection
between the parent and the child. A jealous husband, indeed, notwithstanding the moral connection, notwithstanding the child's having been educated in his own house, often
regards with hatred and aversion that unhappy child which
he supposes to be the offspring of his wife's infidelity. It
is the lasting monument of a most disagreeable adventure—of his own dishonour, and of the disgrace of his
family.

Among well-disposed people the necessity or conveniency
of mutual accommodation very frequently produces a friendship not unlike that which takes place among those who
are born to live in the same family. Colleagues in office,
partners in trade, call one another brothers, and frequently
feel towards one another as if they really were so. Their
good agreement is an advantage to all; and, if they are
tolerably reasonable people, they are naturally disposed to
agree. We expect that they should do so; and their disagreement is a sort of a small scandal. The Romans expressed this sort of attachment by the word *necessitudo*, which,

from the etymology, seems to denote that it was imposed by
the necessity of the situation.

Even the trifling circumstance of living in the same
neighbourhood has some effect of the same kind. We respect the face of a man whom we see every day, provided
he has never offended us. Neighbours can be very convenient, and they can be very troublesome, to one another.
If they are good sort of people, they are naturally disposed
to agree. We expect their good agreement; and to be a
bad neighbour is a very bad character. There are certain
small good offices, accordingly, which are universally allowed to be due to a neighbour in preference to any other
person who has no such connection.

This natural disposition to accommodate and to assimilate,
as much as we can, our own sentiments, principles, and feelings, to those which we see fixed and rooted in the persons
whom we are obliged to live and converse a great deal with,
is the cause of the contagious effects of both good and bad
company. The man who associates chiefly with the wise
and the virtuous, though he may not himself become either
wise or virtuous, cannot help conceiving a certain respect,
at least, for wisdom and virtue; and the man who associates chiefly with the profligate and the dissolute, though he
may not himself become profligate and dissolute, must soon
lose at least all his original abhorrence of profligacy and
dissolution of manners. The similarity of family characters, which we so frequently see transmitted through several
successive generations, may, perhaps, be partly owing to
this disposition, to assimilate ourselves to those whom we
are obliged to live and converse a great deal with. The
family character, however, like the family countenance,
seems to be owing not altogether to the moral but partly
too to the physical connection. The family countenance is
certainly altogether owing to the latter.

But of all attachments to an individual, that which is founded altogether upon esteem and approbation of his good conduct and behaviour, confirmed by much experience and long acquaintance, is by far the most respectable. Such friendships, arising not from a constrained sympathy, not from a sympathy which has been assumed and rendered habitual for the sake of convenience and accommodation, but from a natural sympathy, from an involuntary feeling that the persons to whom we attach ourselves are the natural and proper objects of esteem and approbation, can exist only among men of virtue. Men of virtue only can feel that entire confidence in the conduct and behaviour of one another, which can at all times assure them that they can never either offend or be offended by one another. Vice is always capricious—virtue only is regular and orderly. The attachment which is founded upon the love of virtue, as it is certainly of all attachments the most virtuous, so it is likewise the happiest, as well as the most permanent and secure. Such friendships need not be confined to a single person, but may safely embrace all the wise and virtuous with whom we have been long and intimately acquainted, and upon whose wisdom and virtue we can upon that account entirely depend. They who would confine friendship to two persons, seem to confound the wise security ot friendship with the jealousy and folly of love. The hasty, fond, and foolish intimacies of young people, founded commonly upon some slight similarity of character altogether unconnected with good conduct, upon a taste, perhaps, for the same studies, the same amusements, the same diversions, or upon their agreement in some singular principle or opinion not commonly adopted ; those intimacies which a freak begins, and which a freak puts an end to, how agreeable soever they may appear while they last, can by no means deserve the sacred and venerable name of friendship.

Of all the persons, however, whom nature points out for our peculiar beneficence, there are none to whom it seems more properly directed than to those whose beneficence we have ourselves already experienced. Nature, which formed men for that mutual kindness so necessary for their happiness, renders every man the peculiar object of kindness to the persons to whom he himself has been kind. Though their gratitude should not always correspond to his beneficence, yet the sense of his merit, the sympathetic gratitude of the impartial spectator, will always correspond to it. The general indignation of other people against the baseness of their ingratitude will even sometimes increase the general sense of his merit. No benevolent man ever lost altogether the fruits of his benevolence. If he does not always gather them from the persons from whom he ought to have gathered them, he seldom fails to gather them, and with a tenfold increase, from other people. Kindness is the parent of kindness ; and if to be beloved by our brethren be the great object of our ambition, the surest way of obtaining it is by our conduct to shew that we really love them.

After the persons who are recommended to our beneficence, either by their connection with ourselves, by their personal qualities, or by their past services, come those who are pointed out, not indeed to what is called our friendship, but to our benevolent attention and good offices; those who are distinguished by their extraordinary situation—the greatly fortunate and the greatly unfortunate, the rich and the powerful, the poor and the wretched. The distinction of ranks, the peace and order of society, are in a great measure founded upon the respect which we naturally conceive for the former. The relief and consolation of human misery depend altogether upon our compassion for the latter. The peace and order of society is of more importance than even the relief of the miserable. Our respect for the great, accordingly, is most apt to offend by its excess—our fellow-feeling for the miserable, by its defect. Moralists exhort us to charity and compassion. They warn us against the fascination of greatness. This fascination, indeed, is so powerful, that the rich and the great are too often preferred to the wise and the virtuous. Nature has wisely judged that the distinction of ranks, the peace and order of society, would rest more securely upon the plain and palpable difference of birth and fortune, than upon the invisible and often uncertain difference of wisdom and virtue. The undistinguishing eyes of the great mob of mankind can well enough perceive the former : it is with difficulty that the nice discernment of the wise and the virtuous can sometimes distinguish the latter. In the order of all those recommendations, the benevolent wisdom of nature is equally evident.

It may, perhaps, be unnecessary to observe, that the combination of two, or more, of those exciting causes of kindness, increases the kindness. The favour and partiality which, when there is no envy in the case, we naturally bear to greatness, are much increased when it is joined with wisdom and virtue. If, notwithstanding that wisdom and virtue, the great man should fall into those misfortunes, those dangers and distresses, to which the most exalted stations are often the most exposed, we are much more deeply interested in his fortune than we should be in that of a person equally virtuous, but in a more humble situation. The most interesting subjects of tragedies and romances are the misfortunes of virtuous and magnanimous kings and princes. If by the wisdom and manhood of their exertions they should extricate themselves from those misfortunes, and recover completely their former superiority and security, we cannot help viewing them with the most enthusiastic and even extravagant admiration. The grief which we felt for their distress, the joy which we feel for their prosperity, seem to combine together in enhancing that partial admiration which we naturally conceive both for the station and the character.

When those different beneficent affections happen to draw different ways, to determine by any precise rules in what cases we ought to comply with the one, and in what with the other, is perhaps altogether impossible. In what cases friendship ought to yield to gratitude, or gratitude to friendship—in what cases the strongest of all natural affections ought to yield to a regard forthe safety of those superiors upon whose safety often depends that of the whole society—and in what cases natural affection may, without impropriety, prevail over that regard—must be left altogether to the decision of the man within the breast, the supposed impartial spectator, the great judge and arbiter of our conduct. If we place ourselves completely in his situation, if we really view ourselves with his eyes and as he views us, and listen with diligent and reverential attention to what he suggests to us, his voice will never deceive us. We shall stand in need of no casuistic rules to direct our conduct. These it is often impossible to accommodate to all the different shades and gradations of circumstance, character, and situation, to differences and distinctions which, though not imperceptible, are, by their nicety and delicacy, often altogether undefinable. In that beautiful tragedy of Voltaire, The Orphan of China, while we admire the magnanimity of Zamti, who is willing to sacrifice the life of his own child in order to preserve that of the only feeble remnant of his ancient sovereigns and masters, we not only pardon but love the maternal tenderness of Idame, who, at the risk of discovering the important secret of her husband, reclaims her infant from the cruel hands of the Tartars, into which it had been delivered.

CHAPTER II.

Of the order in which Societies are by nature recommended to our Beneficence.

THE same principles that direct the order in which individuals are recommended to our beneficence, direct that likewise in which societies are recommended to it. Those to which it is, or may be of most importance, are first and principally recommended to it.

The state or sovereignty in which we have been born and educated, and under the protection of which we continue to live, is, in ordinary cases, the greatest society upon whose happiness or misery our good or bad conduct can have much influence. It is accordingly by nature most strongly recommended to us. Not only we ourselves, but all the objects of our kindest affections, our children, our parents, our relations, our friends, our benefactors, all those whom we naturally love and revere the most, are commonly comprehended within it; and their prosperity and safety depend, in some measure, upon its prosperity and safety. It is by nature, therefore, endeared to us, not only by all our selfish, but by all our private benevolent affections. Upon account of our own connection with it, its prosperity and glory seem to reflect some sort of honour upon ourselves. When we compare it with other societies of the same kind, we are proud of its superiority, and mortified, in some degree, if it appears in any respect below them. All the illustrious characters which it has produced in former times (for against those of our own times envy may sometimes prejudice us a little), its warriors, its statesmen, its poets, its philosophers, and men of letters of all kinds, we are disposed to view with the most partial admiration, and to rank them (sometimes most unjustly) above those of all other nations. The patriot who lays down his life for the safety, or even for the vainglory of this society, appears to act with the most exact propriety. He appears to view himself in the light in which the impartial spectator naturally and necessarily views him, as but one of the multitude, in the eye of that equitable judge, of no more consequence than any other in it, but bound at all times to sacrifice and devote himself to the safety, to the service, and even to the glory, of the greater number. But though this sacrifice appears to be perfectly just and proper, we know how difficult it is to make it, and how few people are capable of making it. His conduct, therefore, excites not only our entire approbation, but our highest wonder and admiration, and seems to merit all the applause which can be due to the most heroic virtue. The traitor, on the contrary, who, in some peculiar situation, fancies he can promote his own little interest by betraying to the public enemy that of his native country ; who, regardless of the judgment of the man within the breast, prefers himself, in this respect, so shamefully and so basely, to all those with whom he has any connection, appears to be of all villains the most detestable.

The love of our own nation often disposes us to view, with the most malignant jealousy and envy, the prosperity and aggrandisement of any other neighbouring nation. Independent and neighbouring nations, having no common superior to decide their disputes, all live in continual dread and suspicion of one another. Each sovereign, expecting little justice from his neighbours, is disposed to treat them with as little as he expects from them. The regard for the laws of nations, or for those rules which independent states profess or pretend to think themselves bound to observe in their dealings with one another, is often very little more than mere pretence and profession. From the smallest in-

terest, upon the slightest provocation, we see those rules
every day either evaded or directly violated without shame
or remorse.   Each nation foresees, or imagines it foresees,
its own subjugation in the increasing power and aggrandisement of any of its neighbours; and the mean principle of
national prejudice is often founded upon the noble one of
the love of our own country.   The sentence with which the
elder Cato is said to have concluded every speech which he
made in the senate, whatever might be the subject, " *It is
my opinion, likewise, that Carthage ought to be destroyed,*"
was the natural expression of the savage patriotism of a
strong but coarse mind, enraged almost to madness against
a foreign nation from which his own had suffered so much.
The more humane sentence with which Scipio Nasica is said
to have concluded all his speeches, " *It is my opinion, likewise, that Carthage ought not to be destroyed,*" was the liberal
expression of a more enlarged and enlightened mind, who
felt no aversion to the prosperity even of an old enemy,
when reduced to a state which could no longer be formidable to Rome.   France and England may each of them
have some reason to dread the increase of the naval and
military power of the other; but for either of them to envy
the internal happiness and prosperity of the other, the cultivation of its lands, the advancement of its manufactures,
the increase of its commerce, the security and number of
its ports and harbours, its proficiency in all the liberal arts
and sciences, is surely beneath the dignity of two such great
nations.   These are the real improvements of the world we
live in.   Mankind are benefited, human nature is ennobled
by them.   In such improvements each nation ought not
only to endeavour itself to excel, but, from the love of mankind, to promote, instead of obstructing, the excellence of
its neighbours.   These are all proper objects of national
emulation, not of national prejudice or envy.

The love of our own country seems not to be derived

from the love of mankind. The former sentiment is altogether independent of the latter, and seems sometimes even
to dispose us to act inconsistently with it. France may
contain, perhaps, near three times the number of inhabitants
which Great Britain contains. In the great society of mankind, therefore, the prosperity of France should appear to
be an object of much greater importance than that of Great
Britain. The British subject, however, who upon that account should prefer upon all occasions the prosperity of the
former to that of the latter country, would not be thought a
good citizen of Great Britain. We do not love our country
merely as a part of the great society of mankind—we love
it for its own sake, and independently of any such consideration. That wisdom which contrived the system of human affections, as well as that of every other part of nature,
seems to have judged that the interest of the great society
of mankind would be best promoted by directing the principal attention of each individual to that particular portion
of it which was most within the sphere both of his abilities
and of his understanding.

National prejudices and hatreds seldom extend beyond
neighbouring nations. We very weakly and foolishly, perhaps, call the French our natural enemies ; and they, perhaps, as weakly and foolishly consider us in the same manner. Neither they nor we bear any sort of envy to the
prosperity of China or Japan. It very rarely happens, however, that our good-will towards such distant countries can
be exerted with much effect.

The most extensive public benevolence which can commonly be exerted with any considerable effect is that of the
statesmen, who project and form alliances among neighbouring or not very distant nations, for the preservation
either of what is called the balance of power, or of the
general peace and tranquillity of the states within the circle

of their negotiations. The statesmen, however, who plan and execute such treaties, have seldom any thing in view but the interest of their respective countries. Sometimes, indeed, their views are more extensive. The Count d'Avaux, the plenipotentiary of France, at the treaty of Munster, would have been willing to sacrifice his life (according to the Cardinal de Retz, a man not over-credulous in the virtue of other people), in order to have restored, by that treaty, the general tranquillity of Europe. King William seems to have had a real zeal for the liberty and independency of the greater part of the sovereign states of Europe ; which, perhaps, might be a good deal stimulated by his particular aversion to France, the state from which, during his time, that liberty and independency were principally in danger. Some share of the same spirit seems to have descended to the first ministry of Queen Anne.

Every independent state is divided into many different orders and societies, each of which has its own particular powers, privileges, and immunities. Every individual is naturally more attached to his own particular order or society than to any other. His own interest, his own vanity, the interest and vanity of many of his friends and companions, are commonly a good deal connected with it : he is ambitious to extend its privileges and immunities—he is zealous to defend them against the encroachments of every other order or society.

Upon the manner in which any state is divided into the different orders and societies which compose it, and upon the particular distribution which has been made of their respective powers, privileges, and immunities, depends what is called the constitution of that particular state.

Upon the ability of each particular order or society to maintain its own powers, privileges, and immunities, against the encroachments of every other, depends the stability of that particular constitution. That particular constitution is necessarily more or less altered, whenever any of its subordinate parts is either raised above or depressed below whatever had been its former rank and condition.

All those different orders and societies are dependent upon the state to which they owe their security and protection. That they are all subordinate to that state, and established only in subserviency to its prosperity and preservation, is a truth acknowledged by the most partial member of every one of them. It may often, however, be hard to convince him that the prosperity and preservation of the state require any diminution of the powers, privileges, and immunities of his own particular order or society. This partiality, though it may sometimes be unjust, may not upon that account be useless. It checks the spirit of innovation. It tends to preserve whatever is the established balance among the different orders and societies into which the state is divided; and while it sometimes appears to obstruct some alterations of government which may be fashionable and popular at the time, it contributes in reality to the stability and permanency of the whole system.

The love of our country seems, in ordinary cases, to involve in it two different principles ; first, a certain respect and reverence for that constitution or form of government which is actually established; and, secondly, an earnest desire to render the condition of our fellow-citizens as safe, respectable, and happy as we can. He is not a citizen who is not disposed to respect the laws and to obey the civil magistrate ; and he is certainly not a good citizen who does not wish to promote, by every means in his power, the welfare of the whole society of his fellow-citizens.

In peaceable and quiet times those two principles gene-

·ally coincide and lead to the same conduct. The support of the established government seems evidently the best expedient for maintaining the safe, respectable, and happy situation of our fellow-citizens—when we see that this government actually maintains them in that situation. But in times of public discontent, faction, and disorder, those two different principles may draw different ways, and even a wise man may be disposed to think some alteration necessary in that constitution or form of government which, in its actual condition, appears plainly unable to maintain the public tranquillity. In such cases, however, it often requires, perhaps, the highest effort of political wisdom to determine when a real patriot ought to support and endeavour to re-establish the authority of the old system, and when he ought to give way to the more daring, but often dangerous, spirit of innovation.

Foreign war and civil faction are the two situations which afford the most splendid opportunities for the display of public spirit. The hero who serves his country successfully in foreign war gratifies the wishes of the whole nation, and is upon that account the object of universal gratitude and admiration. In times of civil discord the leaders of the contending parties, though they may be admired by one-half of their fellow-citizens, are commonly execrated by the other. Their characters, and the merit of their respective services, appear commonly more doubtful. The glory which is acquired by foreign war is, upon this account, almost always more pure and more splendid than that which can be acquired in civil faction.

The leader of the successful party, however, if he has authority enough to prevail upon his own friends to act with proper temper and moderation (which he frequently has not), may sometimes render to his country a service much more essential and important than the greatest victories and the most extensive conquests. He may re-establish and improve the constitution, and from the very doubtful and ambiguous character of the leader of a party, he may assume the greatest and noblest of all characters, that of the reformer and legislator of a great state; and, by the wisdom of his institutions, secure the internal tranquillity and happiness of his fellow-citizens for many succeeding generations.

Amidst the turbulence and disorder of faction, a certain spirit of system is apt to mix itself with that public spirit which is founded upon the love of humanity, upon a real fellow-feeling with the inconveniencies and distresses to which some of our fellow-citizens may be exposed. This spirit of system commonly takes the direction of that more gentle public spirit, always animates it, and often inflames it, even to the madness of fanaticism. The leaders of the discontented party seldom fail to hold out some plausible plan of reformation, which, they pretend, will not only remove the inconveniencies and relieve the distresses immediately complained of, but will prevent in all time coming any return of the like inconveniencies and distresses. They often propose, upon this account, to new-model the constitution, and to alter in some of its most essential parts that system of government under which the subjects of a great empire have enjoyed, perhaps, peace, security, and even glory, during the course of several centuries together. The great body of the party are commonly intoxicated with the imaginary beauty of this ideal system, of which they have no experience, but which has been represented to them in all the most dazzling colours in which the eloquence of their leaders could paint it. Those leaders themselves, though they originally may have meant nothing but their own aggrandizement, become, many of them, in time the dupes of their own sophistry, and are as eager for this great reformation as the weakest and foolishest of their followers.

Even though the leaders should have preserved their own heads, as, indeed, they commonly do, free from this fanaticism, yet they dare not always disappoint the expectation of their followers, but are often obliged, though contrary to their principle and their conscience, to act as if they were under the common delusion. The violence of the party refusing all palliatives, all temperaments, all reasonable accommodations, by requiring too much, frequently obtains nothing; and those inconveniencies and distresses which, with a little moderation, might, in a great measure, have been removed and relieved, are left altogether without the hope of a remedy.

The man whose public spirit is prompted altogether by humanity and benevolence, will respect the established powers and privileges even of individuals, and still more those of the great orders and societies into which the state is divided. Though he should consider some of them as in some measure abusive, he will content himself with moderating, what he often cannot annihilate without great violence. When he cannot conquer the rooted prejudices of the people by reason and persuasion, he will not attempt to subdue them by force, but will religiously observe what by Cicero is justly called the divine maxim of Plato, never to use violence to his country, no more than to his parents. He will accommodate, as well as he can, his public arrangements to the confirmed habits and prejudices of the people, and will remedy, as well as he can, the inconveniencies which may flow from the want of those regulations which the people are averse to submit to. When he cannot establish the right, he will not disdain to ameliorate the wrong; but, like Solon, when he cannot establish the best system of laws, he will endeavour to establish the best that the people can bear.

The man of system, on the contrary, is apt to be very

wise in his own conceit, and is often so enamoured with the supposed beauty of his own ideal plan of government, that he cannot suffer the smallest deviation from any part of it. He goes on to establish it completely and in all its parts, without any regard either to the great interests or to the strong prejudices which may oppose it: he seems to imagine that he can arrange the different members of a great society with as much ease as the hand arranges the different pieces upon a chess-board; he does not consider that the pieces upon the chess-board have no other principle of motion besides that which the hand impresses upon them; but that, in the great chess-board of human society, every single piece has a principle of motion of its own, altogether different from that which the legislature might choose to impress upon it. If those two principles coincide and act in the same direction, the game of human society will go on easily and harmoniously, and is very likely to be happy and successful. If they are opposite or different, the game will go on miserably, and the society must be at all times in the highest degree of disorder.

Some general, and even systematical, idea of the perfection of policy and law, may no doubt be necessary for directing the views of the statesman. But to insist upon establishing, and upon establishing all at once, and in spite of all opposition, every thing which that idea may seem to require, must often be the highest degree of arrogance. It is to erect his own judgment into the supreme standard of right and wrong. It is to fancy himself the only wise and worthy man in the commonwealth, and that his fellow-citizens should accommodate themselves to him, and not he to them. It is upon this account that of all political speculators sovereign princes are by far the most dangerous. This arrogance is perfectly familiar to them. They entertain no doubt of the immense superiority of their own judgment. When such imperial and royal reformers, therefore, condescend to con-

template the constitution of the country which is committed
to their government, they seldom see any thing so wrong
in it as the obstructions which it may sometimes oppose to
the execution of their own will. They hold in contempt the
divine maxim of Plato, and consider the state as made for
themselves, not themselves for the state. The great object
of their reformation, therefore, is to remove those obstructions—to reduce the authority of the nobility—to take away
the privileges of cities and provinces, and to render both
the greatest individuals and the greatest orders of the state
as incapable of opposing their commands as the weakest
and most insignificant.

CHAPTER III.

Of universal Benevolence.

THOUGH our effectual good offices can very seldom be extended to any wider society than that of our own country, our good will is circumscribed by no boundary, but may embrace the immensity of the universe. We cannot form the idea of any innocent and sensible being whose happiness we should not desire, or to whose misery, when distinctly brought home to the imagination, we should not have some degree of aversion. The idea of a mischievous, though sensible being, indeed naturally provokes our hatred; but the ill-will which in this case we bear to it is really the effect of our universal benevolence. It is the effect of the sympathy which we feel with the misery and resentment of those other innocent and sensible beings whose happiness is disturbed by its malice.

This universal benevolence, how noble and generous soever, can be the source of no solid happiness to any man who is not thoroughly convinced that all the inhabitants of the universe, the meanest as well as the greatest, are under the immediate care and protection of that great, benevolent, and all-wise Being, who directs all the movements of nature, and who is determined, by his own unalterable perfections, to maintain in it at all times the greatest possible quantity of happiness. To this universal benevolence, on the contrary, the very suspicion of a fatherless world must be the most melancholy of all reflections; from the thought that all the unknown regions of infinite and incomprehensible space may be filled with nothing but endless misery and wretchedness. All the splendour of the highest prosperity can never enlighten the gloom with which so dreadful an idea must necessarily overshadow the imagination; nor, in a wise and virtuous man, can all the sorrow of the most afflicting adversity ever dry up the joy which necessarily springs from the habitual and thorough conviction of the truth of the contrary system.

The wise and virtuous man is at all times willing that his own private interest should be sacrificed to the public interest of his own particular order or society. He is at all times willing, too, that the interest of this order or society should be sacrificed to the greater interest of the state or sovereignty of which it is only a subordinate part : he should, therefore, be equally willing that all those inferior interests should be sacrificed to the greater interest of the universe, to the interest of that great society of all sensible and intelligent beings, of which God himself is the immediate administrator and director. If he is deeply impressed with the habitual and thorough conviction that this benevolent and all-wise Being can admit into the system of his government no partial evil which is not necessary for the universal good, he must consider all the misfortunes which may befall himself, his friends, his society, or his country, as necessary for the prosperity of the universe, and, therefore, as what he ought not only to submit to with resignation, but as what he himself, if he had known all the connections and dependencies of things, ought sincerely and devoutly to have wished for.

Nor does this magnanimous resignation to the will of the great Director of the universe seem in any respect beyond the reach of human nature. Good soldiers, who both love and trust their general, frequently march with more gaiety and alacrity to the forlorn station, from which they never expect to return, than they would to one where there was neither difficulty nor danger. In marching to the latter, they could feel no other sentiment than that of the dulness of ordinary duty—in marching to the former, they feel that they are making the noblest exertion which it is possible for man to make. They know that their general would not have ordered them upon this station had it not been necessary for the safety of the army, for the success of the war : they cheerfully sacrifice their own little systems to the prosperity of a greater system : they take an affectionate leave of their comrades, to whom they wish all happiness and success, and march out, not only with submissive obedience, but often with shouts of the most joyful exultation, to that fatal but splendid and honourable station to which they are appointed. No conductor of any army can deserve more unlimited trust, more ardent and zealous affection, than the great Conductor of the universe. In the greatest public as well as private disasters, a wise man ought to consider that he himself, his friends and countrymen, have only been ordered upon the forlorn station of the universe ; that had it not been necessary for the good of the whole, they would not have been so ordered ; and that it is their duty, not only with humble resignation to submit to this allotment, but to endeavour to embrace it with alacrity and joy. A wise man should surely be capable of doing what a good soldier holds himself at all times in readiness to do.

The idea of that divine Being, whose benevolence and wisdom have from all eternity contrived and conducted the immense machine of the universe so as at all times to produce the greatest possible quantity of happiness, is certainly, of all the objects of human contemplation, by far the most sublime. Every other thought necessarily appears mean in the comparison. The man whom we believe to be principally occupied in this sublime contemplation, seldom fails to be the object of our highest veneration ; and though his life should be altogether contemplative, we often regard him with a sort of religious respect, much superior to that with which we look upon the most active and useful servant of the commonwealth. The meditations of Marcus Antoninus, which turn principally upon this subject, have contributed more, perhaps, to the general admiration of his character than all the different transactions of his just, merciful, and beneficent reign.

The administration of the great system of the universe, however, the care of the universal happiness of all rational and sensible beings, is the business of God, and not of man. To man is allotted a much humbler department, but one much more suitable to the weakness of his powers, and to the narrowness of his comprehension—the care of his own happiness, of that of his family, his friends, his country : that he is occupied in contemplating the more sublime, can never be an excuse for his neglecting the more humble department ; and he must not expose himself to the charge which Avidius Cassius is said to have brought, perhaps unjustly, against Marcus Antoninus, that while he employed himself in philosophical speculations, and contemplated the prosperity of the universe, he neglected that of the Roman empire. The most sublime speculation of the contemplative philosopher can scarce compensate the neglect of the smallest active duty.

SECTION III.

OF SELF-COMMAND.

THE man who acts according to the rules of perfect prudence, of strict justice, and of proper benevolence, may be said to be perfectly virtuous. But the most perfect knowledge of those rules will not alone enable him to act in this manner ; his own passions are very apt to mislead him —sometimes to drive him, and sometimes to seduce him, to violate all the rules which he himself, in all his sober and cool hours, approves of. The most perfect knowledge, if it is not supported by the most perfect self-command, will not always enable him to do his duty.

Some of the best of the ancient moralists seem to have considered those passions as divided into two different classes ; first, into those which it requires a considerable exertion of self-command to restrain even for a single moment ; and, secondly, into those which it is easy to restrain for a single moment, or even for a short period of time ; but which, by their continual and almost incessant solicitations, are, in the course of a life, very apt to mislead into great deviations.

Fear and anger, together with some other passions which are mixed or connected with them, constitute the first class. The love of ease, of pleasure, of applause, and of many other selfish gratifications, constitute the second. Extravagant fear and furious anger it is often difficult to restrain even for a single moment. The love of ease, of pleasure, of applause, and other selfish gratifications, it is always easy to restrain for a single moment, or even for a short period of time ; but, by their continual solicitations, they often mislead us into

many weaknesses which we have afterwards much reason
to be ashamed of. The former set of passions may often be
said to drive, the latter to seduce, us from our duty. The
command of the former was, by the ancient moralists above
alluded to, denominated fortitude, manhood, and strength
of mind; that of the latter, temperance, decency, modesty,
and moderation.

The command of each of those two sets of passions, independent of the beauty which it derives from its utility, from
its enabling us upon all occasions to act according to the
dictates of prudence, of justice, and of proper benevolence,
has a beauty of its own, and seems to deserve, for its own
sake, a certain degree of esteem and admiration. In the
one case, the strength and greatness of the exertion excites
some degree of that esteem and admiration; in the other,
the uniformity, the equality, and unremitting steadiness, of
that exertion.

The man who, in danger, in torture, upon the approach
of death, preserves his tranquillity unaltered, and suffers no
word, no gesture, to escape him which does not perfectly
accord with the feelings of the most indifferent spectator,
necessarily commands a very high degree of admiration. If
he suffers in the cause of liberty and justice, for the sake of
humanity and the love of his country, the most tender compassion for his sufferings, the strongest indignation against
the injustice of his persecutors, the warmest sympathetic
gratitude for his beneficent intentions, the highest sense of
his merit, all join and mix themselves with the admiration
of his magnanimity, and often inflame that sentiment into
the most enthusiastic and rapturous veneration. The heroes
of ancient and modern history, who are remembered with
the most peculiar favour and affection, are many of them
those who, in the cause of truth, liberty, and justice, have
perished upon the scaffold, and who behaved there with that

ease and dignity which became them. Had the enemies of Socrates suffered him to die quietly in his bed, the glory even of that great philosopher might possibly never have acquired that dazzling splendour in which it has been beheld in all succeeding ages. In the English history, when we look over the illustrious heads which have been engraven by Vertue and Howbraken, there is scarce any body, I imagine, who does not feel that the axe, the emblem of having been beheaded, which is engraved under some of the most illustrious of them—under those of the Sir Thomas Mores, of the Raleighs, the Russels, the Sydneys, &c.—sheds a real dignity and interestingness over the characters to which it is affixed, much superior to what they can derive from all the futile ornaments of heraldry with which they are sometimes accompanied.

Nor does this magnanimity give lustre only to the characters of innocent and virtuous men. It draws some degree of favourable regard even upon those of the greatest criminals; and when a robber or highwayman is brought to the scaffold, and behaves there with decency and firmness, though we perfectly approve of his punishment, we often cannot help regretting that a man who possessed such great and noble powers should have been capable of such mean enormities.

War is the great school both for acquiring and exercising this species of magnanimity. Death, as we say, is the king of terrors; and the man who has conquered the fear of death is not likely to lose his presence of mind at the approach of any other natural evil. In war, men become familiar with death, and are thereby necessarily cured of that superstitious horror with which it is viewed by the weak and unexperienced. They consider it merely as the loss of life, and as no further the object of aversion than as life may happen to be that of desire: they learn from experience, too, that many seemingly great dangers are not so great as they appear; and that with courage, activity, and presence of mind, there is often a good probability of extricating themselves, with honour, from situations where at first they could see no hope. The dread of death is thus greatly diminished, and the confidence or hope of escaping it augmented. They learn to expose themselves to danger with less reluctance ; they are less anxious to get out of it, and less apt to lose their presence of mind while they are in it. It is this habitual contempt of danger and death which ennobles the profession of a soldier, and bestows upon it, in the natural apprehensions of mankind, a rank and dignity superior to that of any other profession. The skilful and successful exercise of this profession in the service of their country seems to have constituted the most distinguishing feature in the character of the favourite heroes of all ages.

A great warlike exploit, though undertaken contrary to every principle of justice, and carried on without any regard to humanity, sometimes interests us, and commands even some degree of a certain sort of esteem for the very worthless characters which conduct it. We are interested even in the exploits of the Buccaneers, and read with some sort of esteem and admiration the history of the most worth less men, who, in pursuit of the most criminal purposes, endured greater hardships, surmounted greater difficulties, and encountered greater dangers, than perhaps any which the ordinary course of history gives an account of.

The command of anger appears, upon many occasions, not less generous and noble than that of fear. The proper expression of just indignation composes many of the most splendid and admired passages both of ancient and modern eloquence. The Philippics of Demosthenes, the Catilinarians of Cicero, derive their whole beauty from the noble propriety with which this passion is expressed. But this just indignation is nothing but anger restrained and properly attempered to what the impartial spectator can enter into The blustering and noisy passion which goes beyond this is always odious and offensive, and interests us, not for the angry man, but for the man with whom he is angry. The nobleness of pardoning appears, upon many occasions, superior even to the most perfect propriety of resenting. When either proper acknowledgments have been made by the offending party, or, even without any such acknowledgments, when the public interest requires that the most mortal enemies should unite for the discharge of some important duty, the man who can cast away all animosity, and act with confidence and cordiality towards the person who had most grievously offended him, seems justly to merit our highest admiration.

The command of anger, however, does not always appear in such splendid colours. Fear is contrary to anger, and is often the motive which restrains it; and, in such cases, the meanness of the motive takes away all the nobleness of the restraint. Anger prompts to attack, and the indulgence of it seems sometimes to shew a sort of courage and superiority to fear. The indulgence of anger is sometimes an object of vanity; that of fear never is. Vain and weak men, among their inferiors, or those who dare not resist them, often affect to be ostentatiously passionate, and fancy that they shew what is called spirit in being so. A bully tells many stories of his own insolence, which are not true, and imagines that he thereby renders himself, if not more amiable and respectable, at least more formidable to his audience. Modern manners which, by favouring the practice of duelling, may be said in some cases to encourage private revenge, contribute, perhaps, a good deal to render, in modern times, the restraint of anger by fear still more contemptible than it might otherwise appear to be. There is always something dignified in the command of fear, whatever may be the motive upon which it is founded. It is not so with the command of anger; unless it is founded altogether in the sense of decency, of dignity, and propriety, it never is perfectly agreeable.

To act according to the dictates of prudence, of justice, and proper beneficence, seems to have no great merit where there is no temptation to do otherwise. But to act with cool deliberation in the midst of the greatest dangers and difficulties; to observe religiously the sacred rules of justice, in spite both of the greatest interests which might tempt and the greatest injuries which might provoke us to violate them; never to suffer the benevolence of our temper to be damped or discouraged by the malignity and ingratitude of the individuals towards whom it may have been exercised, is the character of the most exalted wisdom and virtue. Self-command is not only itself a great virtue, but from it all the other virtues seem to derive their principal lustre.

The command of fear, the command of anger, are always great and noble powers. When they are directed by justice and benevolence, they are not only great virtues, but increase the splendour of those other virtues. They may, however, sometimes be directed by very different motives; and in this case, though still great and respectable, they may be excessively dangerous. The most intrepid valour may be employed in the cause of the greatest injustice. Amidst great provocations, apparent tranquillity and good-humour may sometimes conceal the most determined and cruel resolution to revenge. The strength of mind requisite for such dissimulation, though always and necessarily contaminated by the baseness of falsehood, has, however, been often much admired by many people of no contemptible judgment. The dissimulation of Catharine of Medicis is often celebrated by the profound historian Davila; that of Lord Digby, afterwards Earl of Bristol, by the grave and conscientious Lord Clarendon; that of the first Ashley, Earl of Shaftesbury, by the judicious Mr Locke. Even Cicero seems to consider this deceitful character, not indeed as of the highest dignity, but as not unsuitable to a certain flexibility of manners, which he thinks may, notwithstanding, be upon the whole both agreeable and respectable. He exemplifies it by the characters of Homer's Ulysses, of the Athenian Themistocles, of the Spartan Lysander, and of the Roman Marcus Crassus. This character of dark and deep dissimulation occurs most commonly in times of great public disorder—amidst the violence of faction and civil war. When law has become in a great measure impotent, when the most perfect innocence cannot alone insure safety, regard to self-defence obliges the greater part of men to have recourse to dexterity, to address, and to apparent accommodation to whatever happens to be at the moment the prevailing party. This false character, too, is frequently accompanied with the coolest and most determined courage. The proper exercise of it imposes that courage, as death is commonly the certain consequence of detection. It may be employed indifferently, either to exasperate or to allay those furious animosities of adverse factions which impose the necessity of assuming it; and though it may sometimes be useful, it is at least equally liable to be excessively pernicious.

The command of the less violent and turbulent passions seems much less liable to be abused to any pernicious purpose. Temperance, decency, modesty, and moderation, are always amiable, and can seldom be directed to any bad end. It is from the unremitting steadiness of those gentler exertions of self-command that the amiable virtue of chastity, that the respectable virtues of industry and frugality, derive all that sober lustre which attends them. The conduct of all those who are contented to walk in the humble paths of private and peaceable life, derives from the same principle

the greater part of the beauty and grace which belong to
it ; a beauty and grace which, though much less dazzling,
is not always less pleasing than those which accompany the
more splendid actions of the hero, the statesman, or the
legislator.

After what has already been said in several different
parts of this discourse concerning the nature of self-command, I judge it unnecessary to enter into any further detail
concerning those virtues.   I shall only observe at present,
that the point of propriety, the degree of any passion which
the impartial spectator approves of, is differently situated in
different passions.   In some passions the excess is less disagreeable than the defect ; and in such passions the point
of propriety seems to stand high, or nearer to the excess
than to the defect.   In other passions the defect is less disagreeable than the excess ; and in such passions the point
of propriety seems to stand low, or nearer to the defect than
to the excess.   The former are the passions which the
spectator is most, the latter those which he is least disposed
to sympathize with.   The former, too, are the passions of
which the immediate feeling or sensation is agreeable to the
person principally concerned, the latter those of which it is
disagreeable.   It may be laid down as a general rule, that
the passions which the spectator is most disposed to sympathize with, and in which, upon that account, the point of
propriety may be said to stand high, are those of which the
immediate feeling or sensation is more or less agreeable to
the person principally concerned ; and that, on the contrary,
the passions which the spectator is least disposed to sympathize with, and in which, upon that account, the point of
propriety may be said to stand low, are those of which the
immediate feeling or sensation is more or less disagreeable,
or even painful, to the person principally concerned.   This
general rule, so far as I have been able to observe,
admits not of a single exception.   A few examples will

at once both sufficiently explain it and demonstrate tho truth of it.

The disposition to the affections which tend to unite men in society, to humanity, kindness, natural affection, friendship, esteem, may sometimes be excessive. Even the excess of this disposition, however, renders a man interesting to every body. Though we blame it, we still regard it with compassion, and even with kindness, and never with dislike. We àre more sorry for it than angry at it. To the person himself, the indulgence even of such excessive affections is, upon many occasions, not only agreeable but delicious. Upon some occasions, indeed, especially when directed, as is too often the case, towards unworthy objects, it exposes him to much real and heartfelt distress. Even upon such occasions, however, a well-disposed mind regards him with the most exquisite pity, and feels the highest indignation against those who affect to despise him for his weakness and imprudence. The defect of this disposition, on the contrary, what is called hardness of heart, while it renders a man insensible to the feelings and distresses of other people, renders other people equally insensible to his; and, by excluding him from the friendship of all the world, excludes him from the best and most comfortable of all social enjoyments.

The disposition to the affections which drive men from one another, and which tend, as it were, to break the bands of human society; the disposition to anger, hatred, envy, malice, revenge, is, on the contrary, much more apt to offend by its excess than by its defect. The excess renders a man wretched and miserable in his own mind, and the object of hatred, and sometimes even of horror, to other people. The defect is very seldom complained of. It may, however, be defective. The want of proper indignation is a most essential defect in the manly character, and, upon many occasions, renders a man incapable of protecting either himself or his friends from insult and injustice. Even that principle, in the excess and improper direction of which consists the odious and detestable passion of envy, may be defective. Envy is that passion which views with malignant dislike the superiority of those who are really entitled to all the superiority they possess. The man, however, who, in matters of consequence, tamely suffers other people, who are entitled to no such superiority, to rise above him or get before him, is justly condemned as mean-spirited. This weakness is commonly founded in indolence, sometimes in good-nature, in an aversion to opposition, to bustle and solicitation, and sometimes, too, in a sort of ill-judged magnanimity, which fancies that it can always continue to despise the advantage which it then despises, and therefore so easily gives up. Such weakness, however, is commonly followed by much regret and repentance; and what had some appearance of magnanimity in the beginning, frequently gives place to a most malignant envy in the end, and to a hatred of that superiority which those who have once attained it may often become really entitled to, by the very circumstance of having attained it. In order to live comfortably in the world, it is upon all occasions as necessary to defend our dignity and rank, as it is to defend our life or our fortune.

Our sensibility to personal danger and distress, like that to personal provocation, is much more apt to offend by its excess than by its defect. No character is more contemptible than that of a coward—no character is more admired than that of the man who faces death with intrepidity, and maintains his tranquillity and presence of mind amidst the most dreadful dangers. We esteem the man who supports pain and even torture with manhood and firmness; and we can have little regard for him who sinks under them, and abandons himself to useless outcries and womanish lamentations. A fretful temper, which feels with too much sensibility every little cross accident, renders a man miserable in himself and offensive to other people. A calm one, which does not allow its tranquillity to be disturbed, either by the small injuries or by the little disasters incident to the usual course of human affairs, but which, amidst the natural and moral evils infesting the world, lays its account and is contented to suffer a little from both, is a blessing to the man himself, and gives ease and security to all his companions.

Our sensibility, however, both to our own injuries and to our own misfortunes, though generally too strong, may likewise be too weak. The man who feels little for his own misfortunes must always feel less for those of other people, and be less disposed to relieve them. The man who has little resentment for the injuries which are done to himself, must always have less for those which are done to other people, and be less disposed either to protect or to avenge them. A stupid insensibility to the events of human life necessarily extinguishes all that keen and earnest attention to the propriety of our own conduct, which constitutes the real essence of virtue. We can feel little anxiety about the propriety of our own actions when we are indifferent about the events which may result from them. The man who feels the full distress of the calamity which has befallen him, who feels the whole baseness of the injustice which has been done to him, but who feels still more strongly what the dignity of his own character requires; who does not abandon himself to the guidance of the undisciplined passions which his situation might naturally inspire; but who governs his whole behaviour and conduct according to those restrained and corrected emotions which the great inmate, the great demigod within the breast prescribes and approves of; is alone the real man of virtue, the only real and proper object of love, respect, and admiration. Insensibility and that noble firmness, that exalted self-command

which is founded in the sense of dignity and propriety, are
so far from being altogether the same, that in proportion
as the former takes place, the merit of the latter is in many
cases entirely taken away.

But though the total want of sensibility to personal injury, to personal danger and distress, would, in such situations, take away the whole merit of self-command, that sensibility, however, may very easily be too exquisite, and it
frequently is so. When the sense of propriety, when the
authority of the judge within the breast, can control this
extreme sensibility, that authority must no doubt appear
very noble and very great.   But the exertion of it may be
too fatiguing—it may have too much to do. The individual,
by a great effort, may behave perfectly well; but the contest between the two principles, the warfare within the
breast, may be too violent to be at all consistent with internal tranquillity and happiness.   The wise man whom
nature has endowed with this too exquisite sensibility, and
whose too lively feelings have not been sufficiently blunted
and hardened by early education and proper exercise, will
avoid, as much as duty and propriety will permit, the situations for which he is not perfectly fitted.   The man whose
feeble and delicate constitution renders him too sensible to
pain, to hardship, and to every sort of bodily distress,
should not wantonly embrace the profession of a soldier.
The man of too much sensibility to injury should not rashly
engage in the contests of faction. Though the sense of propriety should be strong enough to command all those sen-
sibilities, the composure of the mind must always be disturbed in the struggle.   In this disorder the judgment cannot always maintain its ordinary acuteness and precision;
and though he may always mean to act properly, he may
often act rashly and imprudently, and in a manner which
he himself will, in the succeeding part of his life, be for ever
ashamed of. A certain intrepidity, a certain firmness of

nerves and hardiness of constitution, whether natural or acquired, are undoubtedly the best preparatives for all the great exertions of self-command.

Though war and faction are certainly the best schools for forming every man to this hardiness and firmness of temper, though they are the best remedies for curing him of the opposite weaknesses, yet if the day of trial should happen to come before he has completely learned his lesson, before the remedy has had time to produce its proper effect, the consequences might not be agreeable.

Our sensibility to the pleasures, to the amusements and enjoyments of human life, may offend, in the same manner, either by its excess or by its defect. Of the two, however, the excess seems less disagreeable than the defect. Both to the spectator and to the person principally concerned, a strong propensity to joy is certainly more pleasing than a dull insensibility to the objects of amusement and diversion. We are charmed with the gaiety of youth, and even with the playfulness of childhood; but we soon grow weary of the flat and tasteless gravity which too frequently accompanies old age. When this propensity, indeed, is not restrained by the sense of propriety, when it is unsuitable to the time or to the place, to the age or to the situation of the person, when to indulge it he neglects either his interest or his duty, it is justly blamed as excessive, and as hurtful both to the individual and to the society. In the greater part of such cases, however, what is chiefly to be found fault with is not so much the strength of the propensity to joy as the weakness of the sense of propriety and duty. A young man who has no relish for the diversions and amusements that are natural and suitable to his age, who talks of nothing but his book or his business, is disliked as formal and pedantic; and we give him no credit for his abstinence

even from improper indulgences, to which he seems to have
so little inclination.

The principle of self-estimation may be too high, and it
may likewise be too low.   It is so very agreeable to think
highly, and so very disagreeable to think meanly, of ourselves, that to the person himself it cannot well be doubted but that some degree of excess must be much less disagreeable than any degree of defect.   But to the impartial
spectator it may perhaps be thought things must appear
quite differently, and that to him the defect must always be
less disagreeable than the excess.   And in our companions,
no doubt, we much more frequently complain of the latter
than of the former.   When they assume upon us, or set
themselves before us, their self-estimation mortifies our own.
Our own pride and vanity prompt us to accuse them of pride
and vanity, and we cease to be the impartial spectators of
their conduct.   When the same companions, however, suffer
any other man to assume over them a superiority which
does not belong to him, we not only blame them, but often
despise them as mean-spirited.   When, on the contrary,
among other people they push themselves a little more forward, and scramble to an elevation disproportioned, as we
think, to their merit, though we may not perfectly approve
of their conduct, we are often upon the whole diverted
with it; and where there is no envy in the case, we are almost always much less displeased with them than we should
have been had they suffered themselves to sink below their
proper station.

In estimating our own merit, in judging of our own character and conduct, there are two different standards to
which we naturally compare them.   The one is the idea of
exact propriety and perfection, so far as we are each of us
capable of comprehending that idea.   The other is that

degree of approximation to this idea which is commonly attained in the world, and which the greater part of our friends and companions, of our rivals and competitors, may have actually arrived at. We very seldom (I am disposed to think we never) attempt to judge of ourselves without giving more or less attention to both these different standards. But the attention of different men, and even of the same man at different times, is often very unequally divided between them, and is sometimes principally directed towards the one, and sometimes towards the other.

So far as our attention is directed towards the first standard, the wisest and best of us all can, in his own character and conduct, see nothing but weakness and imperfection; can discover no ground for arrogance and presumption, but a great deal for humility, regret, and repentance. So far as our attention is directed towards the second, we may be affected either in the one way or in the other, and feel ourselves either really above or really below the standard to which we compare ourselves.

The wise and virtuous man directs his principal attention to the first standard—the idea of exact propriety and perfection. There exists in the mind of every man an idea of this kind, gradually formed from his observations upon the character and conduct both of himself and of other people. It is the slow, gradual, and progressive work of the great demigod within the breast, the great judge and arbiter of conduct. This idea is in every man more or less accurately drawn, its colouring is more or less just, its outlines are more or less exactly designed, according to the delicacy and acuteness of that sensibility with which those observations were made, and according to the care and attention employed in making them. In the wise and virtuous man they have been made with the most acute and delicate sensibility, and the utmost care and attention have been employed in making them. Every day some feature is improved—every day some blemish is corrected. He has studied this idea more than other people; he comprehends it more distinctly; he has formed a much more correct image of it, and is much more deeply enamoured of its exquisite and divine beauty: he endeavours as well as he can to assimilate his own character to this archetype of perfection. But he imitates the work of a divine artist, which can never be equalled. He feels the imperfect success of all his best endeavours, and sees, with grief and affliction, in how many different features the mortal copy falls short of the immortal original: he remembers, with concern and humiliation, how often, from want of attention, from want of judgment, from want of temper, he has, both in words and actions, both in conduct and conversation, violated the exact rules of perfect propriety, and has so far departed from that model, according to which he wished to fashion his own character and conduct. When he directs his attention towards the second standard, indeed, that degree of excellence which his friends and acquaintances have commonly arrived at, he may be sensible of his own superiority; but as his principal attention is always directed towards the first standard, he is necessarily much more humbled by the one comparison than he ever can be elevated by the other. He is never so elated as to look down with insolence even upon those who are really below him: he feels so well his own imperfection, he knows so well the difficulty with which he attained his own distant approximation to rectitude, that he cannot regard with contempt the still greater imperfection of other people. Far from insulting over their inferiority, he views it with the most indulgent commiseration, and, by his advice as well as example, is at all times willing to promote their further advancement. If in any particular qualification they happen to be superior to him (for who is so perfect as not to have many superiors in many different qualifications?) far from envying their superiority, he who knows how difficult it is to excel, esteems and honours their excellence, and never fails to bestow upon it the full measure of applause which it deserves. His whole mind, in short, is deeply impressed, his whole behaviour and deportment are distinctly stamped with the character of real modesty; with that of a very moderate estimation of his own merit, and, at the same time, of a full sense of the merit of other people.

In all the liberal and ingenious arts, in painting, in poetry, in music, in eloquence, in philosophy, the great artist feels always the real imperfection of his own best works, and is more sensible than any man how much they fall short of that ideal perfection of which he has formed some conception, which he imitates as well as he can, but which he despairs of ever equalling. It is the inferior artist only who is ever perfectly satisfied with his own performances. He has little conception of this ideal perfection, about which he has little employed his thoughts ; and it is chiefly to the works of other artists, of perhaps a still lower order, that he deigns to compare his own works. Boileau, the great French poet (in some of his works, perhaps not inferior to the greatest poet of the same kind, either ancient or modern), used to say that no great man was ever completely satisfied with his own works. His acquaintance Santeuil (a writer of Latin verses, and who, on account of that school-boy accomplishment, had the weakness to fancy himself a poet) assured him that he himself was always completely satisfied with *his* own. Boileau replied, with perhaps an arch ambiguity, that he certainly was the only great man that ever was so. Boileau, in judging of his own works, compared them with the standard of ideal perfection which, in his own particular branch of the poetic art, he had, I presume, meditated as deeply, and conceived as distinctly, as it is possible for man to conceive it. Santeuil, in judging of *his* own works, compared them, I

suppose, chiefly to those of the other Latin poets of his own
time, to the greater part of whom he was certainly very
far from being inferior.   But to support and finish off, if I
may so say, the conduct and conversation of a whole life to
some resemblance of this ideal perfection, is surely much
more difficult than to work up to an equal resemblance any
of the productions of any of the ingenious arts.   The artist
sits down to his work undisturbed, at leisure, in the full
possession and recollection of all his skill, experience, and
knowledge.   The wise man must support the propriety of
his own conduct in health and in sickness, in success and
in disappointment, in the hour of fatigue and drowsy indolence, as well as in that of the most awakened attention.
The most sudden and unexpected assaults of difficulty and
distress must never surprise him.   The injustice of other
people must never provoke him to injustice.   The violence
of faction must never confound him.   All the hardships and
hazards of war must never either dishearten or appal him.

Of the persons who, in estimating their own merit, in
judging of their own character and conduct, direct by far
the greater part of their attention to the second standard, to
that ordinary degree of excellence which is commonly attained by other people, there are some who really and justly
feel themselves very much above it, and who, by every
intelligent and impartial spectator, are acknowledged to be
so.   The attention of such persons, however, being always
principally directed, not to the standard of ideal, but to that
of ordinary, perfection, they have little sense of their own
weaknesses and imperfections ; they have little modesty ;
are often assuming, arrogant, and presumptuous ; great admirers of themselves, and great contemners of other people.
Though their characters are in general much less correct,
and their merit much inferior to that of the man of real and
modest virtue, yet their excessive presumption, founded
upon their own excessive self-admiration, dazzles the multi-

tude, and often imposes even upon those who are much superior to the multitude. The frequent, and often wonderful, success of the most ignorant quacks and impostors, both civil and religious, sufficiently demonstrate how easily the multitude are imposed upon by the most extravagant and groundless pretensions. But when those pretensions are supported by a very high degree of real and solid merit, when they are displayed with all the splendour which ostentation can bestow upon them, when they are supported by high rank and great power, when they have often been successfully exerted, and are upon that account attended by the loud acclamations of the multitude, even the man of sober judgment often abandons himself to the general admiration. The very noise of those foolish acclamations often contributes to confound his understanding; and while he sees those great men only at a certain distance, he is often disposed to worship them with a sincere admiration, superior even to that with which they appear to worship themselves. When there is no envy in the case we all take pleasure in admiring, and are upon that account naturally disposed, in our own fancies, to render complete and perfect in every respect the characters which, in many respects, are so very worthy of admiration. The excessive self-admiration of those great men is well understood, perhaps, and even seen through, with some degree of derision, by those wise men who are much in their familiarity, and who secretly smile at those lofty pretensions which, by people at a distance, are often regarded with reverence, and almost with adoration. Such, however, have been in all ages the greater part of those men who have procured to themselves the most noisy fame, the most extensive reputation—a fame and reputation, too, which have often descended to the remotest posterity.

Great success in the world, great authority over the

sentiments and opinions of mankind, have very seldom been
acquired without some degree of this excessive self-admiration. The most splendid characters, the men who have
performed the most illustrious actions, who have brought
about the greatest revolutions, both in the situations and
opinions of mankind ; the most successful warriors, the
greatest statesmen and legislators, the eloquent founders
and leaders of the most numerous and most successful
sects and parties ; have many of them been not more distinguished for their very great merit than for a degree of
presumption and self-admiration altogether disproportioned even to that very great merit. This presumption was,
perhaps, necessary not only to prompt them to undertakings
which a more sober mind would never have thought of, but
to command the submission and obedience of their followers
to support them in such undertakings. When crowned with
success, accordingly, this presumption has often betrayed
them into a vanity that approached almost to insanity and
folly. Alexander the Great appears not only to have wished that other people should think him a god, but to have
been at least very well disposed to fancy himself such. Upon
his death-bed—the most ungodlike of all situations—he re-
quested of his friends that, to the respectable list of deities
into which himself had long before been inserted, his old
mother Olympia might likewise have the honour of being
added. Amidst the respectful admiration of his followers
and disciples, amidst the universal applause of the public,
after the oracle, which probably had followed the voice of
that applause, had pronounced him the wisest of men, the
great wisdom of Socrates, though it did not suffer him to
fancy himself a god, yet was not great enough to hinder
him from fancying that he had secret and frequent intima-
tions from some invisible and divine Being. The sound
head of Cæsar was not so perfectly sound as to hinder him
from being much pleased with his divine genealogy from

the goddess Venus ; and, before the temple of this pretended great-grandmother, to receive, without rising from his
seat, the Roman senate, when that illustrious body came to
present him with some decrees conferring upon him the most
extravagant honours.   This insolence, joined to some other
acts of an almost childish vanity, little to be expected from
an understanding at once so very acute and comprehensive,
seems, by exasperating the public jealousy, to have embol-
dened his assassins, and to have hastened the execution of
their conspiracy. The religion and manners of modern times
give our great men little encouragement to fancy themselves
either gods or even prophets.   Success, however, joined to
great popular favour, has often so far turned the heads of
the greatest of them, as to make them ascribe to themselves
both an importance and an ability much beyond what they
really possessed ; and, by this presumption, to precipitate
themselves into many rash and sometimes ruinous adventures.   It is a characteristic almost peculiar to the great
Duke of Marlborough, that ten years of such uninterrupted
and such splendid success as scarce any other general could
boast of, never betrayed him into a single rash action, scarce
into a single rash word or expression.   The same temperate coolness and self-command cannot, I think, be ascribed
to any other great warrior of later times—not to Prince
Eugene, not to the late King of Prussia, not to the great
Prince of Condé, not even to Gustavus Adolphus. Turenne
seems to have approached the nearest to it ; but several
different transactions of his life sufficiently demonstrate
that it was in him by no means so perfect as in the great
Duke of Marlborough.

   In the humble projects of private life, as well as in the
ambitious and proud pursuits of high stations, great abilities and successful enterprise in the beginning, have frequently encouraged to undertakings which necessarily led to
bankruptcy and ruin in the end.

The esteem and admiration which every impartial spectator conceives for the real merit of those spirited, magnanimous, and high-minded persons, as it is a just and well-founded sentiment, so it is a steady and permanent one, and altogether independent of their good or bad fortune. It is otherwise with that admiration which he is apt to conceive for their excessive self-estimation and presumption. While they are successful, indeed, he is often perfectly conquered and overborne by them. Success covers from his eyes, not only the great imprudence, but frequently the great injustice, of their enterprises; and, far from blaming this defective part of their character, he often views it with the most enthusiastic admiration. When they are unfortunate, however, things change their colours and their names. What was before heroic magnanimity, resumes its proper appellation of extravagant rashness and folly; and the blackness of that avidity and injustice, which was before hid under the splendour of prosperity, comes full into view, and blots the whole lustre of their enterprise. Had Cæsar instead of gaining, lost the battle of Pharsalia, his character would at this hour have ranked a little above that of Catiline, and the weakest man would have viewed his enterprise against the laws of his country in blacker colours than perhaps even Cato, with all the animosity of a party-man, ever viewed it at the time. His real merit, the justness of his taste, the simplicity and elegance of his writings, the propriety of his eloquence, his skill in war, his resources in distress, his cool and sedate judgment in danger, his faithful attachment to his friends, his unexampled generosity to his enemies, would all have been acknowledged; as the real merit of Catiline, who had many great qualities, is acknowledged at this day. But the insolence and injustice of his all-grasping ambition would have darkened and extinguished the glory of all that real merit. Fortune has in this, as well as in some other respects already mentioned, great influence over the moral sentiments of mankind, and, according as

she is either favourable or adverse, can render the same
character the object either of general love and admiration
or of universal hatred and contempt. This great disorder
in our moral sentiments is by no means, however, without
its utility ; and we may on this, as well as on many other
occasions, admire the wisdom of God, even in the weakness
and folly of man. Our admiration of success is founded
upon the same principle with our respect for wealth and
greatness, and is equally necessary for establishing the dis
tinction of ranks and the order of society. By this admiration of success we are taught to submit more easily to those
superiors whom the course of human affairs may assign to
us ; to regard with reverence, and sometimes even with a
sort of respectful affection, that fortunate violence which we
are no longer capable of resisting ; not only the violence of
such splendid characters as those of a Cæsar or an Alexander,
but often that of the most brutal and savage barbarians, of
an Attila, a Gengis, or a Tamerlane. To all such mighty
conquerors the great mob of mankind are naturally disposed to look up with a wondering, though no doubt with a
very weak and foolish admiration. By this admiration,
however, they are taught to acquiesce with less reluctance
under that government which an irresistible force imposes
upon them, and from which no reluctance could deliver them.

Though in prosperity, however, the man of excessive
self-estimation may sometimes appear to have some advantage over the man of correct and modest virtue ; though
the applause of the multitude, and of those who see them
both only at a distance, is often much louder in favour
of the one than it ever is in favour of the other ; yet, all
things fairly computed, the real balance of advantage is
perhaps in all cases greatly in favour of the latter and
against the former. The man who neither ascribes to himself, nor wishes that other people should ascribe to him, any
other merit besides that which really belongs to him,

fears no humiliation, dreads no detection, but rests contented and secure upon the genuine truth and solidity of his own
character. His admirers may neither be very numerous nor
very loud in their applauses; but the wisest man who sees
him the nearest, and who knows him the best, admires him
the most. To a real wise man, the judicious and well-
weighed approbation of a single wise man gives more heartfelt satisfaction than all the noisy applauses of ten thousand
ignorant though enthusiastic admirers. He may say with
Parmenides, who, upon reading a philosophical discourse
before a public assembly at Athens, and observing that, except Plato, the whole company had left him, continued notwithstanding to read on, and said that Plato alone was
audience sufficient for him.

It is otherwise with the man of excessive self-estimation.
The wise men who see him the nearest admire him the least.
Amidst the intoxication of prosperity, their sober and just
esteem falls so far short of the extravagance of his own
self-admiration, that he regards it as mere malignity and
envy. He suspects his best friends; their company becomes
offensive to him; he drives them from his presence; and
often rewards their services not only with ingratitude but
with cruelty and injustice: he abandons his confidence to
flatterers and traitors, who pretend to indolize his vanity and
presumption; and that character which in the beginning,
though in some respects defective, was upon the whole both
amiable and respectable, becomes contemptible and odious
in the end. Amidst the intoxication of prosperity Alexander killed Clytus for having preferred the exploits of his
father Philip to his own; put Calisthenes to death in torture for having refused to adore him in the Persian manner;
and murdered the great friend of his father, the venerable
Parmenio, after having, upon the most groundless suspicions,
sent first to the torture, and afterwards to the scaffold, the
only remaining son of that old man, the rest having all

before died in his own service. This was that Parmenio of whom Philip used to say, that the Athenians were very fortunate who could find ten generals every year, while he himself in the whole course of his life could never find one but Parmenio. It was upon the vigilance and attention of this Parmenio that he reposed at all times with confidence and security, and, in his hours of mirth and jollity, used to say, let us drink, my friends, we may do it with safety, for Parmenio never drinks. It was this same Parmenio with whose presence and counsel it had been said Alexander gained all his victories; and without whose presence and counsel he had never gained a single victory. The humble. admiring, and flattering friends, whom Alexander left in power and authority behind him, divided his empire among themselves, and after having thus robbed his family and kindred of their inheritance, put one after another every single surviving individual of them, whether male or female, to death.

We frequently not only pardon but thoroughly enter into and sympathize with the excessive self-estimation of those splendid characters in which we observe a great and distinguished superiority above the common level of mankind. We call them spirited, magnanimous, and high-minded— words which all involve in their meaning a considerable degree of praise and admiration. But we cannot enter into and sympathize with the excessive self-estimation of those characters in which we can discern no such distinguished superiority. We are disgusted and revolted by it; and it is with some difficulty that we can either pardon or suffer it. We call it pride or vanity—two words of which the latter always, and the former for the most part, involve in their meaning a considerable degree of blame.

Those two vices, however, though resembling in some respects, as being both modifications of excessive self-estimation, are yet in many respects very different from one another.

The proud man is sincere, and in the bottom of his heart is convinced of his own superiority ; though it may sometimes be difficult to guess upon what that conviction is founded. He wishes you to view him in no other light than that in which, when he places himself in your situation, he really views himself : he demands no more of you than what he thinks justice. If you appear not to respect him as he respects himself, he is more offended than mortified, and feels the same indignant resentment as if he had suffered a real injury. He does not even then, however, deign to explain the grounds of his own pretensions : he disdains to court your esteem : he affects even to despise it, and endeavours to maintain his assumed station, not so much by making you sensible of his superiority as of your own meanness : he seems to wish not so much to excite your esteem for *himself* as to mortify *that* for *yourself.*

The vain man is not sincere, and, in the bottom of his heart, is very seldom convinced of that superiority which he wishes you to ascribe to him. He wishes you to view him in much more splendid colours than those in which, when he places himself in your situation, and supposes you to know all that he knows, he can really view himself. When you appear to view him, therefore, in different colours, perhaps in his proper colours, he is much more mortified than offended. The grounds of his claim to that character which he wishes you to ascribe to him he takes every opportunity of displaying, both by the most ostentatious and unnecessary exhibition of the good qualities and accomplishments which he possesses in some tolerable degree, and sometimes even by false pretensions to those which he either possesses in no degree, or in so very slender a degree that he may well enough be said to possess them in no degree. Far from despising your esteem, he courts it with the most anxious assiduity. Far from wishing to mortify your self-estimation, he is happy to cherish it, in hopes that in return you will cherish his own. He flatters in order to be flattered: he studies to please, and endeavours to bribe you into a good opinion of him by politeness and complaisance, and sometimes even by real and essential good offices, though often displayed, perhaps, with unnecessary ostentation.

The vain man sees the respect which is paid to rank and fortune, and wishes to usurp this respect, as well as that for talents and virtues. His dress, his equipage, his way of living, accordingly, all announce both a higher rank and a greater fortune than really belong to him; and in order to support this foolish imposition for a few years in the beginning of his life, he often reduces himself to poverty and distress long before the end of it. As long as he can continue his expense, however, his vanity is delighted with viewing himself, not in the light in which you would view him if you knew all that he knows, but in that in which he imagines he has by his own address induced you actually to view him. Of all the illusions of vanity, this is perhaps the most common. Obscure strangers who visit foreign countries, or who, from a remote province, come to visit for a short time the capital of their own country, most frequently attempt to practise it. The folly of the attempt, though always very great, and most unworthy of a man of sense, may not be altogether so great upon such as upon most other occasions. If their stay is short, they may escape any disgraceful detection; and, after indulging their vanity for a few months or a few years, they may return to their own homes, and repair by future parsimony the waste of their past profusion.

The proud man can very seldom be accused of this folly. His sense of his own dignity renders him careful to preserve his independency, and, when his fortune happens not to be large, though he wishes to be decent, he studies to be frugal and attentive in all his expenses. The ostentatious expense of the vain man is highly offensive to him. It outshines, perhaps, his own. It provokes his indignation as an insolent assumption of a rank which is by no means due; and he never talks of it without loading it with the harshest and severest reproaches.

The proud man does not always feel himself at his ease in the company of his equals, and still less in that of his superiors. He cannot lay down his lofty pretensions, and the countenance and conversation of such company overawe him so much that he dare not display them : he has recourse to humbler company, for which he has little respect, which he would not willingly choose, and which is by no means agreeable to him—that of his inferiors, his flatterers, and dependants : he seldom visits his superiors, or if he does, it is rather to shew that he is entitled to live in such company than for any real satisfaction that he enjoys in it. It is, as Lord Clarendon says of the Earl of Arundel, that he sometimes went to court because he could there only find a greater man than himself; but that he went very seldom, because he found there a greater man than himself.

It is quite otherwise with the vain man. He courts the company of his superiors as much as the proud man shuns it. Their splendour, he seems to think, reflects a splendour upon those who are much about them. He haunts the courts of kings and the levees of ministers, and gives himself the air of being a candidate for fortune and preferment, when in reality he possesses the much more precious happiness, if he knew how to enjoy it, of not being one : he is fond of being admitted to the tables of the great, and still more fond of magnifying to other people the familiarity with which he is honoured there : he associates himself as

much as he can with fashionable people, with those who
are supposed to direct the public opinion—with the witty,
with the learned, with the popular; and he shuns the company of his best friends, whenever the very uncertain current
of public favour happens to run in any respect against them.
With the people to whom he wishes to recommend himself
he is not always very delicate about the means which he
employs for that purpose; unnecessary ostentation, groundless pretensions, constant assentation, frequently flattery,
though for the most part a pleasant and a sprightly flattery,
and very seldom the gross and fulsome flattery of a parasite.
The proud man, on the contrary, never flatters, and is frequently scarce civil to any body.

Notwithstanding all its groundless pretensions, however,
vanity is almost always a sprightly and a gay, and very
often a good-natured passion; pride is always a grave, a
sullen, and a severe one.   Even the falsehoods of the vain
man are all innocent falsehoods, meant to raise himself, not
to lower other people.   To do the proud man justice, he
very seldom stoops to the baseness of falsehood.   When
he does, however, his falsehoods are by no means so innocent.   They are all mischievous, and meant to lower other
people.   He is full of indignation at the unjust superiority,
as he thinks it, which is given to them : he views them with
malignity and envy, and in talking of them often endeavours as much as he can to extenuate and lessen whatever
are the grounds upon which their superiority is supposed to
be founded.   Whatever tales are circulated to their disadvantage, though he seldom forges them himself, yet he
often takes pleasure in believing them, is by no means unwilling to repeat them, and even sometimes with some degree of exaggeration.   The worst falsehoods of vanity are
all what we call white lies ; those of pride, whenever it con-
descends to falsehood, are all of the opposite complexion.

Our dislike to pride and vanity generally disposes us to rank the persons whom we accuse of those vices rather below than above the common level. In this judgment, however, I think we are most frequently in the wrong, and that both the proud and the vain man are often (perhaps for the most part) a good deal above it; though not near so much as either the one really thinks himself, or as the other wishes you to think him. If we compare them with their own pretensions, they may appear the just objects of contempt. But when we compare them with what the greater part of their rivals and competitors really are, they may appear quite otherwise, and very much above the common level. Where there is this real superiority, pride is frequently attended with many respectable virtues—with truth, with integrity, with a high sense of honour, with cordial and steady friendship, with the most inflexible firmness and resolution; vanity with many amiable ones—with humanity, with politeness, with a desire to oblige in all little matters, and sometimes with a real generosity in great ones—a generosity, however, which it often wishes to display in the most splendid colours that it can. By their rivals and enemies, the French in the last century were accused of vanity; the Spaniards of pride, and foreign nations were disposed to consider the one as the more amiable, the other as the more respectable people.

The words *vain* and *vanity* are never taken in a good sense. We sometimes say of a man, when we are talking of him in good-humour, that he is the better for his vanity, or that his vanity is more diverting than offensive; but we still consider it as a foible and a ridicule in his character.

The words *proud* and *pride*, on the contrary, are sometimes taken in a good sense. We frequently say of a man that he is too proud, or that he has too much noble pride, ever to suffer himself to do a mean thing. Pride is in this case confounded with magnanimity. Aristotle, a philosopher who certainly knew the world, in drawing the character of the magnanimous man, paints him with many features which, in the two last centuries, were commonly ascribed to the Spanish character; that he was deliberate in all his resolutions; slow and even tardy in all his actions; that his voice was grave, his speech deliberate, his step and motion slow; that he appeared indolent and even slothful, not at all disposed to bustle about little matters, but to act with the most determined and vigorous resolution upon all great and illustrious occasions; that he was not a lover of danger, or forward to expose himself to little dangers, but to great dangers; and that, when he exposed himself to danger, he was altogether regardless of his life.

The proud man is commonly too well contented with himself to think that his character requires any amendment. The man who feels himself all-perfect naturally enough despises all further improvement. His self-sufficiency and absurd conceit of his own superiority commonly attend him from his youth to his most advanced age; and he dies, as Hamlet says, with all his sins upon his head, unanointed, unanealed.

It is frequently quite otherwise with the vain man. The desire of the esteem and admiration of other people, when for qualities and talents which are the natural and proper objects of esteem and admiration, is the real love of true glory—a passion which, if not the very best passion of human nature, is certainly one of the best. Vanity is very frequently no more than an attempt prematurely to usurp that glory before it is due. Though your son under five-and-twenty years of age should be but a coxcomb, do not upon that account despair of his becoming before he is forty a very wise and worthy man, and a real proficient in all those talents and virtues to which at present he may only be an ostentatious and empty pretender. The great secret of education is to direct vanity to proper objects. Never suffer him to value himself upon trivial accomplishments, but do not always discourage his pretensions to those that are of real importance. He would not pretend to them if he did not earnestly desire to possess them. Encourage this desire; afford him every means to facilitate the acquisition; and do not take take too much offence although he should sometimes assume the air of having attained it a little before the time.

Such, I say, are the distinguishing characteristics of pride and vanity, when each of them acts according to its proper character. But the proud man is often vain; and the vain man is often proud. Nothing can be more natural than that the man who thinks much more highly of himself than he deserves should wish that other people should think still more highly of him; or that the man who wishes that other people should think more highly of him than he thinks of himself should, at the same time, think much more highly of himself than he deserves. Those two vices being frequently blended in the same character, the characteristics of both are necessarily confounded; and we sometimes find the superficial and impertinent ostentation of vanity joined to the most malignant and derisive insolence of pride. We are sometimes upon that account at a loss how to rank a particular character, or whether to place it among the proud or among the vain.

Men of merit considerably above the common level sometimes underrate as well as overrate themselves. Such characters, though not very dignified, are often in private society far from being disagreeable. His companions all feel themselves much at their ease in the society of a man so perfectly modest and unassuming. If those companions, however, have not both more discernment and more gene-

rosity than ordinary, though they may have some kindness
for him they have seldom much respect; and the warmth
of their kindness is very seldom sufficient to compensate
the coldness of their respect. Men of no more than ordinary discernment never rate any person higher than he
appears to rate himself. He seems doubtful himself, they
say, whether he is perfectly fit for such a situation or such
an office, and immediately give the preference to some impudent blockhead who entertains no doubt about his own
qualifications. Though they should have discernment, yet,
if they want generosity, they never fail to take advantage
of his simplicity, and to assume over him an impertinent
superiority which they are by no means entitled to. His
good nature may enable him to bear this for some time;
but he grows weary at last, and frequently when it is too
late, and when that rank which he ought to have assumed
is lost irrecoverably, and usurped, in consequence of his
own backwardness, by some of his more forward, though
much less meritorious, companions. A man of this character
must have been very fortunate in the early choice of his companions if, in going through the world, he meets always
with fair justice even from those whom, from his own past
kindness, he might have some reason to consider as his
best friends; and a youth, too unassuming and to unam-
bitious, is frequently followed by an insignificant, complaining, and discontented old age.

Those unfortunate persons whom nature has formed a
good deal below the common level, seem sometimes to rate
themselves still more below it than they really are. This
humility appears sometimes to sink them into idiotism.
Whoever has taken the trouble to examine idiots with
attention, will find that in many of them the faculties of
the understanding are by no means weaker than in several
other people, who, though acknowledged to be dull and
stupid, are not by any body accounted idiots. Many

'diots, with no more than ordinary education, have been taught to read, write, and account tolerably well. Many persons, never accounted idiots, notwithstanding the most careful education, and notwithstanding that in their advanced age they have had spirit enough to attempt to learn what their early education had not taught them, have never been able to acquire, in any tolerable degree, any one of those three accomplishments. By an instinct of pride, however, they set themselves upon a level with their equals in age and situation, and, with courage and firmness, maintain their proper station among their companions. By an opposite instinct the idiot feels himself below every company into which you can introduce him. Ill usage, to which he is extremely liable, is capable of throwing him into the most violent fits of rage and fury. But no good usage, no kindness or indulgence, can ever raise him to converse with you as your equal. If you can bring him to converse with you at all, however, you will frequently find his answers sufficiently pertinent and even sensible. But they are always stamped with a distinct consciousness of his own great inferiority.

He seems to shrink, and, as it were, to retire from your look and conversation, and to feel when he places himself in your situation, that, notwithstanding your apparent condescension, you cannot help considering him as immensely below you. Some idiots, perhaps the greater part, seem to be so chiefly or altogether, from a certain numbness or torpidity in the faculties of the understanding. But there are others in whom those faculties do not appear more torpid or benumbed than in many other people who are not accounted idiots. But that instinct of pride, necessary to support them upon an equality with their brethren, seems totally wanting in the former, and not in the latter.

That degree of self-estimation, therefore, which contributes most to the happiness and contentment of the person himself, seems likewise most agreeable to the impartial spectator. The man who esteems himself as he ought, and no more than he ought, seldom fails to obtain from other people all the esteem that he himself thinks due. He desires no more than is due to him, and he rests upon it with complete satisfaction.

The proud and the vain man, on the contrary, are constantly dissatisfied. The one is tormented with indignation at the unjust superiority, as he thinks it, of other people; the other is in continual dread of the shame which he foresees would attend upon the detection of his groundless pretensions. Even the extravagant pretensions of the man of real magnanimity, though, when supported by splendid abilities and virtues, and, above all, by good fortune, they impose upon the multitude, whose applauses he little regards, do not impose upon those wise men whose approbation he can only value, and whose esteem he is most anxious to acquire. He feels that they see through, and suspects that they despise, his excessive presumption; and he often suffers the cruel misfortune of becoming, first the jealous and secret, and at last the open, furious, and vindictive enemy of those very persons whose friendship it would have given him the greatest happiness to enjoy with unsuspicious security.

Though our dislike to the proud and the vain often disposes us to rank them rather below than above their proper station, yet, unless we are provoked by some particular and personal impertinence, we very seldom venture to use them ill. In common cases we endeavour for our own ease rather to acquiesce, and, as well as we can, to accommodate ourselves to their folly. But, to the man who underrates himself, unless we have both more discernment and more generosity than belong to the greater part of men, we

seldom fail to do at least all the injustice which he does to
himself, and frequently a great deal more. He is not only
more unhappy in his own feelings than either the proud or
the vain, but he is much more liable to every sort of ill-
usage from other people. In almost all cases it is better
to be a little too proud than in any respect too humble;
and, in the sentiment of self estimation, some degree of
excess seems, both to the person himself and to the impartial spectator, to be less disagreeable than any degree of
defect.

In this, therefore, as well as in every other emotion, passion and habit, the degree that is most agreeable to the impartial spectator is likewise most agreeable to the person
himself; and according as either the excess or the defect is
least offensive to the former, so either the one or the other
is in proportion least disagreeable to the latter.

CONCLUSION OF THE SIXTH PART.

CONCERN for our own happiness recommends to us the virtue of prudence; concern for that of other people, the virtues of justice and beneficence—of which the one restrains us from hurting, the other prompts us to promote that happiness. Independent of any regard either to what are or to what ought to be, or to what upon a certain condition would be the sentiments of other people, the first of those three virtues is originally recommended to us by our selfish, the other two by our benevolent affections. Regard to the sentiments of other people, however, comes afterwards both to enforce and to direct the practice of all those virtues and no man, during either the whole course of his life or that of any considerable part of it, ever trod steadily and uniformly in the paths of prudence, of justice, or of proper beneficence, whose conduct was not principally directed by a regard to the sentiments of the supposed impartial spectator, of the great inmate of the breast, the great judge and arbiter of conduct. If in the course of the day we have swerved in any respect from the rules which he prescribes to us; if we have either exceeded or relaxed in our frugality; if we have either exceeded or relaxed in our industry; if through passion or inadvertency we have hurt in any respect the interest or happiness of our neighbour; if we have neglected a plain and proper opportunity of promoting that interest and happiness—it is this inmate who in the evening calls us to an account for all those omissions and violations, and his reproaches often make us blush inwardly, both for our folly and inattention to our own happiness, and for our still greater indifference and inattention, perhaps, to that of other people.

But though the virtues of prudence, justice, and beneficence, may upon different occasions be recommended to us
almost equally by two different principles ; those of self-
command are, upon most occasions, principally and almost
entirely recommended to us by one—by the sense of propriety, by regard to the sentiments of the supposed impartial spectator. Without the restraint which this principle
imposes, every passion would upon most occasions rush
headlong, if I may say so, to its own gratification. Anger
would follow the suggestions of its own fury—fear those
of its own violent agitations. Regard to no time or place
would induce vanity to refrain from the loudest and most
impertinent ostentation ; or voluptuousness from the most
open, indecent, and scandalous indulgence. Respect for
what are, or for what ought to be, or for what, upon a certain condition, would be the sentiments of other people, is
the sole principle which upon most occasions overawes all
those mutinous and turbulent passions into that tone and
temper which the impartial spectator can enter into and
sympathize with.

Upon some occasions, indeed, those passions are restrained, not so much by a sense of their impropriety as by prudential considerations of the bad consequences which might
follow from their indulgence. In such cases, the passions,
though restrained, are not always subdued, but often remain
lurking in the breast with all their original fury. The man
whose anger is restrained by fear does not always lay aside
his anger, but only reserves its gratification for a more safe
opportunity. But the man who, in relating to some other
person the injury which has been done to him, feels at once
the fury of his passion cooled and becalmed by sympathy
with the more moderate sentiments of his companion, who
at once adopts those more moderate sentiments, and comes
to view that injury, not in the black and atrocious colours

in which he had originally beheld it, but in the much milder and fairer light in which his companion naturally views
it; not only restrains, but in some measure subdues his
anger. The passion becomes really less than it was before,
and less capable of exciting him to the violent and bloody
revenge which at first perhaps he might have thought
of inflicting.

Those passions which are restrained by the sense of propriety are all in some degree moderated and subdued by
it. But those which are restrained only by prudential considerations of any kind are, on the contrary, frequently in-
flamed by the restraint, and sometimes (long after the provocation given, and when nobody is thinking about it) burst
out absurdly and unexpectedly, and with tenfold fury and
violence.

Anger, however, as well as every other passion, may
upon many occasions be very properly restrained by prudential considerations. Some exertion of manhood and self-
command is even necessary for this sort of restraint; and
the impartial spectator may sometimes view it with that sort
of cold esteem due to that species of conduct which he considers as a mere matter of vulgar prudence; but never with
that affectionate admiration with which he surveys the same
passions, when by the sense of propriety, they are moderated and subdued to what he himself can readily enter into. In the former species of restraint he may frequently
discern some degree of propriety, and, if you will, even of
virtue; but it is a propriety and virtue of a much inferior
order to those which he always feels with transport and
admiration in the latter.

The virtues of prudence, justice, and beneficence, have no
tendency to produce any but the most agreeable effects.
Regard to those effects, as it originally recommends them

to the actor, so does it afterwards to the impartial spectator.   In our approbation of the character of the prudent man, we feel with peculiar complacency the security which he must enjoy while he walks under the safeguard of that sedate and deliberate virtue.   In our approbation of the character of the just man, we feel with equal complacency the security which all those connected with him, whether in neighbourhood, society, or business, must derive from his scrupulous anxiety never either to hurt or offend.   In our approbation of the character of the beneficent man, we enter into the gratitude of all those who are within the sphere of his good offices, and conceive with them the highest sense of his merit.   In our approbation of all those virtues, our sense of their agreeable effects, of their utility, either to the person who exercises them or to some other persons, joins with our sense of their propriety, and constitutes always a considerable, frequently the greater, part of that approbation.

But in our approbation of the virtues of self-command, complacency with their effects sometimes constitutes no part, and frequently but a small part, of that approbation. Those effects may sometimes be agreeable, and sometimes disagreeable; and though our approbation is no doubt stronger in the former case, it is by no means altogether destroyed in the latter.   The most heroic valour may be employed indifferently in the cause either of justice or of injustice; and though it is no doubt much more loved and admired in the former case, it still appears a great and respectable quality even in the latter.   In that, and in all the other virtues of self-command, the splendid and dazzling quality seems always to be the greatness and steadiness of the exertion, and the strong sense of propriety which is necessary in order to make and to maintain that exertion. The effects are too often but too little regarded.

THE

THEORY OF MORAL SENTIMENTS.

Part Seventh.

OF SYSTEMS OF MORAL PHILOSOPHY:

CONSISTING OF FOUR SECTIONS.

SECTION I

IF we examine the most celebrated and remarkable of the different theories which have been given concerning the nature and origin of our moral sentiments, we shall find that almost all of them coincide with some part or other of that which I have been endeavouring to give an account of; and that if every thing which has already been said be fully considered, we shall be at no loss to explain what was the view or aspect of nature which led each particular author to form his particular system. From some one or other of those principles which I have been endeavouring to unfold, every system of morality that ever had any reputation in the world has, perhaps, ultimately been derived. As they are all of them in this respect founded upon natural principles, they are all of them in some measure in the right. But as many of them are derived from a partial and imperfect view of nature, there are many of them, too, in some respects in the wrong.

In treating of the principles of morals there are two questions to be considered. First, wherein does virtue consist— or what is the tone of temper, and tenor of conduct, which constitutes the excellent and praiseworthy character, the character which is the natural object of esteem, honour, and approbation? And, secondly, by what power or faculty in the mind is it that this character, whatever it be, is recommended to us? or, in other words, how and by what means does it come to pass, that the mind prefers one tenor of conduct to another; denominates the one right and the other wrong; considers the one as the object of approbation, honour, and reward, and the other of blame, censure, and punishment?

We examine the first question when we consider whether virtue consists in benevolence, as Dr Hutcheson imagines; or in acting suitably to the different relations we stand in, as Dr Clarke supposes ; or in the wise and prudent pursuit of our own real and solid happiness, as has been the opinion of others.

We examine the second question, when we consider whether the virtuous character, whatever it consists in, be recommended to us by self-love, which makes us perceive that this character, both in ourselves and others, tends most to promote our own private interest ; or by reason, which points out to us the difference between one character and another, in the same manner as it does that between truth and falsehood ; or by a peculiar power of perception, called a moral sense, which this virtuous character gratifies and pleases, as the contrary disgusts and displeases it; or, last of all, by some other principle in human nature, such as a modification of sympathy, or the like.

I shall begin with considering the systems which have been formed concerning the first of these questions, and shall proceed afterwards to examine those concerning the second.

SECTION II.

OF THE DIFFERENT ACCOUNTS WHICH HAVE BEEN GIVEN OF THE NATURE OF VIRTUE.

INTRODUCTION.

THE different accounts which have been given of the nature of virtue, or of the temper of mind which constitutes the excellent and praiseworthy character, may be reduced to three different classes. According to some, the virtuous temper of mind does not consist in any one species of affections, but in the proper government and direction of all our affections, which may be either virtuous or vicious, according to the objects which they pursue, and the degree of vehemence with which they pursue them. According to these authors, therefore, virtue consists in propriety.

According to others, virtue consists in the judicious pursuit of our own private interest and happiness, or in the proper government and direction of those selfish affections which aim solely at this end. In the opinion of these authors, therefore, virtue consists in prudence.

Another set of authors make virtue consist in those affections only which aim at the happiness of others, not in those which aim at our own. According to them, therefore, disinterested benevolence is the only motive which can stamp upon any action the character of virtue.

The character of virtue, it is evident, must either be

ascribed indifferently to all our affections, when under proper government and direction, or it must be confined to some one class or division of them. The great division of our affections is into the selfish and the benevolent. If the character of virtue, therefore, cannot be ascribed indifferently to all our affections, when under proper government and direction, it must be confined either to those which aim directly at our own private happiness, or to those which aim directly at that of others. If virtue, therefore, does not consist in propriety, it must consist either in prudence or in benevolence. Besides these three, it is scarce possible to imagine that any other account can be given of the nature of virtue. I shall endeavour to shew hereafter how all the other accounts, which are seemingly different from any of these, coincide at bottom with some one or other of them.

CHAPTER I.

Of those Systems which make Virtue consist in **Propriety.**

ACCORDING to Plato, to Aristotle, and to Zeno, virtue consists in the propriety of conduct, or in the suitableness of the affection from which we act to the object which excites it.

I. In the system of Plato,* the soul is considered as something like a little state or republic, composed of three different faculties or orders.

The first is the judging faculty—the faculty which determines not only what are the proper means for attaining any end, but also what ends are fit to be pursued, and what degree of relative value we ought to put upon each. This faculty Plato called, as it is very properly called, Reason, and considered it as what had a right to be the governing principle of the whole. Under this appellation, it is evident, he comprehended not only that faculty by which we judge of truth and falsehood, but that by which we judge of the propriety or impropriety of desires and affections.

The different passions and appetites, the natural subjects of this ruling principle, but which are so apt to rebel against their master, he reduced to two different classes or orders. The first consisted of those passions which are founded in pride and resentment, or in what the schoolmen call the irascible part of the soul; ambition, animosity, the love of honour and the dread of shame, the desire of victory, superiority, and revenge; all those passions, in short, which

* See Plato de Rep. lib. iv.

are supposed either to rise from, or to denote what, by a metaphor in our language, we commonly call spirit or natural fire. The second consisted of those passions which are founded in the love of pleasure, or in what the schoolmen called the concupiscible part of the soul. It comprehended all the appetites of the body, the love of ease and security, and of all sensual gratifications.

It rarely happens that we break in upon that plan of conduct which the governing principle prescribes, and which in all our cool hours we had laid down to ourselves as what was most proper for us to pursue, but when prompted by one or other of those two different sets of passions—either by ungovernable ambition and resentment, or by the importunate solicitations of present ease and pleasure. But though these two orders of passions are so apt to mislead us, they are still considered as necessary parts of human nature; the first having been given to defend us against injuries, to assert our rank and dignity in the world, to make us aim at what is noble and honourable, and to make us distinguish those who act in the same manner ; the second, to provide for the support and necessities of the body.

In the strength, acuteness, and perfection of the governing principle was placed the essential virtue of prudence, which, according to Plato, consisted in a just and clear discernment, founded upon general and scientific ideas of the ends which were proper to be pursued, and of the means which were proper for attaining them.

When the first set of passions, those of the irascible part of the soul, had that degree of strength and firmness which enabled them, under the direction of reason, to despise all dangers in the pursuit of what was honourable and noble ; it constituted the virtue of fortitude and magnanimity. This order of passions, according to this system, was of a more generous and noble nature than the other. They were considered upon many occasions as the auxiliaries of reason, to check and restrain the inferior and brutal appetites. We are often angry at ourselves, it was observed, we often become the objects of our own resentment and indignation, when the love of pleasure prompts to do what we disapprove of; and the irascible part of our nature is in this manner called in to assist the rational against the concupiscible.

When all those three different parts of our nature were in perfect concord with one another, when neither the irascible nor concupiscible passions ever aimed at any gratification which reason did not approve of, and when reason never commanded any thing but what these of their own accord were willing to perform ; this happy composure, this perfect and complete harmony of soul, constituted that virtue which in their language is expressed by a word which we commonly translate Temperance, but which might more properly be translated good temper, or sobriety and moderation of mind.

Justice, the last and greatest of the four cardinal virtues, took place, according to this system, when each of those three faculties of the mind confined itself to its proper office without attempting to encroach upon that of any other; when reason directed and passion obeyed, and when each passion performed its proper duty, and exerted itself towards its proper object, easily and without reluctance, and with that degree of force and energy, which was suitable to the value of what it pursued. In this consisted that complete virtue, that perfect propriety of conduct, which Plato, after some of the ancient Pythagoreans, denominated Justice.

The word, it is to be observed, which expresses justice in the Greek language has several different meanings ; and as the correspondent word in all other languages, so far as

I know, has the same, there must be some natural affinity among those various significations. In one sense we are said to do justice to our neighbour when we abstain from doing him any positive harm, and do not directly hurt him, either in his person, or in his estate, or in his reputation. This is that justice which I have treated of above, the observance of which may be extorted by force, and the violation of which exposes to punishment. In another sense we are said not to do justice to our neighbour unless we conceive for him all that love, respect, and esteem, which his character, his situation, and his connection with ourselves, render suitable and proper for us to feel, and unless we act accordingly. It is in this sense that we are said to do injustice to a man of merit who is connected with us, though we abstain from hurting him in every respect, if we do not exert ourselves to serve him, and to place him in that situation in which the impartial spectator would be pleased to see him. The first sense of the word coincides with what Aristotle and the schoolmen call commutative justice, and with what Grotius calls the *justitia expletrix*, which consists in abstaining from what is another's, and in doing voluntarily whatever we can with propriety be forced to do. The second sense of the word coincides with what some have called distributive justice,* and with the *justitia attributrix* of Grotius, which consists in proper beneficence, in the becoming use of what is our own, and in the applying it to those purposes, either of charity or generosity, to which it is most suitable in our situation that it should be applied. In this sense justice comprehends all the social virtues. There is yet another sense in which the word justice is sometimes taken, still more extensive than either of the former, though very much akin to the last ; and which

---

* The distributive justice of Aristotle is somewhat different. It consists in the proper distribution of rewards from the public stock of a community. See Aristotle Ethic. Nic. l. v. c. 2.

runs too, so far as I know, through all languages. It is in this last sense that we are said to be unjust, when we do not seem to value any particular object with that degree of esteem, or to pursue it with that degree of ardour which to the impartial spectator it may appear to deserve or to be naturally fitted for exciting. Thus we are said to do injustice to a poem or a picture when we do not admire them enough, and we are said to do them more than justice when we admire them too much. In the same manner we are said to do injustice to ourselves when we appear not to give sufficient attention to any particular object of self-interest. In this last sense, what is called justice means the same thing with exact and perfect propriety of conduct and behaviour, and comprehends in it not only the offices of both commutative and distributive justice, but of every other virtue, of prudence, of fortitude, of temperance. It is in this last sense that Plato evidently understands what he calls justice, and which, therefore, according to him, comprehends in it the perfection of every sort of virtue.

Such is the account given by Plato of the nature of virtue, or of that temper of mind which is the proper object of praise and approbation. It consists, according to him, in that state of mind in which every faculty confines itself within its proper sphere, without encroaching upon that of any other, and performs its proper office with that precise degree of strength and vigour which belongs to it. His account, it is evident, coincides in every respect with what we have said above concerning the propriety of conduct.

II. Virtue, according to Aristotle,* consists in the habit of mediocrity according to right reason. Every particular virtue, according to him, lies in a kind of middle between two opposite vices, of which the one offends from being too

---

* See Aristotle. Ethic. Nic. l. ii. c. 5, et seq. et l. iii. c. 6, et seq.

much, the other from being too little, affected by a particular species of objects. Thus the virtue of fortitude or courage lies in the middle between the opposite vices of cowardice and of presumptuous rashness, of which the one offends from being too much, and the other from being too little, affected by the objects of fear. Thus, too, the virtue of frugality lies in a middle between avarice and profusion, of which the one consists in an excess, the other in a defect, of the proper attention to the objects of self-interest. Magnanimity, in the same manner, lies in a middle between the excess of arrogance and the defect of pusillanimity, of which the one consists in too extravagant, the other in too weak, a sentiment of our own worth and dignity. It is unnecessary to observe, that this account of virtue corresponds too pretty exactly with what has been said above concerning the propriety and impropriety of conduct.

According to Aristotle,* indeed, virtue did not so much consist in those moderate and right affections as in the habit of this moderation. In order to understand this, it is to be observed, that virtue may be considered either as the quality of an action or as the quality of a person. Considered as the quality of an action, it consists, even according to Aristotle, in the reasonable moderation of the affection from which the action proceeds, whether this disposition be habitual to the person or not. Considered as the quality of a person, it consists in the habit of this reasonable moderation, in its having become the customary and usual disposition of the mind. Thus the action which proceeds from an occasional fit of generosity is undoubtedly a generous action, but the man who performs it is not necessarily a generous person, because it may be the single action of the kind which he ever performed. The motive and disposition of heart from which this action was performed may have been

* See Aristotle, Ethic. Nic. lib. ii. ch. 1, 2, 3, and 4.

quite just and proper; but as this happy mood seems to have been the effect rather of accidental humour than of any thing steady or permanent in the character, it can reflect no great honour on the performer. When we denominate a character generous or charitable, or virtuous in any respect, we mean to signify that the disposition expressed by each of those appellations is the usual and customary disposition of the person. But single actions of any kind, how proper and suitable soever, are of little consequence to shew that this is the case. If a single action was sufficient to stamp the character of any virtue upon the person who performed it, the most worthless of mankind might lay claim to all the virtues; since there is no man who has not, upon some occasions, acted with prudence, justice, temperance, and fortitude. But though single actions, how laudable soever, reflect very little praise upon the person who performs them, a single vicious action, performed by one whose conduct is usually very regular, greatly diminishes, and sometimes destroys altogether, our opinion of his virtue. A single action of this kind sufficiently shews that his habits are not perfect, and that he is less to be depended upon than, from the usual train of his behaviour, we might have been apt to imagine.

Aristotle, too,* when he made virtue to consist in practical habits, had it probably in his view to oppose the doctrine of Plato, who seems to have been of opinion, that just sentiments and reasonable judgments concerning what was fit to be done or to be avoided were alone sufficient to constitute the most perfect virtue. Virtue, according to Plato, might be considered as a species of science, and no man, he thought, could see clearly and demonstratively what was right and what was wrong, and not act accordingly. Passion might make us act contrary to doubtful and uncertain

---

* See Aristotle, Mag. Mor. lib. i. ch. 1.

opinions, not to plain and evident judgments. Aristotle, on the contrary, was of opinion, that no conviction of the understanding was capable of getting the better of inveterate habits, and that good morals arose not from knowledge but from action.

III. According to Zeno,* the founder of the Stoical doctrine, every animal was by nature recommended to its own care, and was endowed with the principle of self-love, that it might endeavour to preserve, not only its existence, but all the different parts of its nature, in the best and most perfect state of which they were capable.

The self-love of man embraced, if I may say so, his body and all its different members, his mind and all its different faculties and powers, and desired the preservation and maintenance of them all in their best and most perfect condition. Whatever tended to support this state of existence was, therefore, by nature pointed out to him as fit to be chosen; and whatever tended to destroy it, as fit to be rejected. Thus health, strength, agility, and ease of body, as well as the external conveniencies which could promote these; wealth, power, honours, the respect and esteem of those we live with, were naturally pointed out to us as things eligible, and of which the possession was preferable to the want. On the other hand, sickness, infirmity, unwieldiness, pain of body, as well as all the external inconveniencies which tend to occasion or bring on any of them, poverty, the want of authority, the contempt or hatred of those we live with, were in the same manner pointed out to us as things to be shunned and avoided. In each of those two opposite classes of objects there were some which appeared to be more the objects either of choice or rejection than others in the same

* See Cicero de finibus, lib. iii. ; also Diogenes Laertius in Zenone, lib. vii. segment 84.

class. Thus, in the first class, health appeared evidently preferable to strength, and strength to agility—reputation to power, and power to riches. And thus, too, in the second class, sickness was more to be avoided than unwieldiness of body, ignominy than poverty, and poverty than the loss of power. Virtue and the propriety of conduct consisted in choosing and rejecting all different objects and circumstances according as they were by nature rendered more or less the objects of choice or rejection ; in selecting always from among the several objects of choice presented to us, that which was most to be chosen, when we could not obtain them all; and in selecting, too, out of the several objects of rejection offered to us, that which was least to be avoided, when it was not in our power to avoid them all. By choosing and rejecting with this just and accurate discernment, by thus bestowing upon every object the precise degree of attention it deserved, according to the place which it held in this natural scale of things, we maintained, according to the Stoics, that perfect rectitude of conduct which constituted the essence of virtue. This was what they called to live consistently, to live according to nature, and to obey those laws and directions which nature, or the Author of nature, had prescribed for our conduct.

So far the Stoical idea of propriety and virtue is not very different from that of Aristotle and the ancient Peripatetics.

Among those primary objects which nature had recommended to us as eligible, was the prosperity of our family, of our relations, of our friends, of our country, of mankind, and of the universe in general. Nature, too, had taught us, that as the prosperity of two was preferable to that of one, that of many, or of all, must be infinitely more so. That we ourselves were but one, and that, consequently, wherever our prosperity was inconsistent with that, either of the whole or of any considerable part of the whole, it ought, even in our own choice, to yield to what was so vastly preferable. As all the events in this world were conducted by the providence of a wise, powerful, and good God, we might be assured that whatever happened tended to the prosperity and perfection of the whole. If we ourselves, therefore, were in poverty, in sickness, or in any other calamity, we ought, first of all, to use our utmost endeavours, so far as justice and our duty to others would allow, to rescue ourselves from this disagreeable circumstance. But if, after all we could do, we found this impossible, we ought to rest satisfied that the order and perfection of the universe required that we should, in the meantime, continue in this situation. And as the prosperity of the whole should even to us appear preferable to so insignificant a part as ourselves, our situation, whatever it was, ought from that moment to become the object of our liking, if we would maintain that complete propriety and rectitude of sentiment and conduct in which consisted the perfection of our nature. If, indeed, any opportunity of extricating ourselves should offer, it became our duty to embrace it. The order of the universe, it was evident, no longer required our continuance in this situation, and the great Director of the world plainly called upon us to leave it, by so clearly pointing out the road which we were to follow. It was the same case with the adversity of our relations, our friends, our country. If, without violating any more sacred obligation, it was in our power to prevent or put an end to their calamity, it undoubtedly was our duty to do so. The propriety of action, the rule which Jupiter had given us for the direction of our conduct, evidently required this of us. But if it was altogether out of our power to do either, we ought then to consider this event as the most fortunate which could possibly have happened; because we might be assured that it tended most to the prosperity and order of the whole, which was what we ourselves, if we were wise and equitable, ought most of all to desire. It was our own final interest considered as a part of that whole, of which the prosperity ought to be not only the principal but the sole object of our desire.

" In what sense," says Epictetus, " are some things said to be according to our nature, and others contrary to it ?—it is in that sense in which we consider ourselves as separated and detached from all other things. For thus it may be said to be according to the nature of the foot to be always clean. But if you consider it as a foot, and not as something detached from the rest of the body, it must behove it sometimes to trample in the dirt, and sometimes to tread upon thorns, and sometimes, too, to be cut off for the sake of the whole body ; and if it refuses this, it is no longer a foot. Thus, too, ought we to conceive with regard to ourselves. What are you ?—a man. If you consider yourself as something separated and detached, it is agreeable to your nature to live to old age, to be rich, to be in health. But if you consider yourself as a man, and as a part of a whole, upon account of that whole it will behove you sometimes to be in sickness, sometimes to be exposed to the inconveniency of a sea-voyage, sometimes to be in want ; and at last, perhaps, to die before your time. Why then do you complain? do not you know that by doing so, as the foot ceases to be a foot, so you cease to be a man ?''

A wise man never complains of the destiny of Providence, nor thinks the universe in confusion when he is out of order. He does not look upon himself as a whole, separated and detached from every other part of nature, to be taken care of by itself and for itself: he regards himself in the light in which he imagines the great genius of human nature, and of the world, regards him : he enters, if I may say so, into the sentiments of that divine Being, and considers himself as an atom, a particle, of an immense and infinite system, which must and ought to be disposed of according to the conveniency of the whole   Assured of the wisdom which directs all the events of human life, whatever lot befalls him, he accepts it with joy, satisfied that, if he had known all the connections and dependencies of the different parts of the universe, it is the very lot which he himself would have wished for. If it is life, he is contented to live; and if it is death, as nature must have no further occasion for his presence here, he willingly goes where he is appointed. " I accept," said a cynical philosopher, whose doctrines were in this respect the same as those of the Stoics—" I accept with equal joy and satisfaction whatever fortune can befall me—riches or poverty, pleasure or pain, health or sickness, all is alike; nor would I desire that the gods should in any respect change my destination. If I was to ask of them any thing beyond what their bounty has already bestowed, it should be that they would inform me beforehand what it was their pleasure should be done with me, that I might of my own accord place myself in this situation, and demonstrate the cheerfulness with which I embraced their allotment."—" If I am going to sail," says Epictetus, " I choose the best ship and the best pilot, and I wait for the fairest weather that my circumstances and duty will allow. Prudence and propriety, the principles which the gods have given me for the direction of my conduct, require this of me, but they require no more; and if, notwithstanding, a storm arises, which neither the strength of the vessel nor the skill of the pilot are likely to withstand, I give myself no trouble about the consequence. All that I had to do is done already. The directors of my conduct never command me to be miserable, to be anxious, desponding, or afraid. Whether we are to be drowned, or to come to a harbour, is the business of Jupiter, not mine. I leave it entirely to his determination, nor ever break my rest with considering which way he is likely to decide it, but receive whatever comes with equal indifference and security."

From this perfect confidence in that benevolent wisdom

which governs the universe, and from this entire resignation to whatever order that wisdom might think proper to
establish, it necessarily followed, that to the Stoical wise
man all the events of human life must be in a great measure
indifferent. His happiness consisted altogether, first, in the
contemplation of the happiness and perfection of the great
system of the universe, of the good government of the great
republic of gods and men, of all rational and sensible beings;
and, secondly, in discharging his duty, in acting properly
in the affairs of this great republic whatever little part that
wisdom had assigned to him. The propriety or impropriety
of his endeavours might be of great consequence to him.
Their success or disappointment could be of none at all—
could excite no passionate joy or sorrow, no passionate desire or aversion. If he preferred some events to others, if
some situations were the objects of his choice and others of
his rejection, it was not because he regarded the one as in
themselves in any respect better than the other, or thought
that his own happiness would be more complete in what is
called the fortunate than in what is regarded as the distressful situation; but because the propriety of action, the rule
which the gods had given him for the direction of his conduct, required him to choose and reject in this manner. All
his affections were absorbed and swallowed up in two great
affections—in that for the discharge of his own duty, and in
that for the greatest possible happiness of all rational and
sensible beings. For the gratification of this latter affection, he rested with the most perfect security upon the wisdom and power of the great Superintendent of the universe.
His sole anxiety was about the gratification of the former;
not about the event, but about the propriety of his own endeavours. Whatever the event might be, he trusted to a
superior power and wisdom for turning it to promote that
great end which he himself was most desirous of promoting.

  This propriety of choosing and rejecting, though origi-

nally pointed out to us, and, as it were, recommended and
introduced to our acquaintance by the things, and for the
sake of the things, chosen and rejected ; yet when we had
once become thoroughly acquainted with it, the order, the
grace, the beauty, which we discerned in this conduct, the
happiness which we felt resulted from it, necessarily appeared to us of much greater value than the actual obtaining of
all the different objects of choice, or the actual avoiding of
all those of rejection. From the observation of this pro
priety arose the happiness and the glory; from the neglect
of it the misery and the disgrace of human nature.

But to a wise man, to one whose passions were brought
under perfect subjection to the ruling principles of his nature, the exact observation of this propriety was equally
easy upon all occasions. Was he in prosperity, he returned
thanks to Jupiter for having joined him with circumstances
which were easily mastered, and in which there was little
temptation to do wrong. Was he in adversity, he equally
returned thanks to the director of this spectacle of human
life for having opposed to him a vigorous athlete, over
whom, though the contest was likely to be more violent,
the victory was more glorious, and equally certain. Can
there be any shame in that distress which is brought upon
us without any fault of our own, and in which we behave
with perfect propriety ! There can, therefore, be no evil,
but, on the contrary, the greatest good and advantage. A
brave man exults in those dangers in which, from no rashness of his own, his fortune has involved him. They afford
an opportunity of exercising that heroic intrepidity, whose
exertion gives the exalted delight which flows from the consciousness of superior propriety and deserved admiration.
One who is master of all his exercises has no aversion to
measure his strength and activity with the strongest. And,
in the same manner, one who is master of all his passions
does not dread any circumstance in which the Superintend·

ent of the universe may think proper to place him. The
bounty of that divine Being has provided him with virtues
which render him superior to every situation. If it is pleasure, he has temperance to refrain from it ; if it is pain, he
has constancy to bear it ; if it is danger or death, he has
magnanimity and fortitude to despise it. The events of
human life can never find him unprepared, or at a loss how
to maintain that propriety of sentiment and conduct which,
in his own apprehension, constitutes at once his glory and
his happiness.

Human life the Stoics appear to have considered as a
game of great skill ; in which, however, there was a mixture of chance, or of what is vulgarly understood to be
chance. In such games the stake is commonly a trifle, and
the whole pleasure of the game arises from playing well,
from playing fairly, and playing skilfully. If, notwithstanding all his skill, however, the good player should, by the
influence of chance, happen to lose, the loss ought to be a
matter rather of merriment than of serious sorrow. He has
made no false stroke ; he has done nothing which he ought
to be ashamed of ; he has enjoyed completely the whole
pleasure of the game. If, on the contrary, the bad player,
notwithstanding all his blunders, should in the same manner
happen to win, his success can give him but little satisfaction. He is mortified by the remembrance of all the faults
which he committed. Even during the play he can enjoy
no part of the pleasure which it is capable of affording.
From ignorance of the rules of the game, fear and doubt
and hesitation are the disagreeable sentiments that precede
almost every stroke which he plays ; and when he has played
it, the mortification of finding it a gross blunder commonly
completes the unpleasing circle of his sensations. Human
life, with all the advantages which can possibly attend it,
ought, according to the Stoics, to be regarded but as a mere
twopenny stake—a matter by far too insignificant to merit

any anxious concern. Our only anxious concern ought to be, not about the stake but about the proper method of playing. If we placed our happiness in winning the stake, we placed it in what depended upon causes beyond our power and out of our direction. We necessarily exposed ourselves to perpetual fear and uneasiness, and frequently to grievous and mortifying disappointments. If we placed it in playing well, in playing fairly, in playing wisely and skilfully, in the propriety of our own conduct, in short, we placed it in what, by proper discipline, education, and attention, might be altogether in our own power, and under our own direction. Our happiness was perfectly secure, and beyond the reach of fortune. The event of our actions, if it was out of our power, was equally out of our concern, and we could never feel either fear or anxiety about it, nor ever suffer any grievous or even any serious disappointment.

Human life itself, as well as every different advantage or disadvantage which can attend it, might, they said, according to different circumstances, be the proper object either of our choice or of our rejection. If in our actual situation there were more circumstances agreeable to nature than contrary to it—more circumstances which were the objects of choice than of rejection—life in this case was, upon the whole, the proper object of choice, and the propriety of conduct required that we should remain in it. If, on the other hand, there were in our actual situation, without any probable hope of amendment, more circumstances contrary to nature than agreeable to it—more circumstances which were the objects of rejection than of choice—life itself in this case became to a wise man the object of rejection, and he was not only at liberty to remove out of it, but the propriety of conduct, the rule which the gods had given him for the direction of his conduct, required him to do so. " I am ordered," says Epictetus, " not to dwell at Nicopolis. I do not dwell there. I am ordered not to dwell at Athens. I do not dwell at Athens. I am ordered not to dwell in Rome. I do not dwell in Rome. I am ordered to dwell in the little and rocky island of Gyaræ. I go and dwell there. But the house smokes in Gyaræ. If the smoke is moderate I will bear it, and stay there. If it is excessive, I will go to a house from whence no tyrant can remove me. I keep in mind always that the door is open, that I can walk out when I please, and retire to that hospitable house which is at all times open to all the world; for beyond my undermost garment, beyond my body, no man living has any power over me." If your situation is upon the whole disagreeable —if your house smokes too much for you, said the Stoics, walk forth by all means; but walk forth without repining, without murmuring or complaining. Walk forth calm, contented, rejoicing, returning thanks to the gods, who, from their infinite bounty, have opened the safe and quiet harbour of death, at all times ready to receive us from the stormy ocean of human life; who have prepared this sacred, this inviolable, this great asylum, always open, always accessible—altogether beyond the reach of human rage and injustice, and large enough to contain both all those who wish, and all those who do not wish, to retire to it; an asylum which takes away from every man every pretence of complaining, or even of fancying that there can be any evil in human life except such as he may suffer from his own folly and weakness.

The Stoics, in the few fragments of their philosophy which have come down to us, sometimes talk of leaving life with a gaiety, and even with a levity, which, were we to consider those passages by themselves, might induce us to believe that they imagined we could with propriety leave it whenever we had a mind, wantonly and capriciously, upon the slightest disgust or uneasiness. " When you sup with such a person," says Epictetus, " you complain of the long

stories which he tells you about his Mysian wars. ' Now,
my friend,' says he, ' having told you how I took possession of an eminence at such a place, I will tell you how I
was besieged in such another place.' But if you have a
mind not to be troubled with his long stories, do not accept
of his supper. If you accept of his supper, you have not
the least pretence to complain of his long stories. It is the
same case with what you call the evils of human life. Never
complain of that of which it is at all times in your power to
rid yourself." Notwithstanding this gaiety and even levity
of expression, however, the alternative of leaving life, or of
remaining in it, was, according to the Stoics, a matter of
the most serious and important deliberation. We ought
never to leave it till we were distinctly called upon to do
so by that superintending Power which had originally placed
us in it. But we were to consider ourselves as called upon
to do so, not merely at the appointed and unavoidable term
of human life. Whenever the providence of that superintending Power had rendered our condition in life upon the
whole the proper object rather of rejection than of choice,
the great rule which he had given us for the direction of
our conduct then required us to leave it. We might then
be said to hear the awful and benevolent voice of that divine
Being distinctly calling upon us to do so.

It was upon this account that, according to the Stoics,
it might be the duty of a wise man to remove out of life
though he was perfectly happy ; while, on the contrary, it
might be the duty of a weak man to remain in it, though
he was necessarily miserable. If in the situation of the
wise man there were more circumstances which were the
natural objects of rejection than of choice, the whole situation became the object of rejection, and the rule which the
gods had given him for the direction of his conduct required that he should remove out of it as speedily as particular circumstances might render convenient. He was,

however, perfectly happy, even during the time that he might think proper to remain in it : he had placed this happiness, not in obtaining the objects of his choice or in avoiding those of his rejection, but in always choosing and rejecting with exact propriety; not in the success, but in the fitness of his endeavours and exertions.   If in the situation of the weak man, on the contrary, there were more circumstances which were the natural objects of choice than of rejection, his whole situation became the proper object of choice, and it was his duty to remain in it.   He was unhappy, however, from not knowing how to use those circumstances.   Let his cards be ever so good, he did not know how to play them, and could enjoy no sort of real satisfaction either in the progress or in the event of the game, in whatever manner it might happen to turn out.*

The propriety upon some occasions of voluntary death, though it was perhaps more insisted upon by the Stoics than by any other sect of ancient philosophers, was, however, a doctrine common to them all, even to the peaceable and indolent Epicureans.   During the age in which flourished the founders of all the principal sects of ancient philosophy, during the Peloponnesian war, and for many years after its conclusion, all the different republics of Greece were at home almost always distracted by the most furious factions, and abroad involved in the most sanguinary wars, in which each sought, not merely superiority or dominion, but either completely to extirpate all its enemies, or, what was not less cruel, to reduce them into the vilest of all states, that of domestic slavery, and to sell them, man, woman, and child, like so many herds of cattle, to the highest bidder in the market.   The smallness of the greater part of those states, too, rendered it to each of them no very improbable event that it might itself fall into that very

* See Cicero de finibus, lib. iii. c. 13.   Olivet's edition.

calamity which it had so frequently, either perhaps actually inflicted, or at least attempted to inflict, upon some of its neighbours. In this disorderly state of things the most perfect innocence, joined to both the highest rank and the greatest public services, could give no security to any man that, even at home and among his own relations and fellow-citizens, he was not at some time or another, from the prevalence of some hostile and furious faction, to be condemned to the most cruel and ignominious punishment. If he was taken prisoner in war, or if the city of which he was a member was conquered, he was exposed, if possible, to still greater injuries and insults. But every man naturally, or rather necessarily, familiarizes his imagination with the distresses to which he foresees that his situation may frequently expose him. It is impossible that a sailor should not frequently think of storms and shipwrecks, and foundering at sea, and of how he himself is likely both to feel and to act upon such occasions. It was impossible, in the same manner, that a Grecian patriot or hero should not familiarize his imagination with all the different calamities to which he was sensible his situation must frequently, or rather constantly, expose him. As an American savage prepares his death-song, and considers how he should act when he has fallen into the hands of his enemies, and is by them put to death in the most lingering tortures, and amidst the insults and derision of all the spectators ; so a Grecian patriot or hero could not avoid frequently employing his thoughts in considering what he ought both to suffer and to do in banishment, in captivity, when reduced to slavery, when put to the torture, when brought to the scaffold. But the philosophers of all the different sects very justly represented virtue, that is, wise, just, firm, and temperate conduct, not only as the most probable, but as the certain and infallible road to happiness even in this life. This conduct, however, could not always exempt, and might even sometimes expose the person who followed it to all the calamities which were incident to that unsettled situation of public affairs. They endeavoured, therefore, to shew that happiness was either altogether, or at least in a great measure, independent of fortune; the Stoics, that it was so altogether; the Academic and Peripatetic philosophers, that it was so in a great measure. Wise, prudent, and good conduct was, in the first place, the conduct most likely to ensure success in every species of undertaking; and, secondly, though it should fail of success, yet the mind was not left without consolation. The virtuous man might still enjoy the complete approbation of his own breast, and might still feel that, how untoward soever things might be without, all was calm and peace and concord within. He might generally comfort himself, too, with the assurance that he possessed the love and esteem of every intelligent and impartial spectator, who could not fail both to admire his conduct and to regret his misfortune.

Those philosophers endeavoured at the same time to shew, that the greatest misfortunes to which human life was liable might be supported more easily than was commonly imagined. They endeavoured to point out the comforts which a man might still enjoy when reduced to poverty, when driven into banishment, when exposed to the injustice of popular clamour, when labouring under blindness, under deafness, in the extremity of old age, upon the approach of death: they pointed out, too, the considerations which might contribute to support his constancy under the agonies of pain, and even of torture, in sickness, in sorrow—for the loss of children, for the death of friends and relations, &c. The few fragments which have come down to us of what the ancient philosophers had written upon these subjects form, perhaps, one of the most instructive as well as one of the most interesting remains of antiquity. The spirit and manhood of their doctrines make a wonderful contrast with the desponding, plaintive, and whining tone of some modern systems.

But while those ancient philosophers endeavoured in this manner to suggest every consideration which could, as Milton says, arm the obdured breast with stubborn patience as with triple steel, they at the same time laboured above all to convince their followers that there neither was nor could be any evil in death ; and that, if their situation became at any time too hard for their constancy to support, the remedy was at hand, the door was open, and they might without fear walk out when they pleased. If there was no world beyond the present, death they said could be no evil ; and if there was another world, the gods must likewise be in that other, and a just man could fear no evil while under their protection. Those philosophers, in short, prepared a death-song, if I may say so, which the Grecian patriots and heroes might make use of upon the proper occasions ; and, of all the different sects, the Stoics, I think it must be acknowledged, had prepared by far the most animated and spirited song.

Suicide, however, never seems to have been very common among the Greeks. Excepting Cleomenes, I cannot at present recollect any very illustrious patriot or hero of Greece who died by his own hand. The death of Aristomenes is as much beyond the period of true history as that of Ajax. The common story of the death of Themistocles, though within that period, bears upon its face all the marks of a most romantic fable. Of all the Greek heroes whose lives have been written by Plutarch, Cleomenes appears to have been the only one who perished in this manner. Theramines, Socrates, and Phocian, who certainly did not want courage, suffered themselves to be sent to prison, and submitted patiently to that death to which the injustice of their fellow-citizens had condemned them. The brave Eumenes allowed himself to be delivered up by his own mutinous soldiers to his enemy Antigonus, and was starved to death without attemping any violence. The gallant Philopœmen suffered himself to be taken prisoner by the Messenians, was thrown into a dungeon, and was supposed to have been privately poisoned. Several of the philosophers, indeed, are said to have died in this manner; but their lives have been so very foolishly written, that very little credit is due to the greater part of the tales which are told of them. Three different accounts have been given of the death of Zeno the Stoic. One is, that after enjoying for ninety-eight years the most perfect state of health, he happened, in going out of his school, to fall; and though he suffered no other damage than that of breaking or dislocating one of his fingers, he struck the ground with his hand, and, in the words of the Niobe of Euripides, said, "*I come, why dost thou call me?*" and immediately went home and hanged himself. At that great age one should think he might have had a little more patience. Another account is, that at the same age, and in consequence of a like accident, he starved himself to death. The third account is, that at seventy-two years of age he died in the natural way—by far the most probable account of the three, and supported, too, by the authority of a contemporary who must have had every opportunity of being well informed; of Persæus, originally the slave, and afterwards the friend and disciple of Zeno. The first account is given by Apollonius of Tyre, who flourished about the time of Augustus Cæsar, between two and three hundred years after the death of Zeno. I know not who is the author of the second account. Apollonius, who was himself a Stoic, had probably thought i would do honour to the founder of a sect which talked so much about voluntary death, to die in this manner by his own hand. Men of letters, though after their death they are frequently more talked of than

the greatest princes or statesmen of their times, are generally during their life so obscure and insignificant that their
adventures are seldom recorded by contemporary historians.
Those of after ages, in order to satisfy the public curiosity,
and having no authentic documents either to support or to
contradict their narratives, seem frequently to have fashioned
them according to their own fancy, and almost always with
a great mixture of the marvellous. In this particular case
the marvellous, though supported by no authority, seems to
have prevailed over the probable, though supported by the
best. Diogenes Laertius plainly gives the preference to the
story of Apollonius. Lucian and Lactantius appear both
to have given credit to that of the great age and of the
violent death.

This fashion of voluntary death appears to have been
much more prevalent among the proud Romans than it ever
was among the lively, ingenious, and accommodating Greeks.
Even among the Romans, the fashion seems not to have
been established in the early and what are called the virtuous ages of the republic. The common story of the death
of Regulus, though probably a fable, could never have been
invented had it been supposed that any dishonour could fall
upon that hero from patiently submitting to the tortures
which the Carthaginians are said to have inflicted upon him.
In the later ages of the republic, some dishonour, I apprehend, would have attended this submission. In the different civil wars which preceded the fall of the commonwealth,
many of the eminent men of all the contending parties chose
rather to perish by their own hands than to fall into those
of their enemies. The death of Cato, celebrated by Cicero
and censured by Cæsar, and become the subject of a very
serious controversy between, perhaps, the two most illustrious advocates that the world had ever beheld, stamped a character of splendour upon this method of dying, which it seems
to have retained for several ages after. The eloquence of

Cicero was superior to that of Cæsar. The admiring prevailed greatly over the censuring party, and the lovers of liberty for many ages afterwards looked up to Cato as to the most venerable martyr of the republican party. " The head of a party," the Cardinal de Retz observes, "may do what he pleases; as long as he retains the confidence of his own friends he can never do wrong;" a maxim of whch his eminence had himself upon several occasions an opportunity of experiencing the truth. Cato, it seems, joined to his other virtues that of an excellent bottle companion. His enemies accused him of drunkenness; "but," says Seneca, " whoever objected this vice to Cato, will find it much easier to prove that drunkenness is a virtue than that Cato could be addicted to any vice."

Under the emperors this method of dying seems to have been for a long time perfectly fashionable. In the epistles of Pliny, we find an account of several persons who chose to die in this manner rather from vanity and ostentation, it would seem, than from what would appear, even to a sober and judicious Stoic, any proper or necessary reason. Even the ladies, who are seldom behind in following the fashion, seem frequently to have chosen most unnecessarily to die in this manner; and, like the ladies in Bengal, to accompany upon some occasions their husbands to the tomb. The prevalence of this fashion certainly occasioned many deaths which would not otherwise have happened. All the havoc, however, which this, perhaps the highest exertion of human vanity and impertinence, could occasion, would probably at no time be very great.

The principle of suicide, the principle which would teach us upon some occasions to consider that violent action as an object of applause and approbation, seems to be altogether a refinement of philosophy. Nature in her sound and healthful state seems never to prompt us to suicide.

There is, indeed, a species of melancholy (a disease to which human nature, among its other calamities, is unhappily subject) which seems to be accompanied with what one may call an irresistible appetite for self-destruction. In circumstances often of the highest external prosperity, and sometimes, too, in spite even of the most serious and deeply impressed sentiments of religion, this disease has frequently been known to drive its wretched victims to this fatal extremity. The unfortunate persons who perish in this miserable manner are the proper objects not of censure but of commiseration. To attempt to punish them when they are beyond the reach of all human punishment, is not more absurd than it is unjust. That punishment can fall only on their surviving friends and relations, who are always perfectly innocent, and to whom the loss of their friend in this disgraceful manner must always be alone a very heavy calamity. Nature, in her sound and healthful state, prompts us to avoid distress upon all occasions; upon many occasions to defend ourselves against it, though at the hazard, or even with the certainty, of perishing in that defence. But when we have neither been able to defend ourselves from it, nor have perished in that defence, no natural principle, no regard to the approbation of the supposed impartial spectator, to the judgment of the man within the breast, seems to call upon us to escape from it by destroying ourselves. It is only the consciousness of our own weakness, of our own incapacity to support the calamity with proper manhood and firmness, which can drive us to this resolution. I do not remember to have either read or heard of any American savage who, upon being taken prisoner by some hostile tribe, put himself to death in order to avoid being afterwards put to death in torture, and amidst the insults and mockery of his enemies. He places his glory in supporting those torments with manhood, and in retorting those insults with tenfold contempt and derision.

This contempt of life and death, however, and, at the
same time, the most entire submission to the order of Providence—the most complete contentment with every event
which the current of human affairs could possibly cast up,
may be considered as the two fundamental doctrines upon
which rested the whole fabric of Stoical morality. The
independent and spirited, but often harsh Epictetus, may
be considered as the great apostle of the first of those doctrines—the mild, the humane, the benevolent Antoninus,
of the second.

The emancipated slave of Epaphriditus, who in his
youth had been subjected to the insolence of a brutal
master, who in his riper years was, by the jealousy and
caprice of Domitian, banished from Rome and Athens, and
obliged to dwell at Nicopolis; and who, by the same tyrant,
might expect every moment to be sent to Gyaræ, or perhaps to be put to death, could preserve his tranquillity
only by fostering in his mind the most sovereign contempt
of human life. He never exults so much, accordingly his
eloquence is never so animated, as when he represents the
futility and nothingness of all its pleasures and all its pains.

The good-natured emperor, the absolute sovereign of the
whole civilized part of the world, who certainly had no
peculiar reason to complain of his own allotment, delights
in expressing his contentment with the ordinary course of
things, and in pointing out beauties even in those parts of
it where vulgar observers are not apt to see any. "There
is a propriety and even an engaging grace," he observes, "in
old age as well as in youth; and the weakness and decrepi-
tude of the one state are as suitable to nature as the bloom
and vigour of the other. Death, too, is just as proper a
termination of old age as youth is of childhood, or manhood of youth." "As we frequently say," he remarks upon
another occasion, "that the physician has ordered to such a

man to ride on horseback, or to use the cold bath, or to walk barefooted; so ought we to say that nature, the great conductor and physician of the universe, has ordered to such a man a disease, or the amputation of a limb, or the loss of a child. By the prescriptions of ordinary physicians, the patient swallows many a bitter potion—undergoes many a painful operation. From the very uncertain hope, however, that health may be the consequence, he gladly submits to all. The harshest prescriptions of the great Physician of nature, the patient may, in the same manner, hope will contribute to his own health, to his own final prosperity and happiness; and he may be perfectly assured that they not only contribute, but are indispensably necessary to the health, to the prosperity and happiness of the universe, to the furtherance and advancement of the great plan of Jupiter. Had they not been so, the universe would never have produced them; its all-wise Architect and Conductor would never have suffered them to happen. As all, even the smallest of the co-existent parts of the universe, are exactly fitted to one another, and all contribute to compose one immense and connected system; so all, even apparently the most insignificant of the successive events which follow one another, make parts, and necessary parts, of that great chain of causes and effects which had no beginning, and which will have no end; and which, as they all necessarily result from the original arrangement and contrivance of the whole, so they are all essentially necessary, not only to its prosperity, but to its continuance and preservation. Whoever does not cordially embrace whatever befalls him, whoever is sorry that it has befallen him, whoever wishes that it had not befallen him, wishes, so far as in him lies, to stop the motion of the universe, to break that great chain of succession, by the progress of which that system can alone be continued and preserved, and, for some little conveniency of his own, to disorder and discompose the whole machine of the world."—" O world," says he, in another place, "all things are suitable to me which are suitable to thee. Nothing is too early or too late to me which is seasonable for thee. All is fruit to me which thy seasons bring forth. From thee are all things; in thee are all things; for thee are all things. One man says, O beloved city of Cecrops. Wilt not thou say, O beloved city of God?"

From these very sublime doctrines the Stoics, or at least some of the Stoics, attempted to deduce all their paradoxes.

The Stoical wise man endeavoured to enter into the views of the great Superintendent of the universe, and to see things in the same light in which that divine Being beheld them. But to the great Superintendent of the universe, all the different events which the course of his providence may bring forth, what to us appear the smallest and the greatest, the bursting of a bubble, as Mr Pope says, and that of a world, for example, were perfectly equal, were equally parts of that great chain which he had predestined from all eternity, were equally the effects of the same unerring wisdom, of the same universal and boundless benevolence. To the Stoical wise man, in the same manner, all those different events were perfectly equal. In the course of those events, indeed, a little department, in which he had himself some little management and direction, had been assigned to him. In this department he endeavoured to act as properly as he could, and to conduct himself according to those orders which he understood had been prescribed to him. But he took no anxious or passionate concern either in the success or in the disappointment of his own most faithful endeavours. The highest prosperity and the total destruction of that little department, of that little system which had been in some measure committed to his charge, were perfectly indifferent to him. If those events had depended upon him, he would have chosen the one, and he would have rejected the other;

but as they did not depend upon him, he trusted to a superior wisdom, and was perfectly satisfied that the event which happened, whatever it might be, was the very event which he himself, had he known all the connections and dependencies of things, would most earnestly and devoutly have wished for. Whatever he did under the influence and direction of those principles was equally perfect; and when he stretched out his finger to give the example which they commonly made use of, he performed an action in every respect as meritorious, as worthy of praise and admiration, as when he laid down his life for the service of his country. As to the great Superintendent of the universe, the greatest and the smallest exertions of his power, the formation and dissolution of a world, the formation and dissolution of a bubble, were equally easy, were equally admirable, and equally the effects of the same divine wisdom and benevolence; so, to the Stoical wise man, what we would call the great action, required no more exertion than the little one, was equally easy, proceeded from exactly the same principles, was in no respect more meritorious, nor worthy of any higher degree of praise and admiration.

As all those who had arrived at this state of perfection were equally happy, so all those who fell in the smallest degree short of it, how nearly soever they might approach to it, were equally miserable. As the man, they said, who was but an inch below the surface of the water, could no more breathe than he who was an hundred yards below it; so the man who had not completely subdued all his private, partial, and selfish passions; who had any other earnest desire but that for the universal happiness; who had not completely emerged from that abyss of misery and disorder into which his anxiety for the gratification of those private, partial, and selfish passions had involved him, could no more breathe the free air of liberty and independency, could no more enjoy the security and happiness of the wise man, than he who was most remote from that situation. As all the actions of the wise man were perfect, and equally perfect; so all those of the man who had not arrived at this supreme wisdom were faulty, and, as some Stoics pretended, equally faulty. As one truth, they said, could not be more true, nor one falsehood more false than another, so an honourable action could not be more honourable, nor a shameful one more shameful, than another. As in shooting at a mark, the man who missed it by an inch had equally missed it with him who had done so by a hundred yards ; so the man who, in what to us appears the most insignificant action, had acted improperly and without a sufficient reason, was equally faulty with him who had done so in what to us appears the most important; the man who has killed a cock, for example, improperly and without a sufficient reason, with him who had murdered his father.

If the first of those two paradoxes should appear sufficiently violent, the second is evidently too absurd to deserve any serious consideration. It is, indeed, so very absurd, that one can scarce help suspecting that it must have been in some measure misunderstood or misrepresented. At any rate, I cannot allow myself to believe that such men as Zeno or Cleanthes, men, it is said, of the most simple as well as of the most sublime eloquence, could be the authors either of these or of the greater part of the other Stoical paradoxes, which are in general mere impertinent quibbles, and do so little honour to their system, that I shall give no further account of them. I am disposed to impute them rather to Chrysippus, the disciple and follower indeed of Zeno and Cleanthes, but who, from all that has been delivered down to us concerning him, seems to have been a mere dialectical pedant, without taste or elegance of any kind. He may have been the first who reduced their doctrines into a scholastic or technical system of artificial definitions, divisions, and sub-divisions ; one of the most effectual expedients, perhaps,

for extinguishing whatever degree of good sense there may
be in any moral or metaphysical doctrine. Such a man may
very easily be supposed to have understood too literally
some animated expressions of his masters in describing the
happiness of the man of perfect virtue, and the unhappiness
of whoever fell short of that character.

The Stoics in general seem to have admitted that there
might be a degree of proficiency in those who had not advanced to perfect virtue and happiness. They distributed
those proficients into different classes, according to the degree of their advancement; and they called the imperfect
virtues which they supposed them capable of exercising,
not rectitudes but proprieties, fitnesses, decent and becoming actions, for which a plausible or probable reason could
be assigned, what Cicero expresses by the Latin word *officia*,
and Seneca, I think more exactly, by that of *convenientia*.
The doctrine of those imperfect but attainable virtues, seems
to have constituted what we may call the practical morality
of the Stoics. It is the subject of Cicero's Offices; and is
said to have been that of another book written by Marcus
Brutus, but which is now lost.

The plan and system which nature has sketched out for
our conduct seems to be altogether different from that of the
Stoical philosophy.

By nature, the events which immediately affect that little
department in which we ourselves have some little management and direction, which immediately affect ourselves, our
friends, our country, are the events which interest us the
most, and which chiefly excite our desires and aversions,
our hopes and fears, our joys and sorrows. Should those
passions be, what they are very apt to be, too vehement,
nature has provided a proper remedy and correction. The
real or even the imaginary presence of the impartial specta-

tor, the authority of the man within the breast, is always at hand to overawe them into the proper tone and temper of moderation.

If, notwithstanding our most faithful exertions, all the events which can affect this little department should turn out the most unfortunate and disastrous, nature has by no means left us without consolation. That consolation may be drawn, not only from the complete approbation of the man within the breast, but, if possible, from a still nobler and more generous principle—from a firm reliance upon, and a reverential submission to, that benevolent wisdom which directs all the events of human life, and which, we may be assured, would never have suffered those misfortunes to happen had they not been indispensably necessary for the good of the whole.

Nature has not prescribed to us this sublime contemplation as the great business and occupation of our lives. She only points it out to us as the consolation of our misfortunes. The Stoical philosophy prescribes it as the great business and occupation of our lives. That philosophy teaches us to interest ourselves earnestly and anxiously in no events, external to the good order of our own minds, to the propriety of our own choosing and rejecting, except in those which concern a department where we neither have nor ought to have any sort of management or direction—the department of the great Superintendent of the universe. By the perfect apathy which it prescribes to us, by endeavouring not merely to moderate but to eradicate all our private, partial, and selfish affections, by suffering us to feel for whatever can befall ourselves, our friends, our country, not even the sympathetic and reduced passions of the impartial spectator, it endeavours to render us altogether indifferent and unconcerned in the success or miscarriage of every thing which

nature has prescribed to us as the proper business and occupation of our lives.

The reasonings of philosophy, it may be said, though they
may confound and perplex the understanding, can never
break down the necessary connection which nature has established between causes and their effects. The causes which
naturally excite our desires and aversions, our hopes and
fears, our joys and sorrows, would no doubt, notwithstanding all the reasonings of Stoicism, produce upon each individual, according to the degree of his actual sensibility,
their proper and necessary effects. The judgments of the
man within the breast, however, might be a good deal affected by those reasonings, and that great inmate might be
taught by them to attempt to overawe all our private, partial, and selfish affections, into a more or less perfect tranquillity. To direct the judgments of this inmate is the great
purpose of all systems of morality. That the Stoical philosophy had very great influence upon the character and
conduct of its followers, cannot be doubted; and that,
though it might sometimes incite them to unnecessary violence, its general tendency was to animate them to actions
of the most heroic magnanimity and most extensive benevolence.

IV. Besides these ancient, there are some modern systems, according to which virtue consists in propriety, or in
the suitableness of the affection from which we act to the
cause or object which excites it. The system of Dr Clark,
which places virtue in acting according to the relations of
things, in regulating our conduct according to the fitness or
incongruity which there may be in the application of certain
actions to certain things, or to certain relations : that of Mr
Woollaston, which places it in acting according to the truth
of things, according to their proper nature and essence, or

in treating them as what they really are, and not as what they are not : that of my Lord Shaftesbury, which places it in maintaining a proper balance of the affections, and in allowing no passion to go beyond its proper sphere, are all of them more or less inaccurate descriptions of the same fundamental idea.

None of those systems either give, or even pretend to give, any precise or distinct measure by which this fitness or propriety of affection can be ascertained or judged of. That precise and distinct measure can be found nowhere but in the sympathetic feelings of the impartial and well-informed spectator.

The description of virtue, besides, which is either given, or at least meant and intended to be given, in each of those systems—for some of the modern authors are not very fortunate in their manner of expressing themselves—is no doubt quite just, so far as it goes. There is no virtue without propriety, and wherever there is propriety, some degree of approbation is due. But still this description is imperfect. For though propriety is an essential ingredient in every virtuous action, it is not always the sole ingredient. Beneficent actions have in them another quality by which they appear not only to deserve approbation but recompence. None of those systems account either easily or sufficiently for that superior degree of esteem which seems due to such actions, or for that diversity of sentiment which they naturally excite. Neither is the description of vice more complete. For in the same manner, though impropriety is a necessary ingredient in every vicious action, it is not always the sole ingredient ; and there is often the highest degree of absurdity and impropriety in very harmless and insignificant actions. Deliberate actions, of a pernicious tendency to those we live with, have, besides their impropriety, a peculiar quality of their own, by which they appear to deserve not only disapprobation but punishment, and to be the objects not of dislike merely, but of resentment and revenge; and none of those systems easily and sufficiently account for that superior degree of detestation which we feel for such actions.

CHAPTER II.

Of those Systems which make Virtue consist in Prudence.

THE most ancient of those systems which make virtue consist in prudence, and of which any considerable remains have come down to us, is that of Epicurus, who is said, however, to have borrowed all the leading principles of his philosophy from some of those who had gone before him, particularly from Aristippus ; though it is very probable, notwithstanding this allegation of his enemies, that at least his manner of applying those principles was altogether his own.

According to Epicurus,* bodily pleasure and pain were the sole ultimate objects of natural desire and aversion. That they were always the natural objects of those passions, he thought required no proof. Pleasure might, indeed, appear sometimes to be avoided ; not, however, because it was pleasure, but because, by the enjoyment of it, we should either forfeit some greater pleasure, or expose ourselves to some pain that was more to be avoided than this pleasure was to be desired. Pain, in the same manner, might appear sometimes to be eligible ; not, however, because it was pain, but because by enduring it we might either avoid a still greater pain, or acquire some pleasure of much more importance. That bodily pain and pleasure, therefore, were always the natural objects of desire and aversion, was, he thought, abundantly evident. Nor was it less so, he imagined, that they were the sole ultimate objects of those passions Whatever else was either desired or avoided was

* See Cicero de finibus, lib. i. Diogenes Laert. l. x.

so, according to him, upon account of its tendency to produce one or other of those sensations. The tendency to
procure pleasure rendered power and riches desirable, as the
contrary tendency to produce pain made poverty and insignificancy the objects of aversion. Honour and reputation
were valued, because the esteem and love of those we live
with were of the greatest consequence both to procure pleasure and to defend us from pain. Ignominy and bad fame,
on the contrary, were to be avoided, because the hatred,
contempt, and resentment of those we lived with destroyed
all security, and necessarily exposed us to the greatest
bodily evils.

All the pleasures and pains of the mind were, according
to Epicurus, ultimately derived from those of the body.
The mind was happy when it thought of the past pleasures
of the body, and hoped for others to come; and it was miserable when it thought of the pains which the body had formerly endured, and dreaded the same or greater thereafter.

But the pleasures and pains of the mind, though ultimately
derived from those of the body, were vastly greater than
their originals. The body felt only the sensation of the present instant, whereas the mind felt also the past and the
future, the one by remembrance, the other by anticipation,
and consequently both suffered and enjoyed much more.
When we are under the greatest bodily pain, he observed,
we shall always find, if we attend to it, that it is not the
suffering of the present instant which chiefly torments us,
but either the agonizing remembrance of the past, or the
yet more horrible dread of the future. The pain of each
instant, considered by itself, and cut off from all that goes
before and all that comes after it, is a trifle not worth the regarding. Yet this is all which the body can ever be said to
suffer. In the same manner, when we enjoy the greatest
pleasure, we shall always find that the bodily sensation, the

sensation of the present instant, makes but a small part of our happiness, that our enjoyment chiefly arises either from the cheerful recollection of the past, or the still more joyous anticipation of the future, and that the mind always contributes by much the largest share of the entertainment.

Since our happiness and misery, therefore, depended chiefly on the mind, if this part of our nature was well disposed, if our thoughts and opinions were as they should be, it was of little importance in what manner our body was affected. Though under great bodily pain, we might still enjoy a considerable share of happiness if our reason and judgment maintained their superiority. We might entertain ourselves with the remembrance of past, and with the hopes of future pleasure; we might soften the rigour of our pains by recollecting what it was which, even in this situation, we were under any necessity of suffering. That this was merely the bodily sensation, the pain of the present instant, which by itself could never be very great. That whatever agony we suffered from the dread of its continuance, was the effect of an opinion of the mind, which might be corrected by juster sentiments; by considering that, if our pains were violent, they would probably be of short duration; and that if they were of long continuance, they would probably be moderate, and admit of many intervals of ease; and that, at any rate, death was always at hand and within call to deliver us, which as, according to him, it put an end to all sensation, either of pain or pleasure, could not be regarded as an evil. When we are, said he, death is not; and when death is, we are not; death, therefore, can be nothing to us.

If the actual sensation of positive pain was in itself so little to be feared, that of pleasure was still less to be desired. Naturally the sensation of pleasure was much less pungent than that of pain. If, therefore, this last could take so very little from the happiness of a well-disposed mind, the other

could add scarce any thing to it. When the body was free
from pain, and the mind from fear and anxiety, the super-
added sensation of bodily pleasure could be of very little
importance; and though it might diversify, could not properly be said to increase the happiness of this situation.

In ease of body, therefore, and in security or tranquillity
of mind, consisted, according to Epicurus, the most perfect
state of human nature, the most complete happiness which
man was capable of enjoying. To obtain this great end of
natural desire was the sole object of all the virtues, which, according to him, were not desirable upon their own account, but
upon account of their tendency to bring about this situation.

Prudence, for example, though, according to this philosophy, the source and principle of all the virtues, was not
desirable upon its own account. That careful and laborious
and circumspect state of mind, ever watchful and ever attentive to the most distant consequences of every action,
could not be a thing pleasant or agreeable for its own sake,
but upon account of its tendency to procure the greatest
good and to keep off the greatest evil.

To abstain from pleasure too, to curb and restrain our
natural passions for enjoyment, which was the office of temperance, could never be desirable for its own sake. The
whole value of this virtue arose from its utility, from its
enabling us to postpone the present enjoyment for the sake
of a greater to come, or to avoid a greater pain that might
ensue from it. Temperance, in short, was nothing but prudence with regard to pleasure.

To support labour, to endure pain, to be exposed to danger or to death, the situations which fortitude would often
lead us into, were surely still less the objects of natural desire. They were chosen only to avoid greater evils. We

submitted to labour in order to avoid the greater shame and pain of poverty, and we exposed ourselves to danger and to death in defence of our liberty and property, the means and instruments of pleasure and happiness; or in defence of our country, in the safety of which our own was necessarily comprehended. Fortitude enabled us to do all this cheerfully, as the best which, in our present situation, could possibly be done, and was in reality no more than prudence, good judgment, and presence of mind in properly appreciating pain, labour, and danger, always choosing the less in order to avoid the greater.

It is the same case with justice. To abstain from what is another's was not desirable on its own account, and it could not surely be better for you that I should possess what is my own than that you should possess it. You ought, however, to abstain from whatever belongs to me, because by doing otherwise you will provoke the resentment and indignation of mankind. The security and tranquillity of your mind will be entirely destroyed. You will be filled with fear and consternation at the thought of that punishment which you will imagine that men are at all times ready to inflict upon you, and from which no power, no art, no concealment, will ever, in your own fancy, be sufficient to protect you. That other species of justice which consists in doing proper good offices to different persons, according to the various relations of neighbours, kinsmen, friends, benefactors, superiors, or equals, which they may stand in to us, is recommended by the same reasons. To act properly in all these different relations, procures us the esteem and love of those we live with; as to do otherwise excites their contempt and hatred. By the one we naturally secure, by the other we necessarily endanger, our own ease and tranquillity, the great and ultimate objects of all our desires. The whole virtue of justice, therefore, the most important of all the virtues, is no more than discreet and prudent conduct with regard to our neighbours.

Such is the doctrine of Epicurus concerning the nature of virtue. It may seem extraordinary that this philosopher, who is described as a person of the most amiable manners, should never have observed that, whatever may be the tendency of those virtues, or of the contrary vices, with regard to our bodily ease and security, the sentiments which they naturally excite in others are the objects of a much more passionate desire or aversion than all their other consequences ; that to be amiable, to be respectable, to be the proper object of esteem, is by every well-disposed mind more valued than all the ease and security which love, respect, and esteem can procure us; that, on the contrary, to be odious, to be contemptible, to be the proper object of indignation, is more dreadful than all that we can suffer in our body from hatred, contempt, or indignation ; and that consequently our desire of the one character, and our aversion to the other, cannot arise from any regard to the effects which either of them is likely to produce upon the body.

This system is, no doubt, altogether inconsistent with that which I have been endeavouring to establish. It is not difficult, however, to discover from what phasis, if I may say so, from what particular view or aspect of nature, this account of things derives its probability. By the wise contrivance of the Author of nature, virtue is upon all ordinary occasions, even with regard to this life, real wisdom, and the surest and readiest means of obtaining both safety and advantage. Our success or disappointment in our undertakings must very much depend upon the good or bad opinion which is commonly entertained of us, and upon the general disposition of those we live with, either to assist or to oppose us. But the best, the surest, the easiest, and the readiest way of obtaining the advantageous and of avoiding the

unfavourable judgments of others, is, undoubtedly, to render ourselves the proper objects of the former and not of
the latter. " Do you desire," said Socrates, " the reputation
of a good musician ?—The only sure way of obtaining it
is to become a good musician. Would you desire, in the
same manner, to be thought capable of serving your country
either as a general or as a statesman ?—The best way in this
case too is really to acquire the art and experience of war
and government, and to become really fit to be a general or
a statesman. And, in the same manner, if you would be
reckoned sober, temperate, just, and equitable, the best
way of acquiring this reputation is to become sober, temperate, just, and equitable. If you can really render yourself amiable, respectable, and the proper object of esteem,
there is no fear of your not soon acquiring the love, the
respect, and esteem of those you live with." Since
the practice of virtue, therefore, is in general so advantageous, and that of vice so contrary to our interest, the
consideration of those opposite tendencies undoubtedly
stamps an additional beauty and propriety upon the one,
and a new deformity and impropriety upon the other. Temperance, magnanimity, justice, and beneficence, come thus
to be approved of, not only under their proper characters,
but under the additional character of the highest wisdom
and most real prudence. And in the same manner, the
contrary vices of intemperance, pusillanimity, injustice, and
either malevolence or sordid selfishness, come to be disapproved of, not only under their proper characters, but under the additional character of the most short-sighted folly
and weakness. Epicurus appears in every virtue to have
attended to this species of propriety only. It is that which
is most apt to occur to those who are endeavouring to persuade others to regularity of conduct. When men by their
practice, and perhaps too by their maxims, manifestly shew
that the natural beauty of virtue is not like to have much
effect upon them, how is it possible to move them but by

representing the folly of their conduct, and how much they themselves are in the end likely to suffer by it ?

By running up all the different virtues, too, to this one species of propriety, Epicurus indulged a propensity, which is natural to all men, but which philosophers in particular are apt to cultivate with a peculiar fondness, as the great means of displaying their ingenuity,—the propensity to account for all appearances from as few principles as possible. And he, no doubt, indulged this propensity still further, when he referred all the primary objects of natural desire and aversion to the pleasures and pains of the body. The great patron of the atomical philosophy, who took so much pleasure in deducing all the powers and qualities of bodies from the most obvious and familiar, the figure, motion, and arrangement of the small parts of matter, felt, no doubt, a similar satisfaction, when he accounted in the same manner for all the sentiments and passions of the mind from those which are most obvious and familiar.

The system of Epicurus agreed with those of Plato, Aristotle, and Zeno, in making virtue consist in acting in the most suitable manner to obtain* primary objects of natural desire. It differed from all of them in two other respects ; first, in the account which it gave of those primary objects of natural desire; and, secondly, in the account which it gave of the excellence of virtue, or of the reason why that quality ought to be esteemed.

The primary objects of natural desire consisted, according to Epicurus, in bodily pleasure and pain, and in nothing else ; whereas, according to the other three philosophers, there were many other objects, such as knowledge, such as

---

* Prima naturæ.

the happiness of our relations, of our friends, of our country, which were ultimately desirable for their own sakes.

Virtue, too, according to Epicurus, did not deserve to be pursued for its own sake, nor was itself one of the ultimate objects of natural appetite, but was eligible only upon account of its tendency to prevent pain and to procure ease and pleasure. In the opinion of the other three, on the contrary, it was desirable, not merely as the means of procuring the other primary objects of natural desire but as something which was in itself more valuable than them all. Man, they thought, being born for action, his happiness must consist, not merely in the agreeableness of his passive sensations, but also in the propriety of his active exertions.

CHAPTER III.

Of those Systems which make Virtue consist in Benevolence.

THE system which makes virtue consist in benevolence, though I think not so ancient as all of those which I have already given an account of, is, however, of very great antiquity. It seems to have been the doctrine of the greater part of those philosophers who, about and after the age of Augustus, called themselves Eclectics, who pretended to follow chiefly the opinions of Plato and Pythagoras, and who, upon that account, are commonly known by the name of the later Platonists.

In the divine nature, according to these authors, benevolence or love was the sole principle of action, and directed the exertion of all the other attributes. The wisdom of the Deity was employed in finding out the means for bringing about those ends which his goodness suggested, as his infinite power was exerted to execute them. Benevolence, however, was still the supreme and governing attribute, to which the others were subservient, and from which the whole excellency, or the whole morality, if I may be allowed such an expression, of the divine operations was ultimately derived. The whole perfection and virtue of the human mind consisted in some resemblance or participation of the divine perfections, and, consequently, in being filled with the same principle of benevolence and love which influenced all the actions of the Deity. The actions of men which flowed from this motive were alone truly praiseworthy, or could claim any merit in the sight of the Deity. It was by actions of charity and love only that we could imitate, as became us, the conduct of God ; that we could

express our humble and devout admiration of his infinite perfections ; that by fostering in our own minds the same divine
principle, we could bring our own affections to a greater
resemblance with his holy attributes, and thereby become
more proper objects of his love and esteem ; till at last we
arrived at that immediate converse and communication with
the Deity to which it was the great object of this philosophy to raise us.

This system, as it was much esteemed by many ancient
fathers of the Christian church, so, after the Reformation,
it was adopted by several divines of the most eminent piety
and learning, and of the most amiable manners ; particularly
by Dr Ralph Cudworth, by Dr Henry More, and by Mr
John Smith of Cambridge.   But of all the patrons of this
system, ancient or modern, the late Dr Hutcheson was undoubtedly, beyond all comparison, the most acute, the most
distinct, the most philosophical, and, what is of the greatest
consequence of all, the soberest and most judicious.

That virtue consists in benevolence is a notion supported
by many appearances in human nature.   It has been observed already, that proper benevolence is the most graceful
and agreeable of all the affections ; that it is recommended
to us by a double sympathy ; that as its tendency is necessarily beneficent, it is the proper object of gratitude and
reward ; and that, upon all these accounts, it appears to our
natural sentiments to possess a merit superior to any other.
It has been observed, too, that even the weaknesses of benevolence are not very disagreeable to us, whereas those of
every other passion are always extremely disgusting.   Who
does not abhor excessive malice, excessive selfishness, or
excessive resentment ? But the most excessive indulgence,
even of partial friendship, is not so offensive.   It is the benevolent passions only which can exert themselves without
any regard or attention to propriety, and yet retain some-

thing about them which is engaging. There is something
pleasing even in mere instinctive good-will, which goes on
to do good offices without once reflecting whether, by this
conduct, it is the proper object either of blame or approbation. It is not so with the other passions. The moment
they are deserted, the moment they are unaccompanied by
the sense of propriety, they cease to be agreeable.

As benevolence bestows upon those actions which proceed from it a beauty superior to all others, so the want of
it, and much more the contrary inclination, communicates
a peculiar deformity to whatever evidences such a disposition. Pernicious actions are often punishable for no other
reason than because they shew a want of sufficient attention
to the happiness of our neighbour.

Besides all this, Dr Hutcheson* observed, that whenever
in any action, supposed to proceed from benevolent affections, some other motive had been discovered, our sense of
the merit of this action was just so far diminished as this
motive was believed to have influenced it. If an action,
supposed to proceed from gratitude, should be discovered
to have arisen from an expectation of some new favour, or
if what was apprehended to proceed from public spirit
should be found out to have taken its origin from the hope
of a pecuniary reward, such a discovery would entirely destroy all notion of merit or praiseworthiness in either of
these actions. Since, therefore, the mixture of any selfish
motive, like that of a baser alloy, diminished or took away
altogether the merit which would otherwise have belonged
to any action, it was evident, he imagined, that virtue must
consist in pure and disinterested benevolence alone.

When those actions, on the contrary, which are commonly

* See Inquiry concerning Virtue, sect. i. and ii.

supposed to proceed from a selfish motive, are discovered to have arisen from a benevolent one, it greatly enhances our sense of their merit. If we believed of any person that he endeavoured to advance his fortune from no other view but that of doing friendly offices, and of making proper returns to his benefactors, we should only love and esteem him the more. And this observation seemed still more to confirm the conclusion, that it was benevolence only which could stamp upon any action the character of virtue.

Last of all : what, he imagined, was an evident proof of the justness of this account of virtue, in all the disputes of casuists concerning the rectitude of conduct, the public good, he observed, was the standard to which they constantly referred ; thereby universally acknowledging that whatever tended to promote the happiness of mankind was right, and laudable, and virtuous, and the contrary, wrong, blameable, and vicious. In the late debates about passive obedience and the right of resistance, the sole point in controversy among men of sense was, whether universal submission would probably be attended with greater evils than temporary insurrections, when privileges were invaded ? Whether what, upon the whole, tended most to the happiness of mankind was not also morally good, was never once, he said, made a question.

Since benevolence, therefore, was the only motive which could bestow upon any action the character of virtue, the greater the benevolence which was evidenced by any action, the greater the praise which must belong to it.

Those actions which aimed at the happiness of a great community, as they demonstrated a more enlarged benevolence than those which aimed only at that of a smaller system, so were they likewise proportionally the more virtuous. The most virtuous of all affections, therefore, was that which

embraced as its objects the happiness of all intelligent be·
ings. The least virtuous, on the contrary, of those to which
the character of virtue could in any respect belong, was that
which aimed no further than at the happiness of an individual, such as a son, a brother, a friend.

In directing all our actions to promote the greatest possible good, in submitting all inferior affections to the desire
of the general happiness of mankind, in regarding one's self
but as one of the many, whose prosperity was to be pursued
no further than it was consistent with, or conducive to, that
of the whole, consisted the perfection of virtue.

Self-love was a principle which could never be virtuous
in any degree or in any direction. It was vicious whenever
it obstructed the general good. When it had no other effect
than to make the individual take care of his own happiness,
it was merely innocent, and though it deserved no praise,
neither ought it to incur any blame. Those benevolent actions which were performed, notwithstanding some strong
motive from self-interest, were the more virtuous upon that
account. They demonstrated the strength and vigour of the
benevolent principle.

Dr Hutcheson* was so far from allowing self-love to be
in any case a motive of virtuous action, that even a regard
to the pleasure of self-approbation, to the comfortable applause of our own consciences, according to him, diminished
the merit of a benevolent action. This was a selfish motive,
he thought, which, so far as it contributed to any action,
demonstrated the weakness of that pure and disinterested
benevolence which could alone stamp upon the conduct of
man the character of virtue. In the common judgments of

* Inquiry concerning Virtue, sect. ii. art. 4; also Illustrations on the
Moral Sense, sect. v. last paragraph.

mankind, however, this regard to the approbation of our own minds is so far from being considered as what can, in any respect, diminish the virtue of any action, that it is rather looked upon as the sole motive which deserves the appellation of virtuous.

Such is the account given of the nature of virtue in this amiable system, a system which has a peculiar tendency to nourish and support in the human heart the noblest and the most agreeable of all affections, and not only to check the injustice of self-love, but in some measure to discourage that principle altogether, by representing it as what could never reflect any honour upon those who were influenced by it.

As some of the other systems which I have already given an account of do not sufficiently explain from whence arises the peculiar excellency of the supreme virtue of beneficence, so this system seems to have the contrary defect, of not sufficiently explaining from whence arises our approbation of the inferior virtues of prudence, vigilance, circumspection, temperance, constancy, firmness. The view and aim of our affections, the beneficent and hurtful effects which they tend to produce, are the only qualities at all attended to in this system. Their propriety and impropriety, their suitableness and unsuitableness to the cause which excites them, are disregarded altogether.

Regard to our own private happiness and interest, too, appear upon many occasions very laudable principles of action. The habits of economy, industry, discretion, attention and application of thought, are generally supposed to be cultivated from self-interested motives, and at the same time are apprehended to be very praiseworthy qualities, which deserve the esteem and approbation of every body. The mixture of a selfish motive, it is true, seems often to sully the beauty of those actions which ought to arise from a benevolent affection. The cause of this, however, is not that self-love can never be the motive of a virtuous action, but that the benevolent principle appears in this particular case to want its due degree of strength, and to be altogether unsuitable to its object. The character, therefore, seems evidently imperfect, and, upon the whole, to deserve blame rather than praise. The mixture of a benevolent motive, in an action to which self-love alone ought to be sufficient to prompt us, is not so apt, indeed, to diminish our sense of its propriety, or of the virtue of the person who performs it. We are not ready to suspect any person of being defective in selfishness. This is by no means the weak side of human nature, or the failing of which we are apt to be suspicious. If we could really believe, however, of any man, that, was it not from a regard to his family and friends, he would not take that proper care of his health, his life, or his fortune, to which self preservation alone ought to be sufficient to prompt him, it would undoubtedly be a failing, though one of those amiable failings which render a person rather the object of pity than of contempt or hatred. It would still, however, somewhat diminish the dignity and respectableness of his character. Carelessness and want of economy are universally disapproved of, not, however, as proceeding from a want of benevolence, but from a want of the proper attention to the objects of self-interest.

Though the standard by which casuists frequently determine what is right or wrong in human conduct be its tendency to the welfare or disorder of society, it does not follow that a regard to the welfare of society should be the sole virtuous motive of action, but only that, in any competition, it ought to cast the balance against all other motives.

Benevolence may, perhaps, be the sole principle of action in the Deity, and there are several not improbable arguments which tend to persuade us that it is so. It is not easy to conceive what other motive an independent and all-perfect Being, who stands in need of nothing external, and whose happiness is complete in himself, can act from. But whatever may be the case with the Deity, so imperfect a creature as man, the support of whose existence requires so many things external to him, must often act from many other motives. The condition of human nature were peculiarly hard if those affections which, by the very nature of our being, ought frequently to influence our conduct, could, upon no occasion, appear virtuous, or deserve esteem and commendation from any body.

Those three systems, that which places virtue in propriety, that which places it in prudence, and that which makes it consist in benevolence, are the principal accounts which have been given of the nature of virtue. To one or other of them, all the other descriptions of virtue, how different soever they may appear, are easily reducible.

That system which places virtue in obedience to the will of the Deity, may be counted either among those which make it consist in prudence, or among those which make it consist in propriety. When it is asked, why we ought to obey the will of the Deity, this question, which would be impious and absurd in the highest degree if asked from any doubt that we ought to obey him, can admit but of two different answers. It must either be said that we ought to obey the will of the Deity, because he is a being of infinite power, who will reward us eternally if we do so, and punish us eternally if we do otherwise; or it must be said, that, independent of any regard to our own happiness, or to rewards and punishments of any kind, there is a congruity and fitness that a creature should obey its Creator, that a limited and imperfect being should submit to one of infinite and incomprehensible perfections. Besides one or other of these two, it is impossible to conceive that any other answer can be given to this question. If the first answer be the proper one, virtue consists in prudence, or in the proper pursuit of our own final interest and happiness; since it is upon this account that we are obliged to obey the will of the Deity. If the second answer be the proper one, virtue must consist in propriety, since the ground of our obligation to obedience is the suitableness or congruity of the sentiments of humility and submission to the superiority of the object which excites them.

That system which places virtue in utility, coincides too with that which makes it consist in propriety. According to this system, all those qualities of the mind which are agreeable or advantageous, either to the person himself or to others, are approved of as virtuous, and the contrary disapproved of as vicious. But the agreeableness or utility of any affection depends upon the degree which it is allowed to subsist in. Every affection is useful when it is confined to a certain degree of moderation; and every affection is disadvantageous when it exceeds the proper bounds. According to this system, therefore, virtue consists not in any one affection, but in the proper degree of all the affections. The only difference between it and that which I have been endeavouring to establish, is, that it makes utility, and not sympathy, or the correspondent affection of the spectator, the natural and original measure of this proper degree.

CHAPTER IV.

Of Licentious Systems.

ALL those systems which I have hitherto given an account of suppose that there is a real and essential distinction between vice and virtue, whatever these qualities may consist in. There is a real and essential difference between the propriety and impropriety of any affection, between benevolence and any other principle of action, between real prudence and short-sighted folly or precipitate rashness. In the main, too, all of them contribute to encourage the praiseworthy, and to discourage the blameable disposition.

It may be true, perhaps, of some of them, that they tend in some measure to break the balance of the affections, and to give the mind a particular bias to some principles of action beyond the proportion that is due to them. The ancient systems, which place virtue in propriety, seem chiefly to recommend the great, the awful, and the respectable virtues, the virtues of self-government and self-command ; fortitude, magnanimity, independency upon fortune, the contempt of all outward accidents, of pain, poverty, exile, and death. It is in these great exertions that the noblest propriety of conduct is displayed. The soft, the amiable, the gentle virtues, all the virtues of indulgent humanity, are, in comparison, but little insisted upon, and seem, on the contrary, by the Stoics in particular, to have been often regarded as mere weaknesses, which it behoved a wise man not to harbour in his breast.

The benevolent system, on the other hand, while it fosters and encourages all those milder virtues in the highest degree, seems entirely to neglect the more lawful and respectable qualities of the mind. It even denies them the appellation of virtues. It calls them moral abilities, and treats them as qualities which do not deserve the same sort of esteem and approbation that is due to what is properly denominated virtue. All those principles of action, which aim only at our own interest, it treats, if that be possible, still worse. So far from having any merit of their own, they diminish, it pretends, the merit of benevolence, when they co-operate with it; and prudence, it is asserted, when employed only in promoting private interest, can never even be imagined a virtue.

That system, again, which makes virtue consist in prudence only, while it gives the highest encouragement to the habits of caution, vigilance, sobriety, and judicious moderation, seems to degrade equally both the amiable and respectable virtues, and to strip the former of all their beauty, and the latter of all their grandeur.

But notwithstanding these defects, the general tendency of each of those three systems is to encourage the best and most laudable habits of the human mind; and it were well for society, if either mankind in general, or even those few who pretend to live according to any philosophical rule, were to regulate their conduct by the precepts of any one of them. We may learn from each of them something that is both valuable and peculiar. If it were possible, by precept and exhortation, to inspire the mind with fortitude and magnanimity, the ancient systems of propriety would seem sufficient to do this. Or if it were possible, by the same means, to soften it into humanity, and to awaken the affections of kindness and general love towards those we live with, some of the pictures with which the benevolent system presents us, might seem capable of producing this effect. We may learn from the system of Epicurus, though undoubtedly the most imperfect of all the three, how much the practice of both the amiable and respectable virtues is conducive to our own interest, to our own ease, and safety, and quiet, even in this life. As Epicurus placed happiness in the attainment of ease and security, he exerted himself, in a particular manner, to shew that virtue was not merely the best and the surest, but the only means of acquiring those invaluable possessions. The good effects of virtue upon our inward tranquillity and peace of mind, are what other philosophers have chiefly celebrated. Epicurus, without neglecting this topic, has chiefly insisted upon the influence of that amiable quality on our outward prosperity and safety. It was upon this account that his writings were so much studied in the ancient world by men of all different philosophical parties. It is from him that Cicero, the great enemy of the Epicurean system, borrows his most agree- able proofs, that virtue alone is sufficient to secure happiness. Seneca, though a Stoic, the sect most opposite to that of Epicurus, yet quotes this philosopher more frequently than any other.

There is, however, another system which seems to take away altogether the distinction between vice and virtue, and of which the tendency is, upon that account, wholly pernicious; I mean the system of Dr Mandeville. Though the notions of this author are in almost every respect erroneous, there are, however, some appearances in human nature, which, when viewed in a certain manner, seem at first sight to favour them. These, described and exaggerated by the lively and humorous, though coarse and rustic eloquence of Dr Mandeville, have thrown upon his doctrines an air of truth and probability which is very apt to impose upon the unskilful.

Dr Mandeville considers whatever is done from a sense of propriety, from a regard to what is commendable and

praiseworthy, as being done from a love of praise and commendation, or, as he calls it, from vanity. Man, he observes, is naturally much more interested in his own happiness than in that of others, and it is impossible that, in his
heart, he can ever really prefer their prosperity to his own.
Whenever he appears to do so, we may be assured that he
imposes upon us, and that he is then acting from the same
selfish motives as at all other times. Among his other selfish passions, vanity is one of the strongest, and he is always
easily flattered and greatly delighted with the applauses of
those about him. When he appears to sacrifice his own
interest to that of his companions, he knows that this conduct will be highly agreeable to their self-love; and that
they will not fail to express their satisfaction, by bestowing
upon him the most extravagant praises. The pleasure which
he expects from this, overbalances, in his opinion, the interest which he abandons in order to procure it. His conduct,
therefore, upon this occasion, is, in reality, just as selfish,
and arises from just as mean a motive as upon any other.
He is flattered, however, and he flatters himself with the
belief that it is entirely disinterested, since, unless this were
supposed, it would not seem to merit any commendation
either in his own eyes or in those of others. All public
spirit, therefore, all preference of public to private interest,
is, according to him, a mere cheat and imposition upon mankind; and that human virtue, which is so much boasted of,
and which is the occasion of so much emulation among men,
is the mere offspring of flattery begotten upon pride.

Whether the most generous and public spirited actions
may not, in some sense, be regarded as proceeding from
self-love, I shall not at present examine. The decision of
this question is not, I apprehend, of any importance towards
establishing the reality of virtue, since self-love may frequently be a virtuous motive of action. I shall only endeavour to shew that the desire of doing what is honourable

and noble, of rendering ourselves the proper objects of esteem and approbation, cannot, with any propriety, be called
vanity. Even the love of well grounded fame and reputation, the desire of acquiring esteem by what is really estimable, does not deserve that name. The first is the love of
virtue, the noblest and the best passion of human nature.
The second is the love of true glory, a passion inferior, no
doubt, to the former, but which in dignity appears to come
immediately after it. He is guilty of vanity who desires
praise for qualities which are either not praiseworthy in
any degree, or not in that degree in which he expects to
be praised for them; who sets his character upon the frivolous ornaments of dress and equipage, or upon the equally
frivolous accomplishments of ordinary behaviour. He is guilty
of vanity who desires praise for what, indeed, very well deserves it, but what he perfectly knows does not belong to
him. The empty coxcomb who gives himself airs of importance which he has no title to; the silly liar who assumes
the merit of adventures which never happened; the foolish
plagiary who gives himself out for the author of what he
has no pretensions to, are properly accused of this passion.
He too is said to be guilty of vanity who is not contented
with the silent sentiments of esteem and approbation; who
seems to be fonder of their noisy expressions and acclamations than of the sentiments themselves; who is never satisfied but when his own praises are ringing in his ears, and
who solicits, with the most anxious importunity, all external marks of respect; is fond of titles, of compliments, of
being visited, of being attended, of being taken notice of
in public places with the appearance of deference and attention. This frivolous passion is altogether different from
either of the two former, and is the passion of the lowest
and the least of mankind, as they are of the noblest and
the greatest.

But though these three passions, the desire of rendering

ourselves the proper objects of honour and esteem, or of becoming what is honourable and estimable; the desire of acquiring honour and esteem by really deserving those sentiments; and the frivolous desire of praise at any rate, are widely different; though the two former are always approved of, while the latter never fails to be despised; there is, however, a certain remote affinity among them, which, exaggerated by the humorous and diverting eloquence of this lively author, has enabled him to impose upon his readers. There is an affinity between vanity and the love of true glory, as both these passions aim at acquiring esteem and approbation. But they are different in this, that the one is a just, reasonable, and equitable passion, while the other is unjust, absurd, and ridiculous. The man who desires esteem for what is really estimable, desires nothing but what he is justly entitled to, and what cannot be refused him without some sort of injury. He, on the contrary, who desires it upon any other terms, demands what he has no just claim to. The first is easily satisfied, is not apt to be jealous or suspicious that we do not esteem him enough, and is seldom solicitous about receiving many external marks of our regard. The other, on the contrary, is never to be satisfied, is full of jealousy and suspicion that we do not esteem him so much as he desires, because he has some secret consciousness that he desires more than he deserves. The least neglect of ceremony he considers as a mortal affront, and as an expression of the most determined contempt. He is restless and impatient, and perpetually afraid that we have lost all respect for him, and is upon this account always anxious to obtain new expressions of esteem, and cannot be kept in temper but by continual attendance and adulation.

There is an affinity, too, between the desire of becoming what is honourable and estimable, and the desire of honour and esteem; between the love of virtue and the love of true glory. They resemble one another not only in this respect, that both aim at really being what is honourable and noble, but even in that respect in which the love of true glory resembles what is properly called vanity, some reference to the sentiments of others. The man of the greatest magnanimity, who desires virtue for its own sake, and is most indifferent about what actually are the opinions of mankind with regard to him, is still, however, delighted with the thoughts of what they should be, with the consciousness that though he may neither be honoured nor applauded, he is still the proper object of honour and applause; and that if mankind were cool and candid, and consistent with themselves and properly informed of the motives and circumstances of his conduct, they would not fail to honour and applaud him. Though he despises the opinions which are actually entertained of him, he has the highest value for those which ought to be entertained of him. That he might think himself worthy of those honourable sentiments, and, whatever was the idea which other men might conceive of his character, that when he should put himself in their situation, and consider, not what was, but what ought to be their opinion, he should always have the highest idea of it himself, was the great and exalted motive of his conduct. As even in the love of virtue, therefore, there is still some reference, though not to what is, yet to what in reason and propriety ought to be, the opinion of others, there is, even in this respect, some affinity between it and the love of true glory. There is, however, at the same time, a very great difference between them. The man who acts solely from a regard to what is right and fit to be done, from a regard to what is the proper object of esteem and approbation, though these sentiments should never be bestowed upon him, acts from the most sublime and godlike motive which human nature is even capable of conceiving. The man, on the other hand, who, while he desires to merit approbation, is at the same time anxious to obtain it, though he too is

laudable in the main, yet his motives have a greater mixture of human infirmity. He is in danger of being mortified by the ignorance and injustice of mankind, and his
happiness is exposed to the envy of his rivals and the folly
of the public. The happiness of the other, on the contrary,
is altogether secure and independent of fortune and of the
caprice of those he lives with. The contempt and hatred
which may be thrown upon him by the ignorance of mankind, he considers as not belonging to him, and is not at
all mortified by it. Mankind despise and hate him from a
false notion of his character and conduct. If they knew
him better, they would esteem and love him. It is not him
whom, properly speaking, they hate and despise, but another person whom they mistake him to be. Our friend,
whom we should meet at a masquerade in the garb of our
enemy, would be more diverted than mortified, if, under that
disguise, we should vent our indignation against him. Such
are the sentiments of a man of real magnanimity, when exposed to unjust censure. It seldom happens, however, that
human nature arrives at this degree of firmness. Though
none but the weakest and most worthless of mankind are
much delighted with false glory, yet, by a strange inconsistency, false ignominy is often capable of mortifying those
who appear the most resolute and determined.

Dr Mandeville is not satisfied with representing the frivolous motive of vanity, as the source of all those actions
which are commonly accounted virtuous. He endeavours
to point out the imperfection of human virtue in many other
respects. In every case, he pretends it falls short of that
complete self-denial which it pretends to, and instead of a
conquest, is commonly no more than a concealed indulgence
of our passions. Wherever our reserve with regard to pleasure falls short of the most ascetic abstinence, he treats it as
gross luxury and sensuality. Every thing according to him
is luxury which exceeds what is absolutely necessary for

the support of human nature, so that there is vice even in the use of a clean shirt, or of a convenient habitation. The indulgence of the inclination to sex, in the most lawful union, he considers as the same sensuality with the most hurtful gratification of that passion, and derides that temperance and that chastity which can be practised at so cheap a rate. The ingenious sophistry of his reasoning is here, as upon many other occasions, covered by the ambiguity of language. There are some of our passions which have no other names except those which mark the disagreeable and offensive degree. The spectator is more apt to take notice of them in this degree than in any other. When they shock his own sentiments; when they give him some sort of antipathy and uneasiness; he is necessarily obliged to attend to them, and is from thence naturally led to give them a name. When they fall in with the natural state of his own mind, he is very apt to overlook them altogether, and either gives them no name at all, or, if he give them any, it is one which marks rather the subjection and restraint of the passion, than the degree which it still is allowed to subsist in, after it is so subjected and restrained. Thus the common names* of the love of pleasure and of the love of sex, denote a vicious and offensive degree of those passions. The words temperance and chastity, on the other hand, seem to mark rather the restraint and subjection which they are kept under, than the degree which they are still allowed to subsist in. When he can shew therefore, that they still subsist in some degree, he imagines he has entirely demolished the reality of the virtues of temperance and chastity, and shewn them to be mere impositions upon the inattention and simplicity of mankind. Those virtues, however, do not require an entire insensibility to the objects of the passions which they mean to govern. They only aim at restraining the

* Luxury and lust.

violence of those passions so far as not to hurt the individual, and neither disturb nor offend the society.

It is the great fallacy of Dr Mandeville's book* to represent every passion as wholly vicious, which is so in any degree and in any direction. It is thus that he treats every
thing as vanity which has any reference either to what are,
or to what ought to be, the sentiments of others; and it is
by means of this sophistry that he establishes his favourite
conclusion, that private vices are public benefits. If the
love of magnificence, a taste for the elegant arts and improvements of human life; for whatever is agreeable in
dress, furniture, or equipage; for architecture, statuary,
painting, and music, is to be regarded as luxury, sensuality,
and ostentation, even in those whose situation allows, without any inconveniency, the indulgence of those passions;
it is certain that luxury, sensuality, and ostentation are
public benefits: since, without the qualities upon which he
thinks proper to bestow such approbrious names, the arts
of refinement could never find encouragement, and must
languish for want of employment. Some popular ascetic
doctrines, which had been current before his time, and
which placed virtue in the entire extirpation and anni-
hilation of all our passions, were the real foundation of this
licentious system. It was easy for Dr Mandeville to prove,
first, that this entire conquest never actually took place
among men; and secondly, that if it was to take place universally, it would be pernicious to society, by putting an
end to all industry and commerce, and in a manner to the
whole business of human life. By the first of these propositions he seemed to prove that there was no real virtue,
and that what pretended to be such, was a mere cheat and
imposition upon mankind; and by the second, that private

* Fable of the Bees.

vices were public benefits, since without them no society could prosper or flourish.

Such is the system of Dr Mandeville, which once made so much noise in the world, and which, though perhaps it never gave occasion to more vice than what would have been without it, at least taught that vice, which arose from other causes, to appear with more effrontery, and to avow the corruption of its motives with a profligate audaciousness which had never been heard of before.

But how destructive soever this system may appear, it could never have imposed upon so great a number of persons, nor have occasioned so general an alarm among those who are the friends of better principles, had it not in some respects bordered upon the truth. A system of natural philosophy may appear very plausible, and be for a long time very generally received in the world, and yet have no foundation in nature, nor any sort of resemblance to the truth. The vortices of Des Cartes were regarded by a very ingenious nation, for near a century together, as a most satisfactory account of the revolutions of the heavenly bodies. Yet it has been demonstrated, to the conviction of all mankind, that these pretended causes of those wonderful effects, not only do not actually exist, but are utterly impossible, and, if they did exist, could produce no such effects as are ascribed to them. But it is otherwise with systems of moral philosophy; and an author who pretends to account for the origin of our moral sentiments, cannot deceive us so grossly, nor depart so very far from all resemblance to the truth. When a traveller gives an account of some distant country, he may impose upon our credulity the most groundless and absurd fictions as the most certain matters of fact. But when a person pretends to inform us of what passes in our neighbourhood, and of the affairs of the very parish which we live in; though here too, if we are so careless as not to examine things with our own eyes, he may deceive us in many respects; yet the greatest false-hoods which he imposes upon us must bear some resem-blance to the truth, and must even have a considerable mix-ture of truth in them. An author who treats of natural philosophy, and pretends to assign the causes of the great phenomena of the universe, pretends to give an account of the affairs of a very distant country, concerning which he may tell us what he pleases; and as long as his narration keeps within the bounds of seeming possibility, he need not despair of gaining our belief. But when he proposes to explain the origin of our desires and affections, of our sentiments of approbation and disapprobation, he pretends to give an account, not only of the affairs of the very parish that we live in, but of our own domestic concerns. Though here too, like indolent masters who put their trust in a steward who deceives them, we are very liable to be im-posed upon, yet we are incapable of passing any account which does not preserve some little regard to the truth. Some of the articles, at least, must be just; and even those which are most overcharged must have had some founda-tion, otherwise the fraud would be detected, even by that careless inspection which we are disposed to give. The author who should assign as the cause of any natural senti-ment, some principle which neither had any connection with it, nor resembled any other principle which had some such connection, would appear absurd and ridiculous to the most injudicious and inexperienced reader.

SECTION III.

OF THE DIFFERENT SYSTEMS WHICH HAVE BEEN FORMED CONCERNING THE PRINCIPLE OF APPROBATION.

~~~~~~~~

INTRODUCTION.

AFTER the inquiry concerning the nature of virtue, the next question of importance in Moral Philosophy is concerning the principle of approbation; concerning the power or faculty of the mind which renders certain characters agreeable or disagreeable to us; makes us prefer one tenor of conduct to another; denominate the one right and the other wrong; and consider the one as the object of approbation, honour, and reward; the other as that of blame, censure, and punishment.

Three different accounts have been given of this principle of approbation. According to some, we approve and disapprove both of our own actions and of those of others, from self-love only, or from some view of their tendency to our own happiness or disadvantage; according to others, reason, the same faculty by which we distinguish between truth and falsehood, enables us to distinguish between what is fit and unfit, both in actions and affections; according to others, this distinction is altogether the effect of immediate sentiment and feeling, and arises from the satisfaction or disgust with which the view of certain actions or affections inspires us. Self-love, reason, and sentiment, therefore, are the three different sources which have been assigned for the principle of approbation.

Before I proceed to give an account of those different systems, I must observe, that the determination of this second question, though of the greatest importance in speculation, is of none in practice. The question concerning the nature of virtue necessarily has some influence upon our notions of right and wrong in many particular cases. That concerning the principle of approbation can possibly have no such effect. To examine from what contrivance or mechanism within those different notions or sentiments arise, is a mere matter of philosophical curiosity.

CHAPTER I.

Of those Systems which deduce the Principle of Approbation from Self-Love.

THOSE who account for the principle of approbation from self-love, do not all account for it in the same manner, and there is a good deal of confusion and inaccuracy in all their different systems. According to Mr Hobbes and many of his followers,* man is driven to take refuge in society, not by any natural love which he bears to his own kind, but because, without the assistance of others, he is incapable of subsisting with ease or safety. Society, upon this account, becomes necessary to him, and whatever tends to its support and welfare, he considers as having a remote tendency to his own interest; and, on the contrary, whatever is likely to disturb or destroy it, he regards as in some measure hurtful or pernicious to himself. Virtue is the great support, and vice the great disturber of human society. The former, therefore, is agreeable, and the latter offensive, to every man; as from the one he foresees the prosperity, and from the other the ruin and disorder, of what is so necessary for the comfort and security of his existence.

That the tendency of virtue to promote, and of vice to disturb the order of society, when we consider it coolly and philosophically, reflects a very great beauty upon the one, and a very great deformity upon the other, cannot, as I have observed upon a former occasion, be called in question. Human society, when we contemplate it in a certain abstract and philosophical light, appears like a great, an immense machine, whose regular and harmonious movements

* Puffendorff, Mandeville.

produce a thousand agreeable effects. As in any other
beautiful and noble machine that was the production of
human art, whatever tended to render its movements more
smooth and easy, would derive a beauty from this effect,
and, on the contrary, whatever tended to obstruct them,
would displease upon that account; so virtue, which is, as
it were, the fine polish to the wheels of society, necessarily
pleases; while vice, like the vile rust which makes them
jar and grate upon one another, is as necessarily offensive.
This account, therefore, of the origin of approbation and
disapprobation, so far as it derives them from a regard to
the order of society, runs into that principle which gives
beauty to utility, and which I have explained upon a former
occasion; and it is from thence that this system derives all
that appearance of probability which it possesses. When
those authors describe the innumerable advantages of a
cultivated and social above a savage and solitary life;
when they expatiate upon the necessity of virtue and good
order for the maintenance of the one, and demonstrate how
infallibly the prevalence of vice and disobedience to the
laws tends to bring back the other, the reader is charmed
with the novelty and grandeur of those views which they
open to him; he sees plainly a new beauty in virtue, and
a new deformity in vice, which he had never taken notice of
before; and is commonly so delighted with the discovery,
that he seldom takes time to reflect that this political view,
having never occurred to him in his life before, cannot possibly be the ground of that approbation and disapprobation
with which he has always been accustomed to consider
those different qualities.

When those authors, on the other hand, deduce from self-
love the interest which we take in the welfare of society,
and the esteem which, upon that account, we bestow upon
virtue, they do not mean, that when we in this age applaud
the virtue of Cato, and detest the villany of Catiline, our

sentiments are influenced by the notion of any benefit we receive from the one, or of any detriment we suffer from the other. It was not because the prosperity or subversion of society, in those remote ages and nations, was appre-hended to have any influence upon our happiness or misery in the present times, that, according to those philosophers, we esteemed the virtuous and blamed the disorderly cha-racter. They never imagined that our sentiments were influenced by any benefit or damage which we supposed actually to redound to us from either; but by that which might have redounded to us, had we lived in those distant ages and countries; or by that which might still redound to us, if, in our own times, we should meet with characters of the same kind. The idea, in short, which those authors were groping about, but which they were never able to unfold distinctly, was that indirect sympathy which we feel with the gratitude or resentment of those who received the benefit or suffered the damage resulting from such opposite characters; and it was this which they were indistinctly pointing at when they said that it was not the thought of what we had gained or suffered which prompted our applause or indignation, but the conception or imagination of what we might gain or suffer, if we were to act in society with such associates.

Sympathy, however, cannot, in any sense, be regarded as a selfish principle. When I sympathize with your sorrow or your indignation, it may be pretended, indeed, that my emotion is founded in self-love, because it arises from bring-ing your case home to myself, from putting myself in your situation, and thence conceiving what I should feel in the like circumstances. But though sympathy is very properly said to arise from an imaginary change of situations with the person principally concerned, yet this imaginary change is not supposed to happen to me in my own person and cha-racter, but in that of the person with whom I sympathize.

When I condole with you for the loss of your only son, in order to enter into your grief, I do not consider what I, a person of such a character and profession, should suffer, if I had a son, and if that son was unfortunately to die ; but I consider what I should suffer if I was really you ; and I not only change circumstances with you, but I change persons and characters. My grief, therefore, is entirely upon your account, and not in the least upon my own. It is not, therefore, in the least selfish. How can that be regarded as a selfish passion, which does not arise even from the imagination of any thing that has befallen, or that relates to myself, in my own proper person and character, but which is entirely occupied about what relates to you? A man may sympathize with a woman in child-bed, though it is impossible that he should conceive himself as suffering her pains in his own proper person and character. That whole account of human nature, however, which deduces all sentiments and affections from self-love, which has made so much noise in the world, but which, so far as I know, has never yet been fully and distinctly explained, seems to me to have arisen from some confused misapprehension of the system of sympathy.

CHAPTER II.

Of those Systems which make Reason the Principle of Approbation.

It is well known to have been the doctrine of Mr Hobbes, that a state of nature is a state of war; and that antecedent to the institution of civil government, there could be no safe or peaceable society among men. To preserve society, therefore, according to him, was to support civil government, and to destroy civil government, was the same thing as to put an end to society. But the existence of civil government depends upon the obedience that is paid to the supreme magistrate. The moment he loses his authority, all government is at an end. As self-preservation, therefore, teaches men to applaud whatever tends to promote the welfare of society, and to blame whatever is likely to hurt it; so the same principle, if they would think and speak consistently, ought to teach them to applaud, upon all occasions, obedience to the civil magistrate, and to blame all disobedience and rebellion. The very ideas of laudable and blameable, ought to be the same with those of obedience and disobedience. The laws of the civil magistrate, therefore, ought to be regarded as the sole ultimate standards of what was just and unjust, of what was right and wrong.

It was the avowed intention of Mr Hobbes, by propagating these notions, to subject the consciences of men immediately to the civil, and not to the ecclesiastical powers, whose turbulence and ambition, he had been taught, by the example of his own times, to regard as the principal source of the disorders of society. His doctrine, upon this account, was peculiarly offensive to theologians, who, accordingly, did not fail to vent their indignation against him with great asperity and bitterness. It was likewise offensive to all sound moralists, as it supposed that there was no natural distinction between right and wrong; that these were mutable and changeable, and depended upon the mere arbitrary will of the civil magistrate. This account of things, therefore, was attacked from all quarters, and by all sorts of weapons, by sober reason as well as by furious declamation.

In order to confute so odious a doctrine, it was necessary to prove that, antecedent to all law or positive institution, the mind was naturally endowed with a faculty, by which it distinguished, in certain actions and affections, the qualities of right, laudable, and virtuous, and in others those of wrong, blameable, and vicious.

Law, it was justly observed by Dr Cudworth,* could not be the original source of those distinctions, since, upon the supposition of such a law, it must either be right to obey it, and wrong to disobey it, or indifferent whether we obeyed it or disobeyed it. That law which it was indifferent whether we obeyed or disobeyed, could not, it was evident, be the source of those distinctions; neither could that which it was right to obey and wrong to disobey, since even this still supposed the antecedent notions or ideas of right and wrong, and that obedience to the law was conformable to the idea of right, and disobedience to that of wrong.

Since the mind, therefore, had a notion of those distinctions antecedent to all law, it seemed necessarily to follow, that it derived this notion from reason, which pointed out the difference between right and wrong, in the same manner in which it did that between truth and falsehood; and this

---

* Immutable Morality, l. 1.

conclusion, which, though true in some respects, is rather hasty in others, was more easily received at a time when the abstract science of human nature was but in its infancy, and before the distinct offices and powers of the different faculties of the human mind had been carefully examined and distinguished from one another. When this controversy with Mr Hobbes was carried on with the greatest warmth and keenness, no other faculty had been thought of from which any such ideas could possibly be supposed to arise. It became at this time, therefore, the popular doctrine, that the essence of virtue and vice did not consist in the conformity or disagreement of human actions with the law of a superior, but in their conformity or disagreement with reason, which was thus considered as the original source and principle of approbation and disapprobation.

That virtue consists in conformity to reason is true in some respects; and this faculty may very justly be considered as, in some sense, the source and principle of approbation and disapprobation, and of all solid judgments concerning right and wrong. It is by reason that we discover those general rules of justice by which we ought to regulate our actions ; and it is by the same faculty that we form those more vague and indeterminate ideas of what is prudent, of what is decent, of what is generous or noble, which we carry constantly about with us, and according to which we endeavour, as well as we can, to model the tenor of our conduct. The general maxims of morality are formed, like all other general maxims, from experience and induction. We observe, in a great variety of particular cases, what pleases or displeases our moral faculties, what these approve or disapprove of; and by induction from this experience we establish those general rules. But induction is always regarded as one of the operations of reason. From reason, therefore, we are very properly said to derive

all those general maxims and ideas. It is by these, however, that we regulate the greater part of our moral judgments, which would be extremely uncertain and precarious
if they depended altogether upon what is liable to so many
variations as immediate sentiment and feeling, which the
different states of health and humour are capable of altering so essentially. As our most solid judgments, therefore,
with regard to right and wrong, are regulated by maxims
and ideas derived from an induction of reason, virtue may
very properly be said to consist in a conformity to reason;
and so far this faculty may be considered as the source and
principle of approbation and disapprobation.

But though reason is undoubtedly the source of the general rules of morality, and of all the moral judgments which
we form by means of them, it is altogether absurd and un-
intelligible to suppose that the first perceptions of right and
wrong can be derived from reason, even in those particular
cases upon the experience of which the general rules are
formed. These first perceptions, as well as all other expe-
riments upon which any general rules are founded, cannot
be the object of reason, but of immediate sense and feeling.
It is by finding, in a vast variety of instances, that one
tenor of conduct constantly pleases in a certain manner,
and that another as constantly displeases the mind, that we
form the general rules of morality. But reason cannot render
any particular object either agreeable or disagreeable to the
mind for its own sake. Reason may shew that this object
is the means of obtaining some other which is naturally
either pleasing or displeasing, and in this manner may render it either agreeable or disagreeable, for the sake of something else. But nothing can be agreeable or disagreeable
for its own sake, which is not rendered such by immediate
sense and feeling. If virtue, therefore, in every particular
instance, necessarily pleases for its own sake, and if vice as

certainly displeases the mind, it cannot be reason, but immediate sense and feeling, which in this manner reconciles
us to the one and alienates us from the other.

Pleasure and pain are the great objects of desire and
aversion ; but these are distinguished not by reason but by
immediate sense and feeling.   If virtue, therefore, be desirable for its own sake, and if vice be in the same manner
the object of aversion, it cannot be reason which originally
distinguishes those different qualities, but immediate sense
and feeling.

As reason, however, in a certain sense may justly be
considered as the principle of approbation and disapprobation, these sentiments were, through inattention, long regarded as originally flowing from the operations of this faculty.
Dr Hutcheson had the merit of being the first who distinguished, with any degree of precision, in what respect all
moral distinctions may be said to arise from reason, and in
what respect they are founded upon immediate sense and
feeling.   In his illustrations upon the moral sense, he has
explained this so fully, and, in my opinion, so unanswerably,
that if any controversy is still kept up about this subject,
I can impute it to nothing but either to inattention to what
that gentleman has written, or to a superstitious attachment
to certain forms of expression—a weakness not very uncommon among the learned, especially in subjects so deeply
interesting as the present, in which a man of virtue is often
loath to abandon even the propriety of a single phrase which
he has been accustomed to.

CHAPTER III.

Of those Systems which make Sentiment the Principle of Approbation.

THOSE systems which make sentiment the principle of approbation may be divided into two different classes.

I. According to some, the principle of approbation is founded upon a sentiment of a peculiar nature, upon a particular power of perception exerted by the mind at the view of certain actions or affections; some of which affecting this faculty in an agreeable, and others in a disagreeable manner, the former are stamped with the characters of right, laudable, and virtuous, the latter with those of wrong, blameable and vicious. This sentiment, being of a peculiar nature, distinct from every other, and the effect of a particular power of perception, they give it a particular name, and call it a moral sense.

II. According to others, in order to account for the principle of approbation, there is no occasion for supposing any new power of perception which had never been heard of before : nature, they imagine, acts here, as in all other cases, with the strictest economy, and produces a multitude of effects from one and the same cause; and sympathy, a power which has always been taken notice of, and with which the mind is manifestly endowed, is, they think, sufficient to account for all the effects ascribed to this peculiar faculty.

I. Dr Hutcheson* had been at great pains to prove that the principle of approbation was not founded on self-love.

* Inquiry concerning Virtue.

He had demonstrated, too, that it could not arise from any operation of reason. Nothing remained, he thought, but to suppose it a faculty of a peculiar kind, with which nature had endowed the human mind, in order to produce this one particular and important effect. When self-love and reason were both excluded, it did not occur to him that there was any other known faculty of the mind which could in any respect answer this purpose.

This new power of perception he called a moral sense, and supposed it to be somewhat analogous to the external senses. As the bodies around us, by affecting these in a certain manner, appear to possess the different qualities of sound, taste, odour, colour ; so the various affections of the human mind, by touching this particular faculty in a certain manner, appear to possess the different qualities of amiable and odious, of virtuous and vicious, of right and wrong.

The various senses or powers of perception,* from which the human mind derives all its simple ideas, were, according to this system, of two different kinds, of which the one were called the direct or antecedent, the other the reflex or consequent senses. The direct senses were those faculties from which the mind derived the perception of such species of things as did not presuppose the antecedent perception of any other. Thus sounds and colours were objects of the direct senses. To hear a sound or to see a colour does not presuppose the antecedent perception of any other quality or object. The reflex or consequent senses, on the other hand, were those faculties from which the mind derived the perception of such species of things as presupposed the antecedent perception of some other. Thus harmony and beauty were objects of the reflex senses. In order to perceive the harmony of a sound, or the beauty of a colour, we

* Treatise of the Passions.

must first perceive the sound or the colour. The moral sense was considered as a faculty of this kind. That faculty, which Mr Locke calls reflection, and from which he derived the simple ideas of the different passions and emotions of the human mind, was, according to Dr Hutcheson, a direct internal sense. That faculty, again, by which we perceived the beauty or deformity, the virtue or vice, of those different passions and emotions, was a reflex, internal sense.

Dr Hutcheson endeavoured still further to support this doctrine, by shewing that it was agreeable to the analogy of nature, and that the mind was endowed with a variety of other reflex senses exactly similar to the moral sense; such as a sense of beauty and deformity in external objects; a public sense, by which we sympathize with the happiness or misery of our fellow-creatures; a sense of shame and honour; and a sense of ridicule.

But notwithstanding all the pains which this ingenious philosopher has taken to prove that the principle of approbation is founded in a peculiar power of perception, somewhat analogous to the external senses, there are some consequences which he acknowledges to follow from this doctrine, that will perhaps be regarded by many as a sufficient confutation of it. The qualities, he allows,* which belong to the objects of any sense, cannot, without the greatest absurdity, be ascribed to the sense itself. Who ever thought of calling the sense of seeing, black or white; the sense of hearing, loud or low; or the sense of tasting, sweet or bitter? And, according to him, it is equally absurd to call our moral faculties virtuous or vicious, morally good or evil. These qualities belong to the objects of those faculties, not to the faculties themselves. If any man, therefore, was so absurdly

---

* Illustrations upon the Moral Sense, sect. i. p. 237, et seq.; third edition.

constituted as to approve of cruelty and injustice as the highest virtues, and to disapprove of equity and humanity as the most pitiful vices, such a constitution of mind might indeed be regarded as inconvenient both to the individual and to the society, and likewise as strange, surprising, and unnatural in itself; but it could not, without the greatest absurdity, be denominated vicious or morally evil.

Yet surely, if we saw any man shouting with admiration and applause at a barbarous and unmerited execution which some insolent tyrant had ordered, we should not think we were guilty of any great absurdity in denominating this be-haviour vicious and morally evil in the highest degree, though it expressed nothing but depraved moral faculties, or an absurd approbation of this horrid action, as of what was noble, magnanimous, and great. Our heart, I imagine, at the sight of such a spectator, would forget for a while its sympathy with the sufferer, and feel nothing but horror and detestation at the thought of so execrable a wretch. We should abominate him even more than the tyrant who might be goaded on by the strong passions of jealousy, fear, and resentment, and upon that account be more excusable. But the sentiments of the spectator would appear altogether without cause or motive, and therefore most perfectly and completely detestable. There is no perversion of sentiment or affection which our heart would be more averse to enter into, or which it would reject with greater hatred and in-dignation, than one of this kind; and so far from regarding such a constitution of mind as being merely something strange or inconvenient, and not in any respect vicious or morally evil, we should rather consider it as the very last and most dreadful stage of moral depravity.

Correct moral sentiments, on the contrary, naturally ap·pear in some degree laudable and morally good. The man whose censure and applause are upon all occasions suited with the greatest accuracy to the value or unworthiness of the object, seems to deserve a degree even of moral approbation. We admire the delicate precision of his moral sentiments; they lead our own judgments; and, upon account of their uncommon and surprising justness, they even excite our wonder and applause. We cannot, indeed, be always sure that the conduct of such a person would be in any respect correspondent to the precision and accuracy of his judgments concerning the conduct of others. Virtue requires habit and resolution of mind as well as delicacy of sentiment; and, unfortunately, the former qualities are sometimes wanting where the latter is in the greatest perfection. This disposition of mind, however, though it may sometimes be attended with imperfections, is incompatible with any thing that is grossly criminal, and is the happiest foundation upon which the superstructure of perfect virtue can be built. There are many men who mean very well, and seriously pui pose to do what they think their duty, who, notwithstanding, are disagreeable on account of the coarseness of their moral sentiments.

It may be said, perhaps, that though the principle of approbation is not founded upon any power of perception that is in any respect analogous to the external senses, it may still be founded upon a peculiar sentiment, which answers this one particular purpose and no other. Approbation and disapprobation, it may be pretended, are certain feelings or emotions which arise in the mind upon the view of different characters and actions; and as resentment might be called a sense of injuries, or gratitude a sense of benefits, so these may very properly receive the name of a sense of right and wrong, or of a moral sense.

But this account of things, though it may not be liable to the same objections with the foregoing, is exposed to others which are equally unanswerable.

First of all, whatever variations any particular emotion may undergo, it still preserves the general features which distinguish it to be an emotion of such a kind; and these general features are always more striking and remarkable than any variation which it may undergo in particular cases. Thus anger is an emotion of a particular kind; and, accordingly, its general features are always more distinguishable than all the variations it undergoes in particular cases. Anger against a man is, no doubt, somewhat different from anger against a woman, and that again from anger against a child. In each of those three cases, the general passion of anger receives a different modification from the particular character of its object, as may easily be observed by the attentive. But still the general features of the passion predominate in all these cases. To distinguish these requires no nice observation; a very delicate attention, on the contrary, is necessary to discover their variations : every body takes notice of the former—scarce any body observes the latter. If approbation and disapprobation, therefore, were, like gratitude and resentment, emotions of a particular kind, distinct from every other, we should expect that in all the variations which either of them might undergo, it would still retain the general features which mark it to be an emotion of such a particular kind—clear, plain, and easily distinguishable. But in fact it happens quite otherwise. If we attend to what we really feel when, upon different occasions, we either approve or disapprove, we shall find that our emotion in one case is often totally different from that in another, and that no common features can possibly be discovered between them. Thus the approbation with which we view a tender, delicate, and humane sentiment, is quite different from that with which we are struck by one that appears great, daring, and magnanimous. Our approbation of both may, upon different occasions, be perfect and entire · but we are softened by the one, and we are elevated by the other, and there is no sort of resemblance between the emotions which they excite in us. But, according to that system which I have been endeavouring to establish, this must necessarily be the case. As the emotions of the person whom we approve of are in those two cases quite opposite to one another, and as our approbation arises from sympathy with those opposite emotions, what we feel upon the one occasion can have no sort of resemblance to what we feel upon the other. But this could not happen if approbation consisted in a peculiar emotion, which had nothing in common with the sentiments we approved of, but which arose at the view of those sentiments, like any other passion at the view of its proper object. The same thing holds true with regard to disapprobation. Our horror for cruelty has no sort of resemblance to our contempt for mean-spiritedness. It is quite a different species of discord which we feel at the view of those two different vices, between our own minds and those of the person whose sentiments and behaviour we consider.

Secondly, I have already observed, that not only the different passions or affections of the human mind which are approved or disapproved of appear morally good or evil, but that proper and improper approbation appear, to our natural sentiments, to be stamped with the same characters. I would ask, therefore, how it is that, according to this system, we approve or disapprove of proper or improper approbation? To this question there is, I imagine, but one reasonable answer which can possibly be given. It must be said, that when the approbation with which our neighbour regards the conduct of a third person coincides with our own, we approve of his approbation, and consider it as in some measure morally good; and that, on the contrary, when it does not coincide with our own sentiments, we disapprove of it, and consider it as in some measure morally evil. It must be allowed, therefore, that at least in this one case the coincidence or opposition of sentiments, between the observer and the person observed, constitutes moral approbation or disapprobation. And if it does so in this one case, I would ask, why not in every other?—to what purpose imagine a new power of perception in order to account for those sentiments?

Against every account of the principle of approbation, which makes it depend upon a peculiar sentiment distinct from every other, I would object, that it is strange that this sentiment, which Providence undoubtedly intended to be the governing principle of human nature, should hitherto have been so little taken notice of as not to have got a name in any language. The word moral sense is of very late formation, and cannot yet be considered as making part of the English tongue. The word approbation has but within these few years been appropriated to denote peculiarly any thing of this kind. In propriety of language we approve of whatever is entirely to our satisfaction, of the form of a building, of the contrivance of a machine, of the flavour of a dish of meat. The word conscience does not immediately denote any moral faculty by which we approve or disapprove. Conscience supposes, indeed, the existence of some such faculty, and properly signifies our consciousness of having acted agreeably or contrary to its directions. When love, hatred, joy, sorrow, gratitude, resentment, with so many other passions which are all supposed to be the subjects of this principle, have made themselves considerable enough to get titles to know them by, is it not surprising that the sovereign of them all should hitherto have been so little heeded, that, a few philosophers excepted, nobody has yet thought it worth while to bestow a name upon it?

When we approve of any character or action, the sentiments which we feel are, according to the foregoing system, derived from four sources, which are in some respects different from one another. First, we sympathize with the motives of the agent; secondly, we enter into the gratitude of those who receive the benefit of his actions; thirdly, we observe that his conduct has been agreeable to the general rules by which those two sympathies generally act; and, last of all, when we consider such actions, as making a part of a system of behaviour which tends to promote the happiness either of the individual or of the society, they appear to derive a beauty from this utility, not unlike that which we ascribe to any well-contrived machine. After deducting, in any one particular case, all that must be acknowledged to proceed from some one or other of these four principles, I should be glad to know what remains; and I shall freely allow this overplus to be ascribed to a moral sense, or to any other peculiar faculty, provided any body will ascertain precisely what this overplus is. It might be expected, perhaps, that if there was any such peculiar principle, such as this moral sense is supposed to be, we should feel it, in some particular cases, separated and detached from every other, as we often feel joy, sorrow, hope, and fear, pure and unmixed with any other emotion. This, however, I imagine, cannot even be pretended. I have never heard any instance alleged in which this principle could be said to exert itself alone and unmixed with sympathy or antipathy, with gratitude or resentment, with the perception of the agreement or disagreement of any action to an established rule, or, last of all, with that general taste for beauty and order which is excited by inanimated as well as by animated objects.

II. There is another system which attempts to account for the origin of our moral sentiments from sympathy, distinct from that which I have been endeavouring to establish. It is that which places virtue in utility, and accounts for the pleasure with which the spectator surveys the utility of any quality from sympathy with the happiness of those who are affected by it. This sympathy is different both from that by which we enter into the motives of the agent, and from that by which we go along with the gratitude of the persons who are benefited by his actions. It is the same principle with that by which we approve of a well-contrived machine. But no machine can be the object of either of those two last-mentioned sympathies. I have already, in the fourth part of this discourse, given some account of this system.

SECTION IV.

OF THE MANNER IN WHICH DIFFERENT AUTHORS HAVE TREATED OF THE PRACTICAL RULES OF MORALITY.

It was observed in the third part of this discourse that the rules of justice are the only rules of morality which are precise and accurate ; that those of all the other virtues are loose, vague, and indeterminate ; that the first may be compared to the rules of grammar; the others to those which critics lay down for the attainment of what is sublime and elegant in composition, and which present us rather with a general idea of the perfection we ought to aim at, than afford us any certain and infallible directions for acquiring it.

As the different rules of morality admit such different degrees of accuracy, those authors who have endeavoured to collect and digest them into systems have done it in two different manners; and one set has followed through the whole that loose method to which they were naturally directed by the consideration of one species of virtues ; while another has as universally endeavoured to introduce into their precepts that sort of accuracy of which only some of them are susceptible. The first have written like critics, the second like grammarians.

I. The first, among whom we may count all the ancient moralists, have contented themselves with describing in a general manner the different vices and virtues, and with pointing out the deformity and misery of the one disposition, as well as the propriety and happiness of the other, but have not affected to lay down many precise rules that are to hold good unexceptionably in all particular cases. They have only endeavoured to ascertain, as far as language is capable of ascertaining, first, wherein consists the sentiment of the heart, upon which each particular virtue is founded; what sort of internal feeling or emotion it is which constitutes the essence of friendship, of humanity, of generosity, of justice, of magnanimity, and of all the other virtues, as well as of the vices which are opposed to them; and, secondly, what is the general way of acting; the ordinary tone and tenor of conduct to which each of those sentiments would direct us; or how it is that a friendly, a generous, a brave, a just, and a humane man would, upon ordinary occasions, choose to act.

To characterize the sentiment of the heart upon which each particular virtue is founded, though it requires both a delicate and an accurate pencil, is a task, however, which may be executed with some degree of exactness. It is impossible, indeed, to express all the variations which each sentiment either does or ought to undergo, according to every possible variation of circumstances. They are endless, and language wants names to mark them by. The sentiment of friendship, for example, which we feel for an old man, is different from that which we feel for a young; that which we entertain for an austere man different from that which we feel for one of softer and gentler manners; and that again from what we feel for one of gay vivacity and spirit. The friendship which we conceive for a man is different from that with which a woman affects us, even where there is no mixture of any grosser passion. What author could enumerate and ascertain these and all the other infinite varieties which this sentiment is capable of undergoing? But still the general sentiment of friendship and familiar attachment which is common to them all may be ascertained with a sufficient degree of accuracy. The picture which is drawn of it, though it will always be in many respects incomplete, may, however, have such a resemblance as to make us know the original when we meet with it, and even distinguish it from other sentiments to which it has a considerable resemblance, such as good-will, respect, esteem, admiration.

To describe, in a general manner, what is the ordinary way of acting to which each virtue would prompt us, is still more easy. It is, indeed, scarce possible to describe the internal sentiment or emotion upon which it is founded, without doing something of this kind. It is impossible by language to express, if I may say so, the invisible features of all the different modifications of passion as they shew themselves within. There is no other way of marking and distinguishing them from one another, but by describing the effects which they produce, without the alterations which they occasion in the countenance, in the air and external behaviour, the resolutions they suggest, the actions they prompt to. It is thus that Cicero, in the first book of his Offices, endeavours to direct us to the practice of the four cardinal virtues; and that Aristotle, in the practical parts of his Ethics, points out to us the different habits by which he would have us regulate our behaviour, such as liberality, magnificence, magnanimity, and even jocularity and good humour—qualities which that indulgent philosopher has thought worthy of a place in the catalogue of the virtues, though the lightness of that approbation which we naturally bestow upon them should not seem to entitle them to so venerable a name.

Such works present us with agreeable and lively pictures of manners. By the vivacity of their descriptions they inflame our natural love of virtue, and increase our abhorrence of vice; by the justness as well as delicacy of their observations, they may often help both to correct and to ascertain our natural sentiments with regard to the propriety of conduct, and, suggesting many nice and delicate attentions, form us to a more exact justness of behaviour than what, without such instruction, we should have been apt to think of. In treating of the rules of morality in this manner consists the science which is properly called Ethics —a science which, though like criticism it does not admit of the most accurate precision, is, however, both highly useful and agreeable. It is of all others the most susceptible of the embellishments of eloquence, and, by means of them, of bestowing, if that be possible, a new importance upon the smallest rules of duty. Its precepts, when thus dressed and adorned, are capable of producing upon the flexibility of youth the noblest and most lasting impressions; and, as they fall in with the natural magnanimity of that generous age, they are able to inspire, for a time at least, the most heroic resolutions, and thus tend both to establish and confirm the best and most useful habits of which the mind of man is susceptible. Whatever precept and exhortation can do to animate us to the practice of virtue, is done by this science, delivered in this manner.

II. The second set of moralists, among whom we may count all the casuists of the middle and latter ages of the Christian church, as well as all those who, in this and in the preceding century, have treated of what is called natural jurisprudence, do not content themselves with characterizing in this general manner that tenor of conduct which they would recommend to us, but endeavour to lay down exact and precise rules for the direction of every circumstance of our behaviour. As justice is the only virtue with regard to which such exact rules can properly be given, it is this virtue that has chiefly fallen under the consideration of those two different sets of writers. They treat of it, however, in a very different manner.

Those who write upon the principles of jurisprudence, consider only what the person to whom the obligation is due ought to think himself entitled to exact by force; what every impartial spectator would approve of him for exacting, or what a judge or arbiter, to whom he had submitted his case, and who had undertaken to do him justice, ought to oblige the other person to suffer or to perform. The casuists, on the other hand, do not so much examine what it is that might properly be exacted by force, as what it is that the person who owes the obligation ought to think himself bound to perform, from the most sacred and scrupulous regard to the general rules of justice, and from the most conscientious dread either of wronging his neighbour or of violating the integrity of his own character. It is the end of jurisprudence to prescribe rules for the decisions of judges and arbiters. It is the end of casuistry to prescribe rules for the conduct of a good man. By observing all the rules of jurisprudence, supposing them ever so perfect, we should deserve nothing but to be free from external punishment. By observing those of casuistry, supposing them such as they ought to be, we should be entitled to considerable praise, by the exact and scrupulous delicacy of our behaviour.

It may frequently happen that a good man ought to think himself bound, from a sacred and conscientious regard to the general rules of justice, to perform many things which it would be the highest injustice to extort from him, or for any judge or arbiter to impose upon him by force. To give a trite example : a highwayman, by the fear of death, obliges a traveller to promise him a certain sum of money. Whether such a promise, extorted in this manner by unjust force, ought to be regarded as obligatory, is a question that has been very much debated.

If we consider it merely as a question of jurisprudence,

the decision can admit of no doubt. It would be absurd to suppose that the highwayman can be entitled to use force to constrain the other to perform. To extort the promise was a crime which deserved the highest punishment, and to extort the performance would only be adding a new crime to the former. He can complain of no injury who has been only deceived by the person by whom he might justly have been killed. To suppose that a judge ought to enforce the obligation of such promises, or that the magistrate ought to allow them to sustain action at law, would be the most ridiculous of all absurdities. If we consider this question, therefore, as a question of jurisprudence, we can be at no loss about the decision.

But if we consider it as a question of casuistry, it will not be so easily determined. Whether a good man, from a conscientious regard to that most sacred rule of justice, which commands the observance of all serious promises, would not think himself bound to perform, is at least much more doubtful. That no regard is due to the disappointment of the wretch who brings him into this situation, that no injury is done to the robber, and, consequently, that nothing can be extorted by force, will admit of no sort of dispute. But whether some regard is not in this case due to his own dignity and honour, to the inviolable sacredness of that part of his character which makes him reverence the law of truth, and abhor every thing that approaches to treachery and falsehood, may, perhaps, more reasonably be made a question. The casuists accordingly are greatly divided about it. One party, with whom we may count Cicero, among the ancients; among the moderns, Puffendorf; Barbeyrac his commentator; and, above all, the late Dr Hutcheson, one who, in most cases, was by no means a loose casuist, determine, without any hesitation, that no sort of regard is due to any such promise, and that to think otherwise is mere weakness and superstition. Another

party, among whom we may reckon* some of the ancient
fathers of the church, as well as some very eminent modern
casuists, have been of another opinion, and have judged all
such promises obligatory.

If we consider the matter according to the common sentiments of mankind, we shall find that some regard would
be thought due even to a promise of this kind ; but that
it is impossible to determine how much, by any general rule,
that will apply to all cases without exception. The man
who was quite frank and easy in making promises of this
kind, and who violated them with as little ceremony,
we should not choose for our friend and companion. A
gentleman who should promise a highwayman five pounds
and not perform, would incur some blame. If the sum
promised, however, was very great, it might be more doubtful what was proper to be done. If it was such, for example,
that the payment of it would entirely ruin the family of the
promiser ; if it was so great as to be sufficient for promoting the most useful purposes, it would appear in some
measure criminal, at least extremely improper, to throw it,
for the sake of a punctilio, into such worthless hands. The
man who should beggar himself, or who should throw away
an hundred thousand pounds, though he could afford that
vast sum, for the sake of observing such a parole with a
thief, would appear, to the common sense of mankind, absurd and extravagant in the highest degree. Such profusion would seem inconsistent with his duty, with what he
owed both to himself and others, and what, therefore, regard to a promise extorted in this manner could by no means
authorize. To fix, however, by any precise rule, what degree of regard ought to be paid to it, or what might be the
greatest sum which could be due from it, is evidently impossible. This would vary according to the characters of

* St Augustine, La Placette·

the persons, according to their circumstances, according to
the solemnity of the promise, and even according to the
incidents of the rencounter; and if the promiser had been
treated with a great deal of that sort of gallantry which is
sometimes to be met with in persons of the most abandoned characters, more would seem due than upon other occasions.   It may be said in general, that exact propriety requires the observance of all such promises, wherever it is
not inconsistent with some other duties that are more sacred,
such as regard to the public interest, to those whom gratitude, whom natural affection, or whom the laws of proper
beneficence, should prompt us to provide for.   But, as was
formerly taken notice of, we have no precise rules to determine what external actions are due from a regard to such
motives, nor, consequently, when it is that those virtues are
inconsistent with the observance of such promises.

It is to be observed, however, that whenever such promises are violated, though for the most necessary reasons,
it is always with some degree of dishonour to the person
who made them.   After they are made, we may be convinced of the impropriety of observing them; but still
there is some fault in having made them.   It is at least a
departure from the highest and noblest maxims of magnanimity and honour.   A brave man ought to die rather than
make a promise which he can neither keep without folly
nor violate without ignominy.   For some degree of ignominy always attends a situation of this kind.   Treachery and
falsehood are vices so dangerous, so dreadful, and, at the
same time, such as may so easily, and, upon many occasions,
so safely, be indulged, that we are more jealous of them
than of almost any other.   Our imagination, therefore, attaches the idea of shame to all violations of faith, in every
circumstance and in every situation.   They resemble in
this respect the violations of chastity in the fair sex, a virtue of which for the like reasons, we are excessively jealous;

and our sentiments are not more delicate with regard to the one than with regard to the other. Breach of chastity dishonours irretrievably. No circumstances, no solicitation, can excuse it; no sorrow, no repentance, atone for it. We are so nice in this respect, that even a rape dishonours, and the innocence of the mind cannot, in our imagination, wash out the pollution of the body. It is the same case with the violation of faith, when it has been solemnly pledged, even to the most worthless of mankind. Fidelity is so necessary a virtue, that we apprehend it in general to be due even to those to whom nothing else is due, and whom we think it lawful to kill and destroy. It is to no purpose that the person who has been guilty of the breach of it urges that he promised in order to save his life; and that he broke his promise because it was inconsistent with some other respectable duty to keep it. These circumstances may alleviate, but cannot entirely wipe out his dishonour. He appears to have been guilty of an action with which, in the imaginations of men, some degree of shame is inseparably connected. He has broken a promise which he had solemnly averred he would maintain; and his character, if not irretrievably stained and polluted, has at least a ridicule affixed to it which it will be very difficult entirely to efface; and no man, I imagine, who had gone through an adventure of this kind would be fond of telling the story.

This instance may serve to shew wherein consists the difference between casuistry and jurisprudence, even when both of them consider the obligations of the general rules of justice.

But though this difference be real and essential, though those two sciences propose quite different ends, the sameness of the subject has made such a similarity between them, that the greater part of authors, whose professed design was to treat of jurisprudence, have determined the different questions they examine, sometimes according to the principles of that science, and sometimes according to those of casuistry, without distinguishing, and perhaps without being themselves aware when they did the one and when the other.

The doctrine of the casuists, however, is by no means confined to the consideration of what a conscientious regard to the general rules of justice would demand of us. It embraces many other parts of Christian and moral duty. What seems principally to have given occasion to the cultivation of this species of science was the custom of auricular confession, introduced by the Roman Catholic superstition, in times of barbarism and ignorance. By that institution the most secret actions, and even the thoughts of every person which could be suspected of receding in the smallest degree from the rules of Christian purity, were to be revealed to the confessor. The confessor informed his penitents whether and in what respect they had violated their duty, and what penance it behoved them to undergo before he could absolve them in the name of the offended Deity.

The consciousness, or even the suspicion, of having done wrong, is a load upon every mind, and is accompanied with anxiety and terror in all those who are not hardened by long habits of iniquity. Men, in this as in all other distresses, are naturally eager to disburden themselves of the oppression which they feel upon their thoughts, by unbosoming the agony of their mind to some person whose secrecy and discretion they can confide in. The shame which they suffer from this acknowledgment is fully compensated by that alleviation of their uneasiness which the sympathy of their confidant seldom fails to occasion. It relieves them to find that they are not altogether unworthy of regard, and that however their past conduct may be censured, their present disposition is at least approved of, and is perhaps suf-

ficient to compensate the other, at least to maintain them in
some degree of esteem with their friend.   A numerous and
artful clergy had, in those times of superstition, insinuated
themselves into the confidence of almost every private family.   They possessed all the little learning which the
times could afford, and their manners, though in many respects rude and disorderly, were polished and regular
compared with those of the age they lived in.   They were
regarded, therefore, not only as the great directors of all
religious, but of all moral duties.   Their familiarity gave
reputation to whoever was so happy as to possess it; and
every mark of their disapprobation stamped the deepest
ignominy upon all who had the misfortune to fall under it.
Being considered as the great judges of right and wrong,
they were naturally consulted about all scruples that occurred; and it was reputable for any person to have it
known that he made those holy men the confidants of all
such secrets, and took no important or delicate step in his
conduct without their advice and approbation.   It was not
difficult for the clergy, therefore, to get it established as a
general rule, that they should be intrusted with what it had
already become fashionable to intrust them, and with what
they generally would have been intrusted, though no such
rule had been established.   To qualify themselves for con-
fessors became thus a necessary part of the study of church-
men and divines, and they were thence led to collect what
are called cases of conscience, nice and delicate situations,
in which it is hard to determine whereabouts the propriety
of conduct may lie.   Such works, they imagined, might
be of use both to the directors of consciences and to those
who were to be directed; and hence the origin of books of
casuistry.

The moral duties which fell under the consideration of
the casuists were chiefly those which can, in some measure at
least, be circumscribed within general rules, and of which

the violation is naturally attended with some degree of re- morse and some dread of suffering punishment. The de- sign of that institution which gave occasion to their works was to appease those terrors of conscience which attend upon the infringement of such duties. But it is not every virtue of which the defect is accompanied with any very severe compunctions of this kind; and no man applies to his confessor for absolution, because he did not perform the most generous, the most friendly, or the most magnanimous action which, in his circumstances, it was possible to per- form. In failures of this kind, the rule that is violated is commonly not very determinate, and is generally of such a nature too, that though the observance of it might entitle to honour and reward, the violation seems to expose to no positive blame, censure, or punishment. The exercise of such virtues the casuists seem to have regarded as a sort of work of supererogation, which could not be very strictly exacted, and which it was, therefore, unnecessary for them to treat of.

The breaches of moral duty, therefore, which came be- fore the tribunal of the confessor, and, upon that account, fell under the cognizance of the casuists, were chiefly of three different kinds.

First, and principally, breaches of the rules of justice. The rules here are all express and positive; and the vio- lation of them is naturally attended with the consciousness of deserving, and the dread of suffering, punishment both from God and man.

Secondly, breaches of the rules of chastity. These, in all grosser instances, are real breaches of the rules of jus- tice, and no person can be guilty of them without doing the most unpardonable injury to some other. In smaller instances, when they amount only to a violation of those

exact decorums which ought to be observed in the conversation of the two sexes, they cannot, indeed, justly be considered as violations of the rules of justice. They are
generally, however, violations of a pretty plain rule, and, at
least in one of the sexes, tend to bring ignominy upon the
person who has been guilty of them, and, consequently, to
be attended in the scrupulous with some degree of shame
and contrition of mind.

Thirdly, breaches of the rules of veracity. The violation
of truth, it is to be observed, is not always a breach of justice, though it is so upon many occasions, and, consequently, cannot always expose to any external punishment. The
vice of common lying, though a most miserable meanness,
may frequently do hurt to nobody ; and, in this case, no
claim of vengeance or satisfaction can be due either to the
persons imposed upon, or to others. But though the violation of truth is not always a breach of justice, it is always
a breach of a very plain rule, and what naturally tends to
cover with shame the person who has been guilty of it.

There seems to be in young children an instinctive disposition to believe whatever they are told. Nature seems
to have judged it necessary for their preservation that they
should, for some time at least, put implicit confidence in
those to whom the care of their childhood, and of the earliest and most necessary parts of their education, is intrusted. Their credulity, accordingly, is excessive ; and it requires long and much experience of the falsehood of mankind to reduce them to a reasonable degree of diffidence and
distrust. In grown-up people the degrees of credulity are,
no doubt, very different. The wisest and most experienced
are generally the least credulous. But the man scarce lives
who is not more credulous than he ought to be, and who
does not, upon many occasions, give credit to tales which
not only turn out to be perfectly false, but which a very

moderate degree of reflection and attention might have taught him could not well be true. The natural disposition is always to believe. It is acquired wisdom and experience only that teach incredulity, and they very seldom teach it enough. The wisest and most cautious of us all frequently gives credit to stories which he himself is afterwards both ashamed and astonished that he could possibly think of believing.

The man whom we believe is necessarily, in the things concerning which we believe him, our leader and director, and we look up to him with a certain degree of esteem and respect. But as from admiring other people we come to wish to be admired ourselves, so, from being led and directed by other people, we learn to wish to become ourselves leaders and directors. And as we cannot always be satisfied merely with being admired, unless we can, at the same time, persuade ourselves that we are in some degree really worthy of admiration; so we cannot always be satisfied merely with being believed, unless we are, at the same time, conscious that we are really worthy of belief. As the desire of praise and that of praiseworthiness, though very much akin, are yet distinct and separate desires; so the desire of being believed and that of being worthy of belief, though very much akin too, are equally distinct and separate desires.

The desire of being believed, the desire of persuading, of leading, and directing other people, seems to be one of the strongest of all our natural desires. It is perhaps the instinct upon which is founded the faculty of speech, the characteristical faculty of human nature. No other animal possesses this faculty, and we cannot discover in any other animal any desire to lead and direct the judgment and conduct of its fellows. Great ambition, the desire of real superiority, of leading and directing, seems to be altogether

peculiar to man, and speech is the great instrument of ambition, of real superiority, of leading and directing the
judgments and conduct of other people.

It is always mortifying not to be believed, and it is doubly
so when we suspect that it is because we are supposed to be
unworthy of belief, and capable of seriously and wilfully
deceiving.   To tell a man that he lies, is of all affronts the
most mortal.   But whoever seriously and wilfully deceives,
is necessarily conscious to himself that he merits this affront,
that he does not deserve to be believed, and that he forfeits
all title to that sort of credit from which alone he can derive any sort of ease, comfort, or satisfaction, in the society
of his equals.   The man who had the misfortune to imagine
that nobody believed a single word he said, would feel himself the outcast of human society, would dread the very
thought of going into it, or of presenting himself before it,
and could scarce fail, I think, to die of despair.   It is probable, however, that no man ever had just reason to entertain this humiliating opinion of himself.   The most noto-
rious liar, I am disposed to believe, tells the fair truth at
least twenty times for once that he seriously and deliberately lies ; and, as in the most cautious the disposition to believe is apt to prevail over that to doubt and distrust, so in
those who are the most regardless of truth the natural disposition to tell it prevails, upon most occasions, over that
to deceive, or in any respect to alter or disguise it.

We are mortified when we happen to deceive other people,
though unintentionally, and from having been ourselves deceived.   Though this involuntary falsehood may frequently
be no mark of any want of veracity, of any want of the most
perfect love of truth, it is always, in some degree, a mark
of want of judgment, of want of memory, of improper credulity, of some degree of precipitancy and rashness.   It
always diminishes our authority to persuade, and always

brings some degree of suspicion upon our fitness to lead and direct. The man who sometimes misleads from mistake, however, is widely different from him who is capable of wilfully deceiving. The former may safely be trusted upon many occasions ; the latter very seldom upon any.

Frankness and openness conciliate confidence. We trust the man who seems willing to trust us. We see clearly, we think, the road by which he means to conduct us, and we abandon ourselves with pleasure to his guidance and direction. Reserve and concealment, on the contrary, call forth diffidence. We are afraid to follow the man who is going we do not know where. The great pleasure of conversation and society, besides, arises from a certain correspondence of sentiments and opinions, from a certain harmony of minds, which, like so many musical instruments, coincide and keep time with another. But this most delightful harmony cannot be obtained unless there is a free communication of sentiments and opinions. We all desire, upon this account, to feel how each other is affected, to penetrate into each other's bosoms, and to observe the sentiments and affections which really subsist there. The man who indulges us in this natural passion, who invites us into his heart, who, as it were, sets open the gates of his breast to us, seems to exercise a species of hospitality more delightful than any other. No man, who is in ordinary good temper, can fail of pleasing, if he has the courage to utter his real sentiments as he feels them, and because he feels them. It is this unreserved sincerity which renders even the prattle of a child agreeable. How weak and imperfect soever the views of the open-hearted, we take pleasure to enter into them, and endeavour, as much as we can, to bring down our own understanding to the level of their capacities, and to regard every subject in the particular light in which they appear to have considered it. This passion to discover the real sentiments of others is naturally so strong, that it often degenerates into a troublesome and impertinent curiosity to pry into those secrets of our neighbours which they have very justifiable reasons for concealing ; and upon many occasions it requires prudence and a strong sense of propriety to govern this, as well as all the other passions of human nature, and to reduce it to that pitch which any impartial spectator can approve of. To disappoint this curiosity, however, when it is kept within proper bounds, and aims at nothing which there can be any just reason for concealing, is equally disagreeable in its turn. The man who eludes our most innocent questions, who gives no satisfaction to our most inoffensive inquiries, who plainly wraps himself up in impenetrable obscurity, seems, as it were, to build a wall about his breast. We run forward to get within it with all the eagerness of harmless curiosity, and feel ourselves all at once pushed back with the rudest and most offensive violence.

The man of reserve and concealment, though seldom a very amiable character, is not disrespected or despised. He seems to feel coldly towards us, and we feel as coldly towards him : he is not much praised or beloved, but he is as little hated or blamed. He very seldom, however, has occasion to repent of his caution, and is generally disposed rather to value himself upon the prudence of his reserve. Though his conduct, therefore, may have been very faulty, and sometimes even hurtful, he can very seldom be disposed to lay his case before the casuists, or to fancy that he has any occasion for their acquittal or approbation.

It is not always so with the man who, from false information, from inadvertency, from precipitancy and rashness, has involuntarily deceived. Though it should be in a matter of little consequence, in telling a piece of common news, for example, if he is a real lover of truth, he is ashamed of his own carelessness, and never fails to embrace the first opportunity of making the fullest acknowledgments. If it is in a matter of some consequence, his contrition is still greater; and if any unlucky or fatal consequence has followed from his misinformation, he can scarce ever forgive himself. Though not guilty, he feels himself to be in the highest degree what the ancients called piacular, and is anxious and eager to make every sort of atonement in his power. Such a person might frequently be disposed to lay his case before the casuists, who have in general been very favourable to him, and though they have sometimes justly condemned him for rashness, they have universally acquitted him of the ignominy of falsehood.

But the man who had the most frequent occasion to consult them was the man of equivocation and mental reservation, the man who seriously and deliberately meant to deceive, but who, at the same time, wished to flatter himself that he had really told the truth. With him they have dealt variously. When they approved very much of the motives of his deceit, they have sometimes acquitted him, though, to do them justice, they have in general, and much more frequently, condemned him.

The chief sub ects of the works of the casuists, therefore, were the conscientious regard that is due to the rules of justice; how far we ought to respect the life and property of our neighbour; the duty of restitution; the laws of chastity and modesty, and wherein consisted what in their language are called the sins of concupiscence; the rules of veracity, and the obligation of oaths, promises, and contracts of all kinds.

It may be said in general of the works of the casuists, that they attempted, to no purpose, to direct, by precise rules, what it belongs to feeling and sentiment only to judge of. How is it possible to ascertain by rules the exact point at which, in every case, a delicate sense of justice begins to run into a frivolous and weak scrupulosity of conscience? When it is that secrecy and reserve begin to grow into dissimulation? How far an agreeable irony may be carried, and at what precise point it begins to degenerate into a detestable lie? What is the highest pitch of freedom and ease of behaviour which can be regarded as graceful and becoming, and when it is that it first begins to run into a negligent and thoughtless licentiousness? With regard to all such matters, what would hold good in any one case would scarce do so exactly in any other, and what constitutes the propriety and happiness of behaviour varies in every case with the smallest variety of situation. Books of casuistry, therefore, are generally as useless as they are commonly tiresome. They could be of little use to one who should consult them upon occasion, even supposing their decisions to be just; because, notwithstanding the multitude of cases collected in them, yet, upon account of the still greater variety of possible circumstances, it is a chance if, among all those cases, there be found one exactly parallel to that under consideration. One who is really anxious to do his duty, must be very weak if he can imagine that he has much occasion for them; and with regard to one who is negligent of it, the style of those writings is not such as is likely to awaken him to more attention. None of them tend to animate us to what is generous and noble. None of them tend to soften us to what is gentle and humane. Many of them, on the contrary, tend rather to teach us to chicane with our own consciences, and, by their vain subtilties, serve to authorize innumerable evasive refinements with regard to the most essential articles of our duty. That frivolous accuracy which they attempted to introduce into subjects which do not admit of it, almost necessarily betrayed them into those dangerous errors, and at the same time rendered their works dry and disagreeable, abounding in abstruse and metaphysical distinctions, but incapable of exciting in the heart any of those emotions which it is the principal use of books of morality to excite.

The two useful parts of moral philosophy, therefore, are Ethics and Jurisprudence. Casuistry ought to be rejected altogether; and the ancient moralists appear to have judged much better, who, in treating of the same subjects, did not affect any such nice exactness, but contented themselves with describing, in a general manner, what is the sentiment upon which justice, modesty, and veracity, are founded, and what is the ordinary way of acting to which those virtues would commonly prompt us.

Something, indeed, not unlike the doctrine of the casuists, seems to have been attempted by several philosophers. There is something of this kind in the third book of Cicero's Offices, where he endeavours, like a casuist, to give rules for our conduct in many nice cases, in which it is difficult to determine whereabouts the point of propriety may lie. It appears, too, from many passages in the same book, that several other philosophers had attempted something of the same kind before him. Neither he nor they, however, appear to have aimed at giving a complete system of this sort, but only meant to shew how situations may occur, in which it is doubtful whether the highest propriety of conduct consists in observing or in receding from what, in ordinary cases, are the rules of duty.

Every system of positive law may be regarded as a more or less imperfect attempt towards a system of natural jurisprudence, or towards an enumeration of the particular rules of justice. As the violation of justice is what men will never submit to from one another, the public magistrate is under a necessity of employing the power of the commonwealth to enforce the practice of this virtue. Without this precaution, civil society would become a scene of bloodshed and disorder, every man revenging himself at his own hand whenever he fancied he was injured. To prevent the confusion which would attend upon every man's doing justice to himself, the magistrate, in all governments that have acquired any considerable authority, undertakes to do justice to all, and promises to hear and to redress every complaint of injury. In all well-governed states too, not only judges are appointed for determining the controversies of individuals, but rules are prescribed for regulating the decisions of those judges ; and these rules are, in general, intended to coincide with those of natural justice. It does not, indeed, always happen that they do so in every instance. Sometimes what is called the constitution of the state, that is, the interest of the government; sometimes the interest of particular orders of men who tyrannize the government, warp the positive laws of the country from what natural justice would prescribe. In some countries, the rudeness and barbarism of the people hinder the natural sentiments of justice from arriving at that accuracy and precision which, in more civilized nations, they naturally attain to. Their laws are, like their manners, gross, and rude, and undistinguishing. In other countries, the unfortunate constitution of their courts of judicature hinders any regular system of jurisprudence from ever establishing itself among them, though the improved manners of the people may be such as would admit of the most accurate. In no country do the decisions of positive law coincide exactly, in every case, with the rules which the natural sense of justice would dictate. Systems of positive law, therefore, though they deserve the greatest authority, as the records of the sentiments of mankind in different ages and nations, yet can never be regarded as accurate systems of the rules of natural justice.

It might have been expected that the reasonings of lawyers, upon the different imperfections and improvements of the laws of different countries, should have given occasion to an inquiry into what were the natural rules of justice, independent of all positive institution. It might have been expected that these reasonings should have led them to aim

at establishing a system of what might properly be called
natural jurisprudence, or a theory of the general principles
which ought to run through, and be the foundation of, the
laws of all nations. But though the reasonings of lawyers
did produce something of this kind, and though no man has
treated systematically of the laws of any particular country,
without intermixing in his work many observations of this
sort, it was very late in the world before any such general
system was thought of, or before the philosophy of law was
treated of by itself, and without regard to the particular
institutions of any one nation. In none of the ancient
moralists do we find any attempt towards a particular
enumeration of the rules of justice. Cicero in his Offices,
and Aristotle in his Ethics, treat of justice in the same general manner in which they treat of all the other virtues. In
the laws of Cicero and Plato, where we might naturally have
expected some attempts towards an enumeration of those
rules of natural equity which ought to be enforced by the
positive laws of every country, there is, however, nothing
of this kind. Their laws are laws of police, not of justice.
Grotius seems to have been the first who attempted to give
the world any thing like a system of those principles which
ought to run through, and be the foundation of, the laws of
all nations ; and his treatise of the laws of war and peace,
with all its imperfections, is perhaps at this day the most
complete work that has yet been given upon this subject. I
shall, in another discourse, endeavour to give an account of
the general principles of law and government, and of the
different revolutions they have undergone in the different
ages and periods of society, not only in what concerns justice, but in what concerns police, revenue, and arms, and
whatever else is the object of law. I shall not, therefore, at
present enter into any farther detail concerning the history
of jurisprudence.

CONSIDERATIONS

CONCERNING THE

FIRST FORMATION OF LANGUAGES,

AND THE

DIFFERENT GENIUS OF ORIGINAL AND COMPOUNDED LANGUAGES.

CONSIDERATIONS

CONCERNING THE

FIRST FORMATION OF LANGUAGES. &c.

THE assignation of particular names, to denote particular objects, that is, the institution of nouns substantive, would, probably, be one of the first steps towards the formation of language. Two savages, who had never been taught to speak, but had been bred up remote from the societies of men, would naturally begin to form that language by which they would endeavour to make their mutual wants intelligible to each other, by uttering certain sounds, whenever they meant to denote certain objects. Those objects only which were most familiar to them, and which they had most frequent occasion to mention, would have particular names assigned to them. The particular cave whose covering sheltered them from the weather, the particular tree whose fruit relieved their hunger, the particular fountain whose water allayed their thirst, would first be denominated by the words *cave, tree, fountain,* or by whatever other appellations they might think proper, in that primitive jargon, to mark them. Afterwards, when the more enlarged experience of these savages had led them to observe, and their necessary occasions obliged them to make mention of other caves, and other trees, and other fountains, they would naturally bestow, upon each of those new objects, the same name by which they had been accustomed to express the similar object they were first acquainted with. The new objects had none of them any name of its own, but each of them ex-

actly resembled another object, which had such an appellation. It was impossible that those savages could behold
the new objects, without recollecting the old ones; and the
name of the old ones, to which the new bore so close a resemblance. When they had occasion, therefore, to mention,
or to point out to each other, any of the new objects, they
would naturally utter the name of the correspondent old
one, of which the idea could not fail, at that instant, to present itself to their memory in the strongest and liveliest
manner. And thus those words, which were originally the
proper names of individuals, would each of them insensibly
become the common name of a multitude. A child that is
just learning to speak, calls every person who comes to the
house its papa, or its mamma; and thus bestows upon the
whole species those names which it had been taught to apply to two individuals. I have known a clown, who did
not know the proper name of the river which ran by his own
door. It was *the river*, he said, and he never heard any
other name for it. His experience, it seems, had not led
him to observe any other river. The general word *river*,
therefore, was, it is evident, in his acceptance of it, a proper name signifying an individual object. If this person
had been carried to another river, would he not readily have
called it a river? Could we suppose any person living on
the banks of the Thames so ignorant as not to know the
general word *river*, but to be acquainted only with the particular word *Thames*, if he was brought to any other river,
would he not readily call it *a Thames?* This, in reality, is
no more than what they, who are well acquainted with the
general word, are very apt to do. An Englishman, describing any great river which he may have seen in some foreign
country, naturally says, that it is another Thames. The
Spaniards, when they first arrived upon the coast of Mexico,
and observed the wealth, populousness, and habitations of
that fine country, so much superior to the savage nations
which they had been visiting for some time before, cried out

that it was another Spain. Hence it was called New Spain; and this name has stuck to that unfortunate country ever since. We say, in the same manner, of a hero, that he is an Alexander; of an orator, that he is a Cicero, of a philosopher, that he is a Newton. This way of speaking, which the grammarians call an antonomasia, and which is still extremely common, though now not at all necessary, demonstrates how much all mankind are naturally disposed to give to one object the name of any other, which nearly resembles it, and thus to denominate a multitude, by what originally was intended to express an individual.

It is this application of the name of an individual to a great multitude of objects, whose resemblance naturally recalls the idea of that individual, and of the name which expresses it, that seems originally to have given occasion to the formation of those classes and assortments, which, in the schools, are called genera and species, and of which the ingenious and eloquent M. Rousseau, of Geneva,* finds himself so much at a loss to account for the origin. What constitutes a species is merely a number of objects, bearing a certain degree of resemblance to one another, and, on that account, denominated by a single appellation, which may be applied to express any one of them.

When the greater part of objects had thus been arranged under their proper classes and assortments, distinguished by such general names, it was impossible that the greater part of that almost infinite number of individuals, comprehended under each particular assortment or species, could have any peculiar or proper names of their own, distinct from the general name of the species. When there was occasion, therefore, to mention any particular object, it often became

---

* Origine de l'Inegalité. Partie premiere, p. 376, 377. Edition d'Amsterdam des Oeuvres diverses de J. J. Rousseau.

necessary to distinguish it from the other objects comprehended under the same general name, either, first, by its peculiar qualities ; or, secondly, by the peculiar relation which it stood in to some other things. Hence the necessary origin of two other sets of words, of which the one should express quality ; the other, relation.

Nouns adjective are the words which express quality considered as qualifying, or, as the schoolmen say, in concrete with, some particular subject. Thus the word *green* expresses a certain quality considered as qualifying, or as in concrete with, the particular subject to which it may be applied. Words of this kind, it is evident, may serve to distinguish particular objects from others comprehended under the same general appellation. The words *green tree,* for example, might serve to distinguish a particular tree from others that were withered or blasted.

Prepositions are the words which express relation considered, in the same manner, in concrete with the correlative object. Thus the prepositions, *of, to, for, with, by, above, below,* &c. denote some relation subsisting between the objects expressed by the words between which the prepositions are placed ; and they denote that this relation is considered in concrete with the correlative object. Words of this kind serve to distinguish particular objects from others of the same species, when those particular objects cannot be so properly marked out by any peculiar qualities of their own. When we say, *the green tree of the meadow,* for example, we distinguish a particular tree, not only by the quality which belongs to it, but by the relation which it stands in to another object.

As neither quality nor relation can exist in abstract, it is natural to suppose that the words which denote them considered in concrete, the way in which we always see them subsist, would be of much earlier invention than those which express them considered in abstract, the way in which we never see them subsist. The words *green* and *blue* would, in all probability, be sooner invented than the words *greenness* and *blueness ;* the words *above* and *below*, than the words *superiority* and *inferiority*. To invent words of the latter kind requires a much greater effort of abstraction than to invent those of the former. It is probable, therefore, that such abstract terms would be of much later institution. Accordingly, their etymologies generally shew that they are so, they being generally derived from others that are concrete.

But though the invention of nouns adjective be much more natural than that of the abstract nouns substantive derived from them, it would still, however, require a considerable degree of abstraction and generalization. Those, for example, who first invented the words *green, blue, red,* and the other names of colours, must have observed and compared together a great number of objects, must have remarked their resemblances and dissimilitudes in respect of the quality of colour, and must have arranged them, in their own minds, into different classes and assortments, according to those resemblances and dissimilitudes. An adjective is by nature a general, and, in some measure, an abstract word, and necessarily presupposes the idea of a certain species or assortment of things, to all of which it is equally applicable. The word *green* could not, as we were supposing might be the case of the word *cave*, have been originally the name of an individual, and afterwards have become, by what grammarians call an antonomasia, the name of a species. The word *green* denoting, not the name of a substance, but the peculiar quality of a substance, must, from the very first, have been a general word, and considered as equally applicable to any other substance possessed of the same quality. The man who first distinguished a particular object by the epithet of *green*, must have observed other objects that were not *green*, from which he meant to separate it by this appellation. The institution of this name, therefore, supposes comparison. It likewise supposes some degree of abstraction. The person who first invented this appellation must have distinguished the quality from the object to which it belonged, and must have conceived the object as capable of subsisting without the quality. The invention, therefore, even of the simplest nouns adjective must have required more metaphysics than we are apt to be aware of. The different mental operations, of arrangement or classing, of comparison, and of abstraction, must all have been employed, before even the names of the different colours, the least metaphysical of all nouns adjective, could be instituted. From all which I infer, that when languages were beginning to be formed, nouns adjective would by no means be the words of the earliest invention.

There is another expedient for denoting the different qualities of different substances, which, as it requires no abstraction, nor any conceived separation of the quality from the subject, seems more natural than the invention of nouns adjective, and which, upon this account, could hardly fail, in the first formation of language, to be thought of before them. This expedient is to make some variation upon the noun substantive itself, according to the different qualities which it is endowed with. Thus, in many languages, the qualities both of sex and the want of sex are expressed by different terminations in the nouns substantive, which denote objects so qualified. In Latin, for example, *lupus*, *lupa ; equus, equa ; juvencus, juvenca ; Julius, Julia ; Lucretius, Lucretia*, &c., denote the qualities of male and female in the animals and persons to whom such appellations belong, without needing the addition of any adjective for this purpose. On the other hand, the words *forum*, *pratum*, *plaustrum*, denote, by their peculiar termination, the total absence of sex in the different substances which they stand for. Both sex and the want of all sex being naturally con· sidered as qualities modifying and inseparable from the particular substances to which they belong, it was natural to express them rather by a modification in the noun substantive than by any general and abstract word expressive of this particular species of quality. The expression bears, it is evident, in this way, a much more exact analogy to the idea or object which it denotes than in the other. The quality appears in nature as a modification of the substance, and as it is thus expressed in language by a modification of the noun substantive which denotes that substance, the quality and the subject are in this case blended together, if I may say so, in the expression, in the same manner as they appear to be in the object and in the idea. Hence the origin of the masculine, feminine, and neutral genders, in all the ancient languages. By means of these, the most important of all distinctions, that of substances into animated and inanimated, and that of animals into male and female, seem to have been sufficiently marked without the assist· ance of adjectives, or of any general names denoting this most extensive species of qualifications.

There are no more than these three genders in any of the languages with which I am acquainted; that is to say, the formation of nouns substantive can, by itself, and without the accompaniment of adjectives, express no other qualities but those three above mentioned—the qualities of male, of female, of neither male nor female. I should not, however, oe surprised if, in other languages with which I am unac quainted, the different formations of nouns substantive should be capable of expressing many other different quali· ties. The different diminutives of the Italian, and of some other languages, do in reality sometimes express a great variety of different modifications in the substances denoted by those nouns which undergo such variations.

It was impossible, however, that nouns substantive could, without losing altogether their original form, undergo so great a number of variations as would be sufficient to ex press that almost infinite variety of qualities by which it might, upon different occasions, be necessary to specify and distinguish them. Though the different formation of nouns substantive, therefore, might for some time forestall the necessity of inventing nouns adjective, it was impossible that this necessity could be forestalled altogether. When nouns adjective came to be invented, it was natural that they should be formed with some similarity to the substantives to which they were to serve as epithets or qualifications. Men would naturally give them the same terminations with the substantives to which they were first applied, and from that love of similarity of sound, from that delight in the returns of the same syllables, which is the foundation of analogy in all languages, they would be apt to vary the termination of the same adjective according as they had occasion to apply it to a masculine, to a feminine, or to a neutral substantive. They would say, *magnus lupus*, *magna lupa*, *magnum pratum*, when they meant to express a great *he-wolf*, a great *she-wolf*, a great *meadow*.

This variation in the termination of the noun adjective according to the gender of the substantive, which takes place in all the ancient languages, seems to have been introduced chiefly for the sake of a certain similarity of sound, of a certain species of rhyme, which is naturally so very agreeable to the human ear. Gender, it is to be observed, cannot properly belong to a noun adjective, the signification of which is always precisely the same, to whatever species of substantives it is applied When we say, *a great man, a great woman*, the word *great* has precisely the same meaning in both cases, and the difference of the sex in the subjects to which it may be applied makes no sort of difference in its signification. *Magnus, magna, magnum,* in the same manner, are words which express precisely the same quality, and the change of the termination is accompanied with no sort of variation in the meaning. Sex and gender are qualities which belong to substances, but cannot belong to the qualities of substances. In general, no quality, when considered in concrete, or as qualifying some particular subject, can itself be conceived as the subject of any other quality; though, when considered in abstract, it may. No adjective, therefore, can qualify any other adjective. A *great good man,* means a man who is both *great* and *good.* Both the adjectives qualify the substantive; they do not qualify one another. On the other hand, when we say, the *great goodness* of the man, the word *goodness* denoting a quality considered in abstract, which may itself be the subject of other qualities, is, upon that account, capable of being qualified by the word *great.*

If the original invention of nouns adjective would be attended with so much difficulty, that of prepositions would be accompanied with yet more. Every preposition, as I have already observed, denotes some relation considered in concrete with the correlative object. The preposition *above,* for example, denotes the relation of superiority, not in abstract, as it is expressed by the word *superiority,* but in concrete with some correlative object. In this phrase, for example, *the tree above the cave,* the word *above* expresses a certain relation between the *tree* and the *cave,* and it expresses this relation in concrete with the correlative object, *the cave.* A preposition always requires, in order to complete the sense, some other word to come after it; as may be observed in this particular instance. Now, I say, the original invention of such words would require a yet greater effort of abstraction and generalization than that of nouns adjective. First of all, a relation is in itself a more metaphysical object than a quality. Nobody can be at a loss to explain what is meant by a quality; but few people will find themselves able to express, very distinctly, what is understood by a relation. Qualities are almost always the objects of our external senses; relations never are. No wonder, therefore, that the one set of objects should be so much more comprehensible than the other. Secondly, though prepositions always express the relation which they stand for, in concrete with the correlative object, they could not have originally been formed without a considerable effort of abstraction. A preposition denotes a relation, and nothing but a relation. But before men could institute a word which signified a relation, and nothing but a relation, they must have been able, in some measure, to consider this relation abstractedly from the related objects; since the idea of those objects does not, in any respect, enter into the signification of the preposition. The invention of such a word, therefore, must have required a considerable degree of abstraction. Thirdly, a preposition is, from its nature, a general word, which, from its very first institution, must have been considered as equally applicable to denote any other similar relation. The man who first invented the word *above*, must not only have distinguished, in some measure, the relation of *superiority* from the objects which were so related, but he must also have distinguished this relation from other relations, such as, from the relation of *inferiority* denoted by the word *below*, from the relation of *juxtaposition*, expressed by the word *beside*, and the like. He must have conceived this word, therefore, as expressive of a particular sort or species of relation distinct from every other, which could not be done without a considerable effort of comparison and generalization.

Whatever were the difficulties, therefore which embarrassed the first invention of nouns adjective, the same, and many more, must have embarrassed that of prepositions. If mankind, therefore, in the first formation of languages, seem to have for some time evaded the necessity of nouns adjective, by varying the termination of the names of substances, according as these varied in some of their most important qualities, they would much more find themselves under the necessity of evading, by some similar contrivance, the yet more difficult invention of prepositions. The different cases in the ancient languages is a contrivance of precisely the same kind. The genitive and dative cases, in Greek and Latin, evidently supply the place of the prepositions ; and by a variation in the noun substantive, which stands for the correlative term, express the relation which subsists between what is denoted by that noun substantive, and what is expressed by some other word in the sentence. In these expressions, for example, *fructus arboris, the fruit of the tree ; sacer Herculi, sacred to Hercules ;* the variations made in the correlative words, *arbor* and *Hercules,* express the same relations which are expressed in English by the prepositions *of* and *to.*

To express a relation in this manner, did not require any effort of abstraction. It was not here expressed by a peculiar word denoting relation, and nothing but relation, but by a variation upon the correlative term. It was expressed here, as it appears in nature, not as something separated and detached, but as thoroughly mixed and blended with the correlative object.

To express relation in this manner, did not require any effort of generalization. The words *aboris* and *Herculi,* while they involve in their signification the same relation expressed by the English prepositions *of* and *to,* are not, like those prepositions, general words, which can be applied, to express the same relation between whatever other objects it might be observed to subsist.

To express relation in this manner did not require any effort of comparison. The words *arboris* and *Herculi* are not general words intended to denote a particular species of relations, which the inventors of those expressions meant, in consequence of some sort of comparison, to separate and distinguish from every other sort of relation. The example, indeed, of this contrivance would soon probably be followed, and whoever had occasion to express a similar relation between any other objects, would be very apt to do it by making a similar variation on the name of the correlative object. This, I say, would probably, or rather certainly happen; but it would happen without any intention or fore-sight in those who first set the example, and who never meant to establish any general rule. The general rule would establish itself insensibly, and by slow degrees, in consequence of that love of analogy and similarity of sound which is the foundation of by far the greater part of the rules of grammar.

To express relation, therefore, by a variation in the name of the correlative object, requiring neither abstraction nor generalization, nor comparison of any kind, would, at first, be much more natural and easy, than to express it by those general words called prepositions, of which the first inven-tion must have demanded some degree of all those opera-tions.

The number of cases is different in different languages. There are five in the Greek, six in the Latin, and there are said to be ten in the Armenian language. It must have naturally happened that there should be a greater or a smaller number of cases, according as in the terminations of nouns substantive the first formers of any language happened to have established a greater or a smaller number of variations, in order to express the different relations they had occasion to take notice of, before the invention of those more general and abstract prepositions which could supply their place.

It is, perhaps, worth while to observe, that those prepositions which, in modern languages, hold the place of the ancient cases, are, of all others, the most general, and abstract, and metaphysical; and, of consequence, would probably be the last invented. Ask any man of common acuteness, what relation is expressed by the preposition *above,* and he will readily answer, that of *superiority.* By the preposition *below,* and he will as quickly reply, that of *inferiority.* But ask him, what relation is expressed by the preposition *of,* and, if he has not before-hand employed his thoughts a good deal upon these subjects, you may safely allow him a week to consider of his answer. The prepositions *above* and *below* do not denote any of the relations expressed by the cases in the ancient languages. But the preposition *of* denotes the same relation which is in them expressed by the genitive case, and which it is easy to observe, is of a very metaphysical nature. The preposition *of* denotes relation in general, considered in concrete with the correlative object. It marks that the noun substantive which goes before it, is somehow or other related to that which comes after it, but without in any respect ascertaining, as is done by the preposition *above,* what is the peculiar nature of that relation. We often apply it, therefore, to express the most opposite relations, because the most opposite relations agree so far, that each of them comprehends in it the general idea or nature of a relation. We say, *the father of the son,* and *the son of the father; the fir-trees of the forest,* and the *forest of the fir-trees.* The relation in which the father stands to the son, is, it is evident, a quite opposite relation to that in which the son stands to the father; that in which the parts stand to the whole, is quite opposite to that in which the whole stands to the parts. The word *of*, however, serves very well to denote all those relations, because in itself it denotes no particular relation, but only relation in general; and so far as any particular relation is collected from such expressions, it is inferred by the mind, not from the preposition itself, but from the nature and arrangement of the substantives, between which the preposition is placed.

What I have said concerning the preposition *of*, may, in some measure, be applied to the prepositions *to, for, with, by*, and to whatever other prepositions are made use of in modern languages, to supply the place of the ancient cases. They all of them express very abstract and metaphysical relations, which any man who takes the trouble to try it will find it extremely difficult to express by nouns substantive, in the same manner as we may express the relation denoted by the preposition *above*, by the noun substantive *superiority*. They all of them, however, express some specific relation, and are, consequently, none of them so abstract as the preposition *of*, which may be regarded as by far the most metaphysical of all prepositions. The prepositions, therefore, which are capable of supplying the place of the ancient cases, being more abstract than the other prepositions, would naturally be of more difficult invention. The relations, at the same time, which those prepositions express, are, of all others, those which we have most frequent occasion to mention. The prepositions *above, below, near, within, without, against*, &c. are much more rarely made use of in modern languages than the prepositions *of, to, for, with, from, by*. A preposition of the former kind will not occur twice in a page; we can scarce compose a single sentence without the assistance of one or two of the latter. If these latter prepositions, therefore, which supply the place of the cases, would be of such difficult invention, on account of their abstractedness, some expedient to supply their place must have been of indispensable necessity, on account of the frequent occasion which men have to take notice of the relations which they denote. But there is no expedient so obvious, as that of varying the termination of one of the principal words.

It is, perhaps, unnecessary to observe that there are some of the cases in the ancient languages, which, for particular reasons, cannot be represented by any prepositions. These are the nominative, accusative, and vocative cases. In those modern languages which do not admit of any such variety in the terminations of their nouns substantive, the correspondent relations are expressed by the place of the words, and by the order and construction of the sentence.

As men have frequently occasion to make mention of multitudes as well as of single objects, it became necessary that they should have some method of expressing number. Number may be expressed either by a particular word, expressing number in general, such as the words *many, more.* &c. or by some variation upon the words which express the things numbered. It is this last expedient which mankind would probably have recourse to in the infancy of language. Number, considered in general, without relation to any particular set of objects numbered, is one of the most abstract and metaphysical ideas which the mind of man is capable of forming; and, consequently, is not an idea which would readily occur to rude mortals who were just beginning to form a language. They would naturally, therefore, distinguish when they talked of a single, and when they talked of a multitude of objects, not by any metaphysical adjectives, such as the English *a, an, many,* but by a variation upon the termination of the word which signified the objects numbered. Hence the origin of the singular and plural numbers in all the ancient languages;

and the same distinction has likewise been retained in all the modern languages, at least in the greater part of words.

All primitive and uncompounded languages seem to have a dual as well as a plural number. This is the case of the Greek, and, I am told, of the Hebrew; of the Gothic, and of many other languages. In the rude beginnings of society, *one, two,* and *more,* might possibly be all the numeral distinctions which mankind would have any occasion to take notice of. These they would find it more natural to express, by a variation upon every particular noun substantive, than by such general and abstract words as *one, two, three, four,* &c. These words, though custom has rendered them familiar to us, express, perhaps, the most subtile and refined abstractions which the mind of man is capable of forming. Let any one consider within himself, for example, what he means by the word *three,* which signifies neither three shillings, nor three pence, nor three men, nor three horses, but three in general; and he will easily satisfy himself that a word, which denotes so very metaphysical an abstraction, could not be either a very obvious or a very early invention. I have read of some savage nations, whose language was capable of expressing no more than the three first numeral distinctions. But whether it expressed those distinctions by three general words, or by variations upon the nouns substantive, denoting the things numbered, I do not remember to have met with any thing which could determine.

As all the same relations which subsist between single may likewise subsist between numerous objects, it is evident there would be occasion for the same number of cases in the dual and in the plural, as in the singular number. Hence the intricacy and complexness of the declensions in all the ancient languages. In the Greek there are five cases in each of the three numbers, consequently fifteen in all.

As nouns adjective, in the ancient languages, varied their terminations according to the gender of the substantive to which they were applied, so did they likewise, according to the case and the number. Every noun adjective in the Greek language, therefore, having three genders, and three numbers, and five cases in each number, may be considered as having five-and-forty different variations. The first formers of language seem to have varied the termination of the adjective, according to the case and the number of the substantive, for the same reason which made them vary it according to the gender; the love of analogy, and of a certain regularity of sound. In the signification of adjectives, there is neither case nor number, and the meaning of such words is always precisely the same, notwithstanding all the variety of termination under which they appear. *Magnus vir, magni viri, magnorum virorum, a great man, of a great man, of great men;* in all these expressions the words *magnus, magni, magnorum,* as well as the word *great,* have precisely one and the same signification, though the substantives to which they are applied have not. The difference of termination in the noun adjective is accompanied with no sort of difference in the meaning. An adjective denotes the qualification of a noun substantive. But the different relations in which that noun substantive may occasionally stand, can make no sort of difference upon its qualification.

If the declensions of the ancient languages are so very complex, their conjugations are infinitely more so. And the complexness of the one is founded upon the same principle with that of the other, the difficulty of forming, in the beginnings of language, abstract and general terms.

Verbs must necessarily have been coëval with the very first attempts towards the formation of language. No affirmation can be expressed without the assistance of some verb. We never speak, but in order to express our opinion that something either is, or is not. But the word denoting this event, or this matter of fact, which is the subject of our affirmation, must always be a verb.

Impersonal verbs, which express in one word a complete event, which preserve in the expression that perfect simplicity and unity which there always is in the object and in the idea, and which suppose no abstraction or metaphysical division of the event into its several constitutent members of subject and attribute, would, in all probability, be the species of verbs first invented. The verbs *pluit, it rains ; ningit, it snows ; tonat, it thunders ; lucet, it is day ; turbatur, there is a confusion,* &c. each of them express a complete affirmation, the whole of an event, with that perfect simplicity and unity with which the mind conceives it in nature. On the contrary, the phrases, *Alexander ambulat, Alexander walks ; Petrus sedet, Peter sits*, divide the event, as it were, in two parts, the person or subject, and the attribute, or matter of fact, affirmed of that subject. But in nature, the idea or conception of Alexander walking, is as perfectly and completely one simple conception, as that of Alexander not walking. The division of this event, therefore, into two parts, is altogether artificial, and is the effect of the imperfection of language, which, upon this, as upon many other occasions, supplies, by a number of words, the want of one, which could express at once the whole matter of fact that was meant to be affirmed. Every body must observe how much more simplicity there is in the natural expression, *pluit,* than in the more artificial expressions, *imber decidit, the rain falls ;* or *tempestas est pluvia, the weather is rainy.* In these two last expressions, the simple event, or matter of fact, is artificially split and divided, in the one, into two; in the other, into three parts. In each of them it is expressed by a sort of grammatical circumlocu- tion, of which the significancy is founded upon a certain metaphysical analysis of the component parts of the idea expressed by the word *pluit*. The first verbs, therefore, perhaps even the first words, made use of in the beginnings of language, would, in all probability, be such impersonal verbs. It is observed accordingly, I am told by the He- brew grammarians, that the radical words of their language, from which all the others are derived, are all of them verbs, and impersonal verbs.

It is easy to conceive how, in the progress of language, those impersonal verbs should become personal. Let us suppose, for example, that the word *venit, it comes,* was ori- ginally an impersonal verb, and that it denoted, not the coming of something in general, as at present, but the coming of a particular object, such as *the lion.* The first savage inventors of language, we shall suppose, when they observed the approach of this terrible animal, were accus- tomed to cry out to one another, *venit,* that is, *the lion comes ;* and that this word thus expressed a complete event, without the assistance of any other. Afterwards, when, on the further progress of language, they had begun to give names to particular substances, whenever they observed the approach of any other terrible object, they would naturally join the name of that object to the word *venit,* and cry out, *venit ursus, venit lupus.* By degrees the word *venit* would thus come to signify the coming of any terrible object, and not merely the coming of the lion. It would now, there- fore, express, not the coming of a particular object, but the coming of an object of a particular kind. Having become more general in its signification, it could no longer represent any particular distinct event by itself, and without the as- sistance of a noun substantive, which might serve to ascer-

tain and determine its signification. It would now, therefore, have become a personal, instead of an impersonal verb.
We may easily conceive how, in the further progress of
society, it might still grow more general in its signification,
and come to signify, as at present, the approach of any thing
whatever, whether good, bad, or indifferent.

It is probably in some such manner as this that almost
all verbs have become personal, and that mankind have
learned, by degrees, to split and divide almost every event
into a great number of metaphysical parts, expressed by the
different parts of speech, variously combined in the different
members of every phrase and sentence.* The same sort of
progress seems to have been made in the art of speaking
as in the art of writing. When mankind first began to attempt to express their ideas by writing, every character represented a whole word. But the number of words being
almost infinite, the memory found itself quite loaded and
oppressed by the multitude of characters which it was obliged to retain. Necessity taught them, therefore to divide
words into their elements, and to invent characters which
should represent, not the words themselves, but the elements
of which they are composed. In consequence of this invention, every particular word came to be represented, not
by one character, but by a multitude of characters ; and the
expression of it in writing became much more intricate and

* As the far greater part of verbs express, at present, not an event,
but the attribute of an event, and, consequently, require a subject, or
nominative case, to complete their signification, some grammarians, not
having attended to this progress of nature, and being desirous to make
their common rules quite universal, and without any exception, have insisted that all verbs required a nominative, either expressed or understood ; and have, accordingly, put themselves to the torture to find
some awkward nominatives to those few verbs, which, still expressing
a complete event, plainly admit of none. *Pluit*, for example, according
to *Sanctius*, means *pluvia pluit*, in English, *the rain rains*. See Sanctii
Minerva, l. iii. c. 1.

complex than before. But though particular words were thus represented by a greater number of characters, the whole language was expressed by a much smaller, and about four-and-twenty letters were found capable of supplying the place of that immense multitude of characters which were requisite before. In the same manner, in the beginnings of language, men seem to have attempted to express every particular event, which they had occasion to take notice of, by a particular word, which expressed at once the whole of that event. But as the number of words must, in this case, have become really infinite, in consequence of the really infinite variety of events, men found themselves partly compelled by necessity, and partly conducted by nature, to divide every event into what may be called its metaphysical elements, and to institute words, which should denote not so much the events, as the elements of which they were composed. The expression of every particular event became, in this manner, more intricate and complex, but the whole system of the language became more coherent, more connected, more easily retained and comprehended.

When verbs, from being originally impersonal, had thus, by the division of the event into its metaphysical elements, become personal, it is natural to suppose that they would first be made use of in the third person singular. No verb is ever used impersonally in our language, nor, so far as I know, in any other modern tongue. But in the ancient languages, whenever any verb is used impersonally, it is always in the third person singular. The termination of those verbs, which are still always impersonal, is constantly the same with that of the third person singular of personal verbs. The consideration of these circumstances, joined to the naturalness of the thing itself, may serve to convince us that verbs first became personal in what is now called the third person singular.

But as the event, or matter of fact which is expressed by a verb, may be affirmed either of the person who speaks, or of the person who is spoken to, as well as of some third person or object, it became necessary to fall upon some method of expressing these two peculiar relations of the event. In the English language this is commonly done by prefixing what are called the personal pronouns to the general word which expresses the event affirmed. *I came, you came, he or it came;* in these phrases the event of having come is, in the first, affirmed of the speaker; in the second, of the person spoken to; in the third, of some other person or object. The first formers of language, it may be imagined, might have done the same thing, and prefixing in the same manner the two first personal pronouns to the same termination of the verb which expressed the third person singular, might have said *ego venit, tu venit,* as well as *ille* or *illud venit.* And I make no doubt but they would have done so, if, at the time when they had first occasion to express these relations of the verb, there had been any such words as either *ego* or *tu* in their language. But in this early period of the language which we are now endeavouring to describe, it is extremely improbable that any such words would be known. Though custom has now rendered them familiar to us, they, both of them, express ideas extremely metaphysical and abstract. The word *I,* for example, is a word of a very particular species. Whatever speaks may denote itself by this personal pronoun. The word *I,* therefore, is a general word, capable of being predicated, as the logicians say, of an infinite variety of objects. It differs, however, from all other general words in this respect, that the objects of which it may be predicated, do not form any particular species of objects, distinguished from all others. The word *I,* does not, like the word *man,* denote a particular class of objects, separated from all others by peculiar qualities of their own. It is far from being the name of a species, but, on the contrary, whenever it is made use of, it always denotes a precise individual, the particular person who then speaks. It may be said to be, at once, both what the logicians call a singular, and what they call a common term, and to join in its signification the seemingly opposite qualities of the most precise individuality, and the most extensive generalization. This word, therefore, expressing so very abstract and metaphysical an idea, would not easily or readily occur to the first formers of language. What are called the personal pronouns, it may be observed, are among the last words of which children learn to make use. A child, speaking of itself, says, *Billy walks, Billy sits*, instead of *I walk, I sit.* As in the beginnings of language, therefore, mankind seem to have evaded the invention of at least the more abstract prepositions, and to have expressed the same relations which these *now* stand for, by varying the termination of the correlative term, so they likewise would naturally attempt to evade the necessity of inventing those more abstract pronouns, by varying the termination of the verb according as the event which it expressed was intended to be affirmed of the first, second, or third person. This seems, accordingly, to be the universal practice of all the ancient languages. In Latin, *veni, venisti, venit,* sufficiently denote, without any other addition, the different events expressed by the English phrases, *I came, you came, he* or *it came.* The verb would, for the same reason, vary its termination, according as the event was intended to be affirmed of the first, second, or third persons plural; and what is expressed by the English phrases, *we came, ye came, they came,* would be denoted by the Latin words, *venimus, venistis, venerunt.* Those primitive languages, too, which, upon account of the difficulty of inventing numeral names, had introduced a dual as well as a plural number into the declension of their nouns substantive, would probably, from analogy, do the same thing in the conjugations of their verbs. And thus, in all those original languages, we might expect to find at least six, if not eight or nine variations, in the termination of every verb, according as the event which it denoted was meant to be affirmed of the first, second, or third persons singular, dual, or plural. These variations again being repeated, along with others, through all its different tenses, through all its different modes, and through all its different voices, must necessarily have rendered their conjugations still more intricate and complex than their declensions.

Language would probably have continued upon this footing in all countries, nor would ever have grown more simple in its declensions aud conjugations, had it not become more complex in its composition, in consequence of the mixture of several languages with one another, occasioned by the mixture of different nations. As long as any language was spoken by those only who learned it in their infancy, the intricacy of its declensions and conjugations could occasion no great embarrassment. The far greater part of those who had occasion to speak it, had acquired it at so very early a period of their lives, so insensibly, and by such slow degrees, that they were scarce ever sensible of the difficulty. But when two nations came to be mixed with one another, either by conquest or migration, the case would be very different. Each nation, in order to make itself intelligible to those with whom it was under the necessity of conversing, would be obliged to learn the language of the other. The greater part of individuals too, learning the new language, not by art, or by remounting to its rudiments and first principles, but by rote, and by what they commonly heard in conversation, would be extremely perplexed by the intricacy of its declensions and conjugations. They would endeavour, therefore, to supply their ignorance of these, by whatever shift the language could afford them. Their ignorance of the declensions they would naturally supply by the use of prepositions; and a Lombard, who was attempting to speak Latin, and wanted to express that such a person was a citizen of Rome, or a benefactor to Rome, if he happened not to be acquainted with the genitive and dative cases of the word *Roma*, would naturally express himself by prefixing the prepositions *ad* and *de* to the nominative, and, instead of *Romæ*, would say, *ad Roma*, and *de Roma*. *Al Roma* and *di Roma*, accordingly, is the manner in which the present Italians, the descendants of the ancient Lombards and Romans, express this and all other similar relations. And in this manner prepositions seem to have been introduced in the room of the ancient declensions. The same alteration has, I am informed, been produced upon the Greek language, since the taking of Constantinople by the Turks. The words are, in a great measure, the same as before ; but the grammar is entirely lost, prepositions having come in the place of the old declensions. This change is undoubtedly a simplification of the language, in point of rudiments and principle. It introduces, instead of a great variety of declensions, one universal declension, which is the same in every word, of whatever gender, number, or termination.

A similar expedient enables men, in the situation above mentioned, to get rid of almost the whole intricacy of their conjugations. There is in every language a verb, known by the name of the substantive verb; in Latin, *sum ;* in English, *I am.* This verb denotes not the existence of any particular event, but existence in general. It is, upon this account, the most abstract and metapyhsical of all verbs ; and, consequently, could by no means be a word of early invention. When it came to be invented, however, as it had all the tenses and modes of any other verb, by being joined with the passive participle, it was capable of supplying the place of the whole passive voice, and of rendering this part of their conjugations as simple and uniform as the use of prepositions had rendered their declensions. A Lombard who wanted to say, *I am loved,* but could not recollect the word *amor,* naturally endeavoured to supply his ignorance by saying, *ego sum amatus. Io sono amato,* is at this day the Italian expression, which corresponds to the English phrase above mentioned.

There is another verb, which, in the same manner, runs through all languages, and which is distinguished by the name of the possessive verb ; in Latin, *habeo ;* in English, *I have.* This verb likewise denotes an event of an extremely abstract and metaphysical nature, and, consequently, cannot be supposed to have been a word of the earliest invention. When it came to be invented, however, by being applied to the passive participle, it was capable of supplying a great part of the active voice, as the substantive verb had supplied the whole of the passive. A Lombard who wanted to say, *I had loved,* but could not recollect the word *amaveram,* would endeavour to supply the place of it by saying either *ego habebam amatum,* or *ego habui amatum. Io aveva amato,* or *Io ebbi amato,* are the correspondent Italian expressions at this day. And thus, upon the intermixture of different nations with one another, the conjugations, by means of different auxiliary verbs, were made to approach towards the simplicity and uniformity of the declensions.

In general, it may be laid down for a maxim, that the more simple any language is in its composition, the more complex it must be in its declensions and conjugations ; and, on the contrary, the more simple it is in its declensions and conjugations, the more complex it must be in its composition.

The Greek seems to be, in a great measure, a simple, uncompounded language, formed from the primitive jargon of those wandering savages, the ancient Hellenians and Pelasgians, from whom the Greek nation is said to have been descended. All the words in the Greek language are derived from about three hundred primitives, a plain evidence that the Greeks formed their language almost entirely among themselves, and that when they had occasion for a new word, they were not accustomed, as we are, to borrow it from some foreign language, but to form it either by composition or derivation from some other word or words in their own. The declensions and conjugations, therefore, of the Greek, are much more complex than those of any other European language with which I am acquainted.

The Latin is a composition of the Greek and of the ancient Tuscan languages. Its declensions and conjugations, accordingly, are much less complex than those of the Greek; it has dropt the dual number in both. Its verbs have no optative mood distinguished by any peculiar termination. They have but one future. They have no aorist distinct from the preterite-perfect; they have no middle voice; and even many of their tenses in the passive voice are eked out, in the same manner as in the modern languages, by the help of the substantive verb joined to the passive participle. In both the voices, the number of infinitives and participles is much smaller in the Latin than in the Greek.

The French and Italian languages are each of them compounded, the one of the Latin, and the language of the ancient Franks, the other of the same Latin, and the language of the ancient Lombards. As they are both of them, therefore, more complex in their composition than the Latin, so are they likewise more simple in their declensions and conjugations. With regard to their declensions, they have both of them lost their cases altogether; and with regard to their conjugations, they have both of them lost the whole of the passive and some part of the active voices of their verbs. The want of the passive voice they supply entirely by the substantive verb joined to the passive participle ; and they make out part of the active in the same manner by the help of the possessive verb and the same passive participle.

The English is compounded of the French and the ancient Saxon languages. The French was introduced into Britain by the Norman conquest, and continued, till the time of Edward III., to be the sole language of the law, as well as the principal language of the court. The English, which came to be spoken afterwards, and which continues to be spoken now, is a mixture of the ancient Saxon and this Norman French. As the English language, therefore, is more complex in its composition than either the French or the Italian, so is it likewise more simple in its declensions and conjugations. Those two languages retain at least a part of the distinction of genders, and their adjectives vary their termination according as they are applied to a masculine or to a feminine substantive. But there is no such distinction in the English language, whose adjectives admit of no variety of termination. The French and Italian languages have both of them the remains of a conjugation ; and all those tenses of the active voice which cannot be expressed by the possessive verb joined to the passive participle, as well as many of those which can, are in those languages marked by varying the termination of the principal verb. But almost all those other tenses are in the English eked out by other auxiliary verbs, so that there is in this language scarce even the remains of a conjugation. *I love, I loved, loving,* are all the varieties of termination which the greater part of English verbs admit of. All the different modifications of meaning, which cannot be expressed by any of those three terminations, must be made out by different auxiliary verbs joined to some one or other of them. Two auxiliary verbs supply all the deficiencies of the French and Italian conjugations ; it requires more than half a dozen to supply those of the English, which, besides the substantive and possessive verbs, makes use of *do, did; will, would; shall, should; can, could; may, might.*

It is in this manner that language becomes more simple in its rudiments and principles, just in proportion as it grows more complex in its composition, and the same thing has happened in it which commonly happens with regard to mechanical engines. All machines are generally, when first invented, extremely complex in their principles, and there is often a particular principle of motion for every particular movement which it is intended they should perform. Succeeding improvers observe, that one principle may be so applied as to produce several of those movements ; and thus the machine becomes gradually more and more simple, and produces its effects with fewer wheels and fewer principles of motion. In language, in the same manner, every case of every noun, and every tense of every verb, was originally expressed by a particular distinct word, which served for this purpose and for no other. But succeeding observation discovered, that one set of words was capable of supplying the place of all that infinite number, and that four or five prepositions, and half a dozen auxiliary verbs, were capable of answering the end of all the declensions and of all the conjugations in the ancient languages.

But this simplification of languages, though it arises, perhaps, from similar causes, has, by no means, similar effects with the correspondent simplification of machines. The simplification of machines renders them more and more perfect, but this simplification of the rudiments of languages renders them more and more imperfect, and less proper for many of the purposes of language ; and this for the following reasons.

First of all : Languages are by this simplification rendered more prolix, several words having become necessary to express what could have been expressed by a single word before. Thus the words *Dei* and *Deo*, in the Latin, sufficiently shew, without any addition, what relation the object signified is understood to stand in to the objects expressed by the other words in the sentence. But to express the same relation in English, and in all other modern languages, we must make use of, at least, two words, and say, *of God*, *to God*. So far as the declensions are concerned, therefore, the modern languages are much more prolix than the ancient. The difference is still greater with regard to the conjugations. What a Roman expressed by the single word *amavissem*, an Englishman is obliged to express by four different words, *I should have loved*. It is unnecessary to take any pains to shew how much this prolixness must enervate the eloquence of all modern languages. How much the beauty of any expression depends upon its conciseness, is well known to those who have any experience in composition.

Secondly, This simplification of the principles of languages renders them less agreeable to the ear. The variety of termination in the Greek and Latin, occasioned by their declensions and conjugations, gives a sweetness to their language altogether unknown to ours, and a variety unknown to any other modern language. In point of sweetness, the Italian, perhaps, may surpass the Latin, and almost equal the Greek; but in point of variety, it is greatly inferior to both.

Thirdly, This simplification not only renders the sounds of our language less agreeable to the ear, but it also restrains us from disposing such sounds as we have, in the manner that might be most agreeable. It ties down many words to a particular situation, though they might often be placed in another with much more beauty. In the Greek

and Latin, though the adjective and substantive were separated from one another, the correspondence of their terminations still shewed their mutual reference, and the separation
did not necessarily occasion any sort of confusion. Thus,
in the first line of Virgil,

Tityre tu patulæ recubans sub tegmine fagi ;

we easily see that *tu* refers to *recubans,* and *patulæ*
to *fagi ;* though the related words are separated from one
another by the intervention of several others ; because the
terminations, shewing the correspondence of their cases,
determine their mutual reference. But if we were to translate this line literally into English, and say, *Tityrus, thou of
spreading reclining under the shade beech,* Œdipus himself
could not make sense of it ; because there is here no difference of termination, to determine which substantive each
adjective belongs to. It is the same case with regard to
verbs. In Latin the verb may often be placed, without any
inconvenience or ambiguity, in any part of the sentence.
But in English its place is almost always precisely determined. It must follow the subjective and precede the ob-
jective 'member of the phrase in almost all cases. Thus in
Latin, whether you say, *Joannem verberavit Robertus,* or
Robertus verberavit Joanncm, the meaning is precisely the
same, and the termination fixes John to be the sufferer in
both cases. But in English *John beat Robert,* and *Robert
beat John,* have by no means the same signification. The
place, therefore, of the three principal members of the phrase
is in the English, and for the same reason in the French
and Italian languages, almost always precisely determined ;
whereas in the ancient languages a greater latitude is allowed, and the place of those members is often, in a great
measure, indifferent. We must have recourse to Horace,
in order to interpret some parts of Milton's literal translation ;

> Who now enjoys thee credulous all gold,
> Who always vacant, always amiable
> Hopes thee ; of flattering gales
> Unmindful—

are verses which it is impossible to interpret by any rules of our language. There are no rules in our language by which any man could discover, that, in the first line, *credulous* referred to *who*, and not to *thee ;* or that *all gold* referred to any thing ; or, that in the fourth line, *unmindful* referred to *who* in the second, and not to *thee* in the third ; or, on the contrary, that, in the second line, *always vacant*, *always amiable*, referred to *thee* in the third, and not to *who* in the same line with it. In the Latin, indeed, all this is abundantly plain.

> Qui nunc te fruitur credulus aureâ,
> Qui semper vacuam, semper amabilem
> Sperat te ; nescius auræ fallacis ·

because the terminations in the Latin determine the reference of each adjective to its proper substantive, which it is impossible for any thing in the English to do. How much this power of transposing the order of their words must have facilitated the composition of the ancients, both in verse and prose, can hardly be imagined. That it must greatly have facilitated their versification, it is needless to observe ; and in prose, whatever beauty depends upon the arrangement and construction of the several members of the period, must to them have been acquirable with much more ease, and to much greater perfection, than it can be to those whose expression is constantly confined by the prolixness, constraint, and monotony of modern languages.

THE END

THE ADAM SMITH LIBRARY

Works by Adam Smith

AN INQUIRY INTO THE NATURE AND CAUSES OF THE WEALTH OF NATIONS
[1776]

2 volumes, medium quarto

The first facsimile of the original edition of the most famous book in economics. In two bindings: *de luxe,* bound in full antiqued calf, stamped in gold, with a slip case; library, bound in sturdiest buckram.

THE THEORY OF MORAL SENTIMENTS
[1759]

Adam Smith's first major work; indispensable for an understanding of the basic philosophy underlying *The Wealth of Nations.* A reprint of the latest Bohn Library issue of 1892. x, 506 pp.

LECTURES ON JUSTICE, POLICE, REVENUE AND ARMS
[1763]

Edited with an introduction and notes by EDWIN CANNAN
[1898]

Student notes of Adam Smith's course at the University of Glasgow; his early work on economics. xli, 293 pp.

THE EARLY WRITINGS OF ADAM SMITH
Edited with an introduction by J. RALPH LINDGREN

This volume includes: Preface to William Hamilton's *Poems,* writings in *The Edinburgh Review* of 1755, *Essays on Philosophical Subjects, Considerations Concerning the First Formation of Languages.*

The first complete collection of Adam Smith's early writings. 255 pp.

Books on The Life of Adam Smith

THE LIFE OF ADAM SMITH
[1895]

By JOHN RAE

With an Introduction
"Guide to John Rae's *Life of Adam Smith*" by Jacob Viner

A handsome reprint of the most important *Life*, with an introduction which appraises the present state of knowledge about the life of Adam Smith, written by the leading contemporary authority. 146, xv, 449 pp.

ADAM SMITH, AS STUDENT AND PROFESSOR
[1937]

By WILLIAM R. SCOTT

Second in importance ony to John Rae's *Life*, this book, illustrated with pictures and facsimiles of documents, preserves a wide variety of source material concerning Adam Smith's life and work chiefly at the University of Glasgow. Crown octavo, xxv, 445 pp.

BIOGRAPHICAL MEMOIRS OF ADAM SMITH

By DUGALD STEWART

Written in 1793, Dugald Stewart's *Memoir* is the first biography of Adam Smith, and the only one by a contemporary, friend and fellow student of economics and philosophy. Reprinted from Volume X of Stewart's *Collected Works*, with about 30 pages of notes added in 1811 and further material added in 1858. The complete volume which includes *Memoirs* of William Robertson, Thomas Reid and Dugald Stewart himself is reprinted. clxxvii, 338 pp.

Adam Smith's Own Library

A CATALOGUE OF THE LIBRARY OF ADAM SMITH

By JAMES BONAR

2nd edition, 1932   xxiv, 218 pp.

A FULL AND DETAILED CATALOGUE OF BOOKS
WHICH BELONGED TO ADAM SMITH
[1951]

By YADAO YANAIHARA

ix, 126 pp. and plates

These two volumes list most of the books known to have belonged to Adam Smith. A most detailed account of Adam Smith's library appears in Jacob Viner's introduction to John Rae's *Life of Adam Smith*.

Contemporary Discussions of
The Wealth of Nations

A LETTER FROM GOVERNOR POWNALL TO ADAM SMITH
[1776]

By THOMAS POWNALL

This comment on *The Wealth of Nations*, published in the same year, is one of the first and is particularly interesting since it was written by a governor of the colony of Massachusetts. 48 pp., 8½ x 11.

THE STATE OF THE POOR

Or, A History of the Labouring Classes in England, from the Conquest to the present period . . .

[1797]

By SIR FREDERIC MORTON EDEN

3 vols.   Crown quarto

This great collection of information about the working classes of England in the 18th century forms a valuable background to the ideas of Adam Smith.

AN INQUIRY INTO THE NATURE AND ORIGIN OF PUBLIC WEALTH—AND INTO THE MEANS OF ITS INCREASE

[1804]

By JAMES MAITLAND, 8th Earl of Lauderdale

An early major critique of *The Wealth of Nations*. 500 pp.

OBSERVATONS ON THE SUBJECTS TREATED IN DR. SMITH'S INQUIRY . . . 2nd EDITION

[1817]

By DAVID BUCHANAN

A volume of essays added to Buchanan's edition of *The Wealth of Nations* which was the first annotated edition. Comments from what became the Malthusian point of view. xvi, 316, 88 pp.

A TREATISE ON POLITICAL ECONOMY

[1821]

By JEAN-BAPTISTE SAY

Say's work, written in 1803, translated into English in 1821, is credited with putting Adam Smith's views in a more logical form. It is in this form that Smith's views were widely propagated throughout the nineteenth century and even in our day. lx, 488 pp.

NEW PRINCIPLES ON THE SUBJECT OF POLITICAL ECONOMY
[1834]
By JOHN RAE

A major critique of *The Wealth of Nations,* based on experience of life in the United States and Canada; attacks free trade, emphasizes sociological factors in capital formation; pioneer study of economc development. xvi, 414 pp.

Modern Comment on Adam Smith's Work
MONETARY THEORY BEFORE ADAM SMITH
[1923]
By ARTHUR E. MONROE

The outstanding modern treatise on monetary theory before Adam Smith, with special emphasis on the eighteenth century. xi, 312 pp.

THE SPIRIT OF '76 AND OTHER ESSAYS
[1927]
By CARL BECKER, J. M. CLARK, WILLIAM E. DODD

Lectures in commemoration of the 150th anniversary of *The Wealth of Nations* and *The Declaration of Independence.* 135 pp.

ADAM SMITH 1776-1926
[1928]
By J. M. CLARK, PAUL H. DOUGLAS, JACOB H. HOLLANDER, GLENN R. MORROW, MELCHIOR PALYI, and JACOB VINER

Comments on various aspects of Adam Smith's work and significance 150 years after the publication of *The Wealth of Nations.* ix, 241 pp.

PREDECESSORS OF ADAM SMITH
[1937]
By E. A. J. JOHNSON

The growth of British economic thought before Adam Smith, with an exposition of the ideas of the leading British mercantilist writers, xiii, 423 pp.

For additional information about *The Adam Smith Library,* its privileges and conditions of membership, please write the publisher:

AUGUSTUS M. KELLEY · *Publishers*
24 East 22nd Street, New York, New York 10010